EXPLORING
CHURCH GROWTH

EXPLORING CHURCH GROWTH

Edited by
WILBERT R. SHENK

Grand Rapids, Michigan
WILLIAM B. EERDMANS PUBLISHING COMPANY

Library of Congress Cataloging in Publication Data

Main entry under title:
Exploring church growth.

   1. Church growth—Addresses, essays, lectures.
I. Shenk, Wilbert R.
BV652.25.E96 1983   266   83-1563
ISBN 0-8028-1962-1

CONTENTS

III. THEOLOGICAL ISSUES

PREFACE

THE GROWTH OF THE CHURCH IS IMPORTANT TO EVERY CHRISTIAN. THE PRImary goal of the Christian missionary movement, in its various forms and with changing degrees of intensity over the past nineteen hundred years, has been the winning of new adherents to the faith.

In our day we are witnessing the decline of the church in the West; at the same time the church in Asia, Africa, and Latin America is growing. As a result, it is predicted that by the year 2000 a majority of Christians will be found in the southern tier of the world. The reasons for this ebb and flow would alone be sufficient grounds for inquiring into the phenomenon of church growth. But more basic still is the fact that the church is under mandate to witness to the unbelieving world concerning God's love as revealed in Jesus Christ.

If there has been a "growth industry" in the field of missionary studies during the past twenty-five years, it has been "Church Growth"—as it has come to be known under the dynamic leadership of Donald McGavran. The School of World Mission, Fuller Theological Seminary, has furnished the institutional base for Church Growth studies by faculty and students. This concentrated effort has produced an impressive array of books, articles, reports, and theses.

The Church Growth School has made several contributions to the field of missiology. In the first place, it has offered a new way of understanding the missionary task and encouraged a rereading of the history of Christian missions to highlight the "growth" theme. Second, Church Growth has readily appropriated the tools of cognate disciplines—particularly the social sciences and statistics—in doing its work. A third contribution has been the insistence on ruthless honesty in understanding and evaluating the record in a given country or region. Church Growth has given short shrift to easy rationalizations or woolly reasoning used in defense of time-honored but unproductive methods. Fourth, Church Growth has pioneered a new theoretical construct for the study of church growth worldwide.

The purpose of this volume is to continue the exploration into the phenomenon of church growth. The contributors to this volume would demur from the notion that there is anything approaching a *Complete Book of Church Growth* (Towns 1982) because we believe that church growth is more than empirical data and effective methods. It is a complex phenomenon surrounded by a measure of mystery and, if genuine, is directed and controlled by a sovereign God. We can discern the divine mind in these matters only imperfectly.

While freely acknowledging our debt to the stimulation of the Church Growth School, we wish to probe further into the premises, principles, and goals of church growth. Our aim is not to offer definitive answers, but rather to open up fresh lines of inquiry—historically, experientially, methodologically, and theologically. We are asking: What issues are pertinent to understanding the growth of the church, and how can we avoid methodologies which obscure and distort the results of research? At relevant points we interact with previous studies; but our purpose is not polemics. We hope to contribute fresh insights and encourage students to carry the investigation further.

In the course of preparing this volume we were reminded that church growth is a matter on which no one can remain neutral. One scholar had to withdraw her offer of an essay because of the political sensitivity surrounding the church with which she had had long association in a major nation of Asia. The fact that new Christians have found dignity and hope through faith in Jesus Christ is viewed with deep suspicion and hostility. It seemed the better part of wisdom and Christian charity not to expose these fellow believers to unnecessary further harassment.

It is also necessary to underscore the open-endedness of this project by pointing out other themes which beg for treatment but which we have not taken up here. Despite the fact that the theme of this volume—along with scores of others produced under the rubric of Church Growth—is *church* growth, one of the underworked strands is ecclesiology. The nature and mission of the church ought to tell us much about how it grows. It is to be hoped that this gap will be filled in the future.

Since the Church Growth School has made so much of ethnicity as a key to understanding church growth, it is surprising how underworked this theme is in the literature. Aside from Peter Wagner's writings, little has been done with ethnicity. And yet social scientists have invested considerable energy in the study of ethnicity during the past twenty years. Harvie Conn's contributions to this volume help point up the importance of this theme for missiology. Ethnicity is one of the most dynamic determinants of social and political relations in our world today. We cannot afford to overlook it.

A third theme which deserves to be studied from the standpoint of church growth is eschatology. Peter Berger and Jürgen Moltmann have reminded us how important hope is in all of human experience. The Christian gospel is about hope—God's eschatological answer to the human quest for salvation. The recurrent appearance in history of messiahs, the rising and falling of cultures, and the persistence of evil all suggest the need for a biblical eschatology with which to understand the meaning of Christian witness in our world.

A work such as this is only possible through teamwork. In addition to the genial collaboration of the essayists, I wish to note especially the expert help of Merlin Becker-Hoover and John Bender in the exacting task of copy editing. Jo Ann Preheim and her staff handled the typing and retyping with dispatch. I am also grateful to Paul M. Gingrich, president of Mennonite Board of Missions, for his warm support and encouragement to undertake the project.

WILBERT R. SHENK

REFERENCE CITED

TOWNS, Elmer L., et al.
  1981   *The Complete Book of Church Growth*, Wheaton, Illinois: Tyndale.

I. CASE STUDIES

1. THE DIFFICULTY OF UNDERSTANDING CHURCH GROWTH IN MADAGASCAR

Charles W. Forman

ONLY A FEW OF THE MANY COUNTRIES AND PEOPLES APPROACHED BY MISSIONARIES during the past two centuries have responded with immediacy, rapidity, and unity to the Christian message. The country of Uganda, the Batak and the Minahassa peoples of Indonesia, the people of Fiji and the Polynesian Islands, some tribes in Burma and northeast India, and recently the highland people of New Guinea are the principal cases of such responsiveness.

Africa outside of Uganda hardly belongs in this list because the early response was slow and the rapid spread of Christianity among whole peoples came mostly in the mid-twentieth century, long after missionary labors began. The mass movements among the depressed castes in India also are hardly of this category since they did not include a whole country and seldom even a whole ethnic group.

Madagascar, however, is one country which should certainly be included in the list. There was in that island an immediate response to Christianity which, though slowed by a time of persecution, soon spread through the people. It did not actually include the whole people of the island, the Malagasy, but it did include the whole of the dominant ethnic group, the Merina or Hova. The conversion of the Merina is especially impressive because much of it was carried out in the face of government opposition and persecution, while among the other peoples who gave a ready response there was, except for a short time in Uganda, a favorable attitude from the government.

Our concern here is to find the reasons for such an impressive church growth. But first a survey of the events is needed.

THE RISE OF CHRISTIANITY IN MADAGASCAR

EARLY WELCOME AND BAN

In 1820 the pioneer of the London Missionary Society arrived in Madagascar. King Radama welcomed missionary work because he wanted some of the benefits of Western technology. He was especially happy when the first printing press arrived in 1826. He encouraged the missionaries in their task of reducing the language to a written form and teaching the people to read. He had a model

Charles W. Forman, New Haven, Connecticut, is Professor of Missions at Yale Divinity School. He served as a missionary in India from 1945 to 1950 and is the author of The Island Churches of the South Pacific: Emergence in the Twentieth Century *(Orbis Books, 1982).*

school set up in the capital, though he told the missionaries to hold no public worship with the pupils for fear of offending the populace. He never went to Christian worship or preaching himself.

Radama was succeeded in 1828 by Queen Ranovalona I, who tried to protect the old religion. She forbade Christian preaching by Malagasy and put Christian teachers and students in the army. Since she valued the skills the missionaries brought, she allowed the foreigners to continue to preach and to teach. In 1830 the New Testament was published, and in 1831 the first twenty-one converts were baptized. At that time Christianity was already in disfavor with the government, so the new Christians were putting themselves in jeopardy by their baptism.

The following year all Malagasy were forbidden to take part in the Christian communion service. The Christians insisted they were loyal to the queen and government, but they refused to join in any homage to the national idols, which made it appear that they were antinational and even revolutionary in their sentiments. The parallel to the early behavior of Christians in the days of the Roman Empire are obvious here. The queen was enraged just as the Roman emperors had been.

Soon, in March 1834, came a declaration against Christianity. The practice of this new faith was branded as criminal. The populace was assembled, and after much firing of cannon and intimidating actions and words the Christians were ordered to come forward and confess their beliefs. A large number of the officers of the court were among those who did this, showing how Christianity had been spreading. At that time it was estimated that there were in the country 30,000 people who could read; doubtless all of those had a strong sympathy for the Christian faith. A number of nobles had been impressed with Western culture and tried to influence the queen to a favorable attitude toward Christianity. She, however, began a persecution, attacking especially those people who were denounced by others as attending Christian worship or having such worship in their homes. The missionaries were, strangely enough, still working quietly in the land and even bringing out a published version of the Old Testament. But in 1836 she could tolerate them no more, and all six of those who were working in the country were expelled.

MALAGASY CHRISTIANS CARRY ON

The small band of Malagasy Christians were now on their own. They said that though their teachers were gone, the best teacher of all, the Holy Spirit, was still with them. They held meetings secretly, often on isolated mountaintops. They quietly shared their faith with others and taught others to read. When they were discovered, their property was confiscated and they were sold into slavery, put in jail, or executed.

At least 200 Christians were put to death, at first by spearing, later by burning or by being thrown over the cliff below the queen's palace. Some were chained together with heavy irons and left to wander around the country, often having to carry the weight of those who became ill or died in their chains. Those in jail were kept in heavy fetters. Other Christians secretly served and helped those in jail by bringing food and giving comfort by Bible reading. The bond of brotherhood between them was a great strength. The fortitude and patience shown by those suffering imprisonment or death also made a great impression on the populace. The executions were carried out publicly as a form of intimidation, but they also served as a form of evangelization.

The persecution was dropped from time to time, especially when the crown prince began to show some interest in Christianity and went to some worship services. The prince's cousin even held services in his own house. Evidently the Christian influence was gaining in spite of the harshness of the measures against it. An estimate about 1860 set the number of Merina people sympathetic to the Christian cause as about equal to those who opposed it.

OFFICIAL ACCEPTANCE
So half the population had come to favor Christianity, despite the persecutions. Ranovalona died in 1861. Her son, who ruled only a year, had no interest in continuing her policies; nor did the son's wife, who reigned five years. During this time Christians reappeared in public, and their numbers grew by leaps and bounds. As fast as churches were built they were filled. Missionaries returned. The whole direction of the country was now toward Christianity, though the rulers still kept the old idols.

The next monarch, Ranovalona II, who ascended the throne in 1867, recognized the situation, much as Constantine had recognized the situation in the Roman Empire and had thrown his influence in favor of a hitherto persecuted church. Ranovalona II declared at her accession that she based her kingdom on God; two years later she and her prime minister accepted baptism.

Now the full force of the monarchy which had been fighting Christianity was turned in favor of that new faith. The leading citizens rapidly became Christians, and many became ministers of the church. The Merina people as a whole, following their leaders, became a Christian people. They reached out with their new faith to the other peoples whom they ruled. Governors of outlying provinces urged or required their subjects to attend church services. A congregation was organized in the palace, and it dispatched and supported men of high rank to carry the Christian message to distant areas. The churches of the central province of Imerina also began a six-monthly meeting which sent out missions to other provinces. Madagascar became perhaps the greatest example in modern mission history of a new, self-propagating church (Forman 1962).

SEARCH FOR THE REASONS BEHIND MALAGASY CHURCH GROWTH

Is it possible to ascertain the reasons for this remarkable development? The crucial period to understand is the period before 1869, especially the time of persecutions, 1834-1861.

After 1869 Christianity enjoyed official favor and prestige. It carried many social benefits. Though there were doubtless many deeper reasons why the church grew in that period, the obvious social advantages would be enough to explain church growth. The crucial time, however, was already passed by 1869. Christianity under persecution had already proved its power to survive and even to grow. It had won the sympathy of large numbers of the people, though it had no royal favor or support. The queen, in becoming Christian in 1869, was following a trend, not setting one. The important thing to understand is how it happened that prior to 1869 the church had shown such ability to grow and to become a force in society that an intelligent monarch would decide to join it.

HISTORICAL CAUTION

To understand that earlier period is not easy. In fact most of the reasons we can deduce do not seem adequate to explain the facts. Accounting for historical phenomena is always a dubious enterprise. We historians know what has happened. Then we look behind what happened and pick out all the factors which pointed in that direction and think we have understood the reasons for what happened. We fail to note that there were many factors which pointed in other directions and that consequently the eventual course of events might have been different from what actually transpired. Only because we know the outcome can we claim to grasp the reasons behind it.

When we deal with the present and the future, where the outcome is unknown, we are not normally able to predict what will happen. Our knowledge of the factors at work at the present time is just as good or even better than our knowledge of the factors which were at work in previous times. Yet we do not know where the present factors will lead. If we cannot predict what will happen in the future, it would seem that we do not really know why things happened the way they did in the past. If, on the other hand, we claim to understand events of the past, we should also be able to predict the future. Great care must therefore be exercised in any attempt to understand past events.

POPULAR GROWTH THEORIES

All this argument for carefulness applies preeminently to Malagasy church growth before 1869. Various reasons for the growth have been advanced, but they fall short of a full understanding. These bear closer examination.

Bravery of martyrs. It has been said that the bravery of the Malagasy martyrs and the close bond that existed between the Christians made a great impression on others and attracted people to the faith (Mears 1873:109, 112, 163). Doubtless this is true. Numbers of converts said they were attracted to the faith because of the bravery and fellowship which they had seen among the Christians. But is this to be seen as an important reason for church growth? Christian bravery and fellowship have been known in many other lands where no church growth has occurred. What made the difference? Why did bravery and fellowship evoke interest and response in Madagascar but not everywhere else? Evidently other factors were at work in Madagascar. The bravery and fellowship were part of the process of growth more than the cause of it.

Witness of Christian soldiers. It has been said, further, that a reason for church growth was the devotion evidenced by Christian soldiers in the Merina forces as they moved about the country, holding their own worship services and so expressing their faith before others (Mears 1873:207-08). This suggested reason for growth obviously was in operation mostly after the end of the persecutions when army personnel were more likely to be Christian and were freer to let their worship be known. But even in that latter period this again seems to be more a description of the way the church spread rather than a cause of its spread. The cause which produced such soldiers and made people responsive to their witness must be sought behind this particular activity through which Christianity grew.

All evangelists. The same kind of objection must be urged against another feature of Malagasy Christianity which is fastened on as an explanation of its growth. It is said that the church grew because all Christians were evangelists, telling other people about their faith (Mondain 1920:145-46; Sibree 1924:69). The objection to this must be, again, that it describes the process rather than giving the reason. Furthermore, this process has not always led to church growth, so it cannot be set forward as an adequate cause. In many lands the new Christians have eagerly communicated their faith to others without producing any great growth of the church. What made Madagascar different? And what created such a vigorously self-propagating Christian faith in the first place?

Political unity. A line of reasoning which has often been used to explain the spread of Christianity in the Roman Empire might presumably be applied to Madagascar. It has often been said that the faith spread under Roman rule because of the political unity which was provided over a large area. People and ideas could move about with relative freedom because there were no international boundaries to cross. On a smaller scale Merina rule provided similar conditions for Madagascar. Most of the island had been brought under the sway of a single ruler, and therefore people could move about with an ease that was unknown in the days when the competing tribes divided up the land into small political units. But it must quickly be obvious that while political unity might facilitate church growth, it could never cause it—not in Rome nor in Madagascar. Many lands have had political unity over wide areas. The Chinese Empire and the Mogul Empire are outstanding examples. Yet the faith did not spread rapidly under their unifying power. The reasons must be sought elsewhere.

Persecution. Could persecution possibly be the key? Some have said that oddly enough the persecutions which were intended to destroy the church in fact caused it to spread. They scattered the Christians around the land. They also made those who kept the faith exceptionally strong in character. Persecutions resulted in vigorous Christian leaders who eventually became the most vital force in the country (Mears 1873:175). Though this is all true, there is a certain illogic in seeing persecution itself as the cause of Christian expansion.

No one could say that persecution is needed for church growth. It has certainly not been a part of the picture in most countries where Christianity has spread. The churches of Samoa, Tonga, Minahassa, and New Guinea all grew rapidly without any persecution. So did most of the churches of medieval Europe.

All too often persecution has had the more expected effect of stopping the spread of Christianity. The seventeenth- and eighteenth-century persecutions in China, Japan, and Korea all attest to this normal outcome. Though persecutions do sometimes backfire and help what they are trying to hurt, they are not the cause of the phenomenon they perversely assist. They are not necessary for church growth, nor do they normally even hasten it.

Methodology. Were the methods which the missionaries used or the spirit which they showed sufficiently different from those in other countries to explain the appearance of this rapidly self-propagating church? When we examine the missionaries' work we find it was typical of much of the missionary work done in that period. It consisted of reducing the language to writing, translating the Scriptures, starting schools, teaching the people to read, and preaching the Christian gospel. The introduction of the printing press and various technical skills was also typical of most missionary work. Nothing in these methods would explain why the church grew so much faster in Madagascar than in India or Africa, for example.

Nor can it be said that the missionaries showed a devotion or heroism which was unique and thus inspired the local people to actions which attracted others. The missionaries on Madagascar were spared the dangers of the persecution which their followers had to endure, and though they were certainly devoted they showed no more devotion or heroism than many missionaries in countries where the church did not grow.

Missionary staff. Did the number of missionaries have anything to do with the rapid spread of Christianity? It is usually assumed that a large number of missionaries will result in a large-scale growth of the church. This was obviously not the case in Madagascar.

There were never more than nine missionaries there during any part of the period under consideration, and during most of the time there was none. These small numbers, however, may not be used to prove the opposite of the usual assumption. It cannot be said that few missionaries will result in large church growth. Many places in the world have had few missionaries, and no great results have followed. All that can be said is that there is no reliable correlation between the number of missionaries and the amount of church growth; it cannot be claimed that if the number of missionaries is increased or decreased, church growth will follow.

Cultural sensitivity. Did the missionaries' attitude to the local culture affect church growth? Certainly it would seem likely that any missionary efforts to adapt Christianity to the indigenous culture would make the Christian faith more acceptable to the people. But an examination of the situation in Madagascar and in other lands does not suggest that church growth is usually helped by such efforts.

Missionaries in the nineteenth century were prone to take much of Western culture with them as an essential part of Christianity. Missionaries in the twentieth century have usually moved in the opposite direction and have tried to separate Christian faith from Western culture and to fit the faith into local traditions. But there has not been an increase of church growth in the twentieth century that would correspond to the change in missionary policy. The twentieth-century growth in Africa is more associated with the spread of Western education than with rapprochements to African culture. In fact the conscious adaptation to local culture by missionaries and by indigenous Christian leaders has usually come after the period of greatest church growth is past and a period of inner development and little or no growth has begun. Madagascar seems to fit this general picture.

The Madagascar missionaries, like others in the nineteenth century, imposed European styles of life on the converts in a number of ways. They have been criticized for this by recent scholars (Gow 1979:13). Yet the church grew rapidly. In the mid-twentieth century a number of Merina leaders of the church began to explore the possibilities for restoring traditional ways and tried to open the church to more of the ancient practices of their people, but these new ideas came only at a time when no more Merina were becoming Christians.

We might try to turn the proposition around and suggest that rapid church growth is most likely to come precisely when a foreign culture is being introduced along with Christianity. There is more to be said for this. Many non-Western peoples have been interested in acquiring Western culture, and with that interest they have been attracted to Christianity. The technological achievements of the West have been the things which they have most wanted to secure themselves.

Madagascar lends some credence to this theory because Radama initially welcomed missionaries into his island simply because he wanted the technological skills which they brought with them. But a little further investigation shows the shallowness of this reasoning. Radama did not accept Christianity; he accepted only the technology. Other Merina could have made the same distinction and could have exercised the same selective acceptance.

The ruler of the Zulus a few years later, to take another example, welcomed missionaries for the skills they knew, and he likewise refused to take any interest in their religion. He allowed them to continue at his court only with the hope of securing technological advances from them. No church growth appeared in his country at that time nor for as long as the Zulus remained independent.

Many other lands in the world have in succeeding years accepted Western technology yet have not accepted Christianity. Madagascar could have followed that road. Clearly some other factor must have been in operation among the Malagasy which led them to adopt Christianity. The association with Western culture provides no adequate way of understanding church growth.

CULTURAL FACTORS SHED LIGHT

We have looked at reasons for church growth inside the Christian community both among the Malagasy Christians and among the foreign missionaries, and none of these reasons has proved to be particularly helpful to our understanding. Another direction may well prove more helpful. We need to explore Malagasy culture to see whether there was something outside rather than inside the Christian community which explains what happened.

Nonliteracy. One obvious feature of Malagasy culture was that it was preliterate and had a nonliterary religion. This we may seize upon as a very important reason for the growth of the church. A glance at other parts of the world confirms the importance of this feature. Almost everywhere Christian missions have entered preliterate cultures with nonliterary religions, they have sooner or later found a general acceptance among the people. This was true in medieval Europe. It was also true in the modern period over most of the American continents. It was true in the Pacific. And though Africa was slower in its response than Madagascar, it was eventually true in most of Africa.

Over the centuries Christianity has won small minorities in literate societies, but its large-scale acceptance has come mostly from people without any written corpus of religious beliefs. Virtually all such peoples have accepted Christianity when approached by Christian missionaries. Here then must be a basic reason for the great church growth in Madagascar. The comparison with other places and times confirms this line of understanding rather than throwing doubts upon it.

Language group. A distinction can be made between those preliterate cultures which have responded with immediacy, rapidity, and unity to the Christian message, those few cultures which were mentioned at the beginning of this chapter, and other such cultures which have responded in a more delayed and piecemeal way. Most of Africa and Melanesia belong in the latter category. We naturally wonder what factors in the culture made for the more immediate and united response.

It is noticeable that most of the half dozen peoples who moved rapidly into the church after the initial contact belonged to the Malayo-Polynesian language group. The Merina people were of this group, even though they lived so close to Africa. So, of course, were the Polynesians, and so were the Batak and the Minahassa peoples and, to mention a very small group who were not in the original list, the tribal peoples of the mountains of Taiwan, who have become Christians *en masse* in the present generation.

It would seem that there may be some further cultural factors, beyond the general factor of nonliteracy, which may explain the particular receptiveness among these peoples. If there are such factors, however, they elude any precise identification. It may be that polygamy has not been as great a barrier to conversion among these peoples as it has been in Africa. Polygamy has been practiced among them, but it does not seem to have been so closely intertwined with the demands of political power and social influence as it was among African peoples generally. Certainly it was given up more easily when Christianity entered.

Though a few such cultural factors may be mentioned which made the way for Christianity smoother, they cannot be relied upon because they are not always applicable. There have been other peoples in the Malayo-Polynesian language group whose response to Christian preaching has been much more of the delayed and piecemeal type. The peoples of western Micronesia would be an example, as would many of the Melanesian peoples of the Solomon Islands and Vanuatu. Their response has been more like that of African peoples than like that of the Merina. Evidently we are not able to pick out universally reliable reasons for the rapidity and unity of the Merina response.

CONCLUSION

We are left, then, with one reason which does seem to explain church growth. Growth has come as a large-scale phenomenon among preliterate peoples with a nonliterary religion. At times it has come quickly, and at times it has come after a long period of unresponsiveness, but eventually it has come. Seldom has it come among any other types of people. The various alternative lines of explanation we have examined all appear inadequate. The inner qualities of the church, the friendliness or hostility of the government, the nature of the Christianity that is preached, or the convictions and bravery of the Christians seem to have little to do with the outcome. Likewise the number of missionaries, the methods they use, and the attitudes they have toward the local culture or the foreign cultures they carry seem to have no decisive effect. One factor alone seems to continue to be important while all others eventually have to be eliminated.

At the end the question arises whether we have succeeded in overcoming the limitations of the historian and have indeed understood the reasons for church growth. To an extent, apparently, we have. We are not here martialing a whole list of factors pointing in one direction and ignoring the factors pointing in the opposite direction, operating simply on our knowledge of what eventually happened. All the factors but one in our list have been ruled out because they are not real causes of growth or because in other situations than that of Madagascar they did not lead to church growth. The one factor picked out at the end does seem to be a reliable indicator since in all other situations up to the present it has indeed provided the condition for large-scale church growth.

Presumably this kind of discovery should give the historian the ability to predict the future. That would be the only final test for the adequacy of the historical discovery. It is, admittedly, a test which cannot easily be applied in the future, because there are ever fewer remaining preliterate peoples with a nonliterary religion who have not already been touched by pioneer missionaries. Where there are such, however, the prediction may be ventured that, given missionary contact, they will eventually become Christian—provided only that their Christianization is not precluded by some other literary religion entering the scene.

All in all it would seem that understanding church growth in Madagascar is indeed difficult, but perhaps it is not impossible.

REFERENCES CITED

FORMAN, Charles W.
  1962   "A Study in the Self-Propagating Church: Madagascar," *Frontiers of the Christian World Mission since 1938,* Wilber C. Harr (ed.), New York: Harper.

GOW, Bonar A.
  1979   *Madagascar and the Protestant Impact: The Work of the British Missions 1818-1895,* New York: Africana Publishing Company.

MEARS, John W.
  1873   *The Story of Madagascar,* Philadelphia: Presbyterian Board of Publication.

MONDAIN, Gustave
  1920   *Un Siècle de Mission Protestante à Madagascar,* Paris: Société des Missions Evangéliques.

SIBREE, James
  1924   *Fifty Years in Madagascar,* London: Allen and Unwin.

2. THE CASE OF ETHIOPIA

F. Peter Cotterell

THIS CHAPTER DEALS PRIMARILY WITH SOUTHERN ETHIOPIA AND WITH THE emergence of two Protestant communities, the Evangelical Church Makane Yesus (ECMY) (Arén 1978; Saeverås 1974) and the Kale-Heywet Church (KHC).[1] The former relates to the work of several Lutheran missionary societies and the latter to the work of the Sudan Interior Mission (SIM).

The Swedish Evangelical Mission (SEM) began work in Massawa on the Red Sea coast in 1866.[2] The Sudan Interior Mission began its work in southern Ethiopia under the leadership of Dr. Thomas Lambie in 1927. The Lutheran work gradually reached southward. Through two former Ethiopian Orthodox Church priests work was begun in Wallega province in 1899; in 1904 a start was made in Addis Ababa. The Lutherans generally followed a policy of cooperation with the Orthodox Church and did not, therefore, attempt to establish separate congregations. From the start the Sudan Interior Mission followed the opposite policy; their first congregation was formed in Sidamo in 1932, followed by a church in Walamo in 1933. Our present concern, therefore, directs attention to the Sudan Interior Mission work of this pre-World War II period.

From 1927 to the final total expulsion of missionaries from Sudan by the Italians in 1938 a total of some ninety-two SIM missionaries served in the country. At the end they could count approximately one convert for each one of them.

Less than four years later, when the Italians were driven out and the first missionaries returned, there were something like eighty-one churches and upward of 10,000 Christians, concentrated in Kambatta and Walamo. By 1945 there were 280 churches.

It is extremely important to notice that these churches were established with a minimal contribution from missionaries. In the period *before* the occupation there had been opportunity for the people to observe the various activities

1. See Davis 1966 for the history of the Kale-Heywet ("Word-of-life") Church in its beginnings. The account is extended to 1970 in Cotterell 1973. The details of the earlier period may be supplemented (Duff 1977; 1980).
2. However, the pioneers of the modern missionary movement in Ethiopia were Samuel Gobat and Christian Kugler; they reached the country in 1830 and worked under the auspices of the Church Missionary Society.

F. Peter Cotterell, London, England, is Director of Overseas Studies at London Bible College. He served with the Sudan Interior Mission from 1957 to 1976. His latest book, The Eleventh Commandment, *was published in 1981 by Inter-Varsity Press.*

of the missionaries: learning the language, translating the Bible,[3] planting vegetables and growing flowers, holding conferences, gathering for prayer. They
noted these activities. But the number of believers was so small and the believers
themselves were so scattered that there was no call for the missionaries to develop
any system of interrelationship for the churches. In the period following the
return of the missionaries there was again a minimal contribution from the
missionaries to actual church polity. They were on the outside, looking in,
advisers but without any office.

One potentially divisive decision *was* taken by the missionaries, to establish a comity committee which proceeded to allocate areas of influence for
the various mission agencies (Saeverås 1974:39). The Evangelical Church Makane Yesus and the Kale-Heywet Church ignored the comity arrangements. This
was important since the work of the former quickly reached into the south where
the same explosive growth occurred. By 1975 ECMY churches in the two southern synods totalled 953 (Cotterell 1975) with more than 150,000 members.

The period from 1950 to 1970 was essentially one of rapid growth within
a rather limited geographical area of southern Ethiopia. To the south was the
area of greatest language confusion, known as the fragmentation belt, to the east
the Muslim areas of Arussi and Bale, to the north the Semitic Gurage peoples,
and to the west the barrier of the Omo River. Within the envelope the church
grew rapidly. We look, then, to the general background of this highly individualistic pattern of growth.

Ethiopia[4] consists primarily of a highland massif with an average elevation
of about 7,000 feet, slashed from north to south by the Rift Valley. The region
is confined north, east, and west by the deserts of the Sudan and of the Ogaden,
while to the south lie the tumbled mountains of northern Kenya tailing off into
the deserts of the Northern Frontier District. In a word, the land is isolated.

Ethnically and linguistically the peoples can be divided into three groups:
those speaking Semitic languages (the Amharas of the south, the Tigre of the
north, the Hararis and Gurages); those speaking the tonal languages of the border
with the Sudan, the Nilotes; and the remainder, sometimes termed Cushitic,
perhaps better *Erythraic,* including the Somali of the Ogaden, the Oromo (Galla)
peoples, the Kambattans, and the Wolayta. The church has grown largely among
this third group.

Religiously we again have three principal divisions: the Orthodox Christians of the center and northwest, mainly Semitic speakers; the Muslims of the
north and southeast; and the adherents of what is best described as African
traditional religions, exhibiting aspects of animism, of astral cults and litho-cults

---

3. In Kambatta Matthew was put into the Gudeilla language, and Walter Ohman
was largely responsible for translating John's Gospel into Wolayta. In 1933 the Bible
society published Mark in the Sidamo language and the Scripture Gift Mission published
a selection of Bible passages called *God Has Spoken.* The whole Bible in Amharic had
been published in 1840. See E. Ullendorff's *Ethiopia and the Bible,* the Schweich Lectures for 1967, OUP for the British Academy, 1968.

4. The name "Ethiopia" is preferred to "Abyssinia" because of the supposed
relationship of the latter word to an Arabic root meaning "to mix," casting doubt on the
purity of origins of the Ethiopian peoples. Present-day Ethiopia has little or no relationship
to areas labeled "Ethiopia" in some translations of the Bible, which refer either to Nubia
in the Sudan or to South Arabia.

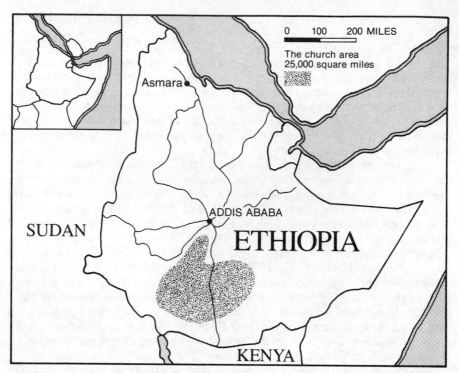

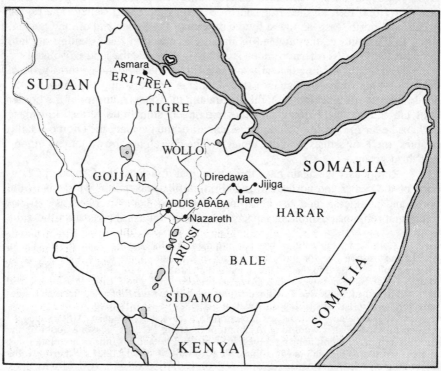

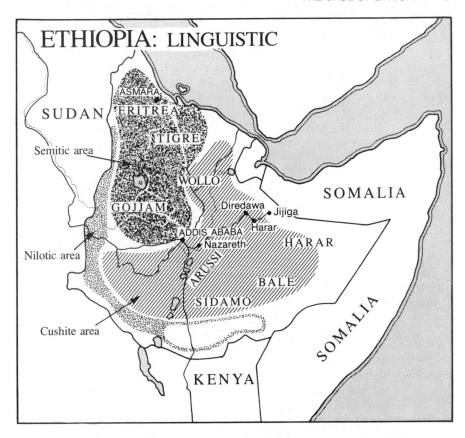

associated with stelae, pillars, and phallic stones which in turn point to fertility rites. It was largely from this third group, the adherents of African traditional religions, that converts to Christianity came.

ANALYSIS

We have already noted that it was not, initially, the policy of the Swedish Evangelical Mission missionaries to form new congregations. Their aim was the revival of the Orthodox Church. The Sudan Interior Mission missionaries, however, had a commitment to church planting and brought with them a clearly thought-out plan. The intention was to use Addis Ababa as a first base, to establish a second base at Jimma, 150 miles to the south, and to use these two as stepping stones to the Kenya border. Lambie, their leader, had passed through the Jimma region in 1920 when he was working with the (American) United Presbyterian Mission, and he knew that there were no missionaries to the south. With Alfred Buxton, formerly of the Heart of Africa Mission, he planned a simultaneous advance on the border area from the Kenya side.

 Along with this clear intention to plant churches was the remarkable influence of the Anglican missiologist Roland Allen on the SIM missionaries.

In particular the missionaries seem unitedly to have adopted strong views on indigeneity. From time to time their views were challenged,[5] but they held to them so that from the outset, so soon as 1933 and the formation of the first church, the missionaries stood back and left church responsibilities to the Ethiopian Christians. Even the well-meant attempt at Soddu, in Walamo, to assist the Ethiopian believers to build a church was ruled out (Cotterell 1973:71).

A third feature was the remarkable way in which the careful planning of the pioneers was set aside. The first journey of the Sudan Interior Mission missionaries was delayed through circumstances over which they had no control.[6] The result was that they left Addis Ababa for Jimma as the rains began. Their way was barred by swollen rivers. Disconcerted they spent a day in prayer before accepting the inevitable: a change of direction. This took them to three towns— Hosanna, Soddu, and Agere Selam—which for half a century to come would delineate a triangle within which the church would grow.

A fourth factor is related to the third: The triangle of land marked out an area of remarkable cultural homogeneity. With the obvious exception of the Amhara administrators, the countryside was inhabited by peoples who had a common culture and interrelated languages. There were, in fact, two blocs of languages, the enormous bloc of Wolayta dialects south and west of Lake Margharita, and the Sidamo language cluster east of the lake and to the north of the triangle. The total area involved measured 25,000 square miles, fairly evenly divided between these two major groupings. Within the triangle the evangelists could travel freely and communicate effectively (Cotterell 1973:ch. 11).

It must again be stressed that the missionaries themselves were not aware of this remarkable cultural and linguistic homogeneity. Indeed it was of less importance for them than it was for the Ethiopian Christians, since the Sudan Interior Mission developed the unfortunate habit of moving missionaries at frequent intervals so that in the postwar period few if any missionaries learned to speak anything other than Amharic with any degree of fluency. Evangelism was the task of the church. The missionaries of the SIM became Bible teachers, academic school teachers, medical auxiliaries, and sometimes very effective assistants to the Ethiopian evangelists.[7]

Flowing from this quartet of factors came a vital life-stream. Witness to Christ did not have to be organized. Each new convert *knew* that what he or she had was good news. In a spontaneous way every Christian became a witness. And there were the recognized traveling witnesses too: unsalaried, living from

5. One missionary was anxious to commence a Bible school in Addis Ababa, but a 1933 conference ruled against it: Bible training must take place in the context of the church (Cotterell 1973:70).

6. The situation was complex. The missionaries were strongly opposed by the leaders of the Orthodox Church. But there was also a major political disturbance in the making, aimed at eliminating Ras Tafari (later Haile Selassie) who was then Regent under Empress Zauditu. There were more important decisions for Ras Tafari to take than those involving a party of missionaries and so the delay (Mosley 1964:ch. 8).

7. Mention must be made, however, of two missionaries in particular who engaged in widespread journeyings for pioneer evangelism: McLellan and Fellows. Even so, neither was a linguist, neither was more than marginally competent even in Amharic, neither learned a second language, and both, therefore, depended on their Ethiopian companions. And, it must be added, both would readily agree to this observation.

the proceeds of their little patches of land which were often cared for on their behalf by other Christians.[8]

The rapid growth of the church did not go unnoticed or unchallenged. The Italian authorities made determined efforts to stamp out the Protestant Church (Lass-Westphal 1972; Cotterell 1969-70), and when the Italians were driven out, the Orthodox Church leadership initiated further persecution. The response of the Christians to persecution tended to a uniform determination to cooperate with lawful authority so far as possible, to disobey where they felt they must, and to accept imprisonment for these acts of disobedience. Only rarely was any formal attempt made to seek redress for their very real grievances.[9]

It is perhaps only fair to make it clear that I lived in Ethiopia from 1957 until 1976, lived within the triangle for part of that time, traveled throughout the region incessantly, spoke the Amharic language with some fluency, and made a point of listening to the Ethiopian Christians as they reminisced. There can be no doubt that the persecution of the Protestant Church from 1947 to 1976 was almost invariably due to the action of Orthodox Church priests, rarely if ever checked by their superiors. Indeed, in Addis Ababa I found the same overt hostility to the Protestants among the Orthodox hierarchy as I had in the rural situation encountered among the often semiliterate priests. Persecution has, in fact, been the lot of the Christians of southern Ethiopia throughout the half century of the existence of the Protestant Church—under the Italians, under the Haile Selassie regime, and more recently under Marxism. It is not clear that persecution leads to growth. It does, however, appear that growth leads to persecution.

AFTER THE MARXIST REVOLUTION

The unsuccessful coup d'etat of 1960 ought to have signaled to authorities the need for political reform. If it did, the authorities failed to perceive the signal, and the still-rebellious soldiers were bought off by the Emperor merely by increasing their wages.[10] Liberalization did not occur, the power of the Orthodox

8. Note Stephen Neill's (1976:55) assessment on growth: "Experience shows that when a church grows . . . by the witness of one to one, by the testimony of the Christian family to its non-Christian relatives, by the service of the unpaid evangelists, by the personal witness of those who have been set on fire by the love of Christ—the church is true to its own nature, manifests its being as the body of Christ, and so grows from strength to strength. Where this does not take place, introversion can only be another name for stagnation and decay."

9. See Cotterell 1973:ch. 15 for a more detailed consideration of the persecution of the church in Ethiopia. It is interesting to note that the Evangelical Church Makane Yesus has invited the intervention of other countries, and particularly the Scandinavian countries, in the matter of the persecution of Christians and general denial of civil rights under the current Marxist regime. But this seems merely to have led to the imprisonment of the Rev. Gudina Tumsa (and his wife), general secretary of the Evangelical Church Makane Yesus, accused of involvement with the Oromo Liberation Front. At the time of writing (March 1982) there is no firm news of the fate of this couple.

10. See in particular Richard Greenfield's (1965:446-49) invaluable work. It is invaluable first because its scholarly objectivity broke with a long tradition of hagiographical writing about the Haile Selassie regime, and second because many of the individuals involved in the 1960 coup died in the progress of the 1974 revolution and are no longer available as sources for this fascinating period of Ethiopian history.

Church was not contained, the vast differentials in wages were not corrected, and the general spirit of nepotism was not checked.

Marxist influence in the university—and later in the high schools—increased. On September 12, 1974, Haile Selassie, Emperor of Ethiopia since 1930, was deposed. Parliament was dissolved, the judiciary was dismissed, and a wide program of doctrinaire Marxism was introduced. Insurance companies and banks were nationalized. So was land. The people were allowed just one dwelling each, and other housing was taken by the government, which, in fact, usually meant the army. In spite of Raul Vivo's claim that this was a people's revolution,[11] this was true only of the very early stages. And this was because the reforms that were introduced (and reform was desperately needed) seemed to be carried through with no sensitivity to the real aspirations of the Ethiopian peasant.

Like Israel, the people wanted nothing better than to sit "each man under his vine and each man under his fig tree." But there was the rub: *his* vine and *his* fig tree. The government, however, could think only in terms of collectivization. The result was rapid disillusionment: Everyone was in favor of revolution, but no one was in favor of *this* revolution (except, perhaps, the army who were the main beneficiaries).

There was, obviously, the question of religion. Antireligious propaganda proliferated. In the pro-China phase of the revolution came a flood of Maoist literature. Mao's *Little Red Book* was everywhere. The phase passed to be replaced by the Russia-Cuba phase, characterized by radio and TV propaganda. In the midst of economic collapse the "toiling masses" spoke ruefully of *dabbo be-radyo*, "bread-on-the-radio."

As the Marxist line hardened, so opposition crystallized. Fighting against the regime spread throughout the provinces.[12] The Christians proved to be convenient whipping boys.

During the opening phase of the revolution, the Christians had found themselves ill-prepared to face the new situation. The Bible schools had been strong on theology but weak on sociology, and few knew even the rudiments of Marxist theory. Study and evaluation convinced them that communism as such presented few problems. After the elitism of the former regime, most could see that communism (as distinct from atheistic Marxism) was more biblical, more conformable to the Christian lifestyle. The church, in general, set to work to cooperate with the new regime in its literacy program and even in its program of collectivization. Few Christians were dragged into the multiplicity of separatist factions.

The Christians handed over their land, accepted the confiscation of tractors and other farm implements, and set up literacy classes. But when China-type "struggle meetings" were introduced in factories and the new communes, Christians were frequently the objects of denunciation. Undoubtedly there *were* aspects of the new society which the Christians would not accept. In particular there was the question of the mass chanting of ideological slogans: "We must

11. Vivo (1978:61) is a Cuban revolutionary and diplomat. He is *not* a historian!
12. The Oromo Liberation Front, the Tigre Liberation Front, the Eritrean Liberation Front, and the Eritrean People's Liberation Front are merely four of more than twenty such opposition groups operating in the country.

destroy our enemies," "Religion is drugging the masses," and even more explicitly, "God is dead." Through 1979 and early 1980 tens of thousands of Christians were imprisoned on charges relating to these slogans.

Indeed, in the middle part of 1980 so many Christians were in prison and so many others had fled their homes that the handful of Christians remaining in the villages were finding it all but impossible to feed them.[13] Even so, theirs was essentially a passive resistance. They obeyed the government where they could, disobeyed where they felt they must, but accepted imprisonment for their disobedience.

In the long term their stand was justified. By later 1980 the economic situation in the country had so far collapsed and famine was so widespread that the authorities no longer had either the heart or the resources to continue to hold the large numbers of prisoners being held, primarily in the south. Unceremoniously they were dismissed from prison.[14] The demand that the clenched fist salute be given and that the slogans should be chanted was dropped.

With the release of the prisoners came an extraordinary flood tide of people into the churches. It happened in the rural areas, but perhaps more markedly in the capital. Churches were forced to hold their services in duplicate and even in triplicate. Discipling the masses of new Christians became an almost insoluble problem. A discipleship class in one church began on Monday and by Thursday had to be discontinued because it had already filled the church and every available overflow area.[15]

THE SECOND PHASE ANALYZED

In this second phase of the account of the growth of the church in southern Ethiopia the importance of the independent assessment of the new situation by the indigenous church is again evident. It is unlikely that Western missionaries could have responded to Maoism and then to doctrinaire Marxism as objectively, as coolly, as biblically, as did the Ethiopian Christians, both in the Evangelical Church Makane Yesus and in the Kale-Heywet Church. The general isolation of Ethiopia from the familiar alignments of East and West, and from traditional associations with already committed international church groupings left them free to decide on the basis of a rational response rather than an emotional response.

13. In the rural areas prisoners must be fed by their friends. Even in the capital, prison diet is not sufficient to sustain life. Obviously I cannot cite sources for the information given in this part of the chapter. Suffice it to say that the information has come from several independent sources which are in substantial agreement with one another. But see the Amnesty International report *Human Rights Violations in Ethiopia* (1978, London) for a sobering summary.

14. In a manner entirely typical of Ethiopian culture the innocent prisoners were accused by their captors of lazing in the prisons at the expense of the state, thus turning the accuser into the accused.

15. The success of the churches in withstanding the opposition of the Marxist regime is admitted in the Dergue policy document originating from the Ministry of Information and National Guidance and somehow leaked to Nairobi. The document was published in *Africa Now* (not to be confused with the mission magazine of the same name) in Nairobi in November 1981. The document comments: "Not only are there funds for the places of worship, but the number of believers . . . is on the increase."

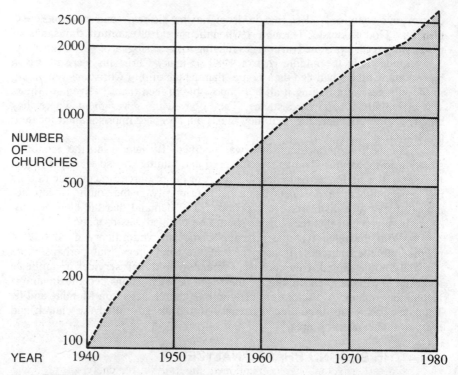

CHURCH GROWTH IN ETHIOPIA:
THE KALE-HEYWET CHURCHES

The Swedish Evangelical Mission had established a congregation in Addis Ababa in 1921, but it remained under a foreign pastor, first of all Swedish and then, during the Italian occupation, Italian, until 1940. In 1941 the congregation constituted itself a church independent of the Swedish Evangelical Mission.[16] It is from this point that the Evangelical Church Makane Yesus has its true beginnings, although it did not formally come into existence until 1959. From that point on the church was genuinely independent, although it continued to be in receipt of generous financial support for its major projects from the Luthern World Federation.

16. See Saeverås (1974) for a full account of the history of the ECMY. It is interesting to note that when the ECMY was first formed its first president was Dr. Emmanuael Gebre-Sellasse and the vice president was the American missionary, H. G. Schaefer. Another missionary, Manfred Lundgren, was treasurer. These appointments are symptomatic of a fundamental difference between the two churches: In the ECMY the churches were not financially independent. The churches, schools, ministers and services, their seminary and its curriculum, their radio station and its programs appeared to me always to reflect this dependence. By contrast the KHC church buildings and Bible schools appeared dowdy, the ministers uncouth. In my view, when the revolution came with its drastic levelling of salaries and cutback in employment and with its savage testing of the Christian's commitment, the KHC was better fitted to face the test.

We have already seen that the Kale-Heywet Church came into existence during the Italian occupation, and that when the missionaries returned to Ethiopia it was to find the church established. They accepted the role of advisers to the churches, and it was in that capacity that they attended church conferences.

Thus the two churches were essentially free from the biased opinions of their related expatriate missionaries. Their response to the revolution was, therefore, an *Ethiopian* response. *Radio Voice of the Gospel* was taken without compensation, but there was no Protestant backlash. The new Evangelical Church Makane Yesus headquarters buildings, scarcely completed, were taken, but again with no subsequent backlash.

The people of the country could scarcely fail to see that here were people who differed radically in their thinking from the military rulers, who were able to relate to them in a very different way from others who took up arms.

The policy of the church, apparently naive but certainly biblical, was ultimately justified. In time the Red Terror and the White Terror coalesced in a welter of blood and brought the war in Addis Ababa to an end through sheer attrition (Legum and Lee 1977:III). Many of the liberation fronts exhausted themselves in confronting the endless flow of armaments that came from Russia. But at the end of it all the church was still there—still expressing its rejection of atheism, still insisting that violence and force could not solve Ethiopia's problems, still demonstrating that even death as the ultimate sanction could not turn Christians away from doing right. Life had meaning beyond death, and for certain principles even death could be accepted.

One other factor must be mentioned: the unity of the church. With some happy exceptions, the missions had not related well to each other. In particular the missionaries of the two largest groups, the Lutheran missions and the Sudan Interior Mission, had a long history of misunderstanding and mistrust.

There were three competing Baptist missionary societies. With the revolution most of these missions were squeezed out altogether, their mission stations expropriated, their schools, clinics, and hospitals Ethiopianized. Those that remained soon found that they could no longer afford the luxury of separatism.

Certainly in the churches a new era of cooperation began. The annual church leaders' conference replaced the sporadic United Christian Conventions of former years. Representatives of all the churches, with the exception of the Orthodox Churches, organized the program and shared the platform.

The revolution had proved a devastating experience for the Orthodox Church. Their extensive lands were confiscated, their state financing brought to an end, their privileged position as the state religion taken from them. The long-suppressed voice of criticism of the church was suddenly very vocal. Even some of the missionaries of the Bible Churchmen's Missionary Society expressed their view that the Orthodox Church had lost all credibility. The Bible Churchmen's Missionary Society (an Anglican mission), which had worked patiently for the revival of the Orthodox Church since 1933, left the country.

An early move for the reform of the Orthodox Church was contained, and the leaders of the church returned to its former preoccupation with cementing an alliance with government. They chose to align themselves with Colonel Atnafu, the second vice chairman of the Dergue,[17] correctly recognizing the power struggle developing between him and Colonel Mengistu, the first vice chairman. They backed the wrong man. Colonel Atnafu was executed and many of his supporters were arrested, including some of the Orthodox hierarchy. The Patriarch was arrested in 1977 and shot without trial in 1980.[18] There is still no sign of genuine revival in the Orthodox Church.

CONCLUSION

The survey presented here offers a great deal of raw material for the missiologist. More detail is readily available from the standard bibliographical materials, and there are still the rather extensive archives of the Sudan Interior Mission, stored in Toronto, awaiting analysis.

There is to my mind little doubt that the two primary factors involved in the growth of the church in southern Ethiopia are indigeneity and the involvement of the masses in the church. The measure in which these two factors are more evident in the Kale-Heywet Church than in the Evangelical Church Makane Yesus is also the measure of the greater growth of the former than the latter.

The importance of this indigeneity in the present situation lies in the freedom of the churches to work out a theology for the present experience, not in terms of Chalcedon but in terms of Cuba, not in terms of Calvin but in terms of Castro, a theology which relates to and meets the challenge of humanism in general and Marxism in particular. The Bible is seen to be the authoritative word from God and to stand as such over against all merely human writings. Christianity is seen to be not merely another religion, one option among many, but a wholistic way of life.

From the missiological standpoint there remains the enigma of the development of a church in Ethiopia within an area of essential cultural homogeneity, and the question of the viability of the expansion beyond the present envelope, especially into the Semitic Gurage peoples to the north. Here two independent Bible translation programs (SIM and Wycliffe) are underway, each representing a faith-expectation that church growth can cross linguistic and cultural barriers. Already a handful of churches have appeared. The boundary once crossed could initiate a new era of growth reaching up to the Semitic north, and into the Orthodox Church.

REFERENCES CITED
Amnesty International
1978 *Human Rights Violations in Ethiopia*, London.

17. The word "Dergue" (although this odd spelling has no linguistic justification) is a nominal form from a root meaning "to act," "to do something." It is thus the executive of the military government. The executive has disposed of Haile Selassie himself (probably murdered, but see the Amnesty International report), of General Aman Andom, the first chairman, of General Teferi Bante, the second chairman, and of Colonel Atnafu, the second vice-chairman. Colonel Mengistu is now president.

18. Private information confirmed by letter from the British Foreign Office. The execution has not been announced in Ethiopia, so far as I am aware.

ARÉN, Gustav
   1978   *Evangelical Pioneers in Ethiopia,* Stockholm: E.F.S. förlaget.
COTTERELL, F. Peter
   1969-70   "An indigenous church in southern Ethiopia," *The Bulletin of the Society for African Church History,* III, 1-2.
   1973   *Born at Midnight,* Chicago: Moody.
   1975   *Ethiopia, a Country Profile,* Addis Ababa: SIM.
DAVIS, R. J.
   1966   *Fire on the Mountain,* Grand Rapids: Zondervan.
DUFF, Clarence
   1977   *God's Higher Ways,* Nutley, New Jersey: Presbyterian and Reformed Publishing Company.
   1980   *Cords of Love,* Nutley, New Jersey: Presbyterian and Reformed Publishing Company.
GREENFIELD, Richard
   1965   *Ethiopia, a New Political History,* London: Pall Mall Press.
LASS-WESTPHAL, Ingeborg
   1972   "Protestant Missions during and After the Italo-Ethiopian War, 1935-1937," *Journal of Ethiopian Studies,* 1 (January).
LEGUM, Colin and LEE, Bill
   1977   *Conflict in the Horn of Africa,* London: Rex Collings.
MOSLEY, Leonard
   1964   *Haile Selassie,* London: Weidenfeld and Nicolson.
NEILL, Stephen
   1976   *Salvation Tomorrow,* Nashville: Abingdon.
SAEVERÅS, Olav
   1974   *On Church-Mission Relations in Ethiopia 1944-1969,* Lunde (Vol. XXVII of *Studia Missionalia Upsaliensia*).
ULLENDORFF, E.
   1967   *Ethiopia and the Bible,* London: Oxford University Press.
VIVO, Raul Valdes
   1978   *Ethiopia's Revolution,* New York: International Publishers.

3. RECENT CHURCH GROWTH IN INDONESIA

Alle G. Hoekema

IN WHAT FOLLOWS WE WILL MAKE A SHORT EVALUATION OF THE GROWTH OF the churches in Indonesia. In 1979 the Indonesian Council of Churches (*Dewan Gereja2 di Indonesia,* or DGI) published a survey of the history, present situation, attitude toward the surrounding culture and other religions, and sense of the future of its member churches (Ukur and Cooley 1979; Cooley 1977:4). This report, *Jerih dan Juang (Exertion and Struggle),* serves as a major source of information for this chapter. Using the same method, Avery Willis (1977) published a dissertation in which the growth figures of five Javanese-speaking churches on Java are compared and analyzed.

Though we have no better sources than the cited references, they offer only partial help in assessing recent church growth in Indonesia. The statistics are incomplete. Another reason for caution is the fact that not all the material which originally should have formed the base for *Jerih dan Juang* was ready at the scheduled time (especially the material about other religions and culture).[1] The conclusions, too, of both studies (and most other, minor studies in this field) are based upon the situation around 1973. Since that time the growth rate of most churches has slowed down. Some possible reasons for the slowed pace will be given at the end of the chapter.

First we will look briefly at the history of the churches in Indonesia, and then we will take a closer look at various reasons for growth.

A LONG HISTORY OF COLONIAL CHRISTIANITY

The history of the Indonesian churches started in 645, according to a Catholic historian (Ukur and Cooley 1979:450); an old source mentions that Nestorian Christians came to Sumatra then. It was not until the time of Portuguese colonization (1520-1615) that Catholic parishes were established in several parts of the archipelago (Cooley 1968:6-7). During the administration of the Dutch East Indies Company (1625-1815) most of those churches turned Protestant, though some strong Catholic bases remained. Starting in the middle of the nineteenth

1. Assessment of Schumann (1979:20-36). Cooley (1979:102-16) also describes the survey.

Alle G. Hoekema, Alkmaar, Netherlands, is pastor of a Mennonite congregation in Alkmaar. From 1969 to 1977 he taught at Wijata Wacana Christian Academy in Pati, Central Java, Indonesia. He has written a number of articles on Indonesian church history and theology.

century, missionary societies also began work on islands, such as Java, which until then were closed to Christianity. Many of the churches which were founded by that missionary endeavor became independent between 1930 and 1940; another part got their independence in the years 1945-50 when Indonesia struggled against the Dutch.

The building of this nation has been an enormous venture. The first president of the Republic, Sukarno, had to deal with people of many languages and cultures, belonging to different religions, and having different political aspirations. The country has a complex economic infrastructure and is overpopulated, especially on Java where more than half of the total population (119 million in 1971; 147 million in 1980) lives. He tried to unite those people while granting sufficient differentiation. Hence the national motto: *Bhinneka tunggal ika* (unity within diversity). Unfortunately Sukarno lost control over the main political groups in the early sixties, and the equilibrium between communist components, nationalists, and the Islamic parties (which never received much more than thirty-five percent of the votes in elections) was lost in a time when the economic situation worsened. The result was an aborted coup on September 30, 1965, inspired by certain groups in the armed forces.

The aftermath of the attempted coup became deeply traumatic to the whole nation. Hundreds of thousands of people were killed, mostly communists or alleged communists who were—and still are—blamed for the coup. The new (semimilitary) government led by Suharto restored law and order. Most Christians credit him for doing so. But this same government periodically has to face both social upheavals within the overpopulated cities and religious tensions. The Muslims draw strength from the Islamic restoration in other parts of the world and therefore claim more influence in Indonesia. But the tendency toward a pluralistic political and religious system cannot be stopped. Within that open system Christians can play an important role.

THE CHURCHES GROW
Already during the colonial time some churches experienced periods of sudden growth. Certain churches in Sumatra grew rapidly in the nineteenth and early twentieth centuries. From 1916 on, the church on the island of Nias was captivated by a revivalistic movement. In 1933 1.8 million people or 2.8 percent of the total population were Christians, most of them living in traditionally Christian areas like the Moluccas, North Sulawesi, and North Sumatra.

During World War II the churches hardly grew. After 1945 both the country and the Christian churches had to recover from Japanese occupation and from the struggle for independence. During the first years of that struggle the Christians often had been suspect because their religion was considered "agama belanda" (Dutch/white religion). In the fifties, when it became clear that they were loyal Indonesians, their churches began to grow again. Growth was significant, but mostly not yet spectacular. Then in the early sixties a number of churches started to grow very fast.

In 1953 the number of Christians within the DGI had increased to 2.5 million; in 1967 there were already 4.5 million; the national census of 1971 gives a total of almost 9 million Christians (or 7.5 percent of the total population). Though all these figures have to be viewed with caution, they nevertheless give a clear indication. If the Christians have grown at the same rate as the total population during the last decade, then there are now (1980 census) almost 11 million Christians in a population of 147 million people. The biggest increases among Christians took place in North Sumatra, Kalimantan, Timor, and Central and East Java.[2]

The reports show a wide variety of reasons for this growth. The *Jerih dan Juang* survey concludes: "The growth of the churches in Indonesia did not start after the abortive coup and was not mainly due to factors which had to do with this event and its aftermath (massacres). The churches in Indonesia grew constantly; that is its character and essence before and after incidents like the coup" (Ukur and Cooley 1979:200). Nevertheless political and socioeconomic factors together account for almost half of the reasons mentioned to join the church (Ukur and Cooley 1979:204).

Willis (1977:223-24; Ukur and Cooley 1979:200-01; Tasdik 1970:11-12) enumerates the following motives for conversion among members of the five Javanese churches which he researched (in order of importance and frequency):

1) the government decision in 1966 that every Indonesian must profess a recognized religion;
2) efforts by the institutional churches, like pastors, evangelistic campaigns, Sunday school or catechism classes;
3) spiritual need, stated as needs of the inner life (*batin*), emptiness of soul, or the lacking of "peace";
4) the appeal of the good news itself to human hearts;
5) factors from society, like influence from village leaders, social groups, or personal witness by neighbors;
6) protection out of fear of being labeled as a communist;
7) family members who played a role in the decision to become a Christian;
8) testimony of day-to-day Christian life;
9) reaction to failures of another religion;
10) service of the churches through schools, hospitals, and so on;
11) miracles like the power to exorcise demons or perform healings.

This list resembles in many aspects the one given by *Jerih dan Juang* and other reports. Some other arguments can be found there, and sometimes another order: notably transmigration and urbanization which loosens ties of tribal religion and causes new needs.[3] Another factor includes the indigenization and autonomy of the churches.

THE BACKGROUND TO CHURCH GROWTH

Most attention has been given to developments in Java, both because of rapid growth in some churches and because most studies have focused on the situation

2. Figures cited by Cooley (1977), Willis (1977:9), and Jones (1976:19-56).
3. "Urbanization is more advanced among Christians than among non-Christians" (Van Akkeren 1970:116). Migration is a very old missionary principle, Van Akkeren says, and he gives the examples of migration from Central Java to East Java (114), according to which principle he quotes Acts 8:1; 11:19-20. Migration of Christians of other tribes and islands to urban areas of Java also accounts partly for the numerical increase on that island. Chinese migrants from Sumatra and West Kalimantan, Bataks from North Sumatra, people from Minahassa, and Moluccas come to Java.

there. There is not always a parallel between what happened on Java and growth processes elsewhere; nevertheless, church growth on Java may be taken as a good example.

EXPANSION OF HINDUISM AND MYSTICAL GROUPS

Clifford Geertz (1972:77ff) mentions that some 20,000 Hindu converts were in the regency of Modjokuto in 1972 in the area where he did research in the years 1957-58. At the time of Geertz's research there were no Hindus in the regency. Some of them may have sought shelter there after the 1965 coup. Most of them belong to the *abangan* people: those Javanese who are tolerant toward the old Javanese religion and negligent toward basic Islamic duties. They stand opposite the so-called *santris*, those who belong to the orthodox Muslim part of Javanese society. These groups are sometimes named the "red" over against the "white," or left over against right (and in a way they belong to each other, like the red-white colors of the Indonesian national banner).

The 1971 census reports that over 300,000 Hindus live outside Bali, some 180,000 of them on Java. But there may be many more. Another publication (Mayor Polak 1973, 1977) gives a number of 334,000 Hindus in East Java alone. Javanese Hinduism existed already before World War II, but after 1965 it got in touch with Balinese Hinduism. Mayor Polak reports a steady growth, and even if we need to accept his estimates with some reserve, nevertheless that growth among common rural people is striking especially because the reasons for conversion are the same as those for conversion into the Christian church.

In a parallel way the *aliran kebatinan* (mystical sects) in Central and East Java also expanded. Specific data on the social background of the adherents of mystical groups is not available, but probably a rather large group belongs to the middle class and so-called *priyayi* (Javanese nobility and civil servants). According to the office of the public prosecutor at Semarang, Central Java had 286 recognized mystical organizations in 1970; thirty-three of those groups had been founded after 1950 and twenty-one after 1960. One of the largest groups, called *Pangestu* (founded in 1949 at Solo), had more than 50,000 members and is also active in East Java (De Jong 1973:17).

Since mysticism shows a high degree of tolerance toward all religions and is rather syncretistic, it can attract many people. Moreover, the present government supports mysticism, and a few years ago the *aliran kebatinan* were put on a par with the official religions. De Jong (1973:13) points to the fact that the insecurity in society leads many people back to the ancestral past, which is depicted as an "ideal-typical" period. This insecurity is felt especially in the cities: People are longing for the reliable atmosphere of a small group. In the *kebatinan* group many people are looking for the fellowship of the *desa* (village) and the *kekeluargaan* (family spirit) which they lost in urban migration. Not the doctrine, but the practical lifestyle makes these groups so attractive to many people.

Neither *Jerih dan Juang* nor Willis has given satisfactory answers to the question what this growth of Hinduism and *kebatinan* means in connection with the growth of the churches there. Others give a theological answer, but sociologically this fact strengthens the force of "external" reasons for conversion to Christianity.

MESSIANIC MOVEMENTS

Both in the nineteenth century and in the first half of the present century messianic movements received much attention and attracted many followers. These movements have been studied seriously by various scholars.[4] Often these *Ratu Adil* (just king) movements arose as a protest against colonial policy and social inequity, but they also exhibited a religious element. This element was also present in the movements which were led by Javanese Christians in the nineteenth century, such as Ibrahim Tunggul Wulung and Sadrach Suropranoto who formed indigenous Christian communities at a time when Dutch missionaries still tried to control everything.[5]

The survey *Jerih dan Juang* does not mention the messianic phenomenon (though some of the reports of member churches of the DGI do so). Apparently the answers given by churches did not indicate that this eschatological factor played a role in the motives for conversion. Nevertheless, there is reason to believe that this type of expectation which had long influenced the hearts and minds of the Javanese also was present during the recent period of church growth.

The social scheme which Van Akkeren (1970:185-86) drafts of Javanese society places the *Ratu Adil* expectations in the same quarter as the progressive Javanism after the independence. Politically this would bring it near the Communist Party. Within the Christian church people such as Tunggul Wulung should be mentioned in this section. With the defeat of the communists these popular expectations eventually also became suspect. Could this be an explanation for the absence of eschatological expectations among the motives for conversion?

Nevertheless, these expectations are alive. The fact that several books with old prophecies about the coming of a just king or a righteous era are still being printed, means that there are people who believe those prophecies. In one village in the Muria area, Karanglegi, a large group of people accepted the gospel after they had read some of those prophecies which can be explained in favor of Christianity (Willis 1977:45, and oral information). There may be more of those examples, since reportedly Hinduism in East Java also grew due to the same kind of prophecies like the prophecy of King Joyoboyo or the Sabdopalon legend (Mayor Polak 1977:17-19; 1973:16; Willis 1977:45).

In 1976 a national scandal arose when a certain Sawito Kartowibowo, a civil servant from West Java, claimed to have a *wahyu*, a revelation, and among his alleged supporters were a chairman of the Council of Churches and a Roman Catholic cardinal. The case, which certainly had a protest character, was closed after the imprisonment of Sawito. It shows how vivid those types of expectations still are as undercurrents of the main political and socioreligious events.

Even today Jesus Christ can be called *Ratu Adil* in the East Javanese church (Van Akkeren 1970:161). Van Akkeren warns against the danger that "the Christian expectation of the future will degenerate into an ornament of the *ratu adil* image," even though this image played and perhaps still plays an important part in the opening of hearts to the preaching of the gospel (Van Akkeren 1970:207).

---

4. Recent scholars include Drewes, Sartono Kartodirdjo, and van der Kroef.

5. On Tunggul Wulung, see Van Akkeren (1970:154-57) and A. G. Hoekema (1979); on Sadrach, recently in Quarles Van Ufford (1980).

Even though this factor was not explicitly mentioned among the motives for conversion, it may have been present both for those who had spiritual needs and for those who sailed at the compass of village leaders or social groups, or reacted at the demonstrated failure of another religion.

CHARISMATIC MOVEMENTS

Some churches grew fast as the result of charismatic experiences. This had happened earlier, as the great spiritual movement on Nias (1916-25) proved. Cooley (1968:72) concludes that "It gave an unusual dimension of personal spiritual experience to many Nias Christians." In the period between 1960 and 1965 the Evangelical Christian Church on Java, located in the Muria area of North Central Java, also had charismatic experiences which brought the moderator of that church to the conclusion that his church had the same Spirit which was present in the church of the apostles. "Does all this belong to the features of the Church? Maybe not yet. But the preachers who have these experiences with the living Spirit, get more courage to go everywhere. They are asked by many to pray in behalf of the sick. And their experiences give real joy to their faith" (Hoekema 1974:36). It is not really clear whether this charismatic spirit clearly influenced the growth of that particular church; the various growth figures are not unanimous.[6]

Perhaps the best-known example of a charismatic movement after 1965 was on Timor. A large number of evangelistic teams brought a revivalistic movement which certainly meant a large gain to the Protestant Church on that island. Nonetheless, Cooley (1975:112-27) comes to the conclusion that the total influence of this movement, which apparently died out after some years, was not greater than the government pressure with regard to numerical growth of the church there. His estimation is supported by *Jerih dan Juang,* though no dependable figures are available for the years 1964-65.

Finally we must mention the growth of several Pentecostal churches which attract many people of Chinese background. The percentage of Chinese Indonesians who have become Christian has grown rapidly. The Pentecostal churches have probably grown rapidly too, but figures are not available. Many of those churches started after 1945.

UNINTENDED EVANGELISM

All reports and publications cite unintentional evangelization or "self-proclamation of the gospel" as a distinguishing factor in the growth of the Indonesian churches. Ardi Soejatno said in 1969 that "the greater part of the church growth of recent years in East Java has been a result of this 'unintentional evangelism' " (Soejatno 1970:5). He quotes Mark 4:26-29 concerning the growing seed which "of itself" (*automatē*) bears fruit. This parable serves also as the *leitmotiv* for the reports from the various churches which together formed the material for *Jerih dan Juang.*

6. Mrs. Martati (1976:90) gives the figures: 1953, 5,260 members; 1963, 17,562 members, which means an annual increase of 23.5 percent (adults and children). In *Jerih dan Juang* (Ukur and Cooley 1979:195) the annual increase for the years 1950 to 1960 is given as 0.7 percent, with 3.7 percent for the period 1964-65. Willis (1977:192) gives the annual increase from 1960 to 1964 as 28.4 percent.

Those reports were published under the common title *Benih yang tumbuh* (The Growing Seed). Tasdik (quoted by Willis 1977:17) explains this by saying that "even though it [Christianity] was a very small lamp, as long as it was still burning, it had a great influence." The church in the fifties and early sixties may have seemed weak and small, but it nevertheless prepared the road along which many people later dared enter!

A similar word is heard in the report I. K. Martati gives about the situation of the Evangelical Christian Church in Java:

> What is called evangelization indeed theoretically is not available here, but in practice it works. Evangelization is expressing in all ways in the midst of the world the existence of Christianity (that is: the church and its members). The existence of the church has to be demonstrated to other groups in society. By this way the church shows its composure, even when she experiences tension and oppression. By its very existence the church tries to help the sick and the suffering ones. Evangelization is here actually done as it were by the Lord himself (Martati 1976:96).

Some pages later she says,

> The matter of evangelization has already become second nature to the hearts of the Christians. Everyone of them knows that he has the task of extending the Kingdom of God with the skills each man has (Martati 1976:98).

When we read lines like these we can understand why *Jerih dan Juang* concludes that there is no clear correlation between having an organized evangelization program and the growth rate of the church which has such a program: Many churches just grow without any program, or even without a clear understanding of what evangelization is (Ukur and Cooley 1979:216, 219).

One might ask why many churches do not have an evangelization program. One reason could be that such a program presupposes a rather high degree of organization and theological reflection. Many rural churches cannot provide that yet. Another reason could be that in regard to the surrounding, non-Christian society, it often seems better not to overemphasize evangelization, but to stress that service and nation-building, unity, and witness together should be called "the mission of the church."

Nevertheless, certainly there is also intentional spreading of the gospel. We have to point, for instance, to the work of the Indonesian Bible Society which translates portions of the Bible into many tribal languages and into modern Indonesian idiom and spreads thousands of copies all over the country. Christian publishing houses and a number of Christian radio stations carry on similar work.

But some churches have clear aims of church planting. One example is the *Gereja Kristen Muria Indonesia* (GKMI or Muria Christian Church of Indonesia), which grew from 550 adult members in 1952 to over 6,000 in 1982, partly because of a rapid expansion outside the Muria area in Central Java where it originally was confined. Such an extension into a large geographical area (including West Kalimantan and South Sumatra) gives reason to rejoice, but it also gives rise to possible difficulties (Yoder 1981:459). The GKMI is a faithful member of the Council of Churches. Up to several years ago almost all of its members were ethnic Chinese Indonesians.

A majority of the churches which have clear concepts of evangelization and programs or campaigns to spread the good news are not members of the Council of Churches—which unites some seventy percent of all Roman Catholic Christians in Indonesia (Wahono 1978:295-305). Some tension can be observed between those churches which often have close ties with evangelical bodies from abroad and those churches which are members of the DGI regarding methods of certain, sometimes "aggressive," evangelization programs.

One church which is not a DGI member and has a rather heavy accent on evangelization is the Baptist. From thirty-nine members in 1953 they grew to almost 11,000 members in 1971, and probably show the highest growth rate of all churches.[7] But then, in 1971 that church employed over 100 foreign missionaries, compared with fewer than 200 foreign co-workers associated with all member-churches of the DGI together. Does this mean that more missionaries mean a larger growth rate? It is hard to compare the figures of the various churches; too many factors have to be taken into account. According to Willis' study, for instance, the comparison with the four Javanese-speaking churches is difficult to make since we do not know exactly the proportion between urban and rural membership, between Javanese and Chinese Indonesians within those churches, nor the influence of Islam at the places where those churches work, whereas the process of indigenization among the Baptists started more recently.

GOVERNMENT PRESSURE

All churches agree that the events of 1965 brought many people into the churches who otherwise would not have sought spiritual shelter there. Among them are members of the Nationalist Party, but also sympathizers of the now-forbidden Communist Party. Many people felt deceived by the ruthless attitude of a number of Muslim leaders and youth groups in the months after the alleged coup. Many of those new members were willing to admit that they always had belonged to the *abangan* and had not been Muslims at all. Others came from several mystical groups which right after 1965 were suspect in the eyes of the authorities. The churches were among the first to take pastoral care of the hundreds of thousands of political prisoners and their families, and this too gave the churches credit.

Tasdik (1970:13) gives examples of how long the duration of catechism was which new members in East and Central Java had to follow: from a period of two weeks to more than two years. But there are also cases in which people were baptized first and only afterward received Christian instruction.

Both the government pressure on those who had not yet chosen an official religion and the imminent fear decreased after some years. But from 1965 on the Christians always felt supported by the government, and this strengthened their position in society and their zeal to evangelize. Later we will see that this situation changed somewhat as government pressure of another kind tried to restrict evangelism in 1978.

7. Willis (1977:192). Cooley (1968:48) made a rather severe judgment of the Baptist Church; it is, however, no longer valid in 1981. The 1979 *Jerih dan Juang* report lists only one church that mentioned a drain of members to the Baptists.

THE ROLE OF EDUCATION AND URBANIZATION

We will have to look at one more factor which eventually influenced the growth of the churches. The figures of the 1971 population census make clear that Christians constitute eight percent of the population of urban areas on Java, whereas this percentage is no more than 0.8 in the rural areas (where eighty-two percent of the total population lives). It also becomes clear that the proportion of Christians aged ten to twenty-nine, compared with those aged thirty and older, is higher than average in Central and East Java and in South Sulawesi.

Urban areas of Central Java (including the university town, Yogyakarta) have sixteen percent Christians among those aged ten to twenty-nine, as compared to 3.3 percent in total Central Java (Jones 1976:31-35). This suggests that in the years before 1971 the gospel attracted especially young people. Maybe they felt impressed by the image of modernization which accompanies the churches in many places. This is valid for Javanese and probably also for Chinese Indonesians on Java. Almost six percent of the total membership of the *Gereja Kristen Indonesia di Jawa Tengah* consists of students. Youth account for more than thirty-five percent of the membership.

Gavin Jones gives the following explanation for this rapid growth among Chinese Indonesians: "This growth appears to represent both a response to intensive missionary efforts and identification in the Indonesian community through espousal of a more acceptable, less 'chinese' religion which at the same time removes the suspicion of communist sympathies" (1976:25).

Though only three percent of those who were interviewed by Willis mentioned *service* as their primary factor for conversion, nevertheless schools may have been harvest places for the churches: Christian schools once again combine gospel and progress. Schools also open doors to better jobs, and often Christian (more often Catholic) schools are among the best schools. The overall figures of 1971 show that only twenty-two percent of the Christians are illiterate as compared to over forty-one percent of the Muslims; in urban areas this proportion is even more significant: 6.4 percent as over against 24.7 percent.

In addition, young people are more receptive to evangelization campaigns, youth camps, and other special activities. The churches, however, have become aware of some problems which can arise here. Young people with a better educational background often are critical of the traditional ways in which many churches are governed; some of them have left the churches out of frustration.

DIFFICULTIES AHEAD

None of the arguments used above can abate our joy about the large growth of many churches in Indonesia during the past decades. We also think that it is not proper to discuss at this place the question whether the Lord of the church or mere outside factors are responsible for this growth. Willis uses the picture of a hand in a glove. He may be right. Nevertheless, one is inclined to be more prudent and less enthusiastic than he is. It is not so easy to divide growth into political and sociological factors on the one hand and into spiritual and church-growth factors on the other. The growth rate of almost all churches has slowed down in the past years. In some churches there even is stagnation. The churches face a number of problems which could not have been foreseen fifteen years ago.

First, the same government which supported the churches by exhorting citizens to make a choice between the officially recognized religions issued some decrees (*Exchange* 1978:47-53) which tried to restrict evangelization or proselytism among people who already adhered to one of those religions. This meant that Christians were no longer allowed to proclaim the gospel to Muslims—only to animists (as in the inlands of Kalimantan) or atheists.

One of the background factors to this new policy was the growing role, both internationally and nationally, of Islam. Although the application and execution of those decrees seems flexible until now, it is nevertheless a warning that the churches cannot always expect a sympathetic government. The firm answer which was formulated in a statement of the Central Committee of the Council of Churches in Indonesia in 1978 proves that the churches felt confident and strengthened: "As long as human history lasts and in any possible circumstances the church will never be able to shirk its duty of proclaiming the Gospel to all creatures (Mark 16:15) who in freedom are willing to listen to it" (Koetsier and de Kuiper 1979:73).

When in 1981 the Muslim *Majelis Ulama* (High Council) issued a decree that Muslims were no longer free to attend Christian Christmas celebrations, again the churches protested with success because consent by the Minister for Religious Affairs to this decree would violate religious tolerance and make evangelization more difficult. This is another example of the inner strength the churches feel in spite of increasing pressure from outside.

A difficulty of a totally different kind involves the growth of tension between urban and rural life. Some churches have a clear urban history (notably those churches with a Chinese background), and the question as it was already put by Van Akkeren twenty years ago is this: Do they "still reflect the socio-economic conditions of the colonial and pre-colonial past? Are these conditions favourable to the mission of the Church—for the confrontation, for example, of the Gospel with Islam and communism?" (Van Akkeren 1970:140).

The same warning is given by an Indonesian theologian, himself belonging to an urban church:

> Christians, numerically a very small minority, but economically and socially rather privileged, are easily tempted to play the psychological game of "over-compensation": building luxurious church buildings, organizing mass evangelistic campaigns, etc. Do we really understand the depth of the meaning of Jesus as the manifestation of the suffering God and the call to be the servant people of the Servant Lord? (Abednego 1974:354).

Yet another sign of emerging problems is the gain by the charismatic movement in the last few years. The large Java Christian Church (Reformed, Central Java) sees this phenomenon as the result of a lack of pastoral care for the thousands who after 1965 joined the church. Insofar as the charismatic movement is accompanied by certain supranatural aspects, it finds a rich soil on Java, where certain mystic groups also make use of miracles.

Recently some research has been done into charismatic groups in Jakarta, Bandung, Surabaya, Malang, Medan, and Menado. In Jakarta there are said to be a thousand small groups, mostly within existing churches, sometimes outside (some meeting in luxurious hotels, some even using the English language!). All reports have the same tenor. The charismatic groups are seen as a correction to the bureaucracy, frozen church life, and sterile liturgical forms within the churches (Peninjau 1980:6-7).

Tasdik, who in 1968 researched the motives for conversion within four groups of new Javanese Christians in East and Central Java, revisited those places ten years later to see what had become of those groups. His conclusion was that proper pastoral care is of more importance to the inner growth and numerical development of the churches than anything else (Tasdik 1978:86).

All these difficulties (and several others) may mean that the present spiritual capacities of the churches have been stretched maximally, and that the churches have to move forward prudently and with wisdom, including some worldly wisdom. Under the present conditions this means abstaining from any form of evangelization which is considered aggressive by people of other faiths, the more so because real dialogue has yet to start.

Also, it must be considered prudent not to make church growth the only aim at all costs; the churches need time to strengthen their own bodies, to find the proper ways of functioning *within* (as an integral part of) the society, and to start the theological reflection about their very existence as churches. The *Jerih dan Juang* survey was only a small start—the smaller since most of the member churches of the DGI belong to the Calvinist or Lutheran heritage.

Nevertheless, the churches have made a big gain during the past decades. They are no longer a marginal group. Even as a marginal group they were able to take a middle position between the mystic-oriented Javanists and the orthodox *santri* Moslems by showing "the signs of justice, peace, harmony and love, which have come among us in Christ" (Van Akkeren 1970:209). Now, almost twenty years and a traumatic coup later, a more openly pluralistic system (Geertz 1972:62-84) is arising in Indonesia. That means even better opportunities are ahead for the churches to become servants of God by serving the needs of men and women in Indonesia.

REFERENCES CITED

ABEDNEGO, Benjamin
   1974   "Church Growth in East Java: The Call to be Servants of God," *International Review of Mission*, Vol. LXIII, No. 251, July.

COOLEY, F. L.
   1968   *Indonesia: Church and Society,* New York: Friendship Press.
   1975   "Gerakan Roh di Timor," *Peninjau, Majalah Lembaga Penelitian dan Studi—DGI,* Vol. 2.
   1977   "The Growing Seed—A descriptive and analytical survey of the church in Indonesia," *Occasional Bulletin of Missionary Research,* Vol. 1, No. 1, January.
   1979   "Makna Proyek Survey Menyeluruh sebagai Peristiwa Dalam Sejarah Gereja di Indonesia," *Theo-doron, Pemberian Allah. Kumpulan karangan dalam rangka menghormati usia 75 tahun Prof. D. Dr. Theodor Mueller-Krueger,* Jakarta: B.P.K. Gunung Mulia.

DE JONG, S.
1973 "Een Javaanse Levenshouding," Wageningen: Veenman en Zn.

EXCHANGE
1978 Text of the decrees in *Exchange, Bulletin of Third World Christian Literature,* No. 21, Leiden: Interuniversity Institute for Missiological and Ecumenical Research.

GEERTZ, Clifford
1972 "Religious Change and Social Order in Soeharto's Indonesia," *Asia,* No. 27, Autumn, New York: The Asia Society.

HOEKEMA, A. G.
1974 "Gesprek met Ds. S. Djojodihardjo," *Doopsgezind Jaarboekje,* Kollum: Algemene Doopsgezinde Societeit.
1979 "Kiai Ibrahim Tunggul Wulung, een Javaanse Apollos," *Nederlands Theologisch Tijdschrift,* Vol. 33, April.

JONES, Calvin
1976 "Religion and Education in Indonesia," *Indonesia,* No. 22, October.

KOETSIER, C. H. and DE KUIPER, A.
1979 "Godsdienstvrijheid in Indonesië in het geding," *Wereld en Zending,* Vol. 8, No. 1.

MARTATI, Insuhardiq Kumaat
1976 *Benih Yang Tumbuh V. Gereja Injili di Tanah Jawa,* Jakarta: Lembaga Penelitian dan Studi—DGI.

MAYOR POLAK, J. B. A. F.
1973 *De herleving van het Hindoeisme op Oost Java,* Voorpublikatie nr. 8, Afdeling Suid—en Zuidoost Azië, Anthropologisch-Sociologisch Centrum, Universiteit van Amsterdam.
1977 *De herleving van het Hindoeisme op Oost-Java (II),* working paper nr. 1, Universiteit van Amsterdam.

PENINJAU
1980 "Gerakan Kharismatik (Suatu Studi Pendahuluan)," Vol. 7, No. 3.

QUARLES VAN UFFORD, Ph.
1980 "Why don't you sit down; Sadrach and the struggle for religious independence in the earliest phase of the Church of Central-Java (1861-1899)," *Man, Meaning and History, Essays in Honour of H. G. Schulte Nordholt,* The Hague: Martinus Nijhoff.

SCHUMANN, Olaf
1979 "Hoe groeien de kerken in Indonesië? Beschrijving van een zelfonderzoek," *Wereld en Zending,* Vol. 8, No. 1.

SOEJATNO, Ardi
1970 "The Evangelistic Methods of the Last Few Years," *Motives for Conversion in East-Java,* Tasdik (ed.), Singapore: The Foundation for Theological Education in South East Asia.

TASDIK
1970 *Motives for Conversion in East-Java,* Singapore: The Foundation for Theological Education in South East Asia.
1978 *Penginjilan dan Penggembalaan,* Yogyakarta: Pusat Penelitian dan Innovasi Pendidikan Duta Wacana.

UKUR, F. and COOLEY, F. L., eds.
  1979   *Jerih dan Juang: Laporan Nasional Survey Menyeluruh Gereja di Indonesia,*
          Jakarta: Lembaga Penelitian dan Studi—DGI.

VAN AKKEREN, Philip
  1970   *Sri and Christ. A Study of the Indigenous Church in East-Java,* London: Lut-
          terworth Press.

WAHONO, Sri Wismoadi
  1978   "Pekabaran Injil Gereja-Gereja Anggota DGI dan Gereja-Gereja non DGI,"
          Peninjau, Majalah Lembaga Penelitian dan Studi—DGI, Vol. 5, Nos. 3-4.

WILLIS, Avery T., Jr.
  1977   *Indonesian Revival: Why Two Million Came to Christ,* South Pasadena: William
          Carey Library.

YODER, Lawrence M.
  1981   *The Church of the Muria: A History of the Muria Christian Church of Indo-
          nesia—GKMI,* Ann Arbor: University Microfilms International.

4. THE KARO BATAK

Martin F. Goldsmith

LIKE PEARLS STRUNG ON A NECKLACE THE ISLANDS OF INDONESIA STRETCH for some 3,000 miles along the equator. Although Java predominates politically and the Javanese outnumber all other races, Indonesia includes a wide range of ethnic groups which have their own languages and cultures. In this chapter we shall look back to personal experience in one relatively small racial group in North Sumatra—the Karo Batak people. With only half a million people they form a tiny part of the 150 million Indonesians. Religiously, too, they differ from many other races. Although some of the Karo people follow Islam, the majority still adhere to their traditional primal faith.

In considering the growth of the church among the Karo Batak, we need to remember the wider context of the Christian church throughout the land. Already by the year 1700 there were about 100,000 Christians in Java alone and another 40,000 on the island of Ambon. The New Testament came out in the local language of Malay in 1688, and the whole Bible followed in 1734. In discussing the Indonesian church we must therefore never forget that it is neither small nor new; in fact it antedates many of our Western denominations and is today considerably larger than most European churches.

When my wife and I went to work in Indonesia, people commonly reckoned that the Christian church there numbered some five million members and was growing by about ten percent a year. Then came the abortive coup by the communists in 1965 which led to a massive turning of people to the church. Statistics are hard to come by in any truly accurate form—an Australian visitor who asked for statistics at that stage of Indonesian history was quietly informed that in Indonesia Christians are too busy to count!

With a history of Dutch colonialism the vast majority of Indonesian churches reflect Dutch denominational traditions: Reformed, Rereformed, or other similar theological backgrounds. The large Toba Batak churches of North Sumatra, founded by the great pioneer missionary Nommensen, stand, however, in communion with the Lutheran World Fellowship, although this discrepancy has in no way caused any break of fellowship with the Reformed churches.

In more recent years a variety of foreign missions have planted all sorts of different denominations, particularly in the outer areas of Kalimantan and West Irian. There is indeed a tragic tendency among some foreign missions to

---

Martin F. Goldsmith, Ware, England, is Lecturer in Missiology at All Nations Christian College. Earlier he and his wife served as missionaries to Indonesia and Malaysia with Overseas Missionary Fellowship. His most recent book is Can My Church Grow? *(Hodder and Stoughton, 1980).*

ignore the existing churches of Indonesia and insist on forming churches pat-
terned after their own home denominations, thus giving Christianity something
of a foreign and divided image. We deeply respect the Anglican CMS (Church
Missionary Society), therefore, for sacrificing its denominational bias in favor
of loaning its workers to the existing Indonesian churches and theological institutions. The interdenominational OMF (Overseas Missionary Fellowship) follows this same approach, which we have found to be highly effective.

What about the Karo Batak Protestant Church? The colonial authorities
longed to have peace and stability on the highland plateau where the Karo culture
is centered, for fruit and vegetables flourish in its fertile soil. The Dutch thought
that the Karos were cannibals like their Toba Batak neighbors and so offered
financial inducements to encourage missions to Christianize the people. Toward
the end of the nineteenth century Neumann and others grasped the opportunity
and began the evangelization of the Karo people. At first the people were suspicious and resistant, but gradually some turned to the Lord. But even in 1960
there were only 20,000 Karo Christians. Like other churches throughout Indonesia the Karo church was growing steadily by about ten percent a year in the
early 1960s, and then from 1965 to 1968 it mushroomed to a membership of
some 75,000. Since then it has grown more slowly to a figure of about 150,000
in 1982.

LESSONS FROM CHURCH GROWTH
EXPERIENCE IN INDONESIA

WIN THE WINNABLE?

As I pointed out in my earlier book *Can My Church Grow?* (1980), the simplistic
adage that we should deploy our resources to concentrate on the "winnable"
may have some strategic significance, but in practice it does not work. The word
"winnable" is a relative term, and the whole concept ignores the overruling
guidance of God and his long-term plans for the world.

We have already noted that the early years of mission among the Karos
were relatively fruitless, while other more advanced areas of Indonesia were
already yielding abundant harvests, though they too had earlier experienced
periods of rugged resistance to the gospel. History has proved the rightness of
those early missionaries' perseverance. Today's considerable church growth is
built on the foundation of their much harder labors.

When we were working in the market town of Kabanjahe, local Christians
caught the vision for evangelizing the villages around the town. One church
leader led a small team of Christians to a totally unevangelized village of about
3,000 souls. They visited the local coffee shop where the men would gather in
the evenings. Here they shared the gospel once a week for three weeks. Then
the elder became aware of the biblical injunctions not to cast our pearls before
swine and to wipe the dust off our feet when people reject our message. He
came to our home in some uncertainty. Should he abandon evangelism there?
Should he move on to riper fields? After three evenings only about thirty people
had been converted! I had to inform him that in my country such success in
evangelism would be written up as a mini-revival.

CREATE A VACUUM

The early missionaries among the Karos not only attempted to win men and women for Jesus Christ, but they also set out to undermine the traditional animistic beliefs and prepare the whole culture for a Christian takeover. In *The Puritan Hope* Iain Murray (1971) criticizes "millenarian missionaries" for aiming only at the conversion of souls from the world without at the same time seeking to prepare whole societies and cultures for the advent of the Christian faith.

"Anyone who sets foot on this sacred field will fall sick and die." So said the Karo people in former times. The missionary called the local village people together at the edge of the sacred field. He prayed aloud in the name of Jesus Christ and then solemnly strode across the untrodden green. A frightened silence fell on the crowd as they waited for the spirits to vent their anger. But nothing happened. And so they were forced to face the question: Is the Christian God more powerful than the spirits?

By the time my wife and I came to North Sumatra, many of the Karos had come to assume that the old ways no longer satisfied them. The Christian faith seemed the inevitable and natural answer to their spiritual vacuum. This was symbolized for us by an event in our first week in Indonesia.

We were busy unpacking, getting our new home into some order, meeting crowds of new faces, entertaining visitors galore, going to innumerable church meetings, and generally settling into our new life. Finally one afternoon we felt it was time to lay down tools, get on our cycles, and go out. We decided to visit a local village in order to see the beautiful and interesting old houses which the Karos used to build. Each house held eight families with fifty to sixty people. Topped with a high, curved roof of sago-palm thatch with buffalo horns standing defiantly at each end, these houses attracted the tourist spirit within us. In the War of Independence against the Dutch the towns and many of the villages had been burned down, but I knew that this village of Lingga still gloried in its traditional eight-family houses.

And so we cycled some five potholed miles through the beauty of the countryside. The local volcano dominated the background, gently puffing smoke up into the clear blue sky. Wild flowers and poinsettias added to the beauty. And then we free-wheeled down the rough path into the village. We heard one lady calling out to her neighbor, "Look, here comes our minister!" We were amazed, for this was a totally unevangelized community. "Our minister"—how could complete non-Christians say that? The preparatory work of those early missionaries was proving its worth. We had the joy of reaping where they had sown. When the church in our town caught the vision for evangelizing Lingga, a church sprang into being and has drawn into its folds many hundreds of souls.

But the early missionaries were not always successful in destroying the influence of the primal religion. In one village there was a traditional story of a girl who became pregnant without marriage and gave birth to triplets—a beautiful green princess, a large iron cannon, and a snake with immense eyes (Goldsmith 1974). In one of the tall eight-family houses the villagers kept a hair from the green princess. It was several miles long. The missionary laughed at such a ridiculous story and challenged the elders to bring out the hair and unwind it for him. In front of a large crowd they did so. It certainly seemed to be a hair, not a cord. No sign of a joint in the hair appeared. What was the explanation? The missionary had no answer. Even in the sixties this village remained hard against the Christian faith, for they knew the reality of their animistic beliefs. The missionaries' attempt to create a spiritual vacuum failed because they did not fully reckon with the power of the spirit world.

We have to be careful how we carry over the rationalistic approach which so influences even Christians in the West. The reality and power of the spirit world cannot be safely ignored. Missionaries need to be trained in spiritual warfare if they are to engage in such a battle. If we discount this battle, we shall be irrelevant to the real needs of the people.

REALITY BRINGS GROWTH

During the War of Independence from 1945 until about 1950 the Karo people engaged in a fierce struggle against the colonial power. A scorched-earth policy was conducted by both sides. The Karos retreated into the surrounding jungle and remoter parts of the countryside. Those were hard times. Starvation stared the people in the face. Hand-to-hand fighting brought fearful casualties.

The Christians not only faced the same hardships as everyone else, but in addition they were distrusted by their Indonesian compatriots. Because the church had been under Dutch leadership, many felt that Christianity was an imperialistic religion. The Christians were often hated and persecuted by their fellow countryfolk because of their association with the Dutch colonialists. Some were even martyred.

"I watched my uncle in the jungle during the War," said a visitor to our house one day. "His God really helped him. When he prayed, his God gave him food." Quite a few people told us how impressed they had been with the life and testimony of the Christians in those days of extreme difficulty. The Christian God seemed to meet the daily needs of his people. And the Christians stood firm in the face of persecution and hardship.

"My uncle's God is the one I want for my family," my visitor said. "How can we become his followers?"

Obvious reality and vitality of faith will lead to the growth of the church in due course. We found this to be true also in the village of the green princess, where the gospel faced such steadfast resistance.

One Sunday I preached on assurance of salvation at the little church of about fifty Christians. The leading young person in the church had never before heard this teaching and was thrilled at the prospect. She took her Bible home with her and read it from cover to cover without stopping for meals or sleep. Could she really know that she would go to be with Christ when she died? As she read, it came clear to her that it was true. As a result she took poison and killed herself. As Paul said, "My desire is to depart and be with Christ, for that is far better" (Phil 1:23). I had not realized the need to say in my sermon that the Christian needs to exercise patience and wait for the Lord's call to go and be with him. The poison took several hours to work, during which time she went around the village joyfully informing everyone of the glories of heaven. She was on her way to glory!

The obvious reality and joy of this girl's testimony led to many others inquiring about the Christian way.

THE CHURCH IS INDONESIAN

Under the Dutch the church suffered a foreign image. Most of the finances came from overseas. And when it is so easy for Europeans to give large sums of money, why should we Indonesians scrape and sacrifice to give our mites?! Power and leadership were also largely in Dutch hands.

But in the War of Independence the missionaries had been thrown out. The Karo church struggled to maintain itself with a desperate shortage of finances and of national leadership. Gradually the wobbly legs of the church began to straighten and stand firm.

Many of the externals of the church remained obviously Dutch—the architecture of the buildings, the robes of the ministers, the Reformed liturgy, and the organizational structures. But even these obviously foreign accretions had been in Indonesia so long that they had largely ceased to have that foreign feel. And now the church was entirely independent. They did not look to any overseas power either for money or personnel. No one could manipulate them any longer with the strings of economic neo-imperialism.

Locally the church was now seen to belong to Indonesia and not to be a pawn of some foreign mission. People saw nothing but Indonesian faces. Evangelism and every other church activity were entirely in the hands of local people. There were no foreign missionaries any more.

In days of strong reaction to the previous history of colonialism, it is of course vitally important for the witness of the gospel that the church is seen to be truly Indonesian and not what Roland Allen (1912) calls "an exotic."

Sadly the immense growth of the church in Indonesia has attracted a large number of foreign missionaries desiring to jump on the bandwagon of success. The majority of such missionaries refuse to inject their endeavors into the existing Indonesian churches, but rather insist on developing new movements which are often in rivalry to the national churches. Such missionaries also have little patience with national Christians and therefore push themselves into leadership positions and steal the limelight. The danger is that we may again give the image of foreignness to the Christian church in Indonesia. If we do so, we shall have damaged the Indonesian churches and the long-term prospects for the progress of the gospel of Jesus Christ.

MISSIONARIES AND THE CHURCH

Having suffered missionary domination for many years, the Karo church had no intention of returning to this after the War of Independence. For some years they continued without any overseas missionary personnel. Then they saw the benefits obtained by other churches from the input of members of the Overseas Missionary Fellowship and agreed to sponsor my wife and me. But they were understandably anxious lest we push ourselves into too much influence and power in the church. They therefore laid down strict conditions for our coming to work with them.

First, we were not to bring any foreign money into the church. We could give an offering on Sunday, but it was not to be more than an average Indonesian teacher would give. Second, we were to live in the house the church chose for us and lent to us. Third, we were not to open our mouth in any church meeting unless asked to do so. Soon after our arrival in Indonesia I attended the annual church synod meetings and sat in silence for five days, for no one asked me for my opinion on any subject.

The house given to us by the church was far from palatial. It consisted of one room downstairs and one upstairs with an outside staircase. We cooked in the space under the staircase, which was partly open to the elements. There was a place behind the church for washing and toilet. We had neither running water nor electricity. The walls were made of unseasoned wood with many peepholes for curious children to watch us throughout the daylight hours. Our neighbors also could look through into our house, and we could of course hear every word from the homes on either side.

Living at this level and sharing their sufferings when food was short or water ran out in the town, we were accepted as friends. People felt free to share with us, and they accepted the message of God from our lips. The fact that we had no car helped further. People saw us on our cycles, in the local buses, and walking from village to village.

God used an apparently insignificant event to open doors for ministry. On my first Sunday in the church I was asked to stand at the door and be welcomed by the thousand or so members. I had been told by another worker in Indonesia not to put my left hand under my right forearm when shaking hands, as this is only done by Muslims. In other Southeast Asian countries it is also done by Christians, so I needed to learn this. However, the first elder to shake hands with me used the "Muslim" handshake. I wondered what to do. Quickly I followed his example and duly used that form of handshake with everyone in the congregation. I later discovered that in the Karo culture this was a sign of humility. The elder had by his handshake been saying that he reckoned me to be superior to him because I was a white missionary—a remnant of the colonial era. In reply I had signaled that every Karo believer is superior to me—the colonial era is over! This unwitting humility opened doors galore for the Word.

The importance in Indonesia of the principle that the missionary should not be in the limelight was underlined to us in the question of village evangelism. During that tourist visit to the village of Lingga we had met many people who said to us, "If someone came to our village to teach us the Christian way, we would turn and believe." We were excited at such openness and wondered if this was God's invitation to us to start church planting there. We consulted with a local Christian friend, an elder in the church.

He told us frankly that we should not initiate anything—we were mere foreigners. He warned us that if we started such church planting, it would further encourage the spirit of dependence which had been implanted in colonial times.

Following his advice we waited. We prayed much, for we saw that amazing openness all around us and longed that the many villages near Kabanjahe should be given the opportunity to turn to Christ. We talked to people about village evangelism. We preached about it and prayed yet more. After some time another leader in the church caught the vision. He organized the six area house meetings in Kabanjahe each to take responsibility for church planting in one village. Five of them succeeded. The result was five new churches. Then others saw that Kabanjahe Christians could plant churches without missionary leadership. Surely, they thought, we might be able to do the same. That was the start of a whole new movement in the church as a whole.

We found that in Indonesia the missionary task lay primarily in the area of lay training and Bible teaching in the church rather than in direct evangelism. We were at that stage the only missionaries in that whole area of North Sumatra. But we had a church of more than 20,000 members. We found that the church was like tinder. It just needed a match to set it aflame. Prejudiced by their own backgrounds, some foreigners have rejected such churches because they are affiliated with the Indonesian Council of Churches, are liturgical, and believe in the Reformed doctrine of infant baptism. But working closely with them, we found that their fundamental doctrine was entirely biblical and evangelical. It lacked, however, what we liked to call "personal religion." When the Spirit applied their sound doctrine to their personal lives, life flowed into their veins. Then evangelism and church planting ensued naturally.

GROUP MOVEMENTS

In the excessively individualistic cultures of the West we may dislike the term "group movement" and prefer to disguise it with such expressions as "multi-individual choices" or "people movements," but it remains true that in many cultures people can make decisions together as groups without losing individual personal integrity. We had never witnessed this phenomenon until we went to Indonesia.

Just before we arrived in Sumatra a whole army battalion in our area turned to Jesus Christ. Soon after we left, a secondary school of some 500 teenagers agreed together to follow the Lord. We personally had the joy of seeing various groups making such decisions.

I particularly remember a ward in the local hospital. Every week I went to the hospital to preach in the wards and distribute and sell Christian literature. On one occasion I shared the gospel with the sixteen men in the TB ward. Having preached and sold literature, I suggested that they discuss the gospel together and make a group decision to be converted. The next week as I approached that area of the hospital they called out, "Come over here, we're all Christians now." They told me happily that they now knew the gospel of Jesus to be the true way of life. God's Spirit had done his marvelous work of convicting and converting.

When doing hospital visitation in Britain, we do not look for groups to be converted. We talk secretly to individuals from bed to bed without suggesting to them that they share the gospel message in discussions together. I realized that in practice I had carried over that individualistic approach to evangelism in my work in Thailand before I went to Indonesia. I had not honestly expected whole villages to turn to Christ.

I find that in Britain many people are deeply suspicious when we talk about such people movements. They assume that it leads to nominal Christianity. It is true that without good follow-up teaching, nominalism can ensue. But I have observed that this danger can also be found in areas which have not seen group movements. I visited a pioneer mission area in another country in Asia where missionaries stressed individual conversion only and would not baptize anyone until there were clear signs of spiritual growth. These workers ignored the theological truth that baptism is a sign associated with regeneration, not with sanctification. In that area, however, it was reckoned that within three years of baptism, fifty percent of the Christians had totally backslidden from the church. We do not face that sort of decline in Indonesia. Nominal Christianity is not the result of either individual conversion patterns or of group movements; it comes from a lack of spirituality, teaching, and fellowship in the church.

HOMOGENEOUS CHURCHES

Like many churches in Indonesia, our Karo church is an ethnic group. The different races in North Sumatra all have their own languages, cultures, and churches. There is no doubt that this facilitates evangelism and fellowship among the Karos. But it also has its dangers.

Just to the south of the Karos live the Toba Bataks. They have been almost totally evangelized for many years, and their churches are large and strong. But they form a racial ghetto with little interest in the evangelization of other races. Happily there are some noble exceptions of vital concern for cross-cultural mission. But the danger has been that the energies and dynamic of the Toba Bataks have been directed at internal quarrels and splits instead of at evangelism and mission.

The Karo church today has a long way to go before we can say that the whole Karo people have been brought into the fold of the people of God. But already about thirty percent of the Karos are Christian. The time will surely come when the vast majority of Karos will be Christians. What will happen then? Will they also spend their energies in ungodly splits, or will they be united in outgoing mission?

To the north of the Karos live some solidly non-Christian peoples. Immediately to the north we find the Alas people who have some cultural and language relationship to the Karos. They could form a bridge to the Gayo people to their north and thus finally perhaps to the fanatically non-Christian Aceh. The possibilities are enormous, but a firmly homogeneous church does not find it easy to evangelize other groupings.

FAMILY NETWORKS

The Karo culture has a complicated system of senior and junior relationships within the extended family. Ultimately almost all Karos can trace a relationship with everyone they meet and thus each Karo can distinguish whether he is a senior (*kalimbubu*) or a junior (*anak-beru*). Evangelism was facilitated by this system, for the *kalimbubu* has rights over the *anak-beru*. Thus the *anak-beru's* home is available to his *kalimbubu*, who can initiate evangelistic Bible discussion meeting there. This is obviously helpful when beginning evangelism in a totally unreached area.

Some Christians developed a deep concern for the salvation of their relatives. I remember one friend of ours who traveled widely to meet his cousins and second cousins in order to share the gospel with them.

CONFIDENCE

On meeting a stranger it was customary not only to exchange family backgrounds, but also to ask about religion. Christians would ask strangers whether they were Christians *yet,* while followers of other religions usually only asked whether you belonged to their faith. Non-Christians of all religious backgrounds would answer, "Not yet," while Christians responded, "No, we are Christians!" In a strange way it had become an assumption that sensible people would probably want to become Christians at some stage of their lives.

I notice that in Europe there is a sad lack of confidence in the glories of the Christian faith even among Christians. Many fear that people of quality or intelligence are more likely to leave the Christians faith than to be converted to Christ. Happily this situation is changing, and I observe the beginnings of a new confidence among believers.

Karo Christians just assumed that Christianity is obviously superior to any other way. This did not come from any objectionable sense of triumphalistic pride. They were not even aware of the contrast between their "no" and the "not yet" of the followers of other religions.

Culture or Superstition?

Every church conference put on its agenda this heated topic. Missiologists have noted the great strength of *adat* (culture) in many parts of Indonesia. The Karo church assumed the basic principle that *adat* needs to be Christianized when possible, but it must not allow heathen superstitious elements to enter the church.

In Western cultures we make a sharp distinction between the religious and the secular. This is impossible in most other cultures. Everything in life has religious overtones and connections. The problem for the Christian church is to discern when any particular cultural form has lost its old religious feel. Young people in the city may affirm that something is merely cultural and not religious at all, while older folk in the rural areas may shudder at their naiveté.

When we worked in Sumatra, church members were excommunicated if they used native drums or dances. This was not a missionary decision at all, for no missionaries had power or influence to affect such decisions. The local Christians knew the traditional association of these activities with the spirit world. But now some fifteen to twenty years later the church officially uses both drums and dances in evangelistic outreach. The leaders of the church feel that these cultural forms have become religiously "cool" and there is no doubt that they make the gospel attractive. Some more traditional people still feel the danger of syncretism, allowing the spirit powers of animism to infiltrate the church.

If the church is too slow to use cultural forms, the gospel will lose its appeal and be alien to the culture. If the church is unwisely naive in failing to sense the religious significance of cultural forms, evil spirits will sap its very lifeblood. The growth of the church depends on such questions. Church leaders need the spiritual gift of discernment.

Big and Small Meetings

For healthy growth the church benefits from small meetings for pastoral care, deeper fellowship, and discussion as well as from larger meetings. The latter encourage an awareness of the fact that we belong to the wider body of the church. Large meetings also allow good singing and the chance to hear more gifted speakers.

The Indonesian churches often have quite large church services on Sunday; they may even attract a regular attendance of one or two thousand. On the other hand, both evangelism and midweek Bible teaching have traditionally been conducted through relatively small house groups of twenty to thirty people. In our area the normal pattern was for these meetings to move to a different home each week, thus allowing a wide range of people to invite their neighbors and relatives. Expositions of the Bible passage were given by the head of the home and by two church leaders. This was followed by questions and discussion.

Because of the house meetings and the close links between Christians it was possible for the church elders to know exactly who was present or absent at Sunday services. Church discipline ruled that Christians be warned if they missed church for three weeks. If they persisted in absenting themselves from the worship of God's people, they were excommunicated.

FESTIVALS

Many parts of Indonesia demonstrate an open-hearted religious tolerance. At the major Muslim festivals Christians will happily share with their Muslim neighbors. But likewise at Christmas Muslims will come to Christian celebrations. Neither Muslims nor Christians compromise their beliefs, but both have the opportunity to relate across religious borders and to understand the other's faith a little better.

For several weeks before Christmas the churches and their various branches hold numerous large services of celebration with clear presentations of the gospel. Many of these services last for two or three hours and include perhaps three twenty to thirty minute sermons.

In the towns the churches sometimes combine to hold a united Christmas celebration which attracts thousands of people of all religious backgrounds. Thus in Kabanjahe, a small market town of about 20,000 inhabitants, our big service would bring together some 5,000 to hear the message of Christ. In the neighboring town of Brastagi we paraded through the streets with torches flaming, trumpets sounding, and hymns being sung. We then gathered in the main market square for a service. Almost the whole town came together to hear God's Word proclaimed (cf. Acts 13:44), and I remember preaching on John 3:16.

LITERATURE

Owing to the vagaries of the Indonesian postal system we set up living quarters in Kabanjahe without any money at all. But we had six Bibles. Our senior missionary in the city of Medan had warned us, however, that the Karos were only semiliterate and would not be interested in reading. Within a day or so we had sold all our six Bibles and used the proceeds to buy more at a good discount.

Thus began our literature ministry. We soon had a cardboard box in our front room with a bright cloth over it and a display of books for sale. Christians dropped in to buy books. The bookstall grew until we were selling about twenty-five books or Bibles every day. God wonderfully used this literature. We reckoned on the average to hear at least one testimony a week from someone who had been converted or revived through a book.

One elder bought a book about personal evangelism from our little bookstall. He was thrilled with it. The next week he came to our house and bought thirty more copies to give to all the other elders in his church.

Every Sunday my wife and I journeyed out to some outlying village church to preach at their service and then spend the rest of the day in Bible teaching in homes. After the service we would display the contents of the heavy bag we had carried with us. Normally, the Christians bought every book we had. They then usually insisted on filling the bag with local produce—rice or fruit— so it was just as heavy on the return journey!

RELIGIOUS EDUCATION IN SCHOOLS

Indonesia is not a secular state, but it enshrines in its constitution belief in God. To be a true Indonesian you must therefore believe in God. Any religion which believes in God has the right to teach its faith in the schools, colleges, and universities if there are at least ten adherents of that faith in the student body. In our area of Sumatra we could teach Bible in every educational establishment. In fact this influential ministry was just a small part of our overall work in the seventy-five congregations of the Karo church. We had time to teach in only seven schools and colleges; other Christians also took time off from their full-time ministries or from their jobs to teach in a school or two.

At the start of each academic year the students gathered in the central area of the school. In front of them stood three men—the Muslim imam, the Roman Catholic priest, and the Protestant teacher. Students could choose which person's line they would follow for that year. Again and again we rejoiced to see not only animists but also Muslims and Roman Catholics standing in front of us and thus joining our classes for that year.

We were free to teach whatever we wanted. Usually we began the year by going steadily through the Gospel of Mark, introducing students to the wonder of Jesus Christ. Our bookstall made profits, and we used these to give each of our students in the schools one new Christian book each term. The Holy Spirit worked through this regular Bible teaching. We were encouraged to hear that in 1979 a third of all newly ordained ministers in the Karo church owed their conversion to religious education at school. The influence of this ministry throughout the church is great.

MARRIAGE

"I would love to be a Christian. It must be beautiful to have a sense of security in your marriage. You Christians never seem to divorce your wives." How often we heard such statements! Many were attracted to Christ through seeing Christian marriages.

The Karo church believed strongly in firm church discipline. Divorce was not permitted. If you divorced your spouse, you faced excommunication. As a result, couples with problems worked hard to mend their relationships and find solutions to their tensions. In a fallen world there were of course some tragic situations of failure, but generally the Christian church gave their neighbors a shining example of the security and quality of Christian marriage.

I often say to my students at All Nations Christian College in England that the witness of the church to the power and reality of Christ will depend largely on the marriages we produce. In societies where marriage stands under dire threat, men and women will see the beauty, love, and relevance of Jesus Christ through our marriages and homes. This has certainly been true in Indonesia.

UNITY

The health, witness, and growth of the church has been much enhanced by a real sense of unity among the churches. Non-Christians are not put off by the multitude of different denominations and Christian movements rivaling one another. This is of course particularly important in a Muslim context, for the Qur'an itself criticizes Christians for their disunity. Can the gospel be true when Christians do not love one another? We preach a message of peace, forgiveness, love, and reconciliation; this is obvious hypocrisy if we do not practice it.

Traditionally the churches in Indonesia have worked closely and happily together. Thus our Karo churches were growing fast, but they lacked trained ministers. The Toba Batak church had a minister who happened to speak the Karo language as well as his own native Toba Batak, so they transferred him to the Karo church. No one questioned this or thought it unusual.

NATIONAL CHURCH: KEY TO CHURCH GROWTH

I am often asked whether the huge growth of the church in Indonesia is a spiritual work or just a social and political movement. I reject the question as theologically and biblically incorrect. Our God is sovereign over history, and it is he who determines social and political movements. In Sumatra we saw many different factors which contributed to the growth of the Christian church. I believe that God was in them all.

In this chapter I have listed a few of the many contributory factors which God used. In them all I believe that God's key is the church. Readers will have noticed that the word *church* has occurred frequently in this chapter. Many missionaries are ignoring the national churches in the countries where they are working; but in Indonesia we discovered that fruitfulness depended on working through, with, and even under the national church.

REFERENCES CITED

ALLEN, Roland
   1912   *Missionary Methods: St. Paul's or Ours?* London: World Dominion Press.
GOLDSMITH, E.
   1974   *God Can Be Trusted?* Sevenoaks, Kent, England: Overseas Missionary Fellowship.
GOLDSMITH, Martin F.
   1980   *Can My Church Grow?* Sevenoaks, Kent, England: Hodder and Stoughton.
MURRAY, Iain
   1971   *The Puritan Hope,* Carlisle, Pennsylvania: Banner of Truth Trust.

5. CHURCH GROWTH AMONG THE CHOKOSI OF NORTHERN GHANA

Alfred C. Krass

FROM 1964 TO 1970 I WAS DISTRICT PASTOR FOR THE EVANGELICAL PRESBY-terian Church among the Chokosi, Konkomba, and Komba peoples of Northern Ghana. A missionary of the United Church Board for World Ministries, I was seconded to the Evangelical Presbyterian Church to serve in their new mission in that area. I worked with evangelists and, later, pastors of the Evangelical Presbyterian Church and with missionary and national agricultural, community development, and health workers.

The work received considerable publicity (as, for example, in McGavran 1970:331-34). I was hailed as an example of successful Church Growth methodology in shepherding a "people's movement."

How did I understand what happened in the Chereponi area? I believed that I was the midwife of a people's movement, that the Chokosi—and, to a lesser extent, the other tribes in the area—were "ripe for the gospel," and that I was able to harvest what the Spirit had prepared. I believed that by developing a culturally sensitive missionary praxis I was able to make use of the "bridges of God" to bring rapid growth into the church. By the end of the decade twenty-two new congregations had been brought into being. A number of them included whole villages; others were made up of entire extended family households; only among the Kombas and Konkombas were people added to the church by individual decision.

As I tried to understand why the Chokosi were ripe for the gospel at that particular time, answers were not hard to come by. Modernization was taking place at a rapid rate. Considerable mobility of peoples was going on—Southern Ghanaians, almost all of them at least nominally Christian, were working in Chereponi for various government departments; Chokosis were migrating to other, often Christianized, areas of the country for work and there coming in contact with the church; a number, largely youth, had become Christians elsewhere and returned to Chereponi; through the radio and mobile cinema the wider world came regularly into view.

Alfred C. Krass, Philadelphia, Pennsylvania, is neighborhood minister with Jubilee Fellowship. He has worked as consultant on Evangelism with the National Council of Churches from 1977 to 1979, and the same with the United Church Board for World Ministries from 1971 to 1976. He is the author of Evangelizing Neo-Pagan North America: The Word That Frees *(Herald Press, 1982),* Five Lanterns at Sundown: Evangelism in a Chastened Mood *(Eerdmans, 1978), and* Go . . . and Make Disciples *(SPCK, 1974).*

Then most Chokosis practiced a clan-based, village-centered, traditional religion connected with the graves of ancestors and sacred shrines. Such a local religion could not adapt to the universal dimensions of modern existence. For some, Islam seemed to offer a passport to modernity, but Muslims were not yet militantly evangelistic (as they were in nearby areas and generally through the savannah belt of West Africa).

Furthermore, Chokosi society was stratified, with semi-Muslims in the ruling class, full Muslims (few in number) in a sacerdotal-and-trading class, and the majority of Chokosis in a despised "pagan" class (the Njem). The initial positive response to the gospel came from this third class, a class many of whose members yearned for a more-than-local religion but found the cultural conversion required for Islamization difficult to make.

The Christian faith, as we presented it, was an accepting, culturally receptive faith, a real contrast to Muslim cultural arrogance. It was expressed in the concepts of Chokosi culture and tradition. It sought to affirm what was positive in the Chokosis' experience. Worship was in the Chokosi language. European forms of dress, music, and liturgy which had been imported into Southern Ghana were largely avoided. Translation of the Bible into Chokosi began rapidly, and—as we wrote down the language—a literacy program was immediately begun.

Islam provided the model of a monotheistic, universal faith; Christianity provided Chokosis with access to it. Coming from the USA, where we had just seen the emergence of the phenomenon of Black Muslims, I was amused to hear Chokosis describe Christians as "European Muslims"!

I could see other reasons why the Chokosis were responsive. There was in Chokosi legend and proverb a latent millennialism which we were able to relate to Christian hope. "When the redeemer comes," a proverb stated, "then we will all be at rest." Other proverbs and stories affirmed that the gulf between Nyeme (the sky-God) and humankind was a recent problem—not present at the creation and due to be overcome, by God's grace, someday. Similarly Chokosi legend affirmed the essential unity of all humanity and lamented the present barriers of hostility and warfare among the tribes and races. As early as 1896 the Germans, in establishing their Togo colony, had brought a *pax germanica* to the area. Intertribal warfare had ceased by fiat, but alienation between tribes and clans persisted. The Chokosis yearned for a day when people of all groups would "speak with one mouth" (their idiom for having unity). The example of a mission which brought together Europeans, Americans, Southern Ghanaians of various languages, and Chokosis, Kombas, and Konkombas was a welcome sign that the millennium was dawning.

Much of the positive response to the gospel, I recognized, emerged from considerations of self-interest as well. Foreign tribespeople and Chokosi Muslims dominated trade in the area. Politics and patronage were the province of the royal clan. The majority of Chokosis were thus not deriving the benefits of modernization. Government tractors didn't plow their fields. Demonstration programs were not done on their farms or houses. To get treatment at the new health center they often had to make payoffs. From its inception the mission engaged in advocacy of the disenfranchised and educated them as to their rights under law. People gained a new self-respect and began to stand up for their rights. In the church they had a support network which encouraged them to overcome their fears.

Finally, the development program in which the church engaged from its earliest stages was a powerful attractive force. Water resource development met a vital need of the people. Improved agricultural techniques, new seeds, seed dressings, and reasonably priced hoe blades, sacks, and simple medicines were highly valued by the people. USAID foodstuffs met real needs during the annual hunger months, and used clothing from Church World Service and kits for school children were appreciated.

We were aware of the danger of developing rice Christians. USAID regulations were stringently followed. Apart from serious crises, no general distribution of food was made. Food was given only to hardship cases, as food-for-work in road-building or well-digging programs, and in the leadership-training program for those who were doing literacy training. The distribution to the needy that took place was made with no regard whatsoever to which villages were responding to the gospel. Development projects were done in staunchly traditionalist and Muslim villages as well as in Christian villages.

Those who were responding to the gospel found this hard. Many of them felt they deserved a *quid* for their *quo*. But the appropriate rewards for a spiritual commitment, we told them, were the spiritual rewards of pastoral care, hearing the gospel, learning how to read the Bible, and so on. We sought to develop a mentality of service to the needy rather than one of seeking recompense. Discovering that the Chokosis had a tradition of taking sheaves to the poor and handicapped at harvest time—which had fallen into disuse—we revitalized that tradition. We were confident that we had disarmed the threat of developing rice Christians.

I could see all these reasons why a "people's movement" should have developed in Chereponi during the sixties. The firstfruits had been brought in. "It seems indubitable," I reported in April 1968 to the district and presbytery, "that a great work of the Spirit is being done here, and that God has prepared the hearts of the people of the area to receive the gospel. With continued prayer and effort it should be possible in the next decade to harvest the great majority of the Chokosi and Konkomba and Komba tribes."

Prayer was important. Our strategies alone would not, I was convinced, bring these results. The great watershed in the six and a half years I worked in Chereponi was when we began regular, intercessory prayer each morning for the villages where the church workers were to be working that day. That daily prayer, plus the annual day of fasting and prayer which we initiated with the Catholics and Assemblies of God (for the conversion of the Chokosi nation in both Ghana and Togo), was being heard by God, I was convinced. It was important, I believed, for our prayer to be a prayer of faith, a prayer offered in the confidence that God would hear our requests. The writings of Donald McGavran reinforced my optimism. The conviction of Roland Allen that the church, if not impeded from it, would expand spontaneously strengthened my commitment. The joyous testimonies of those who accepted the gospel and the signs of the Spirit working in bringing new life to their villages urged me on.

THE INTERVENING YEARS

Eleven years have now passed since I left Chereponi. Much has happened there, and much has also happened to me in the interim. I left the work in the hands of two Ghanaian pastors, an experienced Ghanaian literacy worker, their staffs of evangelists and literacy trainers (almost all locally trained young men from our leadership training program), and a missionary couple: an agriculturalist/community development worker and a public health nurse. Shortly after I left, the recently ordained Chokosi pastor was defrocked because of personal irregularities, and the whole burden of superintending the twenty-three congregations and thirty or more preaching stations fell to the Southern Ghanaian pastor (my colleague during my last three years of work). Support from the central church budget in Southern Ghana waned. In the meantime political turmoil and worldwide inflation related to the sudden increase of oil prices created extremely difficult working conditions. A period of demoralization set it.

Halfway through the decade the Southern Ghanaian pastor suddenly died. The church did not replace him immediately. The work of both Chokosi districts was placed under a pastor fifty-six miles away. The literacy worker, a trained teacher-catechist of the Evangelical Presbyterian Church, was sent for an ordination course. For the past two years he has been the district pastor. Regular letters from him described the continued demoralization under which he and his colleagues work. Though there are 1,160 living baptized Christians in twenty-seven congregations (an increase of about fifteen percent in both categories, which—with the region's high mortality rate—probably indicates a somewhat larger amount of growth), church attendance is extremely low, and in many places regular services are not held. Stung by the experience of seeing so many baptized people fail to take their faith seriously, the pastor has resorted to baptizing only individuals—between twenty and thirty per year (a course which the missionary, who distrusted Church Growth methods, told me he also would have found more responsible than my baptism of whole social units). Little attempt is made to reach out to villages in which no congregations are present (eighty or so villages, which contain perhaps fifty percent of the population). The thrust of developing lay leadership has all but ceased. The only significant lay training which has taken place in the past decade has been the training of farmers in methods of bullock-plowing (a training which, under the missionary, was wholistic; many of those trained have become village development animators, and there is a strong discipleship basis for their work and lifestyle).

I believed strongly that trusting in the Spirit meant that when I would leave the work in the hands of national leaders, I would really leave it and not continue to keep my hand in it from afar. I have, therefore, not sought to influence the development of the church work in these eleven years. Nor do I seek to do so now. When I was asked to write these reflections, I agreed to do so for the help it might offer to others interested in primary evangelism, not to influence what the church will now do in Chereponi. This secondary reflection may serve two purposes: it may add an epilogue to my book about the work in Chereponi (Krass 1974), and it serves as a useful reflection for me as I begin a new missional involvement in wholistic mission in urban Philadelphia.

THE INTERCIVILIZATIONAL ENCOUNTER

What happened in the Chereponi area in the sixties? How do I now understand it? The basic difference in my perception today from my perception while I was involved in the work is that I now include two parties in my analysis: both the Chokosis and myself. I see what happened in Chereponi as not only the Chokosis' encounter with the gospel of Jesus Christ, but their encounter with me and the civilization and culture from which I came, and my encounter with them. I see what happened in the sixties as a case study of an intercivilizational encounter.

I—and most of those who will read this study—am still too close to see what happened objectively. My description will of necessity be impressionistic and subject to the limitations of personal and social perception.

As a missionary I imagined that if only I could empty myself of my cultural biases and perceptions I could enable the Chokosis to have a direct encounter with the gospel. I saw the gospel along the model of an artichoke— if you plucked off all the outer leaves, you would finally get to the heart (or core) of it. If we could divest the gospel of all its European and Southern Ghanaian clothing, the Chokosis could reclothe it in their own cultural garments. The model is familiar to all who have read missionary literature of the last several decades and more.

Part of the urgency of "handing over to the nationals" (that I and my mission board and so many others have exemplified in years past) is that it is important to let local people shape the growing church before foreign-developed patterns harden and then become more difficult to change. Living in Southern Ghana I had seen a perfect example of a church (the Presbyterian Church of Ghana) which was more European than African. In the sixties we were becoming aware of what David Barrett and others (Barrett 1968) have shown, that in churches where foreign patterns have been laid down by missionaries, an impulse toward reformation—toward indigenous authenticity—occurs at a later date which may by that time result in painful schism. I was trying to avoid that later schism by seeing to it that the patterns developed in the first generation were themselves legitimate expressions of Chokosi culture.

An ardent student of Chokosi proverbs, fables, and history, I was involved in a six-and-a-half-year search for the essence of Chokosi culture, which I could bring together with the essence of Christian faith, so that a new, indigenous form of Christianity would develop. It would fit the Chokosis like a custom-tailored garment.

I now recognized that I romanticized the Chokosis and underemphasized the ways in which they had already been influenced by modernization. Though I recorded English loan-words in my Chokosi dictionary, I did it reluctantly, not feeling that they were real Chokosi words. Though I accepted the role of being a middleman in purchasing aluminum roofing sheets for congregations which wanted to roof their chapels with them, I really wished that local thatching methods had allowed for strong, watertight roofs to be put on buildings even as large as the chapels that were built. I wished we had not needed to use Western roofing methods. I was also unhappy with the unanimous decision of all villages to make their chapels rectangular rather than round. Sometimes I was more Chokosi than the Chokosis!

Nevertheless I now recognize that I was selective in what I affirmed of Chokosi culture. Though I thought I had a clear biblical rationale for what I accepted and what I rejected, I am no longer so sure that I did. I fought for and won from the Southern church the permission to baptize polygynists and all of their wives, but I accepted the church's stricture that this was only for the first (guiltless) generation and that polygyny could not be engaged in by those who had once heard the gospel. When I discovered that Chokosi religious ceremonies concerning twins were seen to be crucially related to the fertility of the land, I resurrected ancient Christian Rogation Day rites to provide a functional substitute for the pagan twin customs. But pastorally the church offered Chokosis (who believed that in the birth of twins dangerous spiritual powers entered human life and needed to be placated and harnessed) nothing but the assurance that the birth of twins was a purely natural event. (I even explained modern embryology to some of the church leaders!)

I have only in the past decade come to realize how culturally conditioned a thing it is to regard certain events or processes as "natural." Only in these years have I come to recognize how secular our civilization is. When a new convert came to me as his pastor and announced that his wife was pregnant, I could not understand why he came to me. To me—and to my culture—the birth of a child, and the pregnancy which preceded it, was a totally secular event. I recommended that his wife go to the midwife at the clinic and get iron supplements and other prenatal care. What he wanted me to do, I suspect, was to perform a ritual or say a prayer.

I did pray for the sick while in Chereponi—occasionally, when there was no immediate medicinal remedy—but I suspect I did that only because my society had discovered what it called psychosomatic medicine. That legitimated the use of nonmedical means to deal with medical problems. Nothing like that had happened to make prayers for pregnant women legitimate.

I have come to see that I was as much a missionary of a secular worldview as of Christianity. No matter how much I pretended to not want to import Western culture to Chereponi, I brought in much modern technology—what we have learned to call *appropriate* technology, for the most part, but technology nonetheless. I was selective not only in what I validated and what I rejected of Chokosi culture, but also in what I legitimated and what I delegitimated of Western culture. Battery-operated slide projectors were acceptable; movies were not! I shudder to think how many pens, watches, cameras, radios, bicycles, and even handkerchiefs (a high-prestige item) people gave me money to buy for them both while I was in Ghana and since coming home. And yet I cringed when I heard my Southern Ghanaian co-pastor tell the people, "If you want your children to fly in jets like those you see flying overhead, you should become a Christian."

What was the difference? That pastor saw airplanes and Christian faith as part of one world—an indissoluble mixture of modernization and Christianization—while I saw them as coming from two worlds. I was thus a creature of my culture, which divided between the sacred and the secular. I saw watches and radios as neutral, not part of any culture but virgin offspring of the acultural world of technology. The Chokosis saw Christian faith and automobiles as all part of the world of the *Nasaram* (Europeans). "Don't you pray to your car?"

Konkomba village elders asked me when I asked why they made sacrifices to their village shrine. I laughed. Only in the past decade have I recognized how our culture worships the automobile.

By our very presence in Chereponi and by our lifestyle, simple though it was by Western or even missionary standards, we encouraged the growing consumerism of Chokosi society. Though I preached against materialism, that strikes me now as an incredible act of presumption on my part.

Similarly Western civics seemed neutral to me. Parliamentary democracy, a responsible civil service, and democratic forms of government seemed only to be part of the universal inheritance of humanity. I was sure that if bribery and corruption and abuses of power could be dealt with, the system of government the British had brought Ghana would be enormously helpful to Ghanaians and would not make them any less Ghanaian for it. The same went for the Presbyterian system of church polity I enthusiastically spread (it does have affinities with the village elder system of the Northern Ghanaians!)

Another area in which my selectivity is now apparent to me concerns the place of women in society. Soon after I arrived in Chereponi I became aware of a conflict in the society between young men with girlfriends they wanted to marry and (mostly) older men to whom the girls' fathers had promised them. The older men had gone through various customs and made increasingly valuable material gifts to their intended in-laws (it was not customary for them to have any relationship with the promised brides before marriage). In the meantime the girls had almost without exception gotten boyfriends in a socially sanctioned lovers' relationship called *somaya*. In earlier times this had brought about no conflict. Only in modern times have the young men begun to elope with their girlfriends. This provoked expensive litigation and often violent struggles between individual men and between whole communities. Many died through poisonings and other murders as a result of the conflicts.

Despite my romanticism about the Chokosi past, something in me recoiled at the thought of young women being exchanged by their fathers for gifts and promises of other young women in the future. The Bible, it seemed to me, spoke clearly of the autonomy of the individual. A girl, I suggested, should be able to choose whom she would marry. I encouraged the church elders to recommend that Christians not give away their daughters to other men.

I now recognize that the hermeneutical process in which I engaged was far less simple than I thought. It's painful to me to recognize that, though I felt there was a "Christian pattern" in this matter, I could discern no Christian pattern for the generally oppressive relationship of men to women in Chokosi society. The same Bible which seemed to me to support individual autonomy did not support the liberation of women from the generally oppressive ways in which their husbands related to them.

In so many ways I now recognize that the hermeneutic of biblical theology in which I had been trained was a particular, modern, Western approach to Scripture. We thought we were getting back, through the centuries of accretions, to the essential message of the Bible, and that we could then apply what we learned to modern times. We could take the "apostolic kerygma" and, functioning only as midwives, enable a church to come to birth in another part of the world. When I studied Bible translation in 1969, the Bible Societies taught me how to do "dynamic equivalence" translation, so that the new receptors would hear a message which would enable them to respond to it in their own culture and language in a way equivalent to how the original hearers had responded. That's what I thought I had been doing in my preaching.

I now recognize two things: that there are no acultural Christians and that the supposed core of the biblical message cannot be found apart from the particular, enculturated forms in which it was first expressed. Rather than the image of the artichoke, I would now use the image of the onion: You peel away layer after layer, thinking the layers are not the real thing, only to recognize that the structure of Christianity is not a core-and-outside structure; no, Christianity is the whole onion.

As I look back at the catechism I devised for use in Chereponi (from questions many of which Chokosis themselves were asking), I recognize that it was written in 1969 by an American who did biblical theology, who was concerned to see "development" take place, who had this-worldly hopes closely akin to those of John F. Kennedy, and who was a functionalist in this anthropology. He saw no great tensions in society. He assumed that, given knowledge, people would do the right thing and life would be a harmonious, mutually beneficial experience. The kingdom of God which I described was a world I would have been happy in, and which I sought to lead Chokosis to.

I recognize now that my theology—and my sociology and anthropology—had no place for serious, irreconcilable conflict. My eschatology was therefore an incrementalist, developmental process. It knew nothing of biblical apocalyptic. It did not require radical change except in the personal realm. There was no logical reason in it to connect the announcement of the kingdom with the call to repent, as Jesus did (Mk 1:14-15).

Finally I think I failed to recognize that power-dynamics were involved in the very expansion of the church in Chereponi. As I said in the first section, I knew that much of the growth of the church was connected with the self-determination struggle of the despised Chokosi majority against the royal and Muslim classes which had long dominated them. Many of the Njem villages adopted us just as we were seeking to incorporate them into the church. We were inserted into an ongoing power struggle. It was not a struggle on behalf of the poorest of the poor—they were the Kombas—but what we might call a populist struggle to which I, as an American admirer of the populists, progressives, and muckrakers in our own history, could respond.

Part of the power struggle, however, was a peculiarly modern struggle. One group had gained new power in modern times through Western education. By having the ability to write and read and to function in English, this small group of nkalacim (a loan word from the English clerk) wielded considerable power. Many of our most zealous leadership trainees, I suspect, saw in the mission a chance to get what they had been denied in their youth: a position in this new class.

Others, while not hoping to become nkalacim, hoped through their relation to us to get many of the perquisites of modern life. They learned early on that I—who separated church and state, sacred and secular, Christianity and material things—would not give material benefits as a reward for Christian commitment or service to the church. Those who were able to learn that lesson and not become discouraged in their search for access to material gain probably learned how to deal with my peculiar mental categories. If they would appease my religious sense first, they probably learned, and then approach me separately on secular matters, I would often help.

What happened in Chereponi was a complex, but highly interesting example of an intercivilizational encounter. I see that encounter much more clearly today than I did when I was in it.

THE LESSONS

So how do we evaluate all this? I would draw eight lessons from it.

1. We rarely see ourselves as God sees us. Rarely are we possessed of enough self-consciousness to know why we do what we do. We continually interpret our actions in ways that satisfy us, but we cannot claim Olympian objectivity for our interpretations. They are highly ideological, the product of who we are, what culture and civilization we come from, how we have been trained, and what has happened to us.

2. Our work is imperfect, full of error, misperception, and sin. We offer it as such to God. As the Chokosis prayed, so we ask God to "spray it clean with your good saliva and give it back to us."

3. The Evangelical Presbyterian Church's mission to the people of the Chereponi area brought self-confidence to the Chokosis, and especially to their most despised clans. It enabled people to make important changes in their agricultural and health practices and in their relationships with others. At the very least it eased the shock of modernization. It helped many get benefits out of modernization which otherwise would have gone to others, and imbued a number of villages with a renewed sense of the power of self-help.

4. The mission was not a prophetic liberation movement—especially for women, for the Kombas, for the landless, for the urban poor, for Chokosi migrant workers exploited by Southern Ghanaian cocoa farmers. Such a movement, I suspect, cannot be introduced from outside a society. My rhetoric would be exaggerated if I suggested that what we were involved in was a liberation struggle of that sort.

5. "Dynamic equivalence" missionary strategy is not a bad ideal to hold up, but missionary work—or any work dealing with human groups—is far more complex than linguistics and the art of translation. No missionary situation will ever be fully equivalent to another. The church worker, furthermore, is far more than a translator. He or she is an actor in the story. Each village is, in turn, a unique entity, as different from other villages as Lystra was from Philippi. Let us go back to the original models—or at least as far back as Luke will let us get—and continually judge what is happening in our work in light of what the apostles are reported to have done and how the people are reported to have responded. That is a far better model than that of either the nineteenth-century mission station or Coral Ridge Presbyterian Church. But let's recognize that the Risen Christ is alive, that he still goes before us, and that "there is always new light and new truth waiting to break forth from God's Holy Word."

6. There are dangers in seeking to Christianize whole social units, but that does not mean that it should not be tried. It would be an error to conclude from the Chokosi experience that Christianization that proceeds through group decision is mistaken and to retreat into the church's accustomed individualism.

I still hold that there is room on the canvas of God's mission for the larger vision of kingdom proclamation that moved me in Ghana. When one Canadian church worker from Southern Ghana came to visit Chereponi in 1969 and compared what was going on there with what she saw in the South, she said, "You've got an ideology that works to mobilize whole units of society to move toward a fuller life."

The trouble with what we did was twofold. We tried to join together a people's movement with a hierarchical system of church government which bred dependence. Furthermore, we tried to join a short-term mission commitment of money and people to a long-term vision of social renewal. Neither the mission nor the Southern Ghanaian church was committed to seeing that my successors had the same (albeit small by missionary standards) budget or tools for the work as I had. Furthermore, my successors, for all the time they spent with me, had spent far more time with a different concept of church—a church that dealt with the religious dimension of life, a church which grew by individual decisions, a church which operated out of "Christian towns" or "Salems," a church which rejected the cultures in which it was set, a church which had only Western educated leaders.

My successors were also handicapped by the fact that in Chokosi society they were not the automatic recipients of the respect and awe a white person seemed to inspire. They had to do far more to earn the right to be heard.

Nevertheless, I am sure that seeds were planted for a church which operates on a large canvas, which claims the whole of human existence for the kingdom. As I and my co-workers sat by many a village fire at night sharing stories with the people, I suspect that biblical visions got interspersed with the great lore of the Chokosi people, just as Islamic cultural elements had before. This process still, I am sure, goes on. If a pulse of new life emerges from the church in a second generation reformation someday, I would not be surprised to see such visions empower it.

It is unfortunate—for the kind of church which the Chokosi church seems to be today—that the pattern of becoming Christian relatively easily was set up. There may well be a need in the present for a harder individual discipline of Christians. The social basis for the discipline of Christian life did not develop as it had to to make group decisions meaningful.

7. The mission enabled people to transcend clan, tribal, regional, and racial barriers. Whatever does that in a world such as ours is important and significant.

8. I believe the gospel was communicated. We taught many things, a full theology. What got through most effectively, though, was probably the kind of simple but profound teaching expressed in our first Chokosi Christian song, which began:

> Jesus is God's Son,
> He came from heaven above.
> Jesus is our friend,
> He will help us on our way.
> Jesus came to teach us a new way.
> Let us follow his way,
> his way leads to happiness.

The fundamental message which the Chokosis heard and eagerly responded to was the good will and forgiveness of God toward humanity, God's concern that human life not bring despair and frustration but life and joy, and that nothing is closer to God's heart than the unity of the human family.

REFERENCES CITED

BARRETT, David
  1968   *Schism and Renewal,* London, Nairobi: Oxford.
KRASS, Alfred
  1974   *Go . . . and Make Disciples,* London: SPCK.
McGAVRAN, Donald
  1970   *Understanding Church Growth,* Grand Rapids: Eerdmans.

6. TAIWAN: CHURCH GROWTH, ETHNICITY, AND POLITICS

Harvie M. Conn

THE END OF WORLD WAR II PROVIDES A CONVENIENT DIVIDING POINT FOR Taiwan and the history of Christianity on the island. Politically and culturally, 1945 was a stepping-stone into social upheaval and massive change. Ceded to Japan in 1895 after only ten years as a Chinese province, Taiwan was for fifty years under the regime of a colonial government that sought, as it did elsewhere in Asia, to submerge and suffocate a distinct culture into something Japanese.

Japan sought to break Taiwan's traditional and sentimental ties with the continent by making Japanese the national language (Kerr 1974:84). An exception to this policy were the tribal languages, which were not replaced. In contrast with today's officials, the Japanese police and other levels of dignitaries learned the mountain tongues. To create a new mentality among the young Formosans the Japanese sponsored a growing system of elementary education. On the eve of the war 500,000 Formosan students were in school. They were to be made to think of themselves as Japanese subjects. Yet the inequities of the system continually testified to the Japanese colonial goals. The Formosan population approached five million, with the Japanese on Formosa numbering less than 300,000. But Japanese students continued to form the overwhelming majority in the better schools (Kerr 1974:177).

In this setting, fed by the support of Western missionaries who "encouraged younger people to retain a Formosan cultural identity vis-à-vis Japan proper," Formosan nationalism grew (Kerr 1974:202). The majority of missionaries spoke local dialects reasonably well, and this contributed to the identification of Christianity with Formosa's national goals. Missionary opposition to the compulsory veneration of the imperial Japanese family in state Shinto also placed Christianity on a collision course with the Japanese government. Formosan students and populace found their Christian convictions siding, if only by indirection, with Formosan opposition to the Japanese nationalist mythology. In the choice between Jehovah and the Sun Goddess of Japan, the Bible and the "Record of Ancient Matters" (the *Kojiki*), nationalist overtones also tended to identify the issue as more than simply a religious one. It became also a choice of things Formosan or things Japanese.

Following fourteen years of missionary service in Korea, Harvie M. Conn joined the faculty of Westminster Theological Seminary, Philadelphia, Pennsylvania, where he is Professor of Missions. His latest book is Evangelism: Doing Justice and Preaching Grace *(Zondervan, 1982).*

Among the aboriginal tribal peoples living in the mountainous eastern two-thirds of the island, effective Christian leadership combined with their animistic culture (found always to be the most responsive to the gospel) to produce large "people movements" to Christ. From the animistic worldview came the tribal perception that the "spirit" of America must be greater than that of Japan or "it" could not have defeated Japan. Missionary identification with the West reinforced this perception.

The Japanese had been especially concerned over the "mountain people." Through the 1930s and during the years of World War II, they exercised more and more strict control over the tribes and exerted increased pressure on them to learn the Japanese language and accept the Shinto religion. They feared that their mountain fastnesses might become headquarters for enemy guerrilla forces. The Japanese associated this possibility with the mountain people's conversion to Christianity as a turning from traditional loyalties and singled them out for especially severe persecution (Cheng 1965:4-6).

All this produced the opposite effect. The gospel was carried from convert to convert all through the hills, and hundreds were added to the body of Christ. The smoldering fires of faith during wartime sprang into a conflagration after the war. "By 1949 there were 120 churches with 20,000 believers. The numbers increased to 180 churches with 30,000 members in 1954, and doubled again to 360 churches with 60,000 members by 1959" (Cheng 1965:7; Dickson 1948:31-42). A 1968 report estimated that the tribal peoples were then about seventy-five percent Christian (Hwang 1968:15).

The mountain peoples do not, however, play the major role in understanding church growth in Taiwan. For this we turn to the ethnic group commonly called "Taiwanese," those who through the centuries migrated from the south of Fukien province across the straits to Taiwan. Technically known as Minnan Chinese (Mandarin designation for "south of the Min River"),[1] by 1980 they formed about seventy-five percent of the island population (Swanson 1981:7).

Church growth among the Taiwanese was slow in the years before 1945. Including the mountain tribes, only four major churches and a Christian community of 51,000 existed by 1948 to cope with the massive migrations of mainlander refugees during this period. By 1950 Taiwan had a new ethno-social reality with which to deal—almost one million refugees. In 1948 the island population was 6,806,136. Two years later it had climbed to 7,554,399.

In the years that followed this influx, gospel harvesting took place at an unprecedented pace. "Roman Catholics soared from 13,000 after World War II to 180,000 by 1960. The Protestant community shot up from about 37,000 after the war to over 200,000 in the same time period" (Swanson 1981:25; Raber

---

1. The designation "Minnan" is not used by the Taiwanese to describe themselves. Spurning also the term "Zhong-guo Jen" (men of the central kingdom), used by the Chinese to refer to their own ethnic identity, Taiwanese speak of themselves as the "Ho-lo" people. Lim Kieng-bang (1982:9) suggests that the historical origin of the term "Min" was a pejorative designation, used originally not to point to the Min River but to a kind of snake prominent in the area from which the Taiwanese originally came. The Han founders of China always used the names of animals and worms to describe non-Han peoples. This historical note raises serious questions about the legitimacy of mainlander claims on the Taiwanese as "native Chinese."

1978:72). From 1950 to 1960 thirty-five new denominations came into being. In the same period thirty-nine new mission boards entered the field. By 1955 over 300 missionaries had settled in Taiwan, and by 1960 their numbers reached 600 Protestants and an equal number of Catholic priests and nuns (Tong 1961:84).

The harvesting, however, focused among the Mandarin mainlanders. A significant number of mainland missionaries shifted their labors to Taiwan, though they still ethnically identified with the Mandarin. They were augmented by new personnel also oriented to the mainlanders through the strong anti-communist direction of Western support for the Nationalist regime of exiled Chiang Kai-shek (Mendel 1970:171-95). By 1954 117 missionaries were working with mainland Chinese, forty-six with Taiwanese, ten with mountain tribal groups, and three with the fourth ethnic group in Taiwan, the Hakka peoples (Raber 1978:71; Liao 1972:55-68).

The positive results of this concentration were evident by 1960. During the years 1955 to 1958 the Roman Catholic Church registered approximately 69,000 baptisms: 34,834 of these were mainlanders; 19,193 were Taiwanese. A little less than fifty percent of Catholic growth came from the mainlander segment of the island population, calculated at only ten percent of the census total (Swanson 1970:83). As a result of this emphasis, the Catholic Church as late as 1960 had but two Taiwanese priests among a total of 648 (Ronald 1967:35).

Protestant churches new to the island since 1945 often showed similar patterns of membership. Southern Baptist congregations, for example, grew rapidly in these years, averaging about 1,000 baptisms per year. They were mainlander in their orientation and focus. By 1962 the peak had been reached. The seven years following 1962 brought an additional net increase of only 900 new members (Swanson 1970:106). The Lutheran Church in Taiwan, formed in 1954, developed with a similar focus on the mainlanders. Twenty of the thirty-five Lutheran missionaries in Taiwan in 1955 were from mainland China and shaped the ethnic structure of the church. As with the Baptists, the mainlander harvest began to dry up by the late 1950s. When missionaries urged a new focus on the Taiwanese in 1960, this shift in emphasis did not meet with the approval of the entire church. Many still clung to the hope of returning to the mainland (Swanson 1970:128-29). By 1980 one commentator could still describe the Lutheran Church as "for the most part emigrated Mandarin-speaking mainland Chinese" (Kahle 1980:3).

A notable exception to this deliberate focus on the mainlanders was that of the Presbyterian Church in Taiwan. With an eighty-year history by 1945, its roots were deep among the ethnic Taiwanese. It also had taken a long-standing interest in the evangelization of the mountain tribes. By 1964 a Presbyterian Church community of 70,586 was drawn from that ethnic people. About one-third of the total tribal population was listed on their church rolls (Cheng 1965:14).

In 1955 the Presbyterian Church launched its "Double the Church Movement" in commemoration of the church's centennial celebration in 1965. It achieved its goal. In one decade its community increased from 86,064 to 176,255, its churches and chapels from 410 to 839. Aboriginal church growth accounted for over thirty-seven percent of that growth. Substantial gains were noted particularly in its southern synod, the area where the Presbyterian Church was first planted and which had initiated the Movement. The south was the stronghold of Fukien Taiwanese. Mainlander population constituted twenty-five to forty percent of some of the larger northern cities. But the Presbyterian thrust focused on rural villages and traditionally Taiwanese agrarian society in the southern plains.

Following that Movement, Presbyterian growth also seemed to have reached a plateau. But the reasons suggested by scholars like Swanson (1970:99-101) and repeated by Raber (1978:208) are not apparently tied to their ethnic identity with the Taiwanese. Other suggestions are made: a waning of enthusiasm after the initial exhilaration of success; difficulties in accurately tabulating statistics; the enrolling of former adherents not technically listed on church rolls; growing competition from new, non-Presbyterian churches; the financial pressures of so many new churches in so short a time; late blooming awareness of new patterns of urban migration; and the growth of theological liberalism in Presbyterian institutions.

The church of Taiwan in the 1970s would seem in some respects to be "hardly much stronger than when it entered. The figures suggest that the decadal membership growth rate for the 1970s was approximately 15%—less than the 20-plus % decadal growth rate of the general population" (Swanson 1981:33). A two-year research project undertaken by Allen Swanson supported that conclusion. At the same time a clearer picture than ever before has emerged. And there is reason for guarded optimism in some areas. About thirty-nine percent of the churches in Taiwan are growing at a rate faster than the general population rate of twenty-five percent a decade. About 17.5 percent of the churches can be categorized as "slow growing" (less than twenty-five percent but more than four percent a decade). About sixteen percent are neither gaining nor losing members. These are the static, "no growth" churches. The most alarming figure is that of the second largest block of churches, some 27.5 percent of the total sample; these are in a state of decline, with membership in 1979 lower than that of a decade ago.

In terms of ethnic groupings, these statistics are even more significant. The Minnan (Taiwanese) Christians represent over forty percent of the total Christian community, yet they constitute only one percent of the total Minnan community. The next largest group is the mainlander, Mandarin Christian community with about 33.5 percent of the total Christians. Mountain Christians, though less than two percent of the population of Taiwan, are about twenty-three percent of the total Christian constituency (Swanson 1981:41).

Even in terms of Swanson's categories of "good growth," "slow growth," "no growth," and "decline," Minnan churches represent fifty-four percent of that total compared to only forty-six percent for the mainlander community. Fifty-three percent of the Minnan churches are slow growing, compared to only forty-seven percent of the Mandarin grouping. Among the sixteen percent total of "no growth" churches, Minnan groups account for sixty-nine percent of that figure and thirty-one percent the Mandarin. Finally, in the decline category, the percentages are reversed. Sixty-three percent of the declining churches are Mandarin; only thirty-seven percent are Minnan (Swanson 1981:37).

CHURCH GROWTH ANALYSIS

How does one evaluate all these data in terms of strategy planning? What insights have been underlined by those in the Church Growth Movement?

We are fortunate in this connection; there is a wealth of church growth material on Taiwan from which to choose. In November 1971 Donald McGavran conducted the first island Church Growth workshop with over one hundred attending. His appearance was in response to the invitation of the newly formed Taiwan Church Growth Society. Out of that initiative has come a regularly published *Church Growth Bulletin* with focus on Taiwan and a growing program of workshops and seminars.

Coming at a time of growth stagnation and decline, "church growth thinking" has concentrated by and large on factors contributing to the slowdown, with suggestions for future planning. Four Church Growth books have appeared during the 1970s on the church in Taiwan (Swanson 1970; Liao 1972; Bolton 1976; Raber 1978). In 1981 appeared the most extensive and helpful of all the studies, *The Church in Taiwan: Profile 1980. A Review of the Past, A Projection for the Future* (Swanson 1981).

McGavran himself, in books appearing before 1970, had shown an interest in Taiwan. But most of his case-study material came from the aboriginal tribal groups of the island (McGavran 1955:141; 1959:126; 1970:85, 111-12, 138, 342-43). He showed an awareness of the island's ethnic groupings and their significance for church growth (1970:52, 85), and he accurately called for a special concern for the Mandarin population as particularly readily for harvest (1959:3-4). With less accuracy he predicted "the Church may go back into China sooner than we think, and when it does the significance of the Mainlander Churches of Formosa today will be terrific" (1959:8). The orientation of his earlier references seems to be toward Taiwan's role with relation to mainland China (1958:8) and the need for determining which "responsive peoples during the next thirty years will become either Christians or Communists" (1955:141). The 1980 revision of his 1970 work *Understanding Church Growth* adds little to these earlier references, other than an additional paragraph on the Hakka peoples (1980:62-63) and some use of Bolton's 1977 study of church growth along family networks (1980:401-03). Taiwan's static growth patterns and the contrast of growth among Mandarin and Taiwanese ethnic groups are not touched on at all.

The full-length studies that emerged in the 1970s from church growth thinking generally offered a consensus in analyzing growth slowdown. Swanson summarizes them in five categories: growing indifference to the gospel in the face of rising materialism (a particular emphasis of Raber 1978:84-156), increasing clericalism (Swanson 1970:236-46; Bolton 1976:295-96; Raber 1978:306), lack of lay training programs and weaknesses in theological education (Swanson 1980:249-54; Bolton 1976:266-70; Raber 1978:306-10), individualism and lack of sensitivity to growth by homogeneous units (Swanson 1970:251; Bolton 1976:294; Raber 1978:302-03), and paralysis caused by widespread use of subsidy (Swanson 1970:270-76; Raber 1978:310; Swanson 1981:27-29).

The summary is by no means inclusive. Other suggestions for strategy change recur consistently throughout the titles. Raber summarizes them more individually in her work (1978:233-43). When we take into account the different centers of attention of the books, this sameness of the conclusions raises questions as to what degree the case studies are legitimate case studies or come closer to extended illustrations drawn from Taiwan to amplify what critics call a "church growth" ideology. Their heavy indebtedness to McGavran's larger strategy suggestions may be part of the reason for the evident frustration in motivating new growth and methodological progress. Raber's 1978 work was motivated by this frustration. She was urged by her instructors at Fuller Theological Seminary to seek out reasons why, after a decade of careful analysis of evangelistic potential and numerous methodological suggestions, the church continued to do no more than hold its own (Raber 1978:319). This is not to say there is not a vast amount of helpful and striking material in these books. Our suggestion is that, until the work of Swanson (1981), a new direction for analysis had not yet been sufficiently uncovered.

THE ETHNOPOLITICAL DIMENSION

We do not offer ethnopolitical analysis as a definitive answer, but only as a hypothesis which needs further investigation. Nor do we suggest it is the key issue. But it has more importance than most of these studies give to it.

This does not suggest that these works are insensitive to ethnicity as a strong factor in church growth. They uncover this dimension in their call for a "uni-lingual outreach to homogeneous units of society." But the insight gets buried by the order of priorities. There are calls for "sufficient workers," "early training of native workers," and "lay enthusiasm." Robert Bolton's fine book indeed focuses on such an ethnic group, the urban Minnan Chinese. David Liao does the same in his ground-breaking work on the Hakka. We are reminded by Bolton that on the mainland, "about one quarter the number of Christians in the whole of China are to be found" in the Fukien province from which the bulk of Taiwan's island population has come (1976:79). We are even assured that the missions working in this area "considered the Minnan Chinese as specific people." But when Bolton turns to strategy planning for reaching their descendants, seventy-five percent of Taiwan's population, that insight is buried in all sorts of good advice. "Encourage the national church," we are wisely cautioned (1976:263). But which "national church"? The Hakka church? The mainlander church? The Taiwanese church? The church's theology "must be as thoroughly *Chinese* as possible" (1975:267). That's good advice by way of contextualization. But what is "Chinese"? Hakka Chinese? Minnan Chinese? Mandarin Chinese? The "One China/Taiwan" mentality is conquering, submerging the realities of many Taiwans (Conn 1981:10).

Here we draw attention not only to ethnicity. It is also ethnopolitics. Raber comes close to noting the significance of this in her overview of church growth in Taiwan prior to 1964. Among six factors relating to harvesting, she notes that "the political, economic, and social environmental factors in Taiwan were closely associated to the growth of the Church" (Raber 1978:82). She then proceeds to outline the environment in the lengthiest chapter of her book. But the focus is on "rapid social change" (1964-74) with little attention to the political ramifications of ethnicity in Taiwan and government policies toward ethnicity. When she does analyze the political situation on the island, she cites "nation development" as a positive factor aiding receptivity and "unhealthy nationalism" as a negative factor inhibiting receptivity (1978:158-62, 180-81). Her discussions of both of these factors are never related to the conflict of Minnan/Mandarin ethnic groupings on the island. I suspect, in view of her generally supportive commendations of the Kuomintang regime, she may have the Minnan in mind in her vague negative comments on nationalism and those "national workers who confuse indigeneity and nationalism" (1978:180).

Ethnopolitics in Taiwan has been radically shaped by the dominating presence of the Nationalist Party on the island since their migrations from the mainland in the late 1940s. Almost immediately ethnic hostilities surfaced. In 1945, 12,000 mainland troops boarded American ships to accept the formal surrender of the island by the Japanese. The soldiers were undisciplined and treated the Taiwanese as a conquered people. For eighteen months the mainlanders engaged in looting and brutality. "Taiwanese were replaced in government and business posts by inexperienced mainlanders" (Sawatzky 1981:457). The governor of the island, Chen-Yi, instituted a complex program of monopolies, seen by the Taiwanese as designed to drain off local wealth into the pockets of mainlander administrators (Kerr 1976:124-42). Moved by feelings of cultural superiority, reinforced by the wrenching break with the homeland, mainlanders tended "to look down on what Taiwan had to offer compared with the way things used to be on the mainland" (Grichting 1971:348). The Taiwanese, by contrast, had migrated there at about the same time the Pilgrims were landing at Plymouth, Massachusetts, establishing their own self-identity and way of life independent of the mainland. Fifty years under the Japanese, in isolation from the mainland, reinforced that identity. They did "not consider themselves Chinese citizens any more than Americans consider themselves British" (Sawatzky 1981:456).

On February 28, 1947, island-wide rioting broke out against the Mandarin rule. On March 8 Chiang Kai-shek ordered 50,000 troops sent from the mainland; they indiscriminately killed at least 10,000 Taiwanese (Mendel 1970:26-41). Martial law was instated and has remained in effect since 1947.

By the 1960s Formosan memories of Japanese colonialism had become intertwined with the more recent experience of Chinese nationalist administration and the vast influx of mainlander refugees.

With this sad beginning, the Nationalist government heralded the "Chinese" character of Taiwan in its ideological battle with the mainland. Both Peking and Taipei speak of "one China." Peking continues to insist that Taiwan is a part of China. The nationalist government on the island bases its claims on the same proposition. Taiwan, runs the argument, is the only free province of the whole of China, which it claims to represent. Thus two functioning governments are on the island, the larger representing the whole of China in absentia, the other on a provincial level for the island. To preserve that thesis, no national elections have been held since the last one on the mainland in 1948. In fact, they cannot be held until China is liberated. Native Taiwanese, therefore, have only a handful of elected representatives of the "Province" of Taiwan in the National Assembly. The vast majority of the seats remain filled by mainlanders, aging officials still representing provinces they have not seen for over thirty years.

In the face of this political and social orientation to the mainland, it is not hard to understand early missionary focus on the mainlanders and use of the Mandarin language over against the Taiwanese. Other factors would also reinforce this orientation. Western missionaries, trained by their background to think of countries and geographical territories, too often see only one Taiwan, a political entity occupying 13,900 square miles. Evangelistic goals are measured in terms of one of the world's 221 nations. Looking at Taiwan politically rather than ethnopolitically turns the island from a plethora of cultural mosaics and gospel possibilities into a "one China" monolith.

Politically, the strong anti-communist mentality of the missionary, fed by Nationalist information and a censored press, underlines his or her support of the Mandarin cultural push. The history of communism's suppression and manipulation of the church on the mainland since 1949 is more contemporary than classical. Taiwan's spectacular economic success is an easily observed contrast. But even for the missionary who does not have strong feelings, it is almost impossible to be neutral. Frequent government-sponsored conferences are held, and attendance from various mission groups is expected, if not demanded. One private correspondent notes, "It is pressure with a capital P." All these things combine to minimize local cultural conflicts to the level of simple language/translation questions and internal politics. Final judgments are controlled by what emerges as the bigger question on the missionary agenda: Will Taiwan remain an open port for the gospel? The assumption behind that question is that only mainlander rule will insure it remains open (to the Western missionary).

Geographically, missionary deployment on the island also contributes to their orientation. The vast majority of missionaries are located in the northern half of the island, in cities where the mainlander population is concentrated on the island. The current mission emphasis on the cities will reinforce that pattern.

The end result of all this is that, as late as 1979, six out of ten missionaries (61.6%) work primarily in the Mandarin language, the language group of only thirteen percent of the total population and 33.5 percent of the island's Christian community. By contrast, less than two out of ten (15%) work in the Minnan language, a language used by seventy-five percent of the island's people. Only 2.2 percent work in the Hakka language of ten percent of the total population. "It must, of course, be admitted that Mandarin is now widely used among most levels of society under middle-age. It is also the language of education, and many missionaries are involved in some form of training, education, or student work" (Swanson 1981:59). In the face of government policies pressing for language unification, few new missionaries seem to be departing from that practice. Often with an appeal to Romans 13 and an eye on the young islander now learning only Mandarin in the schools, the missionary continues to plan for a Mandarin-speaking church in the distant or near distant future. Yet fifty-three percent of the island's local churches use Minnan Chinese in their Sunday worship, while only forty-five percent use Mandarin (Swanson 1981:179).

In the government's ethnopolitical definition of itself in terms of the mainland, two factors especially play a part that is crucial for the future of evangelization in Taiwan. One is the effect of what Eric Hanson calls the continental political ideology of the Chinese on organized religions within its borders (1980:86). Related to this is the government attitude toward language unification on the island.

In common with other ideological systems, the Chinese scheme represents an effort to formulate a national plan to insure that the various ethnic and religious groups within a given developing nation work together (Verkuyl 1978:375). The ideology comes with a set of strategies and methods, blueprints for the future, to move the masses and guard the social consensus developed by the elite leadership.

The Chinese ideology, marked by a continental outlook in its traditional past, held to its own economic, political, and cultural sufficiency and tolerated no opposition to or competition with established state orthodoxy. This ideology it sought to protect by the "penetration, regulation and control of institutional religion and obliteration of heterodox sects" (Hanson 1980:28). Government policies on the mainland both before and after 1949 are consistent illustrations of this control mindset—and so too with attitudes of the Kuomintang on Taiwan. The difficulties of the church in the People's Republic are not due primarily to Peking's Marxist ideology "but to the re-emergence of a Chinese state with a continental political ideology" (Hanson 1980:86).

So it is with Taiwan. Chinese tradition is marked by the predominance of diffused, over-institutional religion. The organized church, then, in the light of this ideology, is seen as a political threat. And "the greater the split between national and local political institutions, the greater the concomitant religious antagonism and possibility of religious rebellion" (Hanson 1980:52).

How has this affected church growth on Taiwan? Those churches oriented largely to mainlanders have not felt the negative effect of the ideology as much. The government perceived such churches as being domestically friendly. The growth of the Roman Catholic Church in the 1940s and 1950s is a prime example. "First, Catholic membership was disproportionately mainlander. Second, the Catholic hierarchy was composed of either mainlanders or foreign missionaries. Few spoke Taiwanese. Third, Catholics actively participated in government at high levels. . . . Fourth, the government always presented the Taiwanese issue in terms of returning to the mainland" (Hanson 1980:88).

The one major exception to this Catholic mainland orientation was the Maryknoll Diocese of Taichung. These American missioners learned the Taiwanese dialect. This policy pleased their parishioners, but strained relations with both the government and the mainland clergy of other dioceses. However, since the newcomers were apolitical and anti-communist, the Kuomintang tolerated their Taiwanese orientation.

Given this ideology, how does one explain any possible growth of an institutional religion such as Christianity in the context of a Chinese ideology? Only during periods of social disintegration have the Chinese shown any responsiveness to alien ideas. Thus, in the nineteenth century, when China adopted a maritime, rather than a continental, mindset, interacting with Western cultural influences, the church could take root. Similarly, in the late 1940s and 1950s, during the social and political upheaval and crisis, the church grew within the mainlander population.

This same Chinese ideology helps to explain mainlander attitudes toward language in Taiwan. Unlike many missionaries, the Chinese see language as more than simply a tool, and more even than simply an instrument for understanding culture. Culture and language are so intertwined that our view of reality becomes an abridged version of the ideological world that is edited by our language. Language, then, cannot be isolated from culture or ethnopolitics. It is more than simply some sort of systematic inventory of human experiences. It is part of the essential ideological process in shaping that experience. Not a static, passive instrument, it is a self-contained, creative symbolic organization of our worldview. It provides a map of culture, of "seeing" our ideology.

In keeping with that ideological perception of language, the mainland government in the 1960s and especially the 1970s has campaigned for language unification. The threat of the Communist mainland has reinforced this program of language planning. Missionaries have felt both subtle and more overt pressure to work only in the Mandarin language. Soldiers are fined for using Taiwanese on duty; students are penalized for its use in the classroom. Taiwanese grammatical studies are not carried on in academic circles, and grammar books are available only to missionaries at special request and authorization. One person wrote, "I understand that the *Three People's Principles* says that there is to be only *one* language in China, viz., Mandarin." I have not been able to check the legal accuracy of that statement. But most certainly it reflects a working policy.

In January 1975 the policy came into direct relation to evangelization when the government "took the step of confiscating the Bible in Romanized scripts used in the Presbyterian Church for almost a century on the pretext of promoting the 'national' language, Mandarin" (Song 1976:8). In December 1978 this was followed by a government ruling that anyone wishing to read the Bible in any language other than Mandarin had to have a permit. The Romanized translation of Taiwanese may no longer be printed or published unless it appears in a double-column edition. The first such edition appeared in 1980, Mandarin in one column and Romanized Taiwanese in the other. It was held up for nearly two years, as the director of the Bible Societies in Taiwan patiently went to offices of education, security, and so on, until all the permits had been obtained.

Similar actions have been taken with aboriginal translations of the mountain tribes. Earlier I suggested this was rather severe, involving a December 1974 confiscation of the recently published Tyal version of the New Testament (Conn 1981:9). However, I have learned that of ninety-five Tyal churches, seizure took place in only one church. Similar small incidents may have happened in other language groups, too; but were by no means total, nor as severe as the word "confiscated" sounds in the English language. Government regulations have been enacted, but many of them, it would appear, are seldom implemented. However, they *are there* and handy to apply whenever a person becomes a risk to security/control of the regime in power. I have also heard of police appearing suddenly at the home for "inspections," national and expatriate experiencing difficulty because of association with translation projects. "The pressure has been there," the comment was made, "but it has not been absolutely prohibitive." This fits in well with our exposition of the relationship between language policy and Chinese ideology.

Given this ideological bias toward the Mandarin-oriented culture and an unchallenged ethnopolitical view of Taiwanese culture as Chinese, it is to be expected that strategies for church planting would easily be structured around Mandarin receptivity to the gospel.

Two factors in the 1970s, however, indicate these conditions are shifting. One is the growing conflict between the state and the largest of Taiwan's churches, the predominantly Taiwanese Presbyterian Church. The other is the declining growth rate in Mandarin-oriented churches.

Swanson's 1981 study clearly suggests the slowdown and its lack of perception by the missionaries who continue to work preponderantly in the Mandarin language (Swanson 1981:189). During the late 1970s both Hakka and Minnan baptisms have increased and Mandarin baptisms have decreased. Of the total number of baptisms during the 1974-75 period, forty-one percent were Mandarins. From 1978 to 1980 that figure dropped to only 32.5 percent of the total (Swanson 1981:110). There is also a heavier drop-out rate through the back door among the Mandarin churches. "Minnan Churches must baptize 3.3 Christians in order to register a net gain of one. Mandarin losses, however, are much higher with only one member gained for every 6.1 baptized!" (Swanson 1981:225).

Larger problems are also present among the mainlander clergy. Almost thirty percent of Mandarin churches are either without leadership or are pastored by those of Minnan or Hakka background. There is also a serious aging problem among Mandarin pastors. They are older than their Minnan colleagues by an average of 10.6 years. "If the average retirement age is 70, then about two out of three Mandarin pastors will have retired by the end of this century, in less than 20 years" (Swanson 1981:140, 145).

The same aging factor appears in the laity of the ethnic groups.

> Mandarins constitute almost 50 percent of the older Christians, a reflection of the large number who became Christians during the great ingathering of the 1950's. Their decline is receptivity beginning in the 1960's is reflected in their sharp drop in the 30-49 age bracket. Less than one in five (19.2%) of those interviewed from the 40-49 age bracket were Mandarins and only 22.3 percent of the 20-39 age bracket. This poses a serious problem. Do we have a leadership vacuum developing in the Mandarin Christian community? Where have all the early to middle year Mandarins gone? . . . It is apparent that the strength of the middle age Christian community in Taiwan lies with Minnan Christians (Swanson 1981:102).

The possibility of drawing leadership from the children of Christian parents also seems less among the Mandarin.

> If both Minnan parents are active Christians, about 74 percent of all their children who live at home will attend some form of church activity. In Mandarin homes this drops to 59 percent. Again, if one Minnan parent is a Christian, about 38 percent of all children living at home will still attend some church activities. In Mandarin homes this figure drops to 26 percent (Swanson 1981:111).

Is all of this saying that the days of Mandarin receptivity to the gospel are disappearing? Given this, what effect will it have on the Taiwanese-speaking congregations?

A second factor in evaluating the future is the rising conflict between the Chinese ideology and the Presbyterian Church in Taiwan. That conflict had been especially pronounced in the 1970s. The church has issued four public statements in the last decade that raised repeated questions at crucial areas concerning the traditional ideology. "Our National Fate," issued in 1971,

> called for the election of a new representative government through which the people could determine their own destiny. A second statement issued in 1975, following the government confiscation of the new Taiwanese romanized translation of the New Testament, appealed to the government to perserve religious freedom, promote trust between the government and the church, seek reconciliation of all peoples living in Taiwan, preserve human rights and allow the church to participate in world organizations (Sawatzky 1981:460; Presbyterian Church in Taiwan 1976:54-57).

In 1977 a "Declaration on Human Rights," addressed in an open letter to the President of the United States of America, called for the freedom and independence of the people of Taiwan, urging the Taiwan government to make the island a new and independent country.

These declarations have met with severe action by the government. Church leaders are kept under close surveillance, and some missionaries have been expelled for their alleged promotion of Taiwanese independence. The "Declaration of Human Rights" was sent by mail to all its pastors and never delivered. One writer adds, "Pastors learned of the declaration when police visited them. The text was published in the *Taiwan Church Weekly,* 4000 copies of which were destroyed by the post office" (Bailey 1979:6). Delegates to the assembly had been allegedly offered bribes by the ruling Nationalist Party's fifth section if the declaration would be rejected and General Secretary C. M. Kao defeated in his bid for reelection. The assembly approved the document 235-49-10 and reelected Kao 225-49-8.

The battle goes on. Pending legislation was announced in the summer of 1979 for the "supervision" of shrines, temples, and churches. Said by many to be aimed at stifling the voice of the Presbyterian Church, it prompted an official petition from the Presbyterian General Assembly on July 4, 1979. Acknowledging "a life and death crisis" facing "our country," the petition fears the proposed legislation will contravene the constitutionally guaranteed freedom of religion for the people. It predicts unnecessary friction between the government and the people and a growing distrust. "As a result," it continues, "our nation will fall into the trap of the united front struggle by the Communists" (Conn 1981:11).

The regulations were not passed but sent to the executive for further analysis. The latest act in the conflict took place in April 1980, when the general secretary of the church, C. M. Kao, was arrested for allegedly harboring a participant in a Kaohsiung demonstration in favor of human rights. The arrest came four months after the violence that broke out, and Kao was sentenced to seven years in prison (Ecumenical Diary 1980:332-33). Many see the imprisonment as one more act of an intransigent government concerned over religious assaults on its ideological basis (Shaull 1980:12-13).

What has been the outcome of this conflict for church growth? Full statistics for the Presbyterian Church are difficult to obtain. Swanson's 1981 work does not offer figures for any year except 1979. There is reason, however, to be optimistic. Discounting tribal congregations, the church grew from 412 congregations in 1968 to only 431 in 1972 (Bolton 1976:109). However, by 1979 it numbered 558 (including twenty-five Hakka-speaking churches and four Mandarin groups).

Added to this is the renewed drive for evangelism within the church. In May 1978 the church began what has been called "The Ten Plus Movement." Its goal is to increase membership annually by ten percent, thus doubling again the size of the church in ten years (Swanson 1981:32). The mission dimensions of evangelism and social action are being emphasized concurrently.

Beyond the figures is the potential effect of the controversy on how the church is perceived. In 1980 the pastor of a large church, himself in a very exposed position, said to an American visitor:

> As a result of what has happened over the last three months, the Presbyterian Church in Taiwan is no longer a foreign institution; it is now the church of the Taiwanese people. We are attracting many strangers— men and women who are concerned about what is happening in our society—those who are most open and progressive, who are most willing to give of their money and of themselves. A number of people I had not known before have come to me not only to express their solidarity but also to say, "Your God can now be our God" (Shaull 1980:13).

Some church members are upset by the social ostracism they experience and are getting tired of continued harassment. Many others are saying, "We now know what faithfulness to the gospel means. . . ."

Does this pastor speak for others yet to be harvested in Taiwan? What will this conflict mean in terms of the breaking down, or alteration, of the traditional Chinese ideology? Human societies are not static. How far will a continued blurring of lines between these two ethnic groups take them?

QUESTIONS FOR FUTURE STRATEGY

Case studies are always loose-ended, leaving as many questions and issues to study as firm answers. We end this chapter with our legacy of questions, some created by the Church Growth methodology that has studied Taiwan now for a decade. Our desire at this point is not to critique church growth strategy but to ask questions, to create an agenda for future discussion. Taiwan's situation raises some of these questions in a unique enough way to help us all.

Primary focus. Above all else, we see the need for a more careful study of the relationship between evangelization and social issues in their effect on harvesting strategy. Precisely in this area we see a massive lacuna in the thinking of McGavran that has not aided students of Taiwan church growth. McGavran's concern over social issues in developing a strategy of missions has been molded largely by his legitimate fear of evangelism losing its emphasis in a world of mission theory dominated by social concerns. He pleads repeatedly for no tension between mission and the advocates of social action (McGavran 1970:258). He properly reminds us that "when churches multiply in a non-Christian population, they will bring God's purposes for His children to bear on the particular part of the social order which they can influence." But he says little beyond this. His 1980 revision of his 1970 work adds nothing to this section of the book (1980:292-94).

More recently, Peter Wagner has attempted to flesh out this missing segment of Church Growth thinking. Using Luke 4:18-19 and 7:21, he places the signs of the kingdom listed in the passages into two categories: those "social signs or signs applied to a general class of people" and those "personal signs or signs applied to specific individuals" (Wagner 1981:16). The former he sees as related to social action, the latter parallel with social service (1981:36-38). The Church Growth principle he draws from this distinction is that "when churches are involved in social ministries, the churches which specialize in social service tend to attract more new members than the ones specializing in social action" (1981:37).

I am not impressed, first of all, by Wagner's pragmatic division of the signs. This strikes me as a radical imposition on the text of an issue they were not meant to cover. Because of this imposition, the effect is to distort the message of the text and to create a compartmentalization that goes against the thrust of the whole text. With Howard Marshall and many other commentators on this passage, I see the first sign in the list, "proclaiming good news to the poor" (Lk 4:19), in close connection with those that follow it, the infinitival phrases bringing out more fully through various metaphors the significance of the preaching (Marshall 1978:183).

Further, even as a pragmatic distinction, I do not find the division between social action and social service a usable one in strategy planning. It requires a verbally loaded set of meanings not ordinarily given the terms in common parlance. Beyond that I suggest that most churches involved in what Wagner designates social action are also involved in social service. A more pragmatic contrast is that between churches which are involved in social ministries and those which are not, however far those ministries carry them. A more useful Church Growth principle then becomes, "When churches are involved in evangelization, the churches which link evangelism with felt social needs tend to attract more new members than the ones specializing in only evangelism."

Again, patterns in Taiwan support that principle. Swanson notes, "Churches with the highest level of social services are churches that are growing the best. Note that churches that are declining in membership have a very low score on community activities or services" (Swanson 1981:211). Here too, Minnan churches consistently reflect a higher commitment to their local community's needs than do Mandarin churches.

Finally, Wagner's distinction presumably would place the question of ideology confrontation in the arena of social action, signs applied to a general class of people. Yet the major thesis of this chapter is that such questions of ideology are often crucial to church growth, especially in those times when they are being challenged. Ideologies, by their very nature, do not allow distinctions between social action and social service.

Totally missing in Wagner's treatment is this very question of ideologies and church growth. It is, in fact, a study the evangelical missiological community needs urgently to undertake. But it is also a study the evangelical may have great difficulty in carrying out. The rigid walls often built up between evangelism and social concerns, the reticence of Christians living in an ideological state to discuss it, even the Church Growth way of radically differentiating between "discipling" and "perfecting," all work against taking up this strategy challenge for study.

Ethnicity. Closely related to it must be the question of ethnicity. An ideological state like Taiwan demands that the island become an ethnic melting pot and its ethnic diversities be killed or minimized to serve a political design. The Assyrian model that diffused the ten tribes of Israel into an assimilationist culture is repeated. The Babylonian-exile model that allowed the Jews to retain their ethnic identity and paved the way for the dispersion of the gospel among all the nations (Lk 24:47) is discarded.

Wagner does commend an "open society" policy as that most compatible to the homogeneous unit principle (Wagner 1981:179). In connection with that he condemns "assimilationist racism" as an effort on the part of the powerful group to absorb the powerless group. "If enough social pressure can be brought to bear, powerless groups can be eliminated through assimilation. Some have recognized it as an effective form of 'ethnocide,' because it attempts to do away with the socio-cultural unit. It does not kill *people*—it only kills cultures" (Wagner 1981:177).

Does not the present situation in Taiwan come close to Wagner's description? If so, how can this ethnic pogrom be handled on Wagner's level of social service? It demands that congregational structures take action on a wider level (Wagner's social action). But this he warns against (Wagner 1981:193-94). All this simply indicates the need for further exploration and questioning.

Language. Still another topic related to ideologies is that of language. McGavran properly notes that people like to become Christians without crossing language barriers. But does this insight not become superficial when we recognize the ways in which language is manipulated by ideologies? Language then becomes a macrosociological instrument for oppression. Scholars in the area of language planning argue that "while the development of a national language may be highly conducive to the creation and strengthening of national identity, the *deliberate* use of language for purposes of national identity may—at least in a multiethnic state—have more disruptive than unifying consequences" (Kelman 1975:21). Does not the present conflict in Taiwan between the state and the Presbyterian Church illustrate that profoundly? How may we apply that insight to evangelistic strategy? Is there another Church Growth axiom that needs to be examined here? "While the development of a national language (Mandarin) may be highly conducive to the creation and strengthening of Mandarin churches, the *deliberate* use of that language for purposes of national identity may, in a multiethnic state, ultimately retard growth of the church in that language group and alternately encourage the linguistically oppressed churches." Or will it go the other way? Will the Taiwanese, aware of government pressure against their cultural identity, and remembering the Japanese efforts at language planning, identify Christianity as a pro-mainlander ideology? This whole area needs study as well.

I have no desire in raising these questions to put unwarranted emphasis on the ethnopolitical as a reason for the decline of the Mandarin-speaking churches. To tie the declension too closely to language questions is to forget other elements equally or more significant as factors. At the same time, the Taiwanese church (at least that segment of it tied to the Presbyterians) may now be perceived by many as a symbol for independence or nationalism. After the publication of the Declaration of Human Rights in 1977, a large number of factory workers began to visit the church. When asked why they were now interested in coming to services, they responded that they wanted to find out what this Presbyterian Church was that was speaking out for them. From becoming a foreign institution, the church had moved to the status of friend. Now the church may no longer be friend but sister.

Our agenda for study is a large one. Over it all we remember Jim Wallis's warning that evangelism can never be seen "in isolation from the critical questions and events that shape the context in which the gospel must be lived and proclaimed. The scope of our evangelism must be at least as pervasive as the power of sin itself" (Wallis 1976:31). Where do we direct our compassion in Taiwan? Who ultimately are the "sinned against"?

REFERENCES CITED

BAILEY, J. Martin
    1976   "Taiwan: The Church, the Government and American Reality," *The Church Herald*, January 26.
BOLTON, Robert J.
    1976   *Treasure Island. Church Growth Among Taiwan's Urban Minnan Chinese*, South Pasadena: William Carey Library.
    1977   "Gathering a People in Taiwan," *Church Growth Bulletin*, Vol. XIII, No. 3, January.
CHENG, Lien-min
    1965   "A Short History of the Presbyterian Church Among the Mountain Tribes in Taiwan," *Occasional Bulletin from the Missionary Research Library*, Vol. XVI, Nos. 4-5, April-May.
CONN, Harvie M.
    1981   "Many Taiwans and Lordship Evangelism," *International Bulletin of Missionary Research*, Vol. 5, No. 1, January.
DICKSON, James
    1948   *Stranger Than Fiction*, Toronto: Evangelical Publishers.
ECUMENICAL DIARY
    1980   *Ecumenical Review*, Vol. 32, No. 4, October.
GRICHTING, Wolfgang
    1971   *The Value System in Taiwan 1970*, Taipei, Taiwan: No publisher.
HANSON, Eric O.
    1980   *Catholic Politics in China and Korea*, Maryknoll: Orbis Books.
HWANG, C. H.
    1968   *Joint Action for Mission in Formosa*, New York: Friendship Press; Geneva: World Council of Churches.
KAHLE, Roger
    1980   "Taiwan: Crackdown Gets Mixed Reviews," *One World*, No. 55, April.
KELMAN, Herbert C.
    1975   "Language as an Aid and Barrier to Involvement in the National System," *Can Language Be Planned?* Joan Rubin and Bjorn H. Jernudd (eds.), Honolulu: The University Press of Hawaii.

KERR, George H.
1974　*Formosa. Licensed Revolution and the Home Rule Movement, 1895-1945*, Honolulu: The University Press of Hawaii.
1976　*Formosa Betrayed*, New York: Da Capo Press.

LIAO, David C. E.
1972　*The Unresponsive. Resistant or Neglected?* Chicago: Moody Press.

LIM Kieng-bang
1982　"It is Time for Taiwanese to Speak," *Formosa Weekly*, Los Angeles, Vol. 90, May 29.

MARSHALL, I. Howard
1978　*Commentary on Luke. New International Greek Testament Commentary*, Grand Rapids: Eerdmans.

McGAVRAN, Donald A.
1955　*The Bridges of God*, New York: Friendship Press.
1959　*How Churches Grow. The New Frontiers of Mission*, London: World Dominion Press.
1970　*Understanding Church Growth*, Grand Rapids: Eerdmans.
1980　*Understanding Church Growth*, Revised Edition, Grand Rapids: Eerdmans.

MENDEL, Douglas
1970　*The Politics of Formosan Nationalism*, Berkeley and Los Angeles: University of California Press.

PRESBYTERIAN CHURCH IN TAIWAN
1976　"Our Appeal Concerning the Bible, The Church and the Nation," *Study Encounter*, Vol. XII, Nos. 1-2.

RABER, Dorothy A.
1978　*Protestantism in Changing Taiwan: A Call to Creative Response*, South Pasadena: William Carey Library.

RONALD, Robert J.
1967　*Religion in Taiwan*, Hsinchu, Taiwan: Mimeographed.

SAWATZKY, Sheldon
1981　"State-Church Conflict in Taiwan: Its Historical Roots and Contemporary Manifestations," *Missiology*, Vol. IX, No. 4, October.

SHAULL, Richard
1980　"Taiwan's Christians Suffer Continuing Repression," *A.D. Magazine*, June.

SONG, Choan-seng
1976　"Giving Account of Hope in These Testing Times," *Study Encounter*, Vol. XII, Nos. 1-2.

SWANSON, Allen J.
1970　*Taiwan: Mainline Versus Independent Church Growth*, South Pasadena: William Carey Library.
1981　*The Church in Taiwan: Profile 1980. A Review of the Past, A Projection for the Future*, Pasadena: William Carey Library.

TONG, Hollington K.
1961　*Christianity in Taiwan: A History*, Taipei: China Post Publishers.

VERKUYL, Johannes
1978　*Contemporary Missiology: An Introduction*, Grand Rapids: Eerdmans.

WAGNER, C. Peter
1981　*Church Growth and the Whole Gospel*, San Francisco: Harper and Row.

WALLIS, Jim
1976　*Agenda for Biblical People*, New York: Harper and Row.

II. METHODOLOGICAL ISSUES

7. LOOKING FOR A METHOD: BACKGROUNDS AND SUGGESTIONS

Harvie M. Conn

In 1955 World Dominion and Friendship Press released *The Bridges of God* by Donald McGavran, a missionary of the Disciples of Christ with over thirty years of experience in India (McGavran 1974:54-98). Writing against the backdrop of his experience with India's mass, caste movements to Christ in the 1920s and 1930s, McGavran began to focus missionary attention on the way in which societies, tribes, and castes become Christian. How does an endogamous society, in which everyone marries within the social unit, become Christian? How can evangelization of these groupings avoid inferring or actually saying that becoming Christian means leaving that unit and joining a different caste, the church? His concern, among others, was to alert the Christian community to the slowing-down effect that a one-on-one traditional method, associated with the mission-station approach of the past, had on the rapidity with which such groups could be harvested for the gospel. He saw past approaches as leaving converts with the feeling that they had betrayed their people.

Through the years since 1955, McGavran has articulated that concern in what is now called the homogeneous unit principle—people "like to become Christians without crossing racial, linguistic or class barriers" (McGavran 1970:198). Concomitant with it has been his insistence that "the great obstacles to conversion are social, not theological" (McGavran 1970:191).

In the process of explaining this principle, McGavran has created and refined specialized vocabulary. He has become associated with what many regard as a monolithic "School of Church Growth," usually identified with the staff of the School of World Mission at Fuller Theological Seminary. That identification has not been altogether helpful in evaluating McGavran's contributions. The stress on the continuity of the methodology often slights as well the unique contributions of McGavran's colleagues. Coupled with this is the lack of attention to modifications made by McGavran himself in his formulations. Because of these factors, we seek to offer a historical sketch of the program and some radical modifications of the original thesis.

Following fourteen years of missionary service in Korea, Harvie M. Conn joined the faculty of Westminster Theological Seminary, Philadelphia, Pennsylvania, where he is Professor of Missions. His latest book is Evangelism: Doing Justice and Preaching Grace *(Zondervan, 1982).*

HISTORICAL SKETCH

In considering McGavran alone, one can discern refinements in several areas. On a linguistic level, vocabulary has been modified. By 1955 McGavran was speaking of "people movements." This in itself represented some refinements from earlier language used by his India co-researcher, J. Waskom Pickett. Pickett spoke of people movements and mass movements in 1933. Pressed by his students at Northwest Christian College (where the Institute of Church Growth was born in 1961 and housed till 1966), McGavran struggled with the complaint that his references to "group mind" were not doing full justice to the recognition of personal conversion. McGavran's associate and teaching fellow, Alan Tippett, called on his adviser, Homer Barnett, an anthropologist at the University of Oregon, for suggestions. Barnett answered spontaneously, "multi-individual group decision," which Tippett incorporated into his formulations (Tippett 1970:31). By 1970, McGavran was speaking of "multi-individual interdependent decisions." Among McGavran's students, "people movement" has retained its strength as a more popularized and shorthand expression, but the fuller language has remained.

A more problematic formulation made its appearance in McGavran's 1955 work. To describe the process of conversion in a people movement, he coined two new terms with technical force, "discipling" and "perfecting." They became the labels used by McGavran from 1953 to 1971 generally to designate "two separate stages in the establishment of a Christian civilization" (McGavran 1955:13). Tippett considers these two conceptualizations, the notion of the people movement and the differentiation of discipling and perfecting, as two of the three great contributions of McGavran to missiology (Tippett 1973:20).

Drawing the terms from Matthew 28:19-20, McGavran saw discipling as *"the removal of distracting, divisive, sinful gods and spirits and ideas from the corporate life of the people and putting Christ at the centre on the Throne"* (McGavran 1955:14). At this stage, the full understanding of Christ was not the all-important factor. It was rather that he be recognized by the community as their sole spiritual Sovereign. Perfecting then became the second stage, an elaboration of the Great Commission, the call to "teach them to observe all things." It was "the bringing about of an ethical change in the discipled group, an increasing achievement of a thoroughly Christian way of life for the community as a whole, and conversion of the individuals making up each generation as they come to the age of decision" (1955:15). For McGavran, "Distinguishing these two stages is essential for those who lead people to become Christian. *The second stage overlaps the first, but it cannot precede it without destroying it"* (1955:16).

Subsequent controversy has not confirmed this as the wisest of strategic choices. Critics have continued to charge the distinction with creating a dualism, a bifurcation in a biblical wholism that uses a term like disciple in more than a second-stage sense (Newbigin 1978:152-54). To reply to this criticism by arguing that McGavran's statement "is descriptive, not normative," phenomenological, not theological (Wagner 1981:167), is not really helpful. In effect, the distinction functions on both the descriptive and normative levels.

Another motive, however, controlled McGavran's intention. He was using the language to speak about an exclusively corporate action, the turning of *segments of a society* to Christ. Critics also failed to note that *Bridges of God* declared that "converts were required to take the very costly step of renouncing allegiance to the gods" (McGavran 1979:4).

About 1971, McGavran notes, "under the impact of body life, church growth theory, and other movements, the new verb 'disciple' which I had coined, began to be used for three separate events." The early focus on the movement of a society was kept, but it also came to be used

> to describe the initial conversion of *individuals*. . . . Third, the word was used for the later stages of the process by which an individual Christian becomes an informed, illuminated, thoroughly dedicated follower of Jesus Christ. . . . In effect, we had three uses of the word disciple which might be called D1, D2, and D3; but unfortunately people wrote and spoke as if discipling had only one meaning (McGavran 1979:3).

As McGavran in the 1970s began to address himself more to the individualistic American society, D2 and D3 levels of meaning were given more prominence (Wagner 1981:131-33). McGavran argues that critics and students, many of them writing out of experience with individualistic American society, did not see the developing distinctions of usage. Critics charged McGavran with espousing a form of cheap grace, and even advocates were not clear on the point. One person told McGavran "that he found himself arguing that the Bible requires that ethical decisions be deferred by individuals until after the first declaration of loyalty to Jesus Christ has been made" (McGavran 1979:4). McGavran himself viewed these charges as "much ado about nothing." At the same time, the threefold distinction is now said to be useful in understanding also his earlier focus on people movements. Writing of the 30,000 member Mennonite Brethren Church in India's Andhra State, drawn largely from the Madiga caste, he now describes the great turning that took place initially as D1, D2 bringing a stream of individuals within the Christian movement yearly, and D3 perfecting and sanctifying an even smaller but yet considerable number of the total community.

This clarification of usage by McGavran is much needed and helpful. Unfortunately, not even his students and defenders have seen it clearly. McGavran himself has articulated it rather late in the game.

Other problems still remain. In his concern that evangelism not be crowded out of what he calls "missionary missions," McGavran has also pled that the mission society focus on evangelism, "the specific task of discipling the nations" (McGavran 1972:10, 12). He leaves perfecting to the church. In this way, he seeks to recognize the legitimacy of church involvement in social issues, but to delimit it as a goal of the mission society. Thus, he has appeared to use the distinction to differentiate between the task of the mission society and the task of the church, between evangelism and social action. The problem of wholism remains. Van Engen poses three questions that arise from it:

> First, one might ask that *if* the top priority item for the sending church must be proclamation, how does it justify participating in the fight for social justice at all, given the fact of limited resources? Secondly, if proclamation is top priority for the sending church, why should it not be

also for the receiving church? . . . Thirdly, the assumption that converted people will have an effect on the social, economic, and political situation in a given country is to be questioned. True, it is doubtful that one can expect the macrostructures to be changed to any degree by a tiny minority of Christians. However, on the other hand, can it be expected that simply because people have become members of the church they will be concerned for social justice? (Van Engen 1981:350).

Recent discussions on the nature of conversion have sought to preserve McGavran's sensitivity to the ongoing process of movement to Christ as well as his concern for the initiation of the process of evangelism. At a 1978 consultation on the gospel and culture, sponsored by the Lausanne Committee for World Evangelization, papers by Orlando Costas (1980:173-91) and by the author of this chapter (Conn 1980:147-72) argued for a view of conversion as a complex, dynamic, ongoing experience. The intent was not to discredit conversion as a single step from the kingdom of darkness to the kingdom of light, but to see that step as only the first of many to designate "the changed course of life." Conversion, or discipleship, thus becomes an eschatological journey, a pilgrimage, with ever-new challenges, decisions, and returnings to the Lord as the constant point of reference, until he comes (The Willowbank Report 1980:328). In this process, the meanings behind terms like discipling and perfecting are retained in the "dynamic equivalence" of the process, but the sharp lines McGavran insists on are blurred in a desire to preserve the wholism of the experience.

Critics in the 1970s have missed much of McGavran's argument. Defined often in terms of over-concern with numbers, quantity at the expense of quality, these secondary issues dominated both critical and apologetic literature. John H. Yoder has called them "red herrings" (Yoder 1973:27-30). But they continue to be made, and church growth apologists continue to feel they must be answered (Wagner 1981:60-64, 130-48).

In response to this criticism, different emphases have appeared among McGavran and his colleagues. More irenic in tone than McGavran, sensitized by his background in cultural anthropology toward a more wholistic model of evangelism, Alan Tippett has responded consistently to the quantity/quality polarity on a less negative and more creative tone. In his 1967 work *Solomon Islands Christianity,* he introduced three categories of growth as a model for his analysis—conversion, organic, and quality. Not writing primarily to distance himself from McGavran, as Johannes Verkuyl has charged (Verkuyl 1977:32; 1978:191), Tippett aimed his pen at the quantity/quality objectors. He insisted that "for church growth to be really effective, each of these dimensions of growth should be taking place together and interacting under the guidance and blessing of the Holy Spirit" (Tippett 1967:32). This focus on organic growth was reinforced again in his 1970 devotional work *Church Growth and the Word of God.* His intent was to provide a tripartite model and operate from a more wholistic paradigm than that of McGavran. He added to that model an emphasis on equilibrium and the continuity required from generation to generation. Churches have to grow quantitatively, qualitatively, and organically, but all in balance over the process of time. A schematization of this emphasis appears in Tippett's later work *The Deep Sea Canoe* (1977a:64-65). In keeping with this concern for balanced wholism, he has also presented revisions of his own earlier model for incorporation through conversion. His encounter with cargo cults in Papua, New Guinea, in 1973 reinforced for him the effect of neglecting what McGavran calls perfecting and demanded an extension of his paradigm "beyond the stage of incorporation" (Tippett 1977b:218-20).

This anthropologically informed concern for wholism may well be continued by Tippett's successor at Fuller, Paul G. Hiebert. In a 1976 symposium, Hiebert saw wide implications for missions from a wholistic approach to human beings and to their cultures. Wary of a sacred/secular dichotomization of life, he called for attention to such assaults on the humanization of the person as hunger, sickness, and ignorance, and asked for an adequate theology of cultures which will touch such topics as power and resources, politics and economics, poverty and oppression, and human creativity (Hiebert 1976:78-86). How this will relate to McGavran's distinction between discipling and perfecting remains to be seen.

McGavran's writing in this area of cultural understanding may well reveal the strongest areas of discord within the movement. Without an academic background in linguistics or cultural anthropology, he retains a simplicity in this arena which shows particularly in his 1974 book *The Clash Between Christianity and Cultures*. Writing in a popular vein against the impact of cultural relativism, he denounces it for its standardless pluralism and asks how different cultural patterns can be incorporated in Christian living while remaining soundly and biblically Christian. How can the "one Christian culture" be approximated in thousands of cultures all over the world (McGavran 1974:8-9)?

His answer revolves around three proposals—the retention of what he calls a "high view" of Scripture, in which the supracultural, plain meaning of the Bible is the true meaning; the retention of a "high view" of culture, seen as an aggregate of interrelated components rather than an organism; and the retention of the rights of Christian liberty to adjust to cultural differences "when there is no clear biblical directive" (McGavran 1974:76).

Each of his three proposals has been modified and, in some cases, openly criticized by McGavran's colleagues, especially Charles Kraft. Against the first, Kraft refuses to "contend that the Scriptures present us with a culturally unencumbered Christian worldview to which people are to be converted in total replacement of their own cultural worldview (see McGavran 1974:8-9)" (Kraft 1979:349). Rather, he adds, such an ideal, supracultural worldview (if there is one) is never observable except as its influence is manifested in terms of a specific culture. He issues similar warnings against McGavran's optimism regarding "the possibility of such cultural transformation ever proceeding far enough in any culture that one might accurately describe that culture as thoroughly Christian (contra McGavran 1974:8-9)" (Kraft 1979:79).

There is also evidence of more than slight disagreement over McGavran's judgments regarding a "high view" of Scripture and its "plain meaning." Kraft sees such a reference to the "plain meaning" as the language of those unaware of the pervasive influence of their own culture on their interpretations. Their assumption, which he judges as incorrect, is that arriving at most supracultural truth is simply a matter of accepting the "clear" or "plain meanings" of Scripture (Kraft 1979:131).

Beyond that problem, however, may loom a larger one, unaddressed by

either McGavran or Kraft in writing—their views of the nature of biblical inspiration and revelation. Kraft's view especially has aroused much concern on
the part of evangelicals (Henry 1980:153-64). Preferring to see biblical history
as a divinely inspired canonical collection of classical case studies, he calls for
a dynamic view of scriptural inspiration which draws no firm line between the
inspirational work and the illuminating work of the Spirit. Kraft continues to
call the Bible "the repository for divinely revealed truth" (Kraft 1979:213). But
it is just "as much the record of a dynamic and continuing process of divine-
human interaction." From exposure to case studies such as those recorded in the
Bible, he argues, we discover insights into supracultural truth and seek to transform our contemporary conceptual framework in their direction. We have no
clue as to McGavran's reaction to this emphasis.

Wide differences emerge also on the nature of culture. Tippett, more
gently than Kraft, has been frustrated on at least one occasion by the naive
fluidity of McGavran's alternating definitions (Tippett 1975:193). Kraft objects
to McGavran's popularization of cultural relativism as not "taking seriously either
contemporary anthropological understandings or the great potential for Christian
use of the doctrine" (Kraft 1979:50).

Although they are not specifically cited by page reference in either Kraft
or Tippett, one also suspects that behind this concern are some basic differences
between the men on McGavran's concept of culture as an aggregate of components rather than an organism. The functionalist heritage of the anthropologists
would likely place greater emphasis on cultures as functional organisms.

Again, on McGavran's third proposal, Kraft's extremely sophisticated
discussions could be expected to offer resistance. McGavran's treatment does not
take into account Kraft's insistence on recognizing

> distinctions between cultural forms, their functions, their meanings, and
> their usages. . . . When, therefore, we talk about HUs [homogeneous
> units], it is of great importance that we distinguish which of these aspects
> of homogeneity we are talking about. If we say that HUs are bad, are
> we suggesting that the existence of HUs is bad in and of itself? That is,
> is the HU as a cultural *form* a bad thing? Or are we identifying some or
> all of the functions, meanings and usages of HUs as bad? Or, on the
> other hand, if we say that HUs are good, are we talking about form,
> function, meaning or usage? Not until we identify which aspect of the
> problem we are discussing can we properly deal with the matter of alter-
> natives to those things that we identify as undesirable (Kraft 1978:124).

It appears McGavran's 1974 simplified treatment of culture falls under this judgment of Kraft. But both men remain silent about one another. We are left to
hints and guesses.

Still another area of concern emerging with increasing clarity is the usage
of biblical formulations by McGavran and his associates. We will not discuss
here the creedal differences among the men, important as they are in their
approaches to strategy questions. The issue here is the way in which they make
use of Scripture in their hermeneutic of church growth.

McGavran's background academically has consisted largely of studies in
educational theory and has been shaped by over thirty years of missionary experience. One cannot expect him, therefore, to develop his theories out of a

more formal attention to abstract biblical exegesis. Though his 1955 work displays much attention to data in Acts particularly (McGavran 1955:17-33), it is always controlled by his desire to find people movements in the New Testament record.

The 1970 book by Alan Tippett, *Church Growth and the Word of God,* was originally intended to fill this vacuum. Written over an extended period of time as articles in the *Church Growth Bulletin,* the studies appeared when the movement was under fire from evangelicals for not being biblical. Tippett sought, on a devotional level, to satisfy those who wanted to be assured that church growth was biblical. A secondary purpose of the book is reflected in the indexes and its references to some twenty-five or so anthropological concepts which Tippett sought to underline biblically.

With the coming of Arthur Glasser to the faculty at Fuller, the need for more critically exact attention to the biblical text was recognized. Whether subsequent studies have resolved the concerns of some is still questionable. Wilbert R. Shenk noted in 1973, "While fully appreciating Glasser's great concern to respect the authority and intent of the Scriptures, it must be noted that his insistence on reading the Bible according to the presupposition of a biblical-theological hermeneutic is no safeguard against subjectivism, selectivity and distortion when this 'flattening' out obscures the dynamic movement within the biblical record" (Shenk 1973:23). In a 1976 essay, I have taken exception also to the way in which the larger redemptive patterns of Scripture can be mishandled in asking questions they are not intended to answer (Conn 1976:2, 5-6, 14, 16, 19). More recently, René Padilla, in an expansion of a 1977 paper read at a Lausanne Consultation on the Homogeneous Unit Principle, has provided a powerful model of exegetical interaction with the church growth paradigm (Padilla 1982:23-30; 1983:285-303). More than simply challenging church growth concepts of the unity of the church and ethnic pluriformity, Padilla provides an articulate sample of the way in which these questions ought to be approached from a biblical-theological perspective.

Whether Church Growth writing will ever catch up with its exegetical time lag is a moot question. No doubt the Fuller staff take seriously the importance of having a sound biblical structure underlying their work. But Glasser alone cannot compensate for that lapse. C. Peter Wagner emerges increasingly as the successor both in style and interests to McGavran. Of his 1972 book *Frontiers in Missionary Strategy,* Shenk warns against "a particularly casual attitude toward biblical materials" (Shenk 1973:22). Judging from Wagner's recent handling of Luke 4:21-30 and 7:21-22 (Wagner 1981:15-21), this casualness has not lessened. We are still left with the judgment of Van Engen: "Too often the Movement seems to use texts simply to shore up Church Growth theory" (Van Engen 1981:356-57).

HUMANKIND IN COMMUNITY: THE PRINCIPLE RESTATED

In the light of this interaction, we now seek a reformulation which embodies the following presuppositions: (1) Evangelism involves a call to be incorporated into a visible new humanity that includes all kinds of people; the catholicity of the body of Christ is not simply a result of the good news of the kingdom. It is a demonstration-sign of that good news. (2) Because of the fallenness of human-kind, our quest for community will also display demonic elements. It may claim too high a loyalty (and so become idolatrous) or shun outsiders (and so become self-centered). Racism, tribalism, and oppressive wealth are examples of such demonic homogeneity. (3) Any distinction between discipling and perfecting as a strategical description cannot be allowed to drive a wedge between Jesus as Savior and Jesus as Lord. The call of the kingdom is a call for total submission and a call for daily repentance. Discipleship means "submission to a new dis-cipline, adoption of a new lifestyle and incorporation into a new community" (Costas 1979:14). (4) The liberty into which our cultural diversities are brought in Christ demands that we neither level these diversities into a colorless unifor-mity nor impose one culture on another. Reconciliation between Jew and Gentile, black and white, Hausa and Tiv, is not possible without a commitment to the liberating justice of Christ. That liberating justice is built on the recognition of our common humanity in our common imagehood as covenant creatures of our covenant God.

Simply stated, the formulation I propose is this: *All people want to affirm and reject God-given authentic community without losing social and ethnic iden-tity.* In several terminological areas, the statement seeks to correct McGavran's homogeneous unit principle. (1) It seeks to recognize the demonic element in humankind's quest for community. We not only seek to affirm community; we also seek to pervert it. Culture's contexts do not always give us cause for un-guarded optimism regarding our search for commonality. (2) Our commonality is not just a recognition of bonds purely geographical, ethnic, linguistic, social, educational, or a combination of several of these and other factors. All these bonds are expressions of our religious nature as images of God and are therefore, to a greater or lesser degree, religious in character. God-given community is what we seek to affirm and reject. (3) Our quest is directed to the recovery of the universal shalom of paradise lost. Our solidarity in Adam, not our particu-larity, is our holy grail. (4) As fallen creatures this side of the history of Babel, we cannot, in that quest, shed our unique ethnicities. They remain the guardians of God's common grace against the unchecked presumption of an undivided and sinful development of humanity (Gen 11:1-9).

At the same time, this Covenant Solidarity Principle (an awkward ter-minological creation, to be sure) affirms several of McGavran's theses: (1) "The Bible knows nothing of the human being as an individual in isolation; it knows only of a person as a *related* being, a person in relation to other people" (Padilla 1982:23). In corporate solidarity, we have our "is-ness" in the old humanity represented by the first Adam. In corporate solidarity, we are called by the kingdom to the new humanity represented by the last Adam. (2) People often reject the gospel not because they think it is false but because it strikes them as alien to their quest for solidarity. They imagine that in order to become Christian they must renounce that solidarity of "remembrance of things past," identified by them often with their own ethnic or social or economic identity. (3)

> In order to reach them, not only should the evangelist be able to identify
> with them and they with the evangelist; not only must the gospel be
> contextualized in such a way that it communicates with them; but the

church into which they are invited must itself belong to their culture sufficiently for them to feel at home in it. It is when these conditions are fulfilled that men and women are won to Jesus Christ, and subsequently their churches grow (Pasadena Consultation 1978:3).

(4) As an eschatological community, the church is called to be the new society of the new age. It is called to anticipate on earth the life of heaven and thus to develop both cultural richness and heterogeneous fellowship. The diversity of languages and cultures not put aside by our heavenly fellowship (Rev 7:9-10; 21:26; 22:2) must not inhibit but ennoble the catholic fellowship of the redeemed.

COVENANT ROOTS: RELIGION

Where are the roots of homogeneity in societies? They are not simply in any sociological connection abstracted from its more basic covenant character. Rather, the heart of homogeneity is solidarity in religion as covenant. The element of community can never escape some religious expression, even under the secularizing wear and tear of history and divergent cultural patterns.

Thus the Genesis narrative depicts Adam, the father of us all, as image of God, vassal of the Great King, called to live in covenant in the covenant territory, the arena of covenant response. The Pauline commentary on this history, preserved for us in Acts 17:26-27, focuses on the universal kinship of all humankind: "God has made of one man every race of men to live on all the face of the earth. . . ." From covenant headship flows covenant kinship or solidarity. Even in sin, that solidarity is expressed. The curse on Eve was a curse on her role as wife and mother (Gen 3:16). Adam suffered in painful, death-bringing labor for his family. Even his solidarity with the creation is reflected in the curse upon the world of which humankind was vice-regent (Gen 3:17-19).

To fulfill his redemptive purposes for the nations, God preserved their solidarity in his covenant of common grace with Noah and his descendants (Gen 8:21–9:17). That his is the preserving work of grace was reinforced by the history of the so-called Table of Nations immediately following the narrative of chapter ten.

What is striking for our purposes here is that it was a table of nations (Babel, 10:10; Assyria, 10:11; "the great city," 10:12). Yet most of the names appear to be individuals. What has been called a "corporate extension" is even among those under covenant curse (Shedd 1964:19). The bearing of the name of its founder by a city or people implied more than the mere identity of appellation. Covenant identity and solidarity in covenant allowed Malachi to speak of God's hatred for Esau and identify it with judgment on Edom (Mal 1:3-4). The prince of Tyre was addressed in the dirge of Ezekiel 28, but the judgment included the city of the prince. Pharaoh hardened his heart against the Lord, but God judged Egypt.

Similarly, in the breaching of that solidarity of people with people, God will judge even the *ethnē*. He will judge Damascus for threshing Gilead with instruments of sharp iron (Amos 1:3). Tyre will be punished "because they delivered up an entire population to Edom and did not remember the covenant of brotherhood" (1:9). Edom will be pillaged "because of violence to your brother Jacob" (Obad 19).

Like everything else done in rebellion against our covenant nature, the *ethnē* will seek to suppress the covenant fact of solidarity in unrighteousness (Rom 1:18). The solidarity of worship becomes the solidarity of idolatry (1:23). The solidarity of heterosexuality becomes the solidarity of homosexuality (1:26-27). Solidarity in covenant with God becomes salvation through family cult in China or tribal self-deification in Africa or the commonality of class in Europe. A system of tabus, of expiatory sacrifices, becomes a communal structure of reality to substitute for true communion lost at Eden but constantly remembered and sought. Even in westernized cultures, the *ethnē* will seek to express its solidarity and to reject it in covenant rebellion also in solidarity. Mythic solidarity will be fashioned out of politics or wealth or racist exploitation.

This insistence on a religious core to the Covenant Solidarity Principle resolves some of the problems we see in the McGavran formulation. It recognizes explicitly the demonic side of homogeneity, often lost in Church Growth optimism over the HU. The church's struggle to transform or "possess" the ethnic or sociological unit is a concrete manifestation of its ongoing struggle with the powers (Eph 6:12). Further, it inhibits us from even a pseudo-identification of *Volk* with the church growing in a solidarity unit. Family, tribes, cult, social class, or even church are never untainted by the root of sin. It is then not precise to argue that "the great obstacles to conversion are social, not theological" (McGavran 1970:191). For even these great sociological obstacles are, in the solidarity framework from which they emerge, theological in character. There is an intertwining of the religious and social aspects of the cultural unit.

> As a rule, the two are not radically distinguished, because religious life is not felt as the personal relationship of the individual to his God. Religious life is viewed much more as the collective attitude of the tribe or people with respect to the divine powers with which there is such a close connection, because each individual is a part of the holy communion. Social life, on the other hand, can never be regarded as completely outside of the sphere of religious thought. A tribe or people are aware of a sacred sphere in their social life. The practices dominating social life can never be detached or even thought apart from their religious basis (Bavinck 1960:175).

UNIVERSALIZING COMPULSION: CATHOLICITY AND UNITY

McGavran's continued burden is to help us see the diversity of the church manifest in homogeneous units, "the parts which make up the whole," each growing according to its own pattern, encouraged to be itself, not imposing its cultural growth patterns on the other as a matter of faith (Acts 15). For that we must all be deeply appreciative. But do his formulations provide us with sufficient help to ask what he sees as "the crucial issue in all of this," namely, "How much diversity can the Church allow while remaining the Church?" (McGavran 1977:11)? McGavran's HUP makes the concept of human diversity the keystone of God's strategy for the nations. From that keystone pivot he struggles with its compatibility with the unity of the body, flowing out of its catholicity.

We have no desire to minimize his concern for unity, but we argue that his principle begins at the wrong end of the question. The focus of our Corporate Solidarity Principle affirms community, unity, as the capstone of human desires, however perverted or distorted by the effects of sin. To speak of the planting and growth of the church as the first priority in mission is to recognize the unity and catholicity of the church as a first priority. The ultimate orientation of any HUP must not be structured around the ethnic or sociological unit but around the catholicity and unity of the church as essential attribute. Thus the crucial issue is not so much, "How much diversity can the church allow while remaining the church?" but rather, "How shall the church fully express its nature as one and catholic and do justice to those God-given, but sin-warped, dimensions of covenant solidarity still displayed in the peoples of the world?"

Humanity, even in its broken state, seeks to remain humanity in solidarity. It will seek to express that covenant desire for community in those cultural forms like the family which are God-given ("creation ordinances," to use old language). It will seek to do so in those forms which we create for the protection and enrichment of that people or social grouping of which we consider ourselves a part.

That deep desire we see fulfilled in the church as the kingdom community of the Lord (Rev 1:6; I Pet 2:9). The church is to be more than simply, in principle, the new humanity. It is called to live, even in its strategizing, "the reality of the new humanity" (Rooy 1975:191). The old age marked by the solidarity of humanity in the sin of the first Adam must give way to the regal inauguration of the new age at Calvary, now marked by the solidarity of the new humanity in the redemptive obedience of the second Adam (Gal 1:4; I Cor 15:22). So the church borrows from the Egypts of the world its cultural wealth. It remakes eating and drinking into kingdom rituals of praise (I Cor 10:31), culture's ethnic patterns into God-centered pointers (Rom 11:36), homogeneous units like Sodom into the daughters of Jehovah (Ezek 16:53-61), and the Philistines into "a clan in Judah" (Zech 9:7). The ethnic divisions of Samaritan and Jew, baptized by the shalom of the kingdom come in the presence of the Spirit (Rom 14:17), worship neither at Gerizim nor at Jerusalem but "at the city of the living God, the heavenly Jerusalem" (Heb 12:22), the place where the *ethnē*, still *ethnē*, are healed (Rev 22:2).

We have argued that the biblical emphasis falls on the unity of the church as strategically central—in contrast to the strategic emphasis in the HUP as presently defined.

CULTURAL PARTICULARITY: ETHNOSOCIALITY

The great contribution of Church Growth strategy has been to make us all aware of peoplehood and its human diversity as a tool in world evangelization. With Charles Kraft we affirm that "human beings show an overwhelming predisposition to band together with 'their own kind' " (Kraft 1978:121). For that reason, we add to our Covenant Solidarity Principle the crucial modification, "without losing social and ethnic identity."

That, however, is not the problem that plagues us relative to the HUP. It is whether this recognition of peoplehood has not been so exalted by the methodology as to become ultimately and solely a beneficial principle. The church does not repeal social and ethnic differences between peoples. Unity in Christ can hallow diversity. But can ethnicity become so central to strategy that we miss the demonic use to which it is also put in world history? What makes us reluctant, while accepting Kraft's affirmation of peoplehood, to disagree, to some degree, with the second, which he asserts with it, namely, "God accepts this fact and works with it" (Kraft 1978:121)?

Exegetically, Wagner, for example, has sought to defend this divine intention by his positive interpretation of the tower of Babel history in Genesis 11:1-9. He sees the Table of Nations (Gen 10) as a confirmation "that social pluralism was part of God's creational plan" with "no hint that God had intended anything else for the people he had created to populate the earth" (Wagner 1979:112). The Babel incident then "sees the people of the earth making an attempt to *counteract* what they correctly understood to be God's purpose in diversifying the human race. . . . Apparently, then, God punished this early resistance to pluralism" (1979:111-12).

Wagner's position is built on at least two mistaken assumptions: the assumption that the text attributes all cultural differentiation to these events, and denies all linguistic variations before the flood (contra Kline 1970:91); and the assumption that one must see this history either negatively or positively. Much contemporary scholarship sees it as carrying both negative and positive meaning. The Table of Nations is more than a secular genealogy; its placement before the history of Babel, which it chronologically postdates, points to its redemptive character (Vos 1948:71). As such, it has a backward and a forward look. It looks backward to the flood and the prophetic blessing of Noah (Gen 9:25-27). In terms of that connection, it announces the effectiveness of Genesis 9 and the new covenant with the earth: The earth will be filled with a multitude of the nations. "The joy of the Creator has won over his sadness and wrath (cf. Acts 17:26). The world of nations is the result of the peace made with man *after* the Flood" (Blauw 1962:19-20). The nations are simultaneously signs of God's will to peace and of his judgment. They are not to be permanently dismissed from covenant blessing. In the fullness of time, God will return these peoples to the redemptive fold, through the blessing of the Semites in Abraham.

Again, it also has a forward thrust, linking the nations to the curse of Babel. Genesis 11 and the confusion of tongues provide the reason for God's division of the nations. God initiates differentiation in judgment on humankind's arrogant attempt to remedy the divisive impact of sin by establishing unity in their own honor. This element of judgment is also brought out by the parallels between Babel and the life of Abraham which immediately follows. The people of Babel wished to make their name great (11:4). God promised to make Abraham's name great (12:8). The people of Babel looked for a city on earth to challenge God himself. Abraham looked for a heavenly city as a pilgrim of God. The people of Babel determined to stay. God told Abraham to go, and he obeyed.

Viewed from this perspective, the dispersion movement of Genesis 10 appears as a curse, a centrifugal force separating people and retarding the subjugation of the earth (11:6b). Yet in sin's context this curse proved a blessing. God's intervention had an ultimately saving purpose for the nations. The sinful development of humanity would not be allowed to reach such a peak that it would again demand a worldwide catastrophe like the flood. Such a judgment would have interfered with the unfolding of redemption (De Ridder 1971:21).

Wagner's approach to this history minimizes any element of judgment in this history in his overall search for only positive elements to the biblical portrait of ethnicity. We leave untouched his assumption that, given this understanding of the biblical picture as accurate, we may then apply it wholesale to the more technical definition of *ethnē* operative in Church Growth thinking.

Rather we simply affirm with David Bosch that

> the concept "people" . . . as we know and use it today, plays no theological role in Scripture. Naturally the existence and diversity of peoples are acknowledged, but this is in no way constitutive for the believer's conduct and attitude. When Israel is referred to as a "people," we have, in fact, an ambivalent term. Israel, regarded as an ethnic entity, is a people like other peoples; insofar as it is the "people of God," it has theological significance within salvation-history. . . . If the New Testament applies the concept "people of God" to the church, this is only and exclusively a continuation of the Old Testament concept as *salvation-historical* entity. Statements on the believer's relationship and responsibility to this "people of God" may therefore under no circumstances be made applicable to the idea of "people" in a cultural or ethnic sense (Bosch 1977:30).

In fact, the major emphasis of the New Testament, in connection with peoplehood, is generally of a judgmental sort. Wagner minimizes this feature in his treatment of the topic. The optimism with which the HUP is invested makes it difficult to deal with these materials. Bosch notes that all Jewish groupings—Sadducees, Pharisees, Essenes, and Zealots—devoted themselves ardently to the restoration of their peoplehood. Though differing violently on methods and emphases, their commonly shared point of departure was ethnic group solidarity over against Rome. Even the disciples of Jesus after the resurrection still seemed to think in terms of these ethnic categories: "Lord, is it at this time you are to establish once again the sovereignty to Israel?" (Acts 1:6; cf. Lk 24:21). Our Lord's response moved in a different direction (Acts 1:8). Loving one's neighbor cannot be restricted ethnically (Lk 10:36-37). Even family definitions of mother and father and sister and brother lose their ethnic and social value in the kingdom of God (Mk 10:28-29).

All this is to say that the coming of the kingdom of God relativizes the sociocultural absolutes of the cultures of this world. Our heavenly citizenship causes us to sit lightly to cultural loyalties. Paul could be a Jew to the Jews and Gentile to the Gentiles (I Cor 9:19ff). He could speak Aramaic to a Jerusalem crowd and Greek to an official. But Paul served Christ knowing that in Christ there is neither Jew nor Greek, Korean nor Japanese. All these identities do not disappear. But they can no longer demand primary loyalty.

Our mission methodologies may make use of these identities. But they are subservient always to the reality of the church as fulfiller of "the desire of all *ethnē*" (Hag 2:7). The church stands not only as the fulfiller of covenant solidarity in the world, but also as the judge of covenant solidarity against the world. The church plants churches in the homogeneous units of Jerusalem, but the church cannot forget that its final ethnic attachments are with the New Jerusalem. That understanding, not the other, controls the mission method.

I hear McGavran and the Church Growth School saying Amen to much of this. That is why I prefer to call my suggestions reformulations. In any case, they represent questions by no means answered. Meanwhile, the unreached billions make their perilous descent to judgment.

REFERENCES CITED

BAVINCK, J. H.
 1960   *An Introduction to the Science of Missions*, Philadelphia: Presbyterian and Reformed Publishing Company.

BLAUW, Johannes
 1962   *The Missionary Nature of the Church: A Survey of the Biblical Theology of Mission*, London: Lutterworth Press.

BOSCH, David J.
 1977   "The Church and the Liberation of Peoples?" *Missionalia*, Vol. 2, No. 4, October.

CONN, Harvie M.
 1976   "God's Plan for Church Growth: An Overview," *Theological Perspectives on Church Growth*, Harvie M. Conn (ed.), Nutley: Presbyterian and Reformed Publishing House.
 1980   "Conversion and Culture—A Theological Perspective with Reference to Korea," *Down to Earth: Studies in Christianity and Culture*, John R. W. Stott and Robert T. Coote (eds.), Grand Rapids: Eerdmans.

COSTAS, Orlando
 1979   *The Integrity of Mission: The Inner Life and Outreach of the Church*, New York: Harper and Row.
 1980   "Conversion as a Complex Experience—A Personal Case Study," *Down to Earth: Studies in Christianity and Culture*, John R. W. Stott and Robert T. Coote (eds.), Grand Rapids: Eerdmans.

DE RIDDER, Richard
 1971   *The Dispersion of the People of God*, Kampen: J. H. Kok.

HENRY, Carl F. H.
 1980   "The Cultural Relativizing of Revelation," *Trinity Journal*, Vol. 1NS, No. 2, Fall.

HIEBERT, Paul G.
 1976   "An Introduction to Mission Anthropology," *Crucial Dimensions in World Evangelization*, Arthur F. Glasser, Paul G. Hiebert, C. Peter Wagner, Ralph D. Winter (eds.), South Pasadena: William Carey Library.

KLINE, Meredith G.
 1970   "Genesis," *New Bible Commentary, Revised*, D. Guthrie and J. A. Motyer (eds.), London: Inter-Varsity Press.

KRAFT, Charles H.
 1978   "An Anthropological Apologetic for the Homogeneous Unit Principle of Missiology," *Occasional Bulletin of Missionary Research*, Vol. 2, No. 4, October.
 1979   *Christianity in Culture: A Study in Dynamic Biblical Theologizing in Cross-Cultural Perspective*, Maryknoll: Orbis Books.

McGAVRAN, Donald A.
 1955   *The Bridges of God* (revised and enlarged edition, 1981), New York: Friendship Press.
 1970   *Understanding Church Growth*, Grand Rapids: Eerdmans.
 1972   *Crucial Issues in Missions Tomorrow*, Donald A. McGavran (ed.), Chicago: Moody Press.
 1974   *The Clash Between Christianity and Cultures*, Washington, D.C.: Canon Press.
 1979   "A 1979 Perspective on Church Growth," unpublished paper available through the author.

NEWBIGIN, Lesslie
1978   *The Open Secret: Sketches for a Missionary Theology,* Grand Rapids: Eerdmans.

PADILLA, C. René
1982/83   "The Unity of the Church and the Homogeneous Unit Principle," *International Bulletin of Missionary Research,* Vol. 6, No. 1, January/Chapter 22, *Exploring Church Growth,* Grand Rapids: Eerdmans.

PASADENA CONSULTATION
1978   *Pasadena Consultation—Homogeneous Unit. Lausanne Occasional Papers No. 1,* Wheaton: Lausanne Committee for World Evangelization.

ROOY, Sidney
1975   "The Concept of Man in the Missiology of Donald McGavran: A Model of Anglosaxon Missiology in Latin America," *Westminster Theological Journal,* Vol. XXXVII, No. 2, Winter.

SHEDD, Russell P.
1964   *Man in Community,* Grand Rapids: Eerdmans.

SHENK, Wilbert R.
1973   "Church Growth Studies: A Bibliography Overview," *The Challenge of Church Growth: A Symposium,* Elkhart, Indiana: Institute of Mennonite Studies/ Scottdale: Herald Press.

TIPPETT, Alan R.
1967   *Solomon Islands Christianity,* New York: Friendship Press.
1970   *Church Growth and the Word of God,* Grand Rapids: Eerdmans.
1973   "Portrait of a Missiologist by His Colleague," *God, Man and Church Growth,* Alan R. Tippett (ed.), Grand Rapids: Eerdmans.
1975   "The Meaning of Meaning," *Christopaganism or Indigenous Christianity?* Tetsunao Yamamori and Charles R. Taber (eds.), South Pasadena: William Carey Library.
1977a   *The Deep Sea Canoe: The Story of Third World Missionaries in the South Pacific,* South Pasadena: William Carey Library.
1977b   "Conversion as a Dynamic Process in Christian Mission," *Missiology,* Vol. V, No. 2, April.

VAN ENGEN, Charles
1981   *The Growth of the True Church: An Analysis of the Ecclesiology of Church Growth Theory,* Amsterdam: Rodopi.

VERKUYL, Johannes
1977   "The Mission of God and the Missions of the Churches," *Occasional Essays, Latin American Evangelical Center for Pastoral Studies,* Year IV, Nos. 1-2.
1978   *Contemporary Missiology: An Introduction,* Dale Cooper (trans. and ed.), Grand Rapids: Eerdmans.

VOS, Geerhardus
1948   *Biblical Theology,* Grand Rapids: Eerdmans.

WAGNER, C. Peter
1979   *Our Kind of People: The Ethical Dimensions of Church Growth in America,* Atlanta: John Knox Press.
1981   *Church Growth and the Whole Gospel: A Biblical Mandate,* San Francisco: Harper and Row.

WILLOWBANK REPORT, THE
1980   Report on a Consultation on GOSPEL AND CULTURE held at Willowbank, Somerset Bridge, Bermuda from 6th to 13th January 1978. Sponsored by the

Lausanne Theology and Education Group, Lausanne Committee for World Evangelization. Printed in *Down to Earth: Studies in Christianity and Culture,* John R. W. Stott and Robert T. Coote (eds.), Grand Rapids: Eerdmans.

YODER, John H.
  1976   "Church Growth Issues in Theological Perspective," *The Challenge of Church Growth: A Symposium,* Wilbert R. Shenk (ed.), Elkhart, Indiana: Institute of Mennonite Studies/Scottdale: Herald Press.

8. A WHOLISTIC CONCEPT OF CHURCH GROWTH

Orlando E. Costas

WE WITNESS IN OUR DAY AN EXTRAORDINARY INTEREST AMONG LOCAL CHURCHES and denominations of all types and sizes in the growth of the church. Be they large or small, conservative, moderate, or liberal, Catholic, mainline Protestant, conservative evangelical, classical, or neo-Pentecostal, all seem to be keenly concerned with the question of growth and decline.

This is due largely to the decline in church membership and attendance during the last two decades. Whereas in 1958 forty-nine percent of the population in the USA attended religious services, by 1979 it had dropped to forty percent (Jacquet 1981:266). Mainline denominations such as the United Presbyterian Church, the United Methodist Church, the United Church of Christ, the Lutheran Church in America, and the Protestant Episcopal Church experienced from 1960 to 1979 a total accumulated drop in membership of 62.6 percent. Even the Southern Baptist Convention, which grew by 34.5 percent from 1950 to 1960, saw its increase drop to 31.6 percent from 1960 to 1979 (Doyle and Kelly 1979:144ff).

Considering the fact that there are numerous variables that account for and offset these numbers, such as denominational splits and an upward trend in conservative-evangelical and Pentecostal denominations (Hoge 1979:94-122, 179-97; Kelley 1979:334-43; 1977; and Dudley 1979), the situation has nevertheless alarmed the leadership of declining churches. With the drop in membership has come a shortage of funds, a retrenchment in missionary workers, a decrease in seminary enrollment, and a diminishing influential role in the cultural, social, and political spheres.

Such a crisis has had a fourfold effect in North American Protestant Christianity. First, it has led to an avalanche of church growth studies, specialists, and organizations (Towns, Vaughn, and Seifert 1981). Second, it has brought about a renewed effort on the part of certain groups to re-Christianize (or at least re-religionize) North American society and culture (the Moral Majority and related movements). Third, it has given a new impetus for the revitalization of

Orlando E. Costas, Philadelphia, Pennsylvania, is Thornley B. Wood Professor of Missiology and Director of Hispanic Studies, Eastern Baptist Theological Seminary. Previously he was director of the Latin American Center for Pastoral Studies, San José, Costa Rica. He has written The Church and Its Mission: A Shattering Critique from the Third World *(Tyndale, 1974),* Theology of the Crossroads in Contemporary Latin America *(Rodopi, 1976), and* The Integrity of Mission *(Harper & Row, 1979).*

ecclesiastical institutions (the case of several mainline denominations). And fourth, it has provoked a renewed theological warfare with different but related issues (creationism, inerrancy, evangelism, and justice).

The situation cannot but represent a challenge to evangelistically minded and theologically responsible Christians and churches. For one thing, such reactions reflect fear and panic on the part of many church leaders. For another, they reveal a tendency toward simplistic analyses and reductionistic solutions. Above all, they disclose two equally dangerous pitfalls: There is, on the one hand, the danger of becoming so deterministic in one's view of the church and its missional possibilities that one ends up giving up far too soon on some (numerically stagnant) churches or oversupplying with resources other (successfully growing) churches. On the other hand, there is the peril of becoming so entrepreneurial that one will do literally anything to grow a church, including selling down the river basic tenets of the Christian faith.

Thus the challenge: to move beyond fear and panic, simplism and reductionism, determinism and entrepreneurialism in the theory and practice of church growth. In this chapter I respond to this challenge through a wholistic concept of church growth.[1] This requires, however, a brief classification of several aspects of growth, including its dynamic and deformation, and its presence in the life, faith, and mission of the church.

THE DYNAMIC OF GROWTH

The term "growth" suggests mobility and change; it indicates a dynamic reality. Where there is growth, there is increase, expansion, development, and multiplication or reproduction. Where there is growth there is also mutation, transformation, renewal, and creativity. There is thus no growth without change. Where there is no growth, there is stagnation, inertia, illness, and potential decay. Immobility and stasis are warning lights; they are signs of the absence of growth.

Growth also suggests relativity, contextuality, and variety; it depicts a complex phenomenon. To say that an organism is growing means nothing unless one explains *how* and *in what sense* it is growing.

There are different *kinds* of growth. Some of the most obvious are *biological* (multiplication of living organisms and species), *sociological* (expansion of group life), *psychological* (development of the affective, emotional side of life), *intellectual* (the accumulation of knowledge or the broadening of a person's grasp of reality), *cultural* (evolution of a people's way of life), *economic* (maximization and increase of life's resources), and *institutional* (the extension of the range of activities and sphere of influence of particular organizations or specific areas of organized society).

Likewise there are different *qualities* of growth: positive or negative,

1. This concept deepens my quest for a wholistic understanding of church growth in previous writings. See Costas (1974:37-149; 1979:37-60; 1981:2-8). For two works that are built upon the perspective of my previous writings, see Morikawa (1979) and Owens (1981). The latter is a descriptive analysis of ten congregations in the light of the general categories of church growth suggested in my previous writings and to be further elaborated in the present essay.

enriching or damaging, healthy or unhealthy. In fact, every area of life has a particular growth dimension with varying qualitative possibilities.

Growth takes place at various levels, through a variety of means, and at different stages of life. Thus growth cannot be abstracted from its context (environment); it cannot be studied in isolation. To appreciate its significance, one needs to analyze at each level all of its dimensions and take into account all of its expressions. An analysis that does not attempt to take notice of the total dynamic of growth is partial and incomplete.

Growth has one fundamental presupposition, namely, the process of life. Where there is no life, there is no growth. Conversely, where there is no growth, there is an absence of life.

Life is an ongoing, open process. It is the continuous interaction of organisms full of molecules in the service of specific functions. In biological life, these functions fall under the three categories of living organisms: production, consumption, and reduction.

An organism that does not grow is in reality dead; it ceases to act and thus be. The death of an organism can take place at various levels, at different intervals, and through one or more dimensions. The life process can come to a standstill at one level but continue at another; it can be stagnant in one dimension and overdeveloped in another. The point is that a fundamental characteristic of an organism is the continuous interaction of its parts. The stagnation of any of its parts at any level of interaction brings, sooner or later, mortal consequences.

This is a principle that applies not just to specific organisms, but to the whole of life, as illustrated by the problem of ecological imbalance. The destruction of wildlife, for example, can mean fewer resources for consumption; or the destruction of certain insects, birds, or wild animals can mean that waste cannot be reduced, thereby polluting the environment and threatening the future of the entire planet.

My point is that while all living organisms experience death after they have fulfilled their life-functions (or roles), they not only bring about the self-destruction of their life-process, but also damage their environment if they are not allowed to fulfill their normal tasks. Hence growth presupposes not only life, but a *normal process* of life.

GROWTH AS A DEADLY DEFORMATION

Not all growth is authentic or convenient. Growth can be superficial and shallow. Indeed it can be detrimental for an organism. There is such a thing as deformed growth which contributes to the death of an organism.

Take cancer, for instance. It is a disorderly growth of body cells. It produces a rupture in the normal reproduction of cells, which are limited by the requirements of the body for the growth and separation of textures. Cancer is produced by abnormal cells that multiply themselves and push and invade other organs of the body. The abnormal cells interfere and destroy the normal function of the body; they end up killing it.

Something similar occurs with grass. Several years ago our family moved into our first owned house (in San José, Costa Rica). We planted grass but noticed after a while that weeds also began to grow. By the time the grass established its roots, we could not pluck out the weeds. The more profuse the grass, the taller the weeds. We were in the dry season, but that didn't matter. The weeds fed on the water we sprinkled over the grass. We ended up with a messed-up, weed-covered lawn! What grew was what was not convenient, and what had to grow could not. A deadly growth impeded healthy growth. In fact, it made our lawn look like a wilderness.

Another case of damaging growth is that of consumerism. In societies like ours, the pattern of production is not geared to meet *real* needs but rather false ones—needs that are created for consumption. The ensuing result is a consumeristic lifestyle where "you work to earn money, you earn money to buy things and you buy things to find in them values" (Padilla 1976:209). But the only values we find in consumer goods are the creation of more needs. Hence the consumer society lives in a vicious circle: production for consumption and consumption for production. It experiences a deformed economic growth.

A society cannot enjoy true health when it lives of and for consumption. Human beings are more than consumers. As bearers of God's image they have been given creative capacities. They have been designed to live in communion with each other without violating and destroying the natural resources of the earth. But the manufacture and sale of goods that do not meet real needs can, and usually does, damage the physical environment and the quality of human life. Indeed it threatens the very fabric of human society by alienating its members.

Consumeristic production is a deformation the consequences of which are known all too well: intensification of class divisions, social *anomie,* spiritual anxiety, and the corruption of institutions and public offices. It ends up consuming life because it foments a deformed economic growth which reaches certain spaces of human existence and leaves others untouched, stimulates progress in some sectors and diminishes it in others, and satisfies false needs while leaving real ones unsatisfied.

Every organism grows, but not all growth is healthy. In the history of all organisms is always the danger of deformation which can lead to their self-destruction. That is why when considering the growth of an organism it is important to note how it members interact with one another, in which direction it is expanding, and what impact it is having on its parts and the environment as a whole.

THE COMPLEXITY OF CHURCH GROWTH

The foregone is especially applicable to the church. As a living organism, the church is constrained to grow. Its growth is part and parcel of its life. To stop growing is to cease to live. But the church also runs the risk of deformation. Its growth then can be likened to cancer, weeds, and consumeristic production.

To speak of church growth is also to refer to a complex phenomenon. As a life process, church growth needs to be seen as a corporate action, or as Alan R. Tippett has put it, "a body growing, a body of discrete but interacting parts" (1970:3). The growth of this body takes place at various levels and dimensions. To understand the density and complexity of church growth, it is necessary to have a clear idea of the kinds of growth that the church can and should experience. The crux of the problem then is the question: How does the church grow?

Only by the observation, measurement, and comparison of concrete churches can we describe empirically how the church grows. Yet to undertake such analyses one needs certain theoretical postulates, since all human action responds to a minimal vision of life. Human beings not only exist but think. They are acting-reflecting creatures. Accordingly, all human endeavors carry implicitly certain theoretical assumptions.

As a community of women, men, and children, the church not only exists but also reflects on itself and its reason to be. Its expansion is not an accident nor a mere sociological reflex. Whatever else we may say about church growth, this much is certain: As a religious entity, the church grows in accordance with its self-understanding—the vision it has of its nature and mission in the world. That vision is not derived out of the clear blue sky. Rather it is grounded on the body of beliefs that make up the church's faith. The church's faith defines its nature and mission. Therefore, to describe its growth adequately we need in the first place to understand how it is conceived by the Christian faith.

THE CHURCH AS GOD'S CREATION

A fundamental assertion of the Christian faith is that the church has been called into being by God. It is not only the *product* of God's grace, but the very expression of divine love—a God-created and indwelt entity. Since the Christian faith perceives God as a tri-unity, the eternal communion of Father, Son, and Spirit, it follows that the church derives its nature from the trinitarian terms. In fact, this is one of the most characteristic ways by which New Testament writers refer to the church, as made evident in the images of body, fellowship, and people.

The church is the *body of Christ*. It is integrated by many members interacting with one another and having diverse functions. What the head is to the body, Christ is to the church: the cerebrum that directs its movements, balances its posture, and sends messages to and receives them from its various parts, making learning, memory, and reflection possible. By the same token, the church is the hands, feet, and mouth of Christ in history. It is through its mission that the risen Christ continues to carry out his messianic ministry in the world.

The church is also the *fellowship of the Holy Spirit*. As such, it has been brought into being and set apart for service by the Spirit's grace and purifying fire. Thus the church is the company of regenerated and sanctified sinners. The Holy Spirit, on the other hand, is the nervous system which makes efficacious Christ's lordship over his body. The Spirit sustains, preserves, and indwells the church by his power. Conversely, the church is the one place where the Spirit's presence in the world becomes most visible and where the encounter between God and humankind is facilitated.

The church is, moreover, the *covenant people of God*. Made up of discordant elements, it has been called by the Father of our Lord Jesus Christ to bear witness to God's love in the world. The church is a people in formation, marching through history toward its fullness in the consummation of God's kingdom. Consequently, the church is not only chosen and set apart, but is also a people dispersed and sent out to reproduce itself in all cultures, among all nations, and through all the spheres of life.

The church ought to grow in conformity with its divine nature. As the fellowship of the Spirit, it ought to grow in *holiness* and *communion*. As the body of Christ, it ought to grow in *apostolicity* and *unity*. As God's covenant people, it ought to grow in *fidelity* and *maturity*. Such an imperative proceeds from an indicative, namely, the fact that the church, understood theologically, is no historical accident or human creation, but rather the very expression of God and the firstfruits of his work. In other words, the church exists by the will and power of God. A foremost criterion in evaluating church growth must be, therefore, theological.

The Church as the Company of the Committed

But the church is not a divine robot. It is made up of women, men, and children from all walks of life who have freely committed their lives to God through faith in Jesus Christ. The church is the company of the obedient—those who have *heard* the call of the gospel, *repented* from sin, and *trusted* in Christ for their salvation.

A fundamental trait of the church is, therefore, its obedient faith, the fact that it *hears* God's Word and *responds* in *faith* to its message. To be the church is to be in dialogue with God, to walk according to God's will, to be at the service of God's Word. It is to be a committed company of believers who *live* in communion with the Father through the Son in the power of the Spirit, who bear witness to the good news of God's kingdom in all the earth, who are subject to the teaching and guidance of God's Word, and who demonstrate the love of God in unconditional service to humankind.

This notion of the church proceeds from the fact that faith—understood as an act of trust in Jesus Christ, the one who is the fulfillment of God's promises, the Savior of the world, and the ultimate revelation of God's creative Word—is not static. Faith is not buried in the past of a once-and-for-all act, but rather is a continuous *process of trusting* in God. This being the case, the church is not just a company of hearers but of doers, not only of believers in God but of seekers of the will of God. It is a *growing* community of obedient people. It has arrived at neither its numerical nor organic fullness. It needs ever more wisdom from and understanding of God's Word. Its service is neither what it should nor could be. In short, it lives in the continuous need to "grow in all things" (Eph 4:15).

Wholistic Growth of the Church

If the church needs to grow in every aspect of its life, then it follows that to evaluate properly its performance we need a theory of church growth that corresponds to its complex and dynamic nature. Thus this essay advocates a wholistic (well-rounded and wholesome) concept of church growth.

By *wholistic church growth* I mean the process of integral and normal expansion that can and should be expected from the life and mission of the church as the fellowship of the Spirit, the body of Christ, and God's covenant people. It is a process of *normal expansion* because as a living organism the church has the capacity to grow normally and consistently. And it is an *integral*

67066

(or wholistic) *process* because as a community of obedient people the church is to experience growth in length, breadth, height, and depth and at the level of the grass roots and the leadership, the formal and informal group, in the congregation, the denomination, and the ecumenical and parachurch agency.

TOWARD A WHOLISTIC MODEL

To make the aforementioned definition manageable, a wholistic model of church growth is necessary. A model "is a familiar structure or mechanism used as an analogy to interpret a natural phenomenon" (*Encyclopedia Britannica* 1980:958). Models are used to develop or modify theories, or simply to render them more intelligible.[2]

The following model seeks to do justice to the concept of the church growing wholistically. It takes as its starting point the theological affirmation of the church as a divine creation and as a community of women, men, and children immersed in a pilgrimage of faith, in communion with one another, proclaiming the gospel, hearing and responding to God's Word, and serving humanity in love. From this understanding of the church, the model identifies certain theological *qualities* that should characterize church growth, and several *dimensions* that cover the areas where the church should experience growth. The correlation of these qualities and dimensions in a given ecclesial situation can give a profile of a growing church.

QUALITIES OF GROWTH

Three theologically identifiable qualities of growth emanate from the church's trinitarian nature as the fellowship of the Spirit, the body of Christ, and God's covenant people. They are spirituality, incarnation, and faithfulness. These three qualities represent the model's controlling variables. They are the factors against which the various kinds of growth are qualitatively evaluated, or, in other words, the critical principles that test the theological validity of church growth.

Spirituality is related to the presence and dynamic operation of the Holy Spirit in the growth experience of the church. It probes into the vitality of the church's growth. Is it a growth that responds to the inspiration and motivation of the Holy Spirit? Does it reflect "the fruits of the Spirit"? Does it demonstrate a joyful, vibrant, loving, and hopeful faith?

The *incarnational* variable has to do with the historical rooting of the body of Christ in the collective struggles of society and the personal afflictions of children, women, and men. It evaluates the impact that this enfleshment has in the process of church growth. In other words, we must ask to what extent the church is experiencing a growth that bears a concrete (incarnate) witness to the commitment and comprehensive presence of Christ among the harassed and helpless multitudes of the world (Mt 9:36; 25:31-46).

Faithfulness expresses the need for the church to live "in tune" with God's dealings in history. Therefore, it probes into the covenantal relevance of the church's growth. In what sense is that growth consequential with the church's

2. Greeley (1982:2ff) gives an informative discussion on the uses of models in religion.

calling as God's covenant people? To what extent does it correlate with God's purpose and deeds as revealed in the Scriptures and historically understood in the Christian church?

DIMENSIONS OF GROWTH

In the proposed model, four dimensions of growth flow out of the reality of the church as a growing company of committed persons in the journey of faith. As a community on the way to the kingdom of God, whose members live in fellowship with one another, who are hearers and doers of God's Word, and who are unconditionally committed to serve humankind in the love of the gospel, the church should experience growth in four directions: in the reproduction of its members, the development of its organic life, the deepening of its understanding of the faith, and the efficacy of its service in the world. Hence the four dimensions identified in the model: numerical, organic, conceptual, and diaconal.

Numerical growth is the membership reproduction experienced by the church through the proclamation and living witness of the gospel and the incorporation of those who respond to the fellowship of a local congregation. This dimension is a fundamental component of the church's being. The church needs new tissues to keep itself alive. It needs a continuous reproduction of its cells. Moreover, as a pilgrim people on the way to the kingdom it will not be able to reach its goal until all humanity has had a reasonable opportunity to hear and respond to the gospel (Mk 13:10).

Organic growth is the designation given to the internal development of the community of faith, or the strengthening of the system of relationships between its members. This dimension covers the church's form of government, its financial structure, its patterns of leadership, the type of activities in which it invests its time and resources, and its liturgical celebration. As a living organism, the church cannot be satisfied merely with the reproduction of its cells. It needs to be concerned with the effective functioning of all the parts which make up its life system. The latter needs to be strengthened, looked after, stimulated, and well-coordinated for the church to carry out its duties adequately. Otherwise its reproductive labor may be wasted and its pilgrimage of faith blocked, frustrated, or turned aside from its goal.

Conceptual growth implies expansion in what in theology is called the intelligence of faith (*intelligentia fide*). It involves the deepening of the church's self-understanding and its knowledge of the faith, including its understanding of the Scriptures, the historical development of Christian doctrine, and the world in which it lives and ministers. This dimension of growth gives the church intellectual firmness to face up to internal and external assaults on the faith through false doctrines and deceitful theories. It also enables the church to think critically so as to avoid fossilization and to guarantee thereby organic, evangelistic, and ethical creativity.

The intensity of the service the church renders to the world as a concrete demonstration of God's redemptive love is called *diaconal growth*. This dimension covers the impact that the church's reconciling ministry is having on its social environment; the degree of its participation in the life, conflicts, fears, and hopes of society; and the extent that these expressions contribute to the effective alleviation of human pain and the abrogation of the social conditions that keep people in poverty, powerlessness, and oppression. Without this dimension the church loses its authenticity and credibility. Only in the measure in which the church is able to give concrete visibility to its vocation of love and service can it expect to be heard and respected.

Every one of these dimensions is related to some aspect of the life-in-mission of the church. The numerical is linked with the personal life and conflicts of the multitudes of women, men, and children who themselves, along with their neighbors, live alienated from God without love, peace, or hope and in need of reconciliation and incorporation into the church. These are the billions whose spiritual condition constantly challenges the church and to whom it considers itself a debtor for the sake of the gospel.

The organic dimension has to do with culture and contextualization, Christian education and stewardship, *koinonia* and worship. It confronts the church with the need to be a culturally relevant (indigenous) community which forms and disciples its members; manages well its time, talents, and resources; promotes a warm fellowship between its members; and celebrates the faith in the language of the community where it is located, incorporating its symbols, creations, and values and identifying with its socio-historical situation.

The conceptual dimension penetrates the logical and psychosocial spheres of life. It underscores the church's need not only to reflect critically but reverently on the faith, in prayer, and in the light of the Word. It also stresses the need of evaluating honestly and earnestly the images which the church has formed of itself and its mission in the world, in the light of the faith and the concrete socio-historical reality.

As for the diaconal dimension, it is related to the ethical side of the church and its mission. It has to do with the church's role as a community at the service of people in need and its consequent involvement in the collective struggles and structural problems of society.

EVALUATION AND MEASUREMENT

We now come to the nitty-gritty of any church growth model: how to evaluate and measure the church's experience of growth. The proposed model tackles this problem in a twofold way. First, it seeks to gather and compare all the relevant data of each dimension, keeping in mind the principles of spirituality, incarnation, and faithfulness. This implies not only the use of several methods, since not all the dimensions are measurable in the same way, but also the recognition that all measurement efforts are always probable because it is not possible to isolate all the relevant variables. Let us consider some of the most relevant data that need to be gathered for each dimension and some of the ways to do it.

The least complicated dimension to research is the numerical. The objective is to measure how many are coming to faith in Christ, are being incorporated into the church, and are attracted into its "orbit" or sphere of influence (i.e., how many come to its various functions, participate in its activities, and take advantage of its services). This can be done by determining through church records and other relevant sources over a period of ten years[3] the totals of con-

---

3. The ten-year period is a standard way of measuring numerical church growth. It makes comparison easier and evaluation more meaningful. See Waymire and Wagner (1980:16) and Chaney and Lewis (1977:87ff).

version/baptism membership (those who have had no previous contact with a church), biological membership (those who grow up in the church and become members through confirmation or profession of faith), transfer membership, professions of faith, and attendance at the various church meetings and activities.

In evaluating organic growth, the objective is to identify over a ten-year period *variations* on the following factors: financial giving (total income, missionary offering, and per-capita giving), number of leaders and their distribution, type and number of programs, and type of fellowship activities and worship experiences. The aim is also to identify the intensity of worship, fellowship, personal devotion, and participation in the life of the church. Here there is a departure from the diachronic (across a period of time) approach utilized in the examination of variations. To measure intensity, one needs a synchronic (within the same time-span) procedure. Since the goal is to find out what people feel, think, and do, the researcher needs to sample attitudes, feelings, and opinions and set up a scale accordingly to compare the various responses. The sampling can be done between church members or congregations.

In measuring conceptual growth, the objective is to identify the "level" and "variations" of biblical, ecclesial, and theological knowledge and to assess the correlations between faith and practice. The level of knowledge can be identified by testing individual beliefs against an established standard such as the church's doctrinal statement or confession of faith, or simply the researcher's own theological stance.

A questionnaire can be prepared in the light of the set theological standard and be administered to a representative number of persons in a local church (or several churches). A scale can then be set up to categorize the scores by levels. On the other hand, variations in knowledge can be identified by comparing the "spiritual age" of church members with the established theological standard. This can be done on the basis of the length of time a person has been a church member (or confirmed), or the years since conversion and baptism. A scale can then be set up relating spiritual age to theological maturity. Correlation of faith and practice can be accomplished by comparing personal or church faith statements with individual behavior. Thus, for example, if a local church believes in the authority of the Bible but its members hardly read it, we can conclude that in that church there is no correlation between faith and practice.

In diaconal growth, the aim is to identify variations in, and evaluate the efficacy of, the church's diaconal ministry, as well as to appraise the intensity of the church's involvement in society. Variations are identified by examining the number and types of diaconal activities over a ten-year period. The efficacy of the church's liberating and reconciling service is evaluated by examining the concrete results (the positive and negative changes it has brought) over the same ten-year period. The intensity of the church's participation in the struggles of society is appraised through random surveys of its neighbors (to see what image they have of the church) and congregational interviews and surveys (to find out the kinds of social involvement of the membership).

In addition to the collection, collation, and analysis of the aforementioned data gathered through an examination of church records, demographic information, questionnaires, and random surveys and interviews, the proposed model calls for a *critical evaluation* of each dimension on the basis of the threefold qualities of growth mentioned earlier: spirituality, incarnation, and faithfulness. Thus one is able to assess to what extent a church is *really* growing by correlating qualities and dimensions of growth.

By the same token, one will be better equipped to do a profile of a growing congregation. This possibility may be illustrated by the accompanying chart. The chart may be used either to give each dimension an individual quality score on the basis of a previously set scale or to write an evaluative quality statement for each dimension.

	QUALITIES OF GROWTH	DIMENSIONS OF GROWTH			
		Numerical	Organic	Mental	Diaconal
	Spirituality				
	Incarnation				
	Faithfulness				

PROFILE OF A GROWING CONGREGATION

The value of the proposed model is that it enables the researchers not only to get a *quantitatively* comprehensive picture of the numerical, organic, conceptual, and diaconal vitality of the church, but also a *qualitatively* realistic assessment of the theological integrity of a church's growth experience.[4] Thus, for example, in evaluating numerical growth one does not merely seek to determine how many persons are being reached with the gospel, incorporated into the church (through conversion and baptism, confirmation, or transfer), and attracted to its activities. In addition to the quantification of this information, one seeks to evaluate the level of spirituality, incarnation, and faithfulness of the church in the process of growth and decline and the reasons for it. And it is at this juncture that the church is able to show that it is more than a social institution and a voluntary association.

It can be said that the church experiences *well-rounded* growth when it receives new members, expands internally, deepens its understanding of the faith, and serves the world sacrificially. But its development is *qualitatively*

4. This is beginning to be demonstrated in a series of research projects that students at Eastern Theological Seminary are conducting: Scull (1981), Morrison (1981), Hatch (1981), Smith (1981), and Chaya (1980).

wholesome when it experiences a spiritual, incarnated, and faithful numerical, organic, conceptual, and diaconal growth. The numerical by itself becomes ecclesiastical obesity; the organic is confused with bureaucracy; the conceptual degenerates into a theoretical abstraction; and the diaconal is reduced to a cheap social activism.

By the same token, the four dimensions lack theological integrity if they are not motivated and saturated by the presence of the Spirit, if they do not stem from the efficacious incarnation of the body of Christ in the pains and suffering of humankind, and if they do not reveal themselves to be faithful to God's purpose and actions in the history of the world in general and the covenant people in particular.

Only by integrating the four dimensions and correlating them with the trinitarian qualities of growth can we speak of a normal, and therefore healthy, growth for the church and its world mission.

REFERENCES CITED

CHAYA, Paul
  1980   "In-depth Study for the Growth and Development of the Roxborough Baptist Church" (unpublished), Eastern Baptist Theological Center Library, Philadelphia.

CHANEY, Charles L. and LEWIS, Ron S.
  1977   *Design for Church Growth,* Nashville: Broadman Press.

COSTAS, Orlando E.
  1974   *The Church and Its Mission,* Wheaton: Tyndale House Publishers.
  1979   *The Integrity of Mission,* New York: Harper and Row.
  1981   "Church Growth as a Multidimensional Phenomenon: Some Lessons from Chile," *International Bulletin of Missionary Research,* Vol. 5, No. 1 (January).

DOYLE, Ruth T. and KELLY, Sheila M.
  1979   "Comparisons of Trends in Ten Denominations," *Understanding Church Growth and Decline, 1950-1978,* Dean R. Hoge and David A. Roozen (eds.), New York: The Pilgrim Press.

DUDLEY, Carl S.
  1979   *Where Have All Our People Gone?* Wheaton: Tyndale House Publishers.

ENCYCLOPEDIA BRITANNICA, THE NEW MICROPEDIA
  1980   "Model, Scientific," Vol. VI, 15th edition, Chicago: Encyclopedia Britannica, Inc.

GREELEY, Andrew M.
  1982   *Religions: A Secular Theory,* New York: The Free Press.

HATCH, Robert A.
  1981   "The First Spanish Baptist Church of Philadelphia: A Journey of Faith Towards a Life of Hope and a Ministry of Love" (unpublished), Eastern Baptist Theological Seminary Library, Philadelphia.

HOGE, Dean R.
  1979   "National Contextual Factors Influencing Church Trends" and "A Test of Theories of Denominational Growth and Decline," *Understanding Church Growth and Decline, 1950-1978,* Dean R. Hoge and David A. Roozen (eds.), New York: The Pilgrim Press.

JACQUET, Constant H., ed.
1981   *Yearbook of American and Canadian Churches, 1980,* Nashville: Abingdon.

KELLEY, Dean M.
1977   *Why Conservative Churches Are Growing,* second edition, New York: Harper and Row.
1979   "Is Religion a Dependent Variable?" *Understanding Church Growth and Decline, 1950-1978,* Dean R. Hoge and David A. Roozen (eds.), New York: The Pilgrim Press.

MORIKAWA, Jitsuo
1979   *Biblical Dimensions of Church Growth,* Valley Forge: Judson Press.

MORRISON, John Wesley
1981   "Growing as the Body of Christ: A Holistic Model and Its Application to the Rose Tree Park Church of the Nazarene" (unpublished), Eastern Baptist Theological Seminary Library, Philadelphia.

OWENS, Owen D.
1981   *Growing Churches for a New Age,* Valley Forge: Judson Press.

PADILLA, C. René
1976   "Spiritual Conflict," *The New Face of Evangelicalism,* C. René Padilla (ed.), London: Hodder and Stoughton; Downers Grove: Inter-Varsity Press.

SCULL, Raymond P.
1981   "The Spring Mill Baptist Church: A Study of Growth and Revitalization" (unpublished), Eastern Baptist Seminary Library, Philadelphia.

SMITH, Jay
1981   "A Holistic Church Growth Survey of Tenth Presbyterian Church" (unpublished), Eastern Baptist Theological Seminary.

TIPPETT, Alan R.
1970   "A Resume of Church Growth Theology and Current Debate" (unpublished), Fuller Theological Seminary (March).

TOWNS, Elmer L., VAUGHN, John N., and SEIFERT, David J.
1981   *The Complete Book of Church Growth,* Wheaton: Tyndale House Publishers.

WAYMIRE, Bob and WAGNER, C. Peter
1980   *The Church Growth Survey Handbook,* second edition, revised, Santa Clara: The Global Church Growth Bulletin.

9. CHRISTIAN MISSION AND CULTURAL ANTHROPOLOGY

Robert L. Ramseyer

IN THIS CHAPTER WE EXAMINE SOME OF THE WAYS IN WHICH INSIGHTS FROM the discipline of cultural anthropology have been and can be both used and misused in planning for Christian mission. Not only cultural anthropology, but many of the other behavioral sciences have been popular subjects for study for Christian mission in the second half of the twentieth century.

In far too many cases, however, it has been assumed that the gospel is simply a message to be communicated and that whatever these sciences tell us about the communication of messages can be used to facilitate the communication of the gospel. True, some have raised questions about the appropriateness of using these sciences in this way, but these objections have usually been based on a somewhat vague feeling that science and the gospel do not belong together rather than on a careful consideration of the philosophical bases of these sciences and of the nature of the gospel.

THE GOSPEL COMMUNICATES RECONCILIATION AND IDENTIFICATION

Although writers on Christian mission differ widely on the nature of the gospel, what should have priority in mission, who sets the agenda for mission, and so forth, most Christians understand mission as sharing something about Jesus Christ and God's love with other people. Mission is virtually equated with evangelism understood to be sharing, proclaiming, or communicating the gospel. Since the gospel is usually thought of as words (news), anything designed to facilitate communication might be expected to be useful in mission-evangelism. Hence the interest in anything that science might tell us about the communication of messages. However, although it would seem obvious that the content of the gospel ought to have something to say about the way that it is communicated and that ways which are efficient for communicating other messages may not be appropriate for sharing the gospel, this issue is seldom raised by missionary anthropologists.

The gospel is a message about reconciliation and identification. God identified himself with human beings by becoming a human being in Jesus Christ

---

Robert L. Ramseyer, Elkhart, Indiana, is Director of the Overseas Mission Training Center and Professor of Missions and Anthropology at Associated Mennonite Biblical Seminaries. He served as a missionary in Japan from 1954 to 1972 and from 1978 to 1982. He is the author of Sharing the Gospel *(Herald Press, 1982).*

and in Jesus Christ reconciled us to himself. Obviously, then, the gospel can be communicated only in ways that communicate reconciliation and identification.

When God acted to reconcile us to himself in Jesus Christ, he acted from a position of human powerlessness and vulnerability at the bottom of the human power structure (Phil 2:7). Although as God's Son Jesus Christ could have been expected to have access to unlimited power, he never used superior knowledge or power to maneuver people into following him. It follows naturally, then, that gospel communication from a position of similar vulnerability is important. Attempts to communicate the gospel from positions of power can only distort it.

As the revelation of God's love, the gospel is beyond the comprehension of any of us. Our understanding is incomplete and imperfect. Therefore, the gospel is not something which we, having grasped fully ourselves, can now go on to translate for others so that they can understand it fully too. The gospel is not simply "supracultural" in the sense that it transcends cultural boundaries and is relevant for all human beings; it is suprahuman in the sense that it is beyond human comprehension. The gospel then is not a set of clearly defined teachings which a would-be communicator has grasped and now wants to communicate to others. Mission, the sharing of the gospel, is an attempt to communicate and share something which has been only dimly comprehended by the one who wants to share it.

Obviously, then, the gospel brings with it some basic conditions for its communication. It can only be shared in ways that reconcile, that tear down barriers rather than build them up. Gospel communication means identification of the one who would communicate with those with whom the message is to be shared. The gospel can only be shared from a position of human powerlessness and vulnerability. The gospel must be shared with the humility that comes from knowing that the communicator has grasped its fullness only partially and dimly.

As we consider the widespread use of the behavioral sciences in Christian mission, the basic question of the philosophical assumptions implicit in these tools needs to be faced squarely. Science is based on the assumption that it is possible and desirable for an observer to be emotionally detached from that which is being studied so that it can be studied objectively. By its very nature it calls for detachment. Although a cultural anthropologist talks about being a "participant observer," observation obviously takes precedence over participation. Science also places the observer in a position superior to that which is being observed. The scientist is a specialist who is supposed to know as much as possible about what is being studied. That which is being studied may know little or nothing about the scientist. Reciprocity, equality, and real identification between an anthropologist and the people being studied are not possible within the area of study where the relationship is one of subject and object.

However, because a good cultural anthropologist understands the dynamics involved, she or he is often able to compartmentalize his or her role as anthropologist and thus also maintain good relationships with the people being studied, outside the study relationship, as one ordinary human being to others. This is possible precisely because the anthropologist understands what study does to human relationships. Similarly, a good anthropologist understands that science is one cultural way of understanding reality, not reality itself. Science is part of one specific cultural tradition. A good anthropologist will not confuse an anthropological analysis of a sociocultural context with what is actually there.

Finally, cultural anthropology cannot be spoken of as if there is one anthropological way of studying or understanding the human situation. As is the case with any academic discipline, there are wide differences among its practitioners, differences so significant that they lead to radically different ways of understanding the human situation. For example, it makes a tremendous difference whether one understands culture as a kind of environmental given within which human beings function relatively compliantly because they replicate in their individual thought patterns the basic assumptions of that culture, or whether one understands culture as a kind of contract into which people enter in order to live together, each person with a different attitude toward and understanding of that cultural contract.

Similarly, it makes a difference whether one understands culture change as being essentially cumulative, tending to move in the direction of ever-greater complexity, or whether one sees human culture as basically a collection of discrete, fairly tightly integrated cultural communities (often called cultures), emphasizes the differences among them, and believes that it is ethnocentric and mistaken to understand culture change as building on the past and moving in a definable direction.

CHRISTIANITY IN CULTURE: A READING

The fact that the discipline called cultural anthropology is in no sense a neutral tool waiting for the missionary to pick up and use is nowhere more apparent than in Charles H. Kraft's *Christianity in Culture,* a truly monumental attempt to show what cultural anthropology can do for our understanding of Christian faith and mission. As the most complete work in the field, *Christianity in Culture* is also the best example of the way in which our understanding of culture and the cultural process affects our understanding of Christian faith and life. *Christianity in Culture* is especially helpful in this respect because the author is not afraid to follow his anthropological presuppositions to their obvious theological and missiological conclusions. Where his predecessors were content to merely suggest, Kraft spells out in detail the logical conclusions of consistently acting on his understanding of society and culture. Three examples from *Christianity in Culture* will be examined here.

Most writers on anthropology and Christian mission write as if anthropology were a discipline with one point of view, "the anthropological point of view," ignoring the fact that there are as many different anthropologies as there are theologies. Kraft, for example, opts for an essentially functionalist understanding of culture change rather than for an evolutionary understanding because he confuses evolution with the idea of progress (1979:50ff).[1] Not wishing to appear ethnocentric or to adopt a position that would imply that Western civilization is superior to other sociocultural traditions, he rejects the whole idea of direction in sociocultural change.

1. Kraft talks a great deal about the need for dynamic models, for being open to the idea of change. Nevertheless, his understanding of culture and culture change leads him to a basically static position.

Kraft's functionalism leads him to see culture as tightly integrated systems coterminous with human communities. The members of these communities are perceived as sharing within themselves the essential understandings of the cultures of their communities. Kraft sees culture as analogous to language in that the relationship between cultural forms and the meanings which they convey is essentially arbitrary. That is, just as in language there is no intrinsic reason why a particular set of sounds carries a particular meaning, the meaning which a cultural form conveys is only dependent on that which the culture assigns to it. What concerns us here is the way in which these particular understandings of culture and society have affected his understanding of Christian faith and life, particularly his understanding of the Christian mission.

STATIC CULTURE VIEW APPLIED

The effect of opting for a non-evolutionary understanding of culture change is nowhere more apparent than in Kraft's understanding of the relationship between the Old and New Testaments. In *Christianity in Culture* differences in biblical revelation are attributed entirely to God's adapting his ways of communication to the culture of the people involved. Thus there is change as God accommodates his message to changed circumstances in human society, but there is no direction, no fuller, clearer, or higher revelation. "Yet in many ways tradition ('law'), tribe and ceremony in Hebrew culture were the functional equivalents of grace, freedom, and philosophizing in Greek culture. The latter are not necessarily superior ways of expressing the Gospel, just different culturally" (1979:232). Our own preference for New Testament revelation is attributed to our own cultural affinities with the Greek culture of the New Testament world rather than to anything inherently superior in that revelation.

The important thing for us to see here is that Kraft's failure to see any cumulative direction in biblical revelation is not based on insights from cultural anthropology as a value-free science, but on his choice of one particular kind of cultural anthropology in preference to other perspectives which would be equally respectable among anthropologists today.

IMPLICATIONS OF A NONDIRECTIONAL VIEW OF CULTURE CHANGE

Kraft's choice of a rather simplistically nondirectional view of culture change has blinded him to the effect which sharing the gospel has on any traditional society. The whole idea of mission, of offering people either as individuals or as groups an alternative to the status quo which they perceive as having come down essentially unchanged from the beginning of things, is itself a tremendous push toward modern complex society, the mark of which is the availability of choices, the presentation of a number of alternatives.

Christian mission pushes people to step outside their setting and look at themselves from an outside perspective, an act which is inconceivable from within a traditional society. Christian mission in and of itself is part of a process of directional change over which the missionary has little or no control. Missionary efforts to treat societies in which the range of alternatives is very narrow as if they were not on a different level of development from those which offer a broad range of choices is both futile and mistaken. On this basis alone, a non-evolutionary view of culture is less than helpful in Christian mission.

Static functionalism leads to other unhelpful positions as well. It leads Kraft, for example, to miss the profound missiological implications of the shift in the basis of the formation of the people of God between the Old Covenant and the New. For Kraft, "The fact that today in Western cultures we organize the people of God into churches rather than into tribes and nations (like Israel) shows a *cultural* change rather than some drastic alteration of God's method of dealing with human beings" (1979:318). As a matter of fact, tribe and nation and the ties of kinship were important in New Testament times as well, but Jesus went out of his way to confront his society and make very clear that his people were not to be formed on the basis of ethnic and biological ties but on the basis of their faith (Mk 3:31-35). Ethnic and family groupings by their very nature are exclusive. They include some people, exclude others, and frequently lead to enmity between members of different groups. Jesus not only told his followers that his people were to be formed on an entirely different basis, but that they must be prepared to turn their backs on their natural cultural groups whenever this interfered with their allegiance to him.

Kraft's anthropology has led him to miss the fundamental conflict between human culture and the Christian faith today. Because the Christian gospel is a gospel of reconciliation whereas human culture in all of its forms today is a culture of division, we as Christians are always in search of better ways to express reconciliation among all people who are committed to Jesus Christ. True, since we are all cultural beings we are still trapped in exclusive and divisive forms, even in our church life. One thing, however, is clear. Groups which are part of our cultural heritage, groups which set boundaries on some other basis than our faith in Jesus Christ, can never serve as a basis for forming the people of God in any cultural setting.

PEOPLE NOT CAPTIVE TO CULTURE

The understanding of the relationship between culture and the members of a community found in *Christianity in Culture* shows culture as a tightly integrated system which becomes for the individual human being in a society a basic part of the environment over which he or she has little control. Moreover, the basic cultural assumptions of a society are replicated in each member so that it makes little difference whether one speaks of culture or of the thought patterns of the members of a society.

Although he eschews determinism, Kraft believes that the more the members of a society share common understandings, the healthier that society will be, and he can talk about the " 'room to wiggle' *allowed* us by our culture" (1979:70. Emphasis mine). Again, as with his non-evolutionary understanding of culture change, this is a view of culture which has been held by respected anthropologists. As with his understanding of culture change, it ignores much of what has been done in cultural anthropology in the last twenty years.

Anthropologists today recognize what should have been evident from the beginning, that within any sociocultural setting there is a great deal of diversity among individual people. Culture is a sort of organizing contract which enables people to live and function together. What ties them together is not a set of common understandings of their world, but the fact that in their cultural setting they are able to predict with satisfying accuracy what the results of their actions will be.

Understanding culture as a tightly integrated system replicated in the minds of the members of a society, Kraft puts a high value on integration and evaluates negatively anything which would be disruptive. Therefore mission is to be carried on in ways which will minimize traumatic cultural change. Confrontation is to be avoided in favor of gradual orderly change even if this means that infanticide in Nigeria or slavery and racial discrimination in North America ought to have been prolonged (1979:346-47, 361-62). One looks in vain for those missionaries who were accused of turning the world upside down.

Once again his anthropological presuppositions have led Kraft to overlook significant aspects of the sociocultural setting, in this case the way in which those who shared the gospel in New Testament times confronted those societies to which they went. Reading *Christianity in Culture* one would wonder why Christians were ever persecuted. In actuality, a look at the biblical materials impresses one not with orderly change within an integrated society, but with the continued confrontation between prophetic figures and the society as a whole over the radical changes which those prophets called for. Kraft's understanding of culture has led him to see God as continually reacting to human culture, working within the limits which a cultural system imposes, rather than aggressively confronting human society.

Throughout *Christianity in Culture* Kraft confuses God's willingness to accept people where they are and communicate with them in terms that they can understand with presenting a Christian message colored to make it acceptable to people in their traditional society with a minimum of change. Thus he suggests sharing only Old Testament understandings of God with a people in Nigeria because a New Testament understanding of God's forgiveness is too different from the traditional understanding and is disruptive in that setting (1979:352). He can talk about God's coming to Peter in a typically Hebrew vision in Acts 10 (1979:341) and overlook the fact that the content of that vision was in sharp conflict with the basic premises of Hebrew culture. Similarly, although Paul may have theologized in a typically Hellenistic-Hebrew way (1979:342), what he said was in sharp conflict with the thought world of the Hellenistic Jews. *Christianity in Culture* seems strangely unaware of confrontation and conflict in New Testament gospel sharing.

The logic of Kraft's anthropology leads to churches at home in simple, well-integrated cultural settings, those settings which today, whether one likes it or not, are rapidly being incorporated into larger and larger social units. Rather than leading the way in helping people adjust to a new complex society in which they must learn to live with people from many different settings, the church becomes tied to a disappearing, exclusive sociocultural setting, by its nature denies the gospel of reconciliation which it is supposed to express, and will disappear with the cultural setting in which it has become enmeshed.

FORM AND MEANING

One of the greatest temptations in the social sciences is to set up analytical categories and then act as if they had an actual existence apart from the scientist who formulated them. Kraft knows this (1979:23ff), yet this is precisely what he does himself in his discussion of form and meaning. Building on an analogy with language where the relationship between form and meaning is usually demonstrably arbitrary, he posits the same for culture as a whole. As far as the sharing of the gospel is concerned, culture becomes a kind of value-free language for the communication of a supracultural gospel.

Although culture is not language and the relationship between form and meaning in culture is clearly not as arbitrary as Kraft would have us believe, he goes on to build a structure in which form is relatively unimportant while the meaning which it expresses is what counts. "Christianness lies primarily in the 'supracultural' functions and meanings expressed in culture rather than in the mere forms of any given culture" (1979:118. Italics omitted). His understanding of cultural forms as essentially a neutral language able to carry whatever is given it is seen, for example, in his belief that slavery, dictatorship, and warfare are all *forms* which can be given Christian functions in a given cultural setting (1979:108). Thus one is left with a great deal of emphasis on what presumably is in the heads or hearts of people and a minimization of the importance of actual behavior. Meaning comes to be equated with the gospel and Christian faith, form with actual Christian living, in spite of the fact that the New Testament makes clear that Christian faith and Christian living are not separable entities at all.

By reifying his conceptual categories Kraft intellectualizes the task of the Christian missionary. "The task of Christianity vis-a-vis any given culture or subculture is primarily the transformation of the conceptual system (world view) of that culture" (1979:349). Kraft himself recognizes that this sort of intellectualizing is a characteristic of the Western intellectual tradition (1979:180), but apparently he is unable to see that his attempts to split reality into principles and behavior, meaning and form (1979:122ff), are the sort of Western intellectualizing which he warns his readers against. His refusal to see that in culture form and meaning are inseparable leads him to overlook important elements in a setting when he seeks dynamic equivalence translations of Christian faith from one setting to another. This leads to some of the weakest sections of his work in terms of practical help for the Christian missionary. His discussions of baptism and leadership illustrate this well.

Kraft suggests that in traditional societies with initiation rites these rites might serve as functional equivalents of baptism (1979:331-32). He further suggests that among the Higi of Nigeria membership in a royal social class might well be a qualification for church leadership since it is a requirement for leadership in that society (1979:325). In each case, by relativizing forms, he fails to see important aspects of both the New Testament context and the present setting. Initiation rites almost always signify a transition that is not at all a matter of personal volition. Is this what baptism means in the New Testament, or what it should mean anywhere today? In the New Testament both Jesus and the early church are depicted as having gone out of their way to reject anything which would have given them prestige or authority in human society (Phil 2; I Cor 1). Is it conceivable that requiring membership in a royal social class, or in any social class, could be a functional equivalent in any society?

Learning from Jesus and the early church, it seems clear that the gospel is meant to be shared by servants from a position of human powerlessness and vulnerability. In contrast, missionary study of cultural anthropology has frequently led to power for the missionary, to what might be called an applied anthropology mentality, the use of knowledge which one has gained in order to maneuver people into doing what the maneuverer believes is for their own good. Using anthropology in this way contradicts the gospel message. It sets the missionary over against the people with whom the gospel is to be shared rather than identifying with them as God did with us in Jesus Christ. The gospel says that Jesus was fully one of us, not just someone playing a part. The applied anthropology mentality sets the missionary over the people with superior knowledge to which they have no access. The missionary then is not a vulnerable servant but the one who directs and controls the action. To act like door-to-door salesmen limiting the gospel message to "those portions of biblical information that will be most acceptable" (Kraft 1979:255) so that we can persuade them that becoming Christians will not demand too much change or be too difficult for them, treats people as objects and denies our common humanity with them. A gospel shared in this way can only be a gospel which is grossly distorted.[2]

THE SUM

What then do we say? Are the sciences which study human beings, particularly those which study our social and cultural life, unable to help us in sharing the gospel of Jesus Christ with others?

We have seen that science by its very nature sets the scientist apart from that which is being studied. Anthropologists are always drawn both toward immersion among the people whom they study and toward detached reflection about those same people. This, however, is something which all human beings do to a greater or lesser degree. In fact, the ability to stand apart from ourselves and look at both ourselves and the people around us in a somewhat detached way is one of the important qualities which makes us human.

As Christians living in this world, we are continually facing forces which pull us away from faithfulness to the gospel. What we need is not withdrawal, but an awareness of what these forces are so that we can take steps to counteract them as we live with the tensions which life in this world entails. The discipline of cultural anthropology presents this same sort of challenge to our life and mission as Christians. A naive attempt to use some of the insights of cultural anthropology in mission without recognizing all that this involves can lead us toward human relationships which deny the gospel which we want to share.

APPLICATION TO CHRISTIAN MISSION

The role of cultural anthropology in Christian mission begins with self-understanding. Beginning with ourselves forces us to include ourselves with the rest

---

2. In this article I have focused on what I believe are major weaknesses in *Christianity in Culture* which result from a naive attempt to apply insights from one particular kind of cultural anthropology to the Christian mission. However, in spite of the fact that his faulty anthropology leads to faulty theology and missiology, Charles Kraft has produced a book which contains a wealth of extremely helpful ideas and suggestions. He is at his best when he discusses language. Chapter 13 on the translation of the Bible is excellent. After reading *Christianity in Culture* through for the first time I felt strongly that this was at the same time both the best book and the worst book that I had read on this subject. I still feel that way.

of humanity and gives us a new appreciation for the way in which our own thought processes and understandings are conditioned both by the sociocultural setting in which we have been reared and by our subsequent experiences. Cultural anthropology can help us see how our setting and our experiences have helped to shape our understanding of the gospel. Thus a missionary with a good background in cultural anthropology ought to share the gospel with a much greater sense of humility, realizing that what we now see and understand is really like a dim image in a mirror and that in fact our knowledge of the gospel which we want to share is only partial.

Cultural anthropology can lead us away from thinking of and treating the people with whom we work as objects, away from the manipulation to which we are always tempted, and toward identification with others as we come to see more clearly that both we and they are subject to the same kind of sociocultural limitations. This recognition in turn ought to make us more open to the possibility that the Holy Spirit will show other people—with backgrounds different from our own—aspects of the fullness of the gospel which we have been unable to see from our own perspective. Cultural anthropology can help us in sharing together in a worldwide fellowship of Christian people, open to sharing what God has revealed to us and learning from others as they respond in faith to his gospel.

Just as a naive application of cultural anthropology leads to both a distortion of the biblical message and an attempted manipulation of human beings, an awareness of what is involved can help us to identify with others by helping us to see the fullness of their sociocultural setting and what that setting means for them. Cultural anthropology should help us to see that for mutual understanding we need to see people in their total setting, not merely in terms of bits and pieces of that setting. Cultural anthropology can help me to stand in my friend's shoes and see the world from my friend's point of view. If I can learn to do that, then I am also better able to share the gospel with my friend as the good news which I believe that it is.

Cultural anthropology in Christian mission should help us to greater self-understanding, which in turn should help us to identify with and to share with others. This, after all, is what the Christian mission is all about.

REFERENCE CITED

KRAFT, Charles H.
   1979   *Christianity in Culture,* Maryknoll: Orbis Books.

10. CONTEXTUALIZATION

Charles R. Taber

THE PURPOSE OF THIS CHAPTER IS TO EXAMINE THE NEXUS BETWEEN *contextualization*[1] and *Church Growth theory*.[2] I will argue that contextualization as a central missiological emphasis based on the *incarnation* has profound implications for missionary methodology which are not given sufficient attention in Church Growth theory. This is in large part because Church Growth theory— like several other mission models—proceeds deductively and fails to consider some important dimensions of the human context in which mission takes place.

It will become evident that I am in fundamental sympathy with the Church Growth model and that my effort is indeed to strengthen and not to debunk it. Perhaps paradoxically, a part of this attempt will involve relativizing the Church Growth model by placing it within a broader framework.

EXISTING MODELS OF MISSION

A number of writers representing diverse theological perspectives have identified two major Protestant models of mission: the evangelical and the ecumenical.[3] These have come to be identified respectively with the Lausanne Congress (International Congress on World Evangelization 1974) and its constituency, and the World Council of Churches, though both identifications are simplistic. Each of these has certain characteristic emphases. Church Growth theory is an extension and specialization of the evangelical model.

1. The contextualization literature is so voluminous that only a sample can be cited: Coe (1973:233-43), Conn (1977), Khin Maung Din (1976:151-63), Nyamiti (1973), Taber (1978a:53-79), TEF (1972), Von Allmen (1975:37-55).
2. The following are some of the important works in Church Growth theory: Kraft (1979), Kraft and Wisley (1979), McGavran (1955, 1980), Tippett (1970, 1973a, 1973b), Wagner (1971), and Winter (1969:74-89; 1974:121-39).
3. I omit Roman Catholic models, not because they are unimportant, but because I am not thoroughly familiar with them. *Grosso modo,* one can find variants of both traditional Protestant ones, though little or nothing that corresponds to Church Growth theory. More recently, some Catholic missiologists have pioneered the development of incarnational missiology, and one (Donovan 1982) has worked out independently a practical model of indigenous missiology.

Charles R. Taber, Johnson City, Tennessee, is Professor of World Mission at Emmanuel School of Religion. He taught at Milligan College from 1973 to 1979, served as a translation consultant with the United Bible Societies in West Africa from 1969 to 1973, and worked as a research consultant with the American Bible Society from 1966 to 1969. From 1953 to 1960 he was a missionary in the Central African Republic, and from 1960 to 1962 he pastored a congregation. He authored eight articles in the Abingdon Dictionary of Living Religions *(1981).*

The evangelical approach emphasizes the propositional content of the gospel as contained in verbally inspired Scriptures. It sees the world as lost because of the fall and as subject to the wrath of God, but its understanding of sin is primarily personal and individual. Salvation, which is by grace through faith in Jesus Christ, is individual and otherworldly, though increasingly some insist on a here-and-now social dimension in the gospel (ICWE 1974). Evangelization is the proclamation of the gospel with the intent to convert persons to faith in Jesus Christ. As argued by Hoekstra (1979), this approach claims to be identical with that of the orthodox mainstream of the church since the New Testament, so that traditional, evangelical, and biblical are used interchangeably. But this model rests upon a specific package of evangelical assumptions which can be shown to have arisen historically and which demonstrably condition how both the Bible and the world are understood.

The ecumenical model stems in part from perceptions of weakness in the evangelical model: its pietism, its moralism, its privatism, its social irrelevance. When evangelicals claim that society will be reformed if enough individuals are converted, ecumenicals point out that this has not in fact happened in many so-called Christian nations. The ecumenical model therefore finds it necessary to address directly and as such the structural ills of the world, and in fact to make this concern central to mission. There is sometimes, though not always, a jettisoning of personal conversion. The most thoroughgoing versions, such as Liberation Theology, tend to equate salvation with the solution of the world's social problems and to make free use of the Marxist analysis of these problems and often of the Marxist prescription for their solution.

The Church Growth model is founded squarely on the evangelical one, though selectively and with certain additions. Its hermeneutic is quite model-specific. On the basis of this hermeneutic, the church is seen as central to the purpose of God in the world. It is therefore not enough to convert individuals; these must *"become His disciples and dependable members of His Church"* (McGavran 1980:26. Italics in original). The multiplication of congregations and the numerical increase of each one thus becomes the central goal of mission and the single criterion of success and even of faithfulness. From this maxim certain corollaries are explicitly drawn: A field in which church growth is not occurring rapidly is intrinsically less important than one where it is, and merits less attention; in order to maximize growth, one ought to try to convert not individuals but entire cohesive social groups; in order to maximize growth, evangelism and church planting ought to be done separately within the limits of each homogeneous unit rather than among heterogeneous populations; in order to maximize growth, only a bare minimum of simple moral demands ought to be placed on converts, and tougher biblical imperatives postponed to a later time of *perfecting* which is distinct from *discipling*.

Supporting these theological tenets and explicitly underlying Church Growth missionary methodology are certain ideas derived from a structural-functional model of cultural anthropology. There is in Church Growth theory a tendency to define missionary goals *a priori* and then to be totally pragmatic with respect to methods and techniques which are perceived to facilitate reaching these goals.

Despite the differences between these three models, they are all *deduc-*

tive; each starts from its distinctive understandings of the Bible, of the world, of the sending church, and of the receiving context. The evangelical model and its offspring Church Growth theory work from theologically determined interpretations of biblical data taken as normative. The older version of the evangelical model, but not Church Growth theory, takes for granted a close similarity between modern sending churches and the New Testament church. It therefore aims to reproduce this pattern; but since the receiving context is sometimes refractory, it becomes necessary to erect long-lasting structures of control over the younger churches by means of personnel, expertise, and money.

The ecumenical model takes the contemporary world much more seriously, as in the slogan which was current a few years ago that "the world sets the agenda for the church," but it is nevertheless founded on certain values which derive from Western liberal or radical philosophical traditions. Its *a priori* interpretations of the world, of the gospel, and hence of the missionary task stem from these roots.

The Church Growth model works deductively from two foundations and does not always notice the tensions and incompatibilities between them. One foundation is a narrowed-down version of the evangelical hermeneutic and theology. From this basis it deduces that everywhere and in all circumstances the numerical increase of the church is the one goal for which everything else may be sacrificed. The other foundation is a structural-functional model of cultural anthropology. On this basis it builds a set of definitions for certain concepts and a kit of pragmatic techniques for fostering the desired growth. Each of these foundations can be shown to have flaws within its own terms of reference.

More seriously, there are profound philosophical tensions between them. The static view of the world which is inherent in this model of anthropology is such that "cultural givens" take on permanence and rigidity; it suggests that whatever is, endures. This cannot help but undermine the hope of transformation which is central to the gospel. Further, the cultural relativism inherent in anthropology is in conflict with the evangelical understanding of a radically fallen world; it suggests that whatever is, is acceptable. These ideas give a kind of legitimacy to the insistence of Church Growth theorists that one must be realistic about what demands can be made of converts. They are also a reason why Church Growth theorists are sometimes insufficiently critical of existing sociocultural realities, especially on the "mission field."

CONTEXTUALIZATION AND INCARNATION

In contrast with all deductive models is the contextual model, at least when it is pursued to its logical conclusion.

What all true contextualists have in common is the attempt to take the concrete human context in all its dimensions with utmost seriousness. The *particularity* of each milieu becomes the starting point for both the questions and the answers which will shape the evangelistic process and its aftermath in the life of the new church.

The questions that must be asked before authentic evangelism can take place are at least these: What is the nature of the human condition for *these* people in *this* place? What *specific* problems do they face? What does the gospel say about *these* issues? In answering these and related questions, the contextual approach will reject any *a priori* limits on the scope of its inquiry, but will instead insist on being as comprehensive as possible. It will include the spiritual focus of the evangelical model, but also the social, economic, and political focus of the ecumenical model. It is concerned with the individual, but also with the group and with society as a whole. And it is concerned not only with problems which originate within a particular context, but also with the interlocking and interdependent structural problems of nations, regions, and the globe. In being so comprehensive, the contextual model ironically is taking more seriously than the evangelical model the radicalness of the fall and the pervasiveness of its consequences.

The demonic is not exclusively or even chiefly manifested in its control of disordered individual lives, though that is one area of its domain; it is also and even more fully manifested in the systems and structures—political, social, economic, cultural—which shape, distort, and destroy human lives. In being so comprehensive, contextualization also is taking more seriously than the evangelical model the completeness of the gospel to address the entire human predicament rather than a subset of its problems.

But contextualization goes further; it suggests that in important ways the gospel *answer* to the human predicament will be found within the context rather than outside. This is not to say that everything necessary for salvation is already present, but it is to say that God did not arrive for the first time when foreign missionaries came on the scene. Contextualization suggests that religions normally express responses to different degrees of divine revelation, and that the response is a varied and variable mixture of openness and rejection. The exact nature of the mix must be determined by inquiry, not by prejudgment. For instance, when missionaries arrived in many West African societies, they found already present an elaborate doctrine of the creator god. It would have been both pragmatically foolish and theologically indefensible for those missionaries to try to reject as error the incomplete knowledge of God already there; rather, their approach was, quite correctly, to build on the existing foundation.

In the same way, contextualization insists that the chief agents of the gospel in any context must be full participants in the local society. Outsiders may be crucially needed to get the process started, but their role should be kept as small as possible; during their involvement, they should be as closely identified with the local people as possible.

A full-blown contextual model is best constructed on the example of the incarnation. This represents at its core the fact that God took the human context in its irreducible particularity with utmost seriousness. Jesus did not begin his official ministry until he was thoroughly inside the lower-middle-class, artisanal, Galilean, pious context of early first-century Judaism. The essence of the incarnation was to work for radical transformation *from within*; as such, it could be and was profoundly subversive without being in the least alien or imperialistic. So specific was the incarnation that Jesus had little contact with Gentiles. Jesus defined the needs and problems to be addressed, the goals to be aimed at, and the resources and means for attaining those goals in and from the context itself.

Jesus worked on the basis of an understanding, not of the needs of humanity in general, but of the needs of particular people at a particular time and in particular circumstances. The gospel he brought touched directly the needs of persons: it was sight for the blind, healing for the sick, freedom for captives, forgiveness for sinners, respect for the despised. Nor did he, as some claim, shrink from addressing social, political, and economic issues. If we remember that our modern separation of church and state and of religion from politics could not have been imagined in first-century Jerusalem, and if we remember that the *first* and most immediately present form of oppression suffered by the people Jesus identified with was not Roman rule but the official and unofficial structures of authority within Judaism, we begin to see how radical Jesus was. The cleansing of the temple and the clashes with Pharisees and scribes and Sadducees all had unmistakable systemic overtones.

Jesus did not dream up deductively a set of goals—twelve disciples the first year, 120 the next. He simply made his invitation and his warning as clear as possible and was content with the results that emerged. He explicitly recognized that the context established limits for what even the Son of God could do (Mt 15:24; Jn 14:12). If one looks at what Jesus did in the days of his flesh, one might conclude that God's entire purpose was to save the little nation of Jewry—and that he failed at that.

Jesus did not muster outside resources, but made do with what was at hand. His personnel was a band of people whose chief distinction was their willingness to follow him. He was supported by a few devout women (Lk 8:3). His arsenal of concepts and images was found in the language and traditions of the people and the Jewish Scriptures—things already familiar to his hearers. His technique was that of an itinerant rabbi, also familiar in his day. Jesus took seriously the persons he dealt with—their dignity, their knowledge, their individuality. But he also took them seriously enough to tell them the truth.

What about Paul? Superficially, it might seem that he worked in a totally different way. Instead of staying in one area, he spread himself as thin as possible and kept on the move. Yet there are common features between Jesus and Paul that merit consideration.

Paul also identified issues and needs to be addressed in terms of the context. One has only to look at the occasional, *ad hoc* nature of his letters to see that he dealt with each situation in terms intrinsic to itself. He never took refuge in glittering generalities, but named names and identified problems concretely. He did not duck the personal basis of the division in the church at Corinth nor the socioeconomic basis of the perversions of the Lord's Supper there (Bartchy 1979:45-61). He did not address the institution of slavery or other oppressive inequalities in society as a whole, but he did address them in direct terms as they affected the church (Eph 5:21-6:9; Philem).

As regards resources, Paul, like Jesus, made use of what was at hand: his rabbinic education and status, which gave him access to synagogue pulpits; his tentmaking skills, which supported him; his Hellenistic culture, which made him at home in Gentile circles; and his Roman citizenship. He expected and pushed the churches he founded to discover within themselves the people and means to carry on after his departure. As far as the record shows, he never introduced into any context either methods or resources not already there, apart from his temporary team and the gospel he preached.

One kind of local resource of which Paul made free and bold use was the knowledge of God people had, whether much or little. He did not sneer at ignorance, but built on any foundation, however slight (Acts 13:16-31; 14:8-18; 17:22-34).

Before closing this section, we ought to point out that one can also use the model of the incarnation deductively. That is, one may examine the life of Jesus or the practice of the apostles and deduce a set of rules and procedures to be applied today. This was in part what Roland Allen did (1930). Such an approach also underlies all arguments that we ought to limit the scope of our concern to the specific kinds of questions Jesus and the apostles addressed, regardless of the nature of current issues or of the nature of our involvement in them. What I am suggesting is quite different; it is that we do not imitate the specific things Jesus and the apostles did, but take the model of the incarnation itself to heart and discover anew, *as they did,* how to express and embody the gospel *in each context.*

THEORETICAL ISSUES

The contextual model offers clues to the solution of three tensions inherent in deductive missiologies: that between the "essential gospel" and "cultural forms"; that between "cultural universals" and "cultural relativism"; and that between affirming and denying culture. All three tensions—theological, philosophical, and practical—seem to be artifacts of the deductive approach and of the dualistic philosophy that underlies it.

THE THEOLOGICAL TENSION

Often a tension is seen between the essential gospel and the cultural forms in which actual communication of the gospel is couched; this essential gospel, it is argued, exists somewhere—in the mind of God, but also in some sense in the Bible—in a universal and absolute form. It is both the source of our proclamation and the criterion by which we evaluate the fidelity of our preaching and of the understanding of hearers. But to serve such purposes, it must be somewhere accessible—and there's the rub.

This is the hermeneutical equivalent of Archimedes' search for an immovable fulcrum from which to move the earth. For once it is formulated in words and sentences, it is *ipso facto* conditioned by the questions to which it offers answers, by the terms that are used and the worldview they reflect, and by all the other aspects of the contextual conditioning of exegete, preacher, and hearer.

Insofar as the gospel is *news,* there is no gospel apart from concrete correlative acts of proclamation and response. Both of these acts are performed by human beings within the limits of language and culture. An essential gospel is useless, because as long as it is essential it is by definition unavailable, and as soon as it becomes available it is contextually conditioned.

One ought not to be surprised at this, since it is inherent in incarnation, and hence also in Scripture. It is this which will forever frustrate any hermeneutic, positivistic or not, which seeks an algorithm to guarantee correct understanding. It will also frustrate any mechanistically deductive use of Scripture to discover *the* correct missionary method.

What are the implications of all this for missiology? As regards *goals,* one must work within the tension between the ultimate goal—the kingdom of God—and proximate goals which are derived from the concrete needs and the realistic possibilities of the context. First, then, one diagnoses the context to determine where on the way to the kingdom the various persons and groups within it are. This is a bit like the model proposed by Engel (1974:349-58), but it goes beyond the single dimension of "degrees of receptivity" to a verbal gospel message. Major input comes from the felt needs of hearers—what Loewen and Loewen call "scratching where it itches" (1967a:49-72; see also Dayton and Fraser 1980:164).

Needs are, of course, partly defined in terms of cultural and economic circumstances. But it must be added that this fact is not ethically neutral. It may be that the observed greater receptivity of the poor (in New Testament times and since) stems from a less distorted notion of needs than the affluent usually have. The more one's self-definition of need is warped by affluence away from basic human requirements for survival and well-being, the more it may need to be challenged by the gospel rather than pandered to. In any case, whether the evangelist takes felt needs at face value or questions them, those are the needs addressed, not the needs of humanity in general. But the evangelist also needs to go beyond superficial symptoms to the underlying and fundamental issues. This is what John meant when he said Jesus would place the axe at the root of the tree (Mt 3:10).

Little more needs to be said beyond what has already been said about practical approaches to the task. As much as possible, the evangelist identifies resources, means, and methods appropriate to and available in the context, enlists persons indigenous to the context, and introduces as little as possible that is alien. This is intended as an explicit corrective to the argument of McGavran that, at all of these points, everything else is relative to how it fosters or inhibits church growth (McGavran 1980:373-91, esp. 382-85).

THE PHILOSOPHICAL TENSION

The problems of cultural universals and cultural relativity are here raised, though they should pose no insoluble difficulty. *Universal* properly applies to basic requirements for survival and well-being that relate to permanent biological-psychological-social properties of all human beings. *Relative* applies to the diverse ways cultures opt to meet these requirements in terms of environmental possibilities, social conditions, the specific history of each group, and the ingenuity, imagination, and freedom of its members.

Each culture provides its own unique inventory of food and beverages, mechanisms of defense, rules for legitimate mating and marriage, groups for people to belong to, languages, work, play, intellectual inquiry, art, and religion. Each culture represents a more or less coherent configuration of interrelated options made at each point between a range of possibilities, in light of some overarching vision of what is real, what is true, what is good, and what is right.

As regards the mission of the gospel, this suggests that beneath the apparent diversity between religions—indeed, their many contradictions—there will be found universally a desire to understand and to relate to the Ultimate. Now it is a clear teaching of the Bible that God has revealed himself to humankind in a variety of ways. He has spoken through creation (Ps 19; Rom 1:19ff), through the built-in moral sensitivity of persons (Rom 2), through prophets (Heb 1:1), and finally through his Son (Heb 1:2-4). Different human groups thus have different amounts of light, but none is totally bereft (John 1:9; Acts 14:17).

From the human side, the response is also varied. Calvinism emphasized the negative dimensions of the response, which are very real. But there is also in human beings a craving for the presence of God. So each response is a mixture in varying proportions of yes and no. Each religion as a system and as an institution represents a shifting resultant of the tension between whatever light is available and the strategies by which groups try to balance their positive and negative responses. Furthermore, each devotee of a religion has his or her own configuration of understandings and his or her own mix of yes and no to revelation. One cannot therefore answer *a priori* the question of anyone's ultimate status or destiny; one can only discover it empirically in person-to-person encounter: What does this person know? How has she or he responded to that knowledge? One needs to discover both how close or how far each person is from the Light, and which direction that person is facing and moving (Hiebert 1978:24-29).

It is also true that each religion offers its adherents a more or less elaborate and consistent set of terms, conceptual categories, images, and logical or paralogical strategies for validating and perpetuating itself. It may well be that the gospel will find itself in conflict with much of this; but the question is an empirical one, not one which can be answered *a priori*. And even so, one must understand the religion in depth and make use of as much of it as possible. Biblical examples abound: John's use of *logos,* Paul's use of *mystērion* and *plērōma*. These were terms loaded with philosophical-religious meanings, images, and affect, yet the biblical writers used them boldly.

THE PRACTICAL TENSION

The matter boils down to how and to what extent one affirms existing culture, and how and to what extent one rejects it. Two traps await the unwary: the Scylla of uncritical acceptance of what is, and the Charybdis of rejecting what is on *a priori* criteria. But if one has followed the argument so far, it becomes evident that there is no *a priori*, universal answer. One has missed the point if one poses the question in such terms.

It is simplistic, for example, to make lists of good (cultivating yams), bad (polygyny), and neutral (wearing indigo-dyed cloth) cultural traits. Each trait is a complex phenomenon involving form, function, meaning, and intended and unintended consequences; each is integrated into larger configurations which make up the whole culture, so that it is usually impossible to alter one detail arbitrarily and leave the rest unchanged. Because of the divine image in human beings, most traits express some good values; because of the fall, none is untouched by evil.

Sometimes one applauds the avowed intent of a custom but deplores its real effects. Sometimes a practice is beneficial or innocuous when performed by one person, but destructive when performed by another. One finds oneself perpetually weighing relative goods and evils and seldom making categorical judgments. Among Church Growth writers, Kraft, Tippett, and Hiebert are quite sensitive at this point. However, even they find themselves tripped up at times by the structural-functional model they work with and by the dichotomy of ends and means in Church Growth theory, so that they sometimes accept uncritically cultural patterns that may need to be questioned on biblical grounds.

It seems to me self-evident that this task of evaluating, affirming or rejecting, and ultimately transforming a culture belongs chiefly to people who are full members of the local society. First, because it is their lives and well-being that are at stake, no one should have these placed under the control of outsiders, least of all in the name of the Truth that sets people free. Second, only they have the deep inner understanding which comes from full participation (what Kenneth Pike calls the "emic" view). Certainly, as Loewen and Loewen (1967a:49-72; 1967b:145-60) and Ramseyer (1982) have pointed out, there is an important and even necessary role for a sensitive and respectful outsider, even after the original acceptance of the gospel; but it is to be catalysts rather than primary agents (Taber 1970).

IMPLICATIONS FOR CHURCH GROWTH

What does all of this have to do with Church Growth theory? After all, a number of the issues discussed here are mentioned only briefly if at all in Church Growth literature. But it is precisely my point that, to the extent that Church Growth theory has neglected these issues or taken uncritical or unconscious stances with regard to them, it is the weaker.

The contextual or incarnational model requires Church Growth theory to extend its acceptance of the role of context, which is already considerable (especially in the work of Kraft). The context will define not only cultural givens but also proximate goals, results to be expected (not only in terms of receptivity to the gospel), needs to be met, issues to be addressed, methods and resources to be used, and the like. I therefore propose seven criteria by which one may contextually evaluate church growth and the missiology intended to foster church growth.

DEMOGRAPHIC REALISM

A contextual missiology must take seriously demographic realities. Surprisingly, in a theory which makes so much of the social sciences, Church Growth theory sometimes fails at this basic level. That is, it does not take fully into account the implications of the fact that not all communities are equally available for numerical increase in church membership, quite apart from the receptivity question. Churches in the USA which are held up as paradigms of church growth often turn out to be in places with large numbers of non-Christians, places with rapidly increasing populations, or both. Preponderantly, fast-growing churches are in fast-growing suburbs where increase in church membership is merely keeping up with population increase. Further, a good deal of the increase often consists in the task of conserving people who were already Christians elsewhere, which McGavran calls "transfer growth"; though this is important, it is not growth at all in terms of net additions to the body of Christ. It is of course true that some churches in fast-growing communities fail to grow numerically as they should.

On the other hand, it is cruel and unbiblical to suggest that *any* church, whatever its demographic situation, is failing to do its job if it is not increasing in membership. What about those churches, by no means least vital, which serve communities where the only non-Christians are hardened resisters? What about those which are fulfilling a crucial spiritual role in communities which are demographically stagnant or dying? It may take more courage to stay in such a place than to move to a "successful" situation.

Essentially the same argument holds for any other part of the world.

"AGRICULTURAL" REALISM

If we are to use legitimately the biblical imagery of agriculture which Church Growth theory emphasizes so much, it is necessary to take into account the place of a given group in the entire agricultural cycle. Though McGavran (1980:245ff; see also Wagner 1971:106ff) gives considerable space to this fact, he really majors almost exclusively in the harvest, and by neglect if nothing else seems to suggest that prior stages—clearing ground, plowing, planting, watering, cultivating—are intrinsically less important and need less careful attention. But it is not even self-evident, as McGavran claims, that the harvest always requires the most hands and resources. *In no case* does a harvest happen unless someone has taken care of the preliminary steps.

Church Growth theory has been oversimplified by its fixation on those historical cases—almost exclusively among small, technologically simple, non-literate societies—in which the whole process has seemed to be telescoped into a short period of time. As De Ridder has shown (1979), it is a mistake to compare such situations with that which prevailed in the Gentile world in New Testament times, where the apparently instant success of Paul in Corinth and Ephesus was in fact based on centuries of prior exposure to Judaism. It is noteworthy that in the complex, literate non-Christian societies of the Middle East and Asia, resistance based upon a combination of factors continues massively; the optimism of some about supposed imminent breakthroughs in harvesting seems in many places to be naive.

Clearly we need to harvest when the fields are ready; but not all fields are ready, and we need to do more long-range planning beyond praying and watching from a distance for the miracle of receptivity to happen. There is no reason to suppose that it will happen by itself at all. In the meantime, the work of the kingdom, which is more inclusive than the harvest, must go on.

CULTURAL REALISM

In each context, it seems to be the case that there are specific and characteristic idols—religious, social, political, economic—which are the focus of whatever resistance there is to the irruption into that context of the kingdom of God. It is here that we need, in light of what was said above about affirming or rejecting culture, to be most sensitive to the cultural realities. Here is where, in Tippett's terms (1973a), the "power encounter" must take place if people are to become true disciples of the Lord as well as members of a group called church.

As critics like Yoder (1973) have pointed out, this may be one of the weaker points in Church Growth theory. Too often evangelism designed to maximize professions of faith is tempted to evade or soft-pedal those crucial questions which *must* be faced as people decide who is Lord. Merely stating that Jesus is Lord is meaningless until it is given *concrete* religious *and ethical* content (Mt 7:21-23). Such an approach easily offers cheap grace and leads to a fast-growing group which may not in any biblical sense be the church at all. There is all the difference in the world between demanding instant perfection in converts—which is quite unbiblical—and requiring them to face squarely the choice between their specific and concrete idols and Jesus Christ. It will not do to say, as some do, that Jesus was unrealistic in scaring away potential disciples; if Jesus is not our model, we have no model and in fact no gospel.

This is also a chief weakness in the "homogeneous unit" concept, insofar as it tends to justify creating homogeneous churches in all contexts. It is one thing to have a homogeneous church where other kinds of people are absent or far away; it is a quite different thing to maintain such a church in a heterogeneous community where relations between groups may be *the* community agenda, as in many modern cities. In such a case, the purity of the group easily becomes an idol. Similarly, we in the USA typically avoid mentioning in our evangelism the current American idols of economic growth and consumerism, technological progress, and national security. We thus fail to approximate a contextually appropriate form of discipleship. Christians and congregations are in few important ways different from respectable non-Christians. And the salt has lost its taste.

MISSIONARY REALISM

A sound missiology will recognize that not any and every missionary can work in all contexts, so it will decide contextually what kinds of missionaries ought to carry the gospel to each human group. Such factors as nationality, ethnicity, and social class; experience, education, and other preparation; personality; professional role; and lifestyle on the field are all matters to be so determined. All of these will affect credibility if not the actual intelligibility of the gospel. Dayton and Fraser, for instance (1980:403-06), cite the problem of the dissonance in India between the Western idea of a doctor and the Indian idea of a healer.

Fairly voluminous literature, notably in the journal *Practical Anthropology*,[4] deals with aspects of this question. It is not an accident that the discontents and resentments which gave rise a few years ago to the call for moratorium (Nacpil 1971:356-62) were sparked in part by failures of missionaries at this point. It is significant that the call for moratorium and the call for contextualization coincided in time. This is an area where Church Growth theory—especially in the work of Kraft—has gone a good way but needs to go further.

COMMUNICATIONAL REALISM

A contextual missiology will discern and make full use of locally normal patterns of communication and decision making, in keeping with New Testament practice (Acts 10). This is a strong point in the Church Growth model, though others have contributed to it (Rice 1969:264-73).

4. Among relevant articles are the following: Loewen (1964a:145-60; 1964b:193-203), Reyburn (1962:1-8), Nida (1955:90-95), Bare and Reyburn (1963:89-90), and Smalley (1957:101-04).

METHODOLOGICAL REALISM

Contextual missiology will make the greatest possible use of all local resources—material, personal, conceptual, cultural, organizational, technical—and the least possible use of alien resources. It will not permit any permanently essential feature of the emerging church and its life and work to depend on outside personnel, technical expertise, finances, *or ideas*. This has obvious similarities with the old "three-self" formula of indigenous missiology, but it goes much further.

When a mission, for instance, teaches explicitly or implicitly that leadership is achieved by a process of education (whether residential or by extension) and then controls the shape of that education, it is creating a dependent church. Nothing ought to be introduced that would impair the church by being withdrawn. This will be hard to put into practice, so deeply are we Westerners committed to the idea that we know what the job is and how to do it (Taber 1978b).

One problematic area which is just beginning to be highlighted by persons from the Third World (Samuel and Sugden 1981) is that of missionary organizations as such. It is becoming evident that agencies structured like business corporations bring about, intentionally or not, many of the same undesirable effects as the business concerns: There is a similar emphasis on "distribution and promotion of the [uniform] product"; similar tendency to bypass local agencies (the national church) which are in the same "business"; and above all similar control over the process. There may be something at least potentially demonic about operating in this way that may forbid its being justified even in terms of real pragmatic advantages.

This does not mean that any and all methodological concepts that arise from the context are *ipso facto* sanctified. It is necessary rather to work out appropriate methods in the interplay between existing resources and gospel imperatives. Dayton and Fraser have useful ideas here (1980:350-68).

ORGANIC REALISM

All that we have been saying leads up to this: A contextual missiology will strongly foster in the emerging church an internally motivated drive to discover *for itself,* from its own examination of the Scriptures and its own context, what its proximate goals are, what are the needs and possibilities of the context that define its concrete task, what resources it has, and how best it ought to proceed. A contextual missiology will result in a church—large or small, growing or stable in membership—that faithfully understands its relationship to its own context, its nature as the church, its own forms of worship, and its own expressions of Christian discipleship.

In the terms of Costas (1974:89-90), it will be a church able to grow numerically (within its demographic possibilities), organically, conceptually, and incarnationally. Whatever else happens, if this does not, mission has failed. If it does, whatever else does not happen, mission has succeeded, inasmuch as a church is present which faithfully incarnates the gospel in that context, and which is therefore in the most strategic position to press that context toward the kingdom of God.

REFERENCES CITED

ALLEN, Roland
  1930   *Missionary Methods: St. Paul's or Ours?* London: World Dominion Press.

BARE, Garland and REYBURN, William D.
  1963   "Motives in Missionary Identification," *Practical Anthropology,* Vol. 10 (March-April).

BARTCHY, S. Scott
  1979   "Table Fellowship with Jesus and the 'Lord's Supper' at Corinth," *Increase in Learning: Essays in Honor of James G. Van Buren,* R. J. Owens, Jr., and B. E. Hamm (eds.), Manhattan, Kansas: Manhattan Christian College.

COE, Shoki
  1973   "In Search of Renewal in Theological Education," *Theological Education,* Vol. 9 (Summer).

CONN, Harvie M.
  1977   "Contextualization: Where Do We Begin?" *Evangelism and Liberation,* Carl Armerding (ed.), Nutley, New Jersey: Presbyterian and Reformed.

COSTAS, Orlando E.
  1974   *The Church and Its Mission,* Wheaton: Tyndale.

DAYTON, Edward R. and FRASER, David A.
  1980   *Planning Strategies for World Evangelization,* Grand Rapids: Eerdmans.

DE RIDDER, Richard R.
  1979   *Discipling the Nations,* Grand Rapids: Baker Book House.

DONOVAN, Vincent J.
  1982   *Christianity Rediscovered: An Epistle from the Masai* (second ed.), Maryknoll: Orbis.

ENGEL, James F., KORNFIELD, William J., and OLIVER, Victor L.
  1974   "What's Gone Wrong with Our Harvesting?" *Missiology,* Vol. 2 (July).

HIEBERT, Paul G.
  1978   "Conversion, Culture and Cognitive Categories," *Gospel in Context,* Vol. 1 (October).

HOEKSTRA, Harvey T.
  1979   *The World of Council of Churches and the Demise of Evangelism,* Wheaton: Tyndale.

INTERNATIONAL CONGRESS ON WORLD EVANGELIZATION (ICWE)
  1974   "The Lausanne Covenant."

KHIN Maung Din
  1976   "How to Feed His Lambs," *International Review of Mission,* Vol. 65 (April).

KRAFT, Charles H.
  1979   *Christianity in Culture.* Maryknoll: Orbis.

KRAFT, Charles H. and WISLEY, Tom, eds.
  1979   *Readings in Dynamic Indigeneity,* Pasadena: William Carey Library.

LOEWEN, Jacob A.
  1964a   "Reciprocity in Identification," *Practical Anthropology,* Vol. 11 (July-August).
  1964b   "Sponsorship: The Difference Between Good News and Propaganda," *Practical Anthropology,* Vol. 11 (September-October).

LOEWEN, Jacob A. and LOEWEN, Anne
1967a "Religion, Drives and the Place Where It Itches," *Practical Anthropology,* Vol. 14 (March-April).
1967b "Role, Self-Image and Missionary Communication," *Practical Anthropology,* Vol. 14 (July-August).

McGAVRAN, Donald A.
1955 *The Bridges of God,* New York: Friendship Press.
1980 *Understanding Church Growth* (rev. ed.), Grand Rapids: Eerdmans.

NACPIL, Emerito P.
1971 "Mission But Not Missionaries," *International Review of Mission,* Vol. 60 (July).

NIDA, Eugene A.
1955 "Identification, a Major Problem in Modern Missions," *Practical Anthropology,* Vol. 2 (July-August).

NYAMITI, Charles
1973 *The Scope of African Theology,* Kampala: GABA.

RAMSEYER, Robert L.
1982 "Ethical Decision-Making and the Missionary Role," *International Bulletin of Missionary Research,* Vol. 6.

REYBURN, William D.
1962 "Identification—Symptom or Sublimation?" *Practical Anthropology,* Vol. 9 (January-February).

RICE, Delbert
1969 "Evangelism and Decision-Making Processes," *Practical Anthropology,* Vol. 16 (November).

SAMUEL, Vinay K. and SUGDEN, Chris
1981 "Christian Mission in the Eighties—A Third World Perspective." Bangalore: Partnership in Mission—Asia.

SMALLEY, William A.
1957 "Proximity or Neighborliness?" *Practical Anthropology,* Vol. 4 (May-June).

TABER, Charles R.
1970 "The Missionary: Wrecker, Builder or Catalyst?" *Practical Anthropology,* Vol. 17 (July-August).
1978a "The Limits of Indigenization in Theology," *Missiology,* Vol. 6 (January).
1978b "Structures and Strategies for Interdependence in World Mission," *Mission-Focus,* Vol. 4, No. 6. Reprinted in *Mission Focus: Current Issues,* Wilbert R. Shenk (ed.), Scottdale: Herald Press.

THEOLOGICAL EDUCATION FUND (TEF)
1972 *Ministry in Context,* Bromley, U. K.: New Life Press.

TIPPETT, Alan R.
1970 *Church Growth and the Word of God,* Grand Rapids: Eerdmans.
1973a *Verdict Theology and the Word of God* (second ed.), Pasadena: William Carey Library.
1973b (ed.), *God, Man, and Church Growth,* Grand Rapids: Eerdmans.

VON ALLMEN, Daniel
1975 "The Birth of Theology," *International Review of Mission,* Vol. 64 (January).

WAGNER, C. Peter
1971 *Frontiers of Missionary Strategy,* Chicago: Moody.

WINTER, Ralph D.

1969 "The Anatomy of the Christian Mission," *Evangelical Missions Quarterly,* Vol. 5 (Winter).

1974 "The Two Structures of God's Redemptive Mission," *Missiology,* Vol. 2 (January).

YODER, John H.

1973 "Church Growth Issues in Theological Perspective," *The Challenge of Church Growth,* Wilbert R. Shenk (ed.), Scottdale: Herald Press.

11. THE CASE OF SOUTH AFRICA: PRACTICE, CONTEXT, AND IDEOLOGY

W. A. Saayman

ANY MENTION OF THE NAME SOUTH AFRICA PROBABLY CONJURES UP IN THE minds of many people a picture of racism at its worst, embodied in the system of apartheid. In church circles specifically this political system is often linked to the white Afrikaans-speaking churches[1] which, so it is believed, provide the theological justification for this abhorrent system. Whereas in the rest of the world church, racism and institutionalized separation along racial lines stand discredited, here we have the unique situation that these churches actually preach and practice a policy of racially separated churches.

A church has to be firmly convinced of the rightness of its policy and the soundness of its theology to defy the prevailing opinion in the rest of the church to such an extent. An investigation into the development of this policy and its theological underpinnings can therefore be of great importance in the debate on the advisability of any kind of (ethnic or cultural) group approach in mission.

DUTCH REFORMED CHURCH MISSIONARY PRINCIPLES: DEVELOPMENT IN CONTEXT

ROOTS IN GENERAL MISSIONARY POLICY AND PRINCIPLES
One might assume as self-evident that such a unique state of affairs must stem from a particular missionary policy or theology. This is not the case, however. Various eminent South African missionary theologians have studied the development of missionary policy and principles in the Dutch Reformed Church

---

1. There are three Afrikaans Reformed churches of Dutch origin in South Africa: the *Nederduitse Gereformeerde Kerk* (Dutch Reformed Church/DRC), the *Gereformeerde Kerk,* and the *Nederduitsch Hervormde Kerk.* This article deals only with the oldest and largest of these three churches, the DRC. This does not imply that the DRC is the only church following a policy of racially separated churches; all three of the above-mentioned churches follow such a policy (with some variations). The Lutheran Church in South Africa also followed a policy of separate mission churches, while racial separation occurred in practice also in some English-speaking churches (Anglican, Methodist, Presbyterian, and others), although it was never official policy in these churches.

W. A. Saayman, Pretoria, Republic of South Africa, has been Senior Lecturer in Missiology at the University of South Africa since 1978. He has served as a missionary teacher in Zambia from 1966 to 1968 and missionary and lecturer in theology in Namibia from 1974 to 1977. His doctoral thesis at the University of Stellenbosch was Unity and Mission *(1980).*

(which was the only officially recognized church in the early years of the Cape Colony). It is their unanimous conclusion that the missionary principles which guided the early missionary endeavors in the Cape Colony incorporated the main trends in contemporary European and North American missionary theology (de Klerk 1923; du Toit 1967; Gerdener 1911; van der Merwe 1936 and 1967). In the early years (approximately the middle of the seventeenth century), when the DRC was the only church at the Cape, the missionary attitudes of early Protestantism, especially as reflected in the thinking of the Reformed Church in the Netherlands at the time, can be clearly detected (van der Merwe 1936:28-29). The influence of Voetius' formulation of the goal of mission in terms of conversion of the Gentiles, the planting of the church, and the extension of the glory of God, is particularly apparent (Dutch Reformed Church 1950:8).

The growing influence of Pietism on missions also made itself felt in the Cape Colony, especially from the beginning of the eighteenth century. The policy, according to which the DRC was the only church recognized and allowed in the Colony, had by then been relaxed, so that the first Moravian missionary was allowed into the Colony from Germany in 1737. He was followed some time later by missionaries from other European missionary societies. These societies all reflected (to a greater or lesser extent) the strong influence of Pietism on missions. Toward the end of the eighteenth century the Pietistic emphasis gained support from another quarter.

Two young DRC ministers of that time, Van Lier and Vos, while studying in the Netherlands, had both been strongly influenced by the Second Reformation, the Dutch parallel to German and English Pietism, and both were enthusiastic supporters of mission work. It can be said that Pietism, particularly during its early years, did not really have any ecclesiology. The Pietistic influence of the Cape Colony therefore did not *initially* affect to a significant extent the condoned practice of accepting black converts as members of the existing DRC, though it did contribute to the growth of greater missionary enthusiasm with its strong emphasis on the "saving of souls for the Lamb."

Another major trend in nineteenth-century European and North American missionary thinking, concerning the emphasis on the autonomy of younger churches, also left its mark clearly on DRC missionary principles. Thinking on this subject developed along two distinct lines: the Anglo-American and the German. The former found expression especially in the "Three Selfs" theory (self-government, self-support, self-extension) of Venn and Anderson; the latter in the concept of autonomous indigenous churches (*Volkskirchen*). This concept, with its basic concern for the "christianizing of the people," was first proposed by Graul, but developed more fully in the work of the great German missiologist, Gustav Warneck. Warneck attempted to combine the traditional Pietistic aim of mission (the conversion of individuals) with that of Graul (that is, the christianizing of peoples). Later German missiologists (Keysser, Gutmann) emphasized the latter aim to such an extent that it practically eliminated the former. Although the Anglo-American and German emphases can be distinguished in DRC missionary principles, it was Warneck's synthesis particularly which made an indelible impression. This was especially evident in the first three decades of the twentieth century (du Plessis 1932; van der Merwe 1967:51-53; du Toit 1967:268).

The influence of these various, and sometimes successive, schools of thought can be distinguished particularly clearly in the "Mission policy of the Federated Dutch Reformed Churches of South Africa" adopted in 1935. This policy stated: All mission work should be based on the Great Commission. The preaching of the gospel, with a view to "ingathering of souls for the Kingdom of God," should be the first priority. A second priority should be the upbuilding of indigenous churches, which should be self-governing, self-extending, and self-supporting, and which should "not deprive the Native of his language and culture, but must eventually permeate and purify his entire nationalism"—in other words, peoples' churches (quoted in Gerdener 1958:269-75).

It seems quite clear that the DRC missionary principles grew out of and reflected general contemporary Western missionary thinking and practice. It was therefore not a unique set of principles which gave rise to this particular (and peculiar) state of affairs in South African church life. Yet racially separated churches *did* come into being as a product of DRC mission work. It seems necessary, therefore, to examine further the historical circumstances and context surrounding the founding of the first separate church in order to determine what gave rise to this distinctive missionary policy.

FOUNDING OF THE FIRST SEPARATE DUTCH REFORMED MISSION CHURCH

The earliest "objects" of DRC missions were the slaves (mainly imported) and Hottentots (indigenous inhabitants of the southwestern Cape and ancestors of the "Coloreds" or people of mixed descent). Soon after the establishment of the Dutch settlement at the Cape, this work bore fruit, and slaves and Hottentots were baptized. The question of church membership of these converts did not cause any problems at the time. In line with the general policy followed by the Netherlands Reformed Church in Dutch colonies, the converts simply became members of the DRC (which was, of course, overwhelmingly white at that stage). This state of affairs was maintained for more than two centuries after the founding of the colony, and it was the recognized policy when mission work was later also started among Africans.

As stated above, the first representative of a European missionary society (the Moravians) arrived in the Cape Colony in 1737, to be followed some decades later by representatives of other European societies (including the London Missionary Society, Wesleyan Missionary Society, Rhenish Missionary Society, and others). At that stage the DRC was still the officially recognized state church, and one of the early conditions on which missionary societies were allowed to enter the colony was that they would not work within the boundaries of existing DRC congregations.

The missionary societies, as a result of this agreement but also in accordance with their own aims, therefore directed their efforts at blacks (Coloreds and Africans) and also introduced the use of separate places of worship for blacks. The DRC churches, on the other hand, were generally open to white and black alike. Even though the missionary societies were compelled to use separate places of worship, they were nonetheless not allowed to form separate congregations initially; converts had to become members of the state church, the DRC. The official DRC policy of *one* church for both black and white Christians was thus maintained, but a new custom of separate places of worship for black and white was also established, and it gained momentum through the work of the missionary societies.

By the beginning of the nineteenth century, the first signs of possible change in the official policy can be detected. At the first Synod of the DRC in 1824[2] a decision was made to ordain ministers specifically for mission work. These ordained missionaries would not be allowed to minister in existing (at that stage predominantly white) congregations. Although the way was thus opened for separate ministry to blacks, the policy of membership remained unchanged; black converts would therefore still become members of the one DRC. During that period the first signs of growing resistance among white members to blacks in the church were also revealed through the question, brought before the Presbytery of Cape Town in 1928, as to whether communion should be administered simultaneously to black and white members of the congregation. The presbytery decided "that it is compulsory, according to the teachings of Scripture and the spirit of Christianity, to admit such persons simultaneously with born Christians [that is, whites] to the communion table" (van der Merwe 1936:149). This decision of the presbytery was affirmed by the DRC Synod of 1834 as "an unalterable axiom founded on the infallible Word of God." All congregations and each individual Christian were therefore urged "to think and act in accordance with it" (van der Merwe 1936:149).

The clear statement of scriptual principle by both the presbytery and the synod could not, however, allay the growing problem of race relations within the DRC. The Synod of 1857 therefore had to deal again with essentially the same question: Should communion be administered simultaneously to white and black members of the church? As the decision of this synod was later to prove decisive for the development of the DRC missionary policy of separate churches, it is quoted in full.

> Synod regards it as desirable and in accordance with Scripture that converted heathen members [blacks] should be incorporated into existing congregations [predominantly white congregations] wherever it is possible; but where, as a result of the weakness of some, this should be an obstacle to the progress of the Kingdom of Christ among the heathen, the existing heathen congregations, or those heathen congregations still to be established, should exercise their Christian privileges in a separate place of worship (Saayman 1979:108-09).

The following important elements in relation to our investigation into the development of the DRC missionary policy of separate churches should be pointed out.

1. No DRC synod, up to and including that of 1857, could be convinced of any scriptural justification for a policy of racially separated churches. On the contrary, the basic scriptural nature of integrated church membership was established and reconfirmed in clear terms.

2. The concession that black and white members could worship sepa-

---

2. Before this time, the DRC was affiliated to the Netherlands Reformed Church, functioning as part of the classis of Amsterdam. When the British annexed the Cape Colony in 1806 this tie was severed, and after some hesitation the congregations at the Cape organized themselves into an autonomous synod.

rately, owing to "the weakness of some" (which clearly referred to racial prejudice among white church members), was therefore granted on purely *pragmatic* grounds (so that it should not be "an obstacle to the progress of the Kingdom of Christ among the heathen").

3. The decision dealt mainly with the question of separate places of worship, especially for Holy Communion. To regard the decision of 1857 as the potential foundation for a policy of separate churches would be a serious violation of the historical context. (This view is supported by the fact that "during the debate on the decision various speakers stated clearly that this *prejudice among whites had to be combatted,* albeit in a circumspect manner" (Saayman 1979:109).)

In spite of the above comments on the decision of 1857, this decision *did* lead eventually to the founding of the first separate DRC mission church. The Synod of 1880 decided to constitute the *Nederduitse Gereformeerde Sendingkerk* (Dutch Reformed Mission Church) for the black (at that stage mainly Colored) converts who constituted the fruit of its mission work. This church was officially founded in 1881 when four Colored congregations gathered for the first synod. It is important to note that between 1857 and 1881 no synod reconsidered the scriptural principles pertaining to racially separated churches; only practical matters regarding church polity, finance, and the like appeared on the agenda. "In spite, therefore, of the clear and consistent statement of the Scriptural principle to the contrary, the Dutch Reformed Church quietly pursued a course which led ultimately to racially segregated churches" (Saayman 1979:109).

Why? The first half of the nineteenth century was a time of increasing contact and conflict between black and white in the Cape Colony. The move into the interior of an increasing number of white settlers led to a collision course with the simultaneous move southward of a number of black tribes. This led to increasing friction and conflict, erupting in a series of border wars in the Eastern Cape. This caused a serious deterioration of relations between black and white, which was especially noticeable in the development of an entirely negative attitude toward miscegenation during this period (du Preez 1959:189). In this regard particularly an important factor, which was unique to the South African "mission field," has to be borne in mind: In Cape Colony at that time the sending church existed right in the midst of its "mission field." It did not consist simply of a few devoted European missionaries who had been sent to a foreign country far away. Large numbers of European settlers arrived at the Cape, so that a situation developed in which a transplanted older European church came into existence right in its own "mission field." The deteriorating relations between whites and blacks therefore had an immediate and extremely decisive effect on the missionary policy and practice of the DRC.

The idea of a separate missionary ministry, perhaps even separate congregations, introduced to the Cape Colony mainly by the mission societies and strengthened by the fact that these mission societies were not allowed to operate within the boundaries of white congregations, must have seemed an attractive possibility for coping with deteriorating race relations and their detrimental effect on the church's own mission work.

As a result mainly of the sociopolitical situation (Saayman 1979:109) and for purely *practical* considerations, the DRC therefore ignored its own insistence on an integrated church as the goal of its mission work and opted instead for the pragmatic missionary policy of racially separated churches.

SEPARATION AS PRINCIPLE

The policy of separate churches in the Dutch Reformed Church no longer operates simply as a matter of practical missionary policy (as I will point out). From about 1930 onward, this policy has been interpreted increasingly as a matter of theological principle, a principle which has, moreover, come to have important consequences also in the South African political arena.

MISSIONARY POLICY INTERPRETED AS A
THEOLOGICAL/IDEOLOGICAL PRINCIPLE

A general characteristic of the modern Protestant missionary movement was that missionary practice preceded theological reflection on mission. This was the case in a number of mission societies and churches from various confessional traditions. The great danger accompanying such a state of affairs is that the results achieved may come to be accepted unquestioningly as being normative for all future missionary practice (Cronjé 1962:58). The development of the Dutch Reformed Church practice of separate churches on the "mission field" into a theological principle for all mission work seems to have fallen prey precisely to this danger.

Van der Merwe detected the first signs of this shift in emphasis (from practical missionary policy to a fundamental missiological principle) in about the 1930s. At that time

> thoughtful mission students within the DRC . . . tried to relate race relations to evangelism. The old Boer desire for racial purity and maintenance of European civilization was defended by such students. A differentiated cultural development on a religious basis made possible through territorial and political segregation was advocated. In the next few decades this theory was to be worked out more fully and become more popular within the DRC (Van der Merwe 1936:197-98).

The signs of the development of a theory of segregation, with its accompanying theological substructure, were quite obvious in the official missionary policy of the DRC adopted in 1935 (quoted in full in Gerdener 1958:269-75).

The development of racially separated DRC churches was explained as follows:

> Starting from the unity of the Church of Christ as circumscribed above [in this policy], and taking the specific racial situation in South Africa into careful consideration, the Dutch Reformed Church maintains the following standpoint as its policy: (a) That the founding and development of independent indigenous churches for the purpose of evangelizing the native races of South Africa was both necessary and *in accordance with our understanding of the nature of the Church of the Lord Jesus* on earth, and has been richly blessed in the many years that have passed. (b) That since, under the pressure of circumstances, the historical development in the missionary sphere throughout the centuries showed tendencies of unchristian exclusiveness, thus impeding the realization of the true Chris-

tian fellowship between believers, this happened, not through ill-will towards the non-whites, nor with the approval of the official leadership of the Church, but must be seen as the result of uncontrollable circumstances and of general human weakness. (c) That in each congregation both the mother- and the indigenous daughter-churches *reserve the right to regulate their membership* according to the realistic demand of circumstances, and in accordance with the spirit of Christ; but at the same time it is also the Christian duty of the above-mentioned churches to educate their members for and in the practice of a healthy Christian communion of believers, *provided the motives for this are good* and provided the methods used do not give offence (Gerdener 1958:274-75. Italics mine).

When compared to the decisions of 1829, 1834, and 1857, several interesting tendencies indicative of a shift from practice to theological principle are revealed in this policy: There is an acknowledgment in (b) of the "tendencies towards unchristian exclusiveness" in the development of the policy of separate churches. However, whereas the Synod of 1857 saw these tendencies as (white) prejudice which had to be combatted, the missionary policy of 1935 found no ill-will among whites in this development. Additionally, the decisions of 1829, 1834, *and* 1857 stated that according to their understanding of Scripture and the spirit of Christ, the nature of the church should be such that both blacks and whites should be members of the same church. The missionary policy of 1935, however, states that racially separated churches are "in accordance with . . . the nature of the Church." And, whereas even after the decision of 1857 it was still possible for blacks to become members of white DRC congregations, the mother church now reserved the right to regulate its membership (meaning in practice that blacks would no longer be allowed to become members).[3] Furthermore, faith in Christ is no longer sufficient as a basis for admittance to the "communion of believers" (at worship). Good motives have first to be established. The whole trend of the arguments in this policy, and particularly the description of the nature of the church in (a), indicates that racial separation is no longer seen simply as practical missionary policy; the tendency toward exclusiveness is strengthened and a theological justification for this is beginning to be developed.

At the 1949 Synod of the DRC in the Cape Province the policy of racially separated churches, and especially the growing opposition to this policy, was discussed. The Synod then concluded, "We are convinced that we ourselves, and our fathers, practised this policy with a clear conscience before God, in a peaceful way, in mutual agreement and also for practical reasons, in the conviction that we do not act contrary to the Spirit of Christ and Holy Scripture." The argument continued: Because of the "blessed fruits" of this policy since 1857, there could be no other conclusion than that this policy had been formulated under the inspiration of the Holy Spirit and had served the best interests of the church in South Africa (Vorster 1978:44. My translation).

In the process of changing practical missionary policy into missiological (theological) principle, and the need for theological justification for this prin-

3. This indeed proved to be the case; it is impossible for any black Christian to become a member of a white congregation of the DRC. The younger Dutch Reformed churches (those for black converts) never adopted this policy of closed membership, so that there are some white members in all of these churches.

ciple, some interesting differences can be pointed out between the decisions of 1857 and those of 1949. Whereas in 1857 the *unity* of white and black in one church was seen as an "unalterable axiom founded on the Word of God" and separation between white and black Christians was regarded as being *contrary* to the spirit of Christ, in 1949 the *separation* between white and black churches was regarded as being in accordance with Scripture and the Spirit of Christ. The Synod of 1949 was not concerned with a *new* study of the whole problem of separate churches; in that case they might, of course, have come to different conclusions. However, the Synod of 1949 was attempting to interpret the decision of 1857 and the subsequent development. In this context the obvious differences in theological motivation assume great importance.

At the Synod of 1857 no special inspiration by the Holy Spirit was claimed in the formulation of this policy (as was done in 1949), perhaps because the 1857 Synod was not at all convinced that separation would be in the best interests of the church. It is also important to point out that this claim to the inspiration of the Holy Spirit was based on the fact that the policy of separate churches had produced "blessed fruits," meaning that the separate churches had stimulated growth. The possible danger, namely, that the achievement of results determines theological interpretation, seems to have been realized in this case.

In 1950 the Federal Missions Council of the DRC convened a congress of representatives from all DRC synods to discuss "The Native Question." Among the findings of this congress was the following: "There exists an inevitable link between one's own residential area, one's own language, national characteristics (*volksaard*) and tradition on the one hand, and a sense of vocation or religious destiny on the other. . . . We are also children of the Covenant and possess our own confession of faith, and these things are implicated (or prejudiced) if our cultural heritage or racial purity is threatened" (DRC 1950:13. My translation). It is difficult to escape the conclusion that the 1950 congress made matters such as salvation, confession of faith, and even the Covenant, subordinate to racial separation.

It seems fair to conclude, then, that the reluctant concession of 1857, owing to "the weakness of some," had now become (by means of several attempts to justify separation theologically) an (ideological) scriptural imperative for apartheid. This happened in spite of the fact that the 1950 congress admitted that the Synod of 1857 did not provide any fundamental support for separation, and justified its decision on purely pragmatic grounds. Yet the 1950 congress proceeded to do exactly what the Synod of 1857 did *not* want to do. It attempted to find fundamental theological justification for the principle of separation (DRC 1950:15-16).

The various attempts to construct a theological substructure for the policy of separate churches may be said to have culminated eventually in the so-called *Landman Report* of the General Synod of the DRC in 1974.[4] The report contains extensive commentary on the policy of separate churches, but the basic principle of the policy is stated thus: "The existence of separate Dutch Reformed Church affiliations for the various population [read: racial] groups is recognized as being

4. This report, with official commentary, was later published under the title *Human relations and the South African scene in the light of Scripture,* Cape Town, 1976.

in accordance with the plurality of church affiliations described in the Bible. These enable each individual to hear and preach the great deeds of God in the context of his own language, culture and national affiliation" (DRC 1976:82).

In the closing words especially of this decision we encounter a factor which has played an important role in the process in which practical policy has been reinterpreted in order to transform it into theological principle—a factor which has not yet been touched in this account. This is the factor of language, specifically language as representative of various national cultures. The language miracle at Pentecost, which enabled various groups of people present in Jerusalem on that day to hear the great deeds of God proclaimed in their respective languages (Acts 2:5-11), plays an especially important role in this understanding. In DRC thinking on the policy of separate churches, this event is not regarded as having only kerygmatic implications. The language miracle of Pentecost is rather regarded as an affirmation that the confusion of languages at Babel, and subsequent development of various peoples (volke), was a conscious act of God's providence, even of his grace (DRC 1976:14-19, 86-87; du Preez 1959:59, 103).

Language and culture are therefore loaded with theological significance, as is well illustrated in the following words of du Preez (at that time Professor of Systematic Theology at one of the two DRC Theological Faculties): "It is of little value to demonstrate church unity [between various Dutch Reformed churches] by artificial means such as multiracial worship services or joint communion services; some will always remain strangers at such events because they cannot really feel linguistically or culturally at home at such joint worship services" (du Preez 1959:108. My translation). Differences in language and culture are valued so highly here that koinonia, even of believers within one confessional tradition, becomes impossible because of them. "The weakness of some" white Christians of 1857, which had to be overcome, has thus become an ideological/theological principle which functions as a prerequisite for worship and communion services.

When viewed in conjunction with the fact that the 1974 Synod regarded separation according to population groups (races) as being in accordance with Scripture (in direct contrast to the 1857 Synod), the conclusion seems self-evident: What was conceived simply as a matter of practical and temporary missionary policy in order to facilitate evangelization has slowly but surely been reinterpreted and furnished with a theological substructure, to become a rigid theological principle with definite ideological overtones.

This reinterpretation is carried to its utmost limit—and the ideological overtones reveal themselves most clearly—in the following statement of Kriel (at that time professor in theology at the seminary for Colored DRC ministers): "Sporadic and unplanned missionary work grew on an unfamiliar terrain among various population groups, out of which eventually, after several centuries, a people (volk) was born, and among whom an indigenous Mission Church was established. I refer to the Coloured population, born on South African soil, and to the Dutch Reformed Mission Church in South Africa, which was founded among this new nation born here" (Kriel 1963:1. My translation). Here the principle of separation so that "each can hear in his own language" is carried so far that a new "nation" or "people" even had to be created so that they could have their own (separate) church!

THE POLICY OF RACIALLY SEPARATED CHURCHES AND THE POLICY OF APARTHEID OR SEPARATE DEVELOPMENT

As has been stated, the Dutch Reformed Church policy of separate churches has also had a significant influence in the political arena in South Africa. A note of warning must be sounded here, though: The relationship between the policy of separate churches (which was formulated first) and the policy of apartheid or separate development is not to be seen in simplistic terms. The DRC did not simply set out to evangelize South Africa according to its peculiar missionary policy of racially separated churches, thereby providing the impetus and undergirding for the specifically South African political system of institutionalized racism.

I have already pointed out that the DRC missionary policy was initially not so peculiar or particular, but that it developed its peculiarity over a period of two centuries in the South African context. The relationship between the missionary policy of separate churches and the political system of separate development has rather been one of reciprocal interaction. The initial relationship between the DRC and the state (originally represented by the Dutch East India Company) in the Cape Colony was the typical church/state relationship of seventeenth-century Protestantism. It was expected that the state would be intimately involved in the evangelization of its colonies (for whatever motive), and church and state therefore stood in close and contractual relationship. The result was that the state—and the ordering of its political life—at times dominated the church, but that the church was also at times able to exert a strong influence on the direction of sociopolitical affairs.

It has been pointed out above that the DRC, during its first two centuries of existence at the Cape, could not be convinced that racial separation in the church was either desirable or scriptural. In this point of view the DRC was strongly supported by government leaders. At the same time, however, sociopolitical relationships between black and white people grew more and more problematic, erupting eventually in a series of black/white border wars. This deterioration of sociopolitical relationships eventually contributed to a great extent to the reluctant concession of the DRC to racial separation. Once the policy of separate churches became institutionalized, though, that in turn provided momentum for the movement toward institutionalized separation in the political realm as well.

This tangled network of reciprocal interaction is illustrated clearly in the findings of the Bloemfontein congress of 1950. (The congress followed just two years after the victory of the National Party in the general elections of 1948; the National Party fought these elections specifically on the platform of apartheid.) On the one hand, the congress recommended an investigation to determine "on what grounds the policy of apartheid in the social, economic, and political realms can also be applied in the ecclesiastical/religious realm" (DRC 1950:8. My translation).

Somewhat later, on the other hand, the congress stated, "It should be remembered that it was the Afrikaans churches which laid the foundation for the policy of separate development. It is the Afrikaans churches which accepted the principle that there should be apartheid between their white and non-white members. It is mainly due to the influence of the Afrikaans churches that the policy of apartheid between white and non-white in schools has been accepted" (DRC 1950:123. My translation).

The cyclical process of reciprocal interaction is illustrated in these quotations: Missionary policy, which was similar to contemporary missionary policy in the rest of the world, developed in the sociopolitical context of South Africa into an ideological/theological principle of racial separation, which in turn provided the religious substructure for the political superstructure of apartheid (and also helped create the desire for it).

The reciprocal interaction between church/missionary policy and political policy has been largely responsible for the ideological importance attached to the necessity for the survival of white Afrikanerdom in South Africa. It is generally assumed by many whites that their survival (and more specifically, that of white Afrikaners) can be guaranteed only by means of the policy of apartheid or separate development. This survival is considered essential for the survival of Christian civilization in South Africa, and the policy can (and must) therefore be justified on Christian moral grounds (DRC 1950:123). This kind of thinking was articulated well by du Preez: "As surely as the Afrikaner people (*volk*) has a calling to fulfil in this land, as surely as Christians are called to establish Christianity over against barbarism . . . so surely the demand remains for the Afrikaner to maintain himself, not for the sake of himself only, but because he is obliged bravely to defend his God-given calling" (du Preez 1959:141). (The fact that more than seventy percent of the Christians in South Africa are black either does not register with people who reason this way, or else they interpret "the calling of the Afrikaner" as being so important that without it Christianity in South Africa will collapse.)

When this reciprocal interaction between church/missionary policy and political policy is kept in mind, especially the ideological overtones involved in this interaction, it is hardly possible to believe that this all grew out of a seemingly innocuous practical decision taken by the DRC in 1857 in order to facilitate the evangelization of South Africa.

CONCLUSION

It is agreed in many missionary circles that cross-cultural evangelization should be *the* priority for Christians at present in the face of the pressing need for the evangelization of the world. One way in which this cross-cultural evangelization can be facilitated is by using the "people group" approach in which the importance of cultural homogeneity in group evangelization is rated highly. Without in any way implying similarity between this approach and the DRC policy of separate churches, it would seem that people involved in designing and developing such an approach could benefit greatly from studying the history of the DRC missions in South Africa. This would be especially valuable in the area of creating an awareness of the dangers which are inherent in adopting an approach aimed specifically at a certain group, and excluding others, although at the time they may seem nothing more than a practical aid in facilitating evangelism.

The history of the DRC in South Africa illustrates that "the weakness of some" may become "the ideological blinding of many," to the ultimate detriment of the kingdom of God.

REFERENCES CITED

CRONJÉ, J. M.
1962   *Die selfstandigwording van die Bantoekerk*, Bloemfontein: N. G. Spendingpers.

DE KLERK, P. J. S.
1923   *Kerk en sending in Suid-Afrika*, Amsterdam: Van Bottenburg.

DU PLESSIS, J.
1932   *Wie sal gaan? Die sending in teorie en praktyk*, Cape Town: Bible Union.

DU PREEZ, A. B.
1959   *Eiesoortige ontwikkeling tot volksdiens*, Die hoop van Suid-Africa, Pretoria: HAUM.

DUTCH REFORMED CHURCH—DRC
1950   *Die Naturellevraasgstuk. Referate gelewer op die kerklike kongres van die Gefedereerde Ned. Geref. Kerke in Suid-Afrika, byeengeroep deur die Federale Sendingraad, Bloemfontein, April 1950*, Bloemfontein: N. G. Sendingpers.
1976   *Human relations and the South African scene in the light of Scripture*, Cape Town: N. G. Kerkboekhandel.

DU TOIT, H. D. A.
1967   *Die kerstening van die Bantoe*, Pretoria: N. G. Kerkboekhandel.

GERDENER, G. B. A.
1958   *Recent developments in the South African mission field*, Cape Town: N. G. Kerkuitgewers.
1911   *Studies in the evangelisation of South Africa*, London: Longmans, Green & Company.

KRIEL, C. J.
1963   *Die geskiedenis van die Nederduitse Gereformeerde Sendingkerk in Suid-Afrika 1881-1956*, Paarl: Paarlse Drukpers.

LANDMAN, W. A.
1968   *A plea for understanding*, A reply to the Reformed Church in America, Cape Town: N. G. Kerkuitgewers.

SAAYMAN, W. A.
1979   "Separate Dutch Reformed Churches: notes on the historical perspective," in Viljoen, A. C. (red.): *Ekumene onder die Suiderkruis*, Pretoria: UNISA.

VAN DER MERWE, W. J.
1967   *Gesante om Christus wil*, Kaapstad: N. G. Kerkuitgewers.
1936   *The development of missionary attitudes in the Dutch Reformed Church in South Africa*, Cape Town: Nasionale Pers.

VORSTER, J. D., ed.
1978   *Veelvormigheid en eenheid*, Kaapstad: N. G. Kerkuitgewers.

12 THE MUSLIM *UMMA* AND THE GROWTH OF THE CHURCH

David W. Shenk

"WHY DON'T CHRISTIANS FOLLOW THE WAY OF JESUS?" A MUSLIM ASKED. I was dining with a close friend, a Muslim, in the Blue Nile Restaurant in Washington, D.C., when he leaned close and asked that disturbing question.

He continued slowly, pensively, "When I read the gospel, I am overjoyed. The life and teachings of Jesus are wonderful, wonderful, really, truly wonderful. But, please, show me Christians who are willing to follow in the *sunna* (way) of Jesus."

We sipped our cardamom spiced tea in reflective silence, and then he continued. "I have met a few, very few people who try to follow Jesus. But they follow him only in their private lives. Consequently your American society has become very evil. It seems to me that you Christians really do not believe that the *sunna* of Jesus is practical. That makes me very sad."

These comments reminded me of a similar conversation which an acquaintance and some of his clergy colleagues had with Ayatollah Khomeini on Christmas Day 1979. The Ayatollah implored these churchmen to take Jesus more seriously, and then added that if the Christians in America really believed in and followed Jesus, the tragedy of American injustice against Iran would not have happened.

All forms of Christian mission need to reflect the Spirit of Jesus. I have recently read Edward Said's *Orientalism* (1979) and Ali Shari'ati's *On the Sociology of Islam* (1979). I also recall the French Algerian Frantz Fanon's earlier works and have frequently listened to both Christians and Muslims whose homelands are the countries of Islam. In all of these writings and most of these encounters there is a common theme of heartbreak, a deep sense of sorrow that Christianized societies have participated so enthusiastically in wounding Islamized societies. I ask myself whether "strategies for evangelizing homogeneous target groups" in any way mitigate the suspicion by many Muslims that Western Christians are intent on continuing and exacerbating the dismemberment of the Islamic nation, which nineteenth- and twentieth-century Western political and

David W. Shenk, Mountville, Pennsylvania, is secretary for Home Missions with Eastern Mennonite Board of Missions and Charities, Salunga, Pennsylvania. He worked in church administration and education in the Somali Democratic Republic and Kenya from 1963 to 1979. He was lecturer in philosophy and religion at Kenyatta University College Nairobi. He is co-author of Islam and Christianity: A Muslim and a Christian in Dialogue *(Eerdmans, 1981) and* The Holy Book of God, an Introduction *(ACP, 1981).*

economic imperialism began. Is the insensitivity of the language we use any indication of an insensitivity within our spirit?

Surely we should rejoice when people experience grace in Christ. Nevertheless, we need to ask to what extent the church extension models which we use fit into the communication and experience of redemptive grace? To address this concern, we first look at several theological and practical problems Islam presents to Church Growth models of ministry. Second, we pause to listen momentarily to a question which Islam addresses to the church. Third, we evaluate five dimensions of contemporary Church Growth theory and practice. This chapter concludes with a description of the ministry and witness of a particular redemptive fellowship present in a Muslim community.

THEOLOGICAL AND PRACTICAL PROBLEMS

Islam is an embarrassment to theologies of rapid church growth. There are several reasons for the embarrassment.

Islam is a post-Christian movement of God-fearing people. Within the New Testament, God-fearing Gentiles were recognized with appreciation as people who had moved closer to the truth than their polytheistic contemporaries (Acts 10:34-36; 13:26). These pre-Christian God-fearers were exceptionally receptive to Christian faith. Islam, on the other hand, presents a theological problem which has no precedent in the New Testament, a monotheistic faith which is post-Christian, and which originated in a Christianized environment.

In Islam we see the etchings of aspects of Christian faith. Islam is a form of Arian Christianity, but unlike Arianism, Islam has flourished outside the modifying discipline and witness of Christian experience and biblical revelation. Therefore, although Arianism within the church finally withered into oblivion, Islam has thrived as a movement outside the bounds of churchly discipline.

Islam began as the quest of a people for inclusion in the people of God. Islam seeks to embrace and be embraced by all God-fearers. It began as a quest by the Arab people for inclusion, and now invites all people to participate in the blessing of that inclusion.

In the seventh century Arabia, Island of the Arabs, was largely encircled by Christian peoples. The advanced Christianized cultures—Ethiopian, Egyptian, Syrian—on the Arabian periphery had the Bible in their native languages. The pagan, nomadic Arabs were living in ignorance (*jahiliyya*), an ignorance perpetuated through exclusion from the community of the people of the Book. For nascent Islam the Arabic Book (Qur'an) and Arabian Prophet were the good news that the Arab peoples are now also included. The *da'wah* (invitation) of Islam is the good news that all other peoples are also invited to enjoy inclusion in the community of peace, the people of God. The inclusiveness of the invitation, as well as the detestation of all forms of exclusivism, is revealed in the Muslim conviction that everyone everywhere is born a Muslim. The success of Islamic mission is therefore not statistically measurable. All are born Muslim; Islamic mission is to invite people to affirm the reality of inclusion.

Islam's most rapid missionary expansion has been through the Islamization of Christianized societies. Within one century of its birth, Islam had gained control of half of the Christianized world. In all Christianized societies ruled by

Muslim governments, there has been a steady flow of converts from the church to Islam. Political techniques, such as the *dhimmi* (protected) status of the church, or the application of forms of the law of apostasy in relation to Muslims who would convert to Christianity, have combined to assure that the net flow of conversions always favored Islam. In all countries ruled by Muslim governments, shrinking Christian communities vis-à-vis Islam have been the norm. Islam has generally confronted the church with church growth in reverse.

Muslims believe that Islam is the primal, middle, and final religion of humankind, given as a mercy for all people. It is the faith of Adam, Abraham, and Muhammed; in fact all true prophets are Muslims. All necessary truth is succinctly summarized in the Qur'an, which is the criterion of all truth. God-fearers weep with joy when hearing the Qur'an recited. From an Islamic perspective, the fundamental test as to whether one is a person of faith is one's personal response to the Qur'an and belief in the Prophet of Islam. In relation to professed believers in God, the foremost question in the mind of Muslims is this: "What do you believe concerning the Qur'an and the Prophet?" A lack of commitment to the Prophet and the Book suggests that one's professed faith commitment to God is not genuine, and the dialogue is subsequently often broken (Qur'an 84:20-25).

The Islamic commitment to tauhid *(the unity of God) profoundly affects the Muslim commitment to community.* Belief in the unity of God is pragmatically reflected in the unity and harmony of the community which lives under the law of God. According to Ali Shari'ati (1979:82-87) belief in *tauhid* is commitment to the exorcism of all aspects of disequilibrium. All forms of disharmony are *shirk,* that is, the adding of associates to divinity. The *umma* is commanded by God to protect the community of faith from *shirk.* The community must be protected from all forms of disharmony, including the destabilization which can occur through unregulated religious pluralism, or the dichotomization of life into secular and spiritual realms. *Tauhid* is the experience and expression of personal and social integration and harmony under the revealed will of God. Within the framework of *tauhid,* church growth which in any sense seems to threaten the integrity of the *umma,* the *Dar al Islam,* is normally perceived as contributory to disharmony; it is a form of *shirk.*

How should the church respond theologically to the Islamic worldview? It is tempting to sidestep the issues. Most contemporary Church Growth writings are heavily oriented toward communication theory and anthropology, with a parallel dearth of theological reflection. At the Colorado Springs Consultation on Muslim Evangelization (1978) only one of the thirteen foundation papers attempted an in-depth probe of the theological issues. Seven of the papers related to cultural dynamics. The underlying assumption seemed to be that the fundamental objection of Islam to the gospel is Western culture, that if the gospel gets clothed in appropriate cultural forms, the theological objections will be easily surmounted (McCurry 1978).

A QUESTION FROM THE *UMMA* TO THE CHURCH

Could it be that we hesitate to accept theological engagement with Islam because we are embarrassed by the questions which the *umma* addresses to the church?

Yet if we would listen, we might discover that through the questions which Islam addresses to us, our own perceptions of the gospel will be purified, and in the purification process, the gospel itself will become more attractive and life changing for Christians and, we anticipate, also for our Muslim friends.

Many Muslims suspect that we really don't believe in the practicality of Jesus. "How can anyone love his enemy?" I have often been asked. I have frequently gone to mosques in East Africa and listened to the sermons. It is surprising how often Muslim preachers proclaim Islam as the practical faith in contrast to Christianity, which is far too idealistic. Thus the question, "Why don't you follow Jesus?" is also a form of Muslim witness. It is often a form of invitation to follow Muhammed, the pragmatic prophet.

Nevertheless, there is more to the question than a subtle invitation to accept Islam. The question also reflects the Muslim commitment to *tauhid,* the unity of every dimension of life under the rule of God. Muslims who know Christians are often disturbed at the easy manner in which many Western Christians violate *tauhid* by cozily dividing life into secular and sacred, public and private, temporal and spiritual.

Jesus also commanded *tauhid*; in fact from a biblical perspective he is the perfect revelation of *tauhid.* He is the breakthrough into history of cosmic harmony. From a Muslim perspective, cosmic harmony has been marvelously revealed in the Qur'an, whereas the biblical witness is that the eternal Word is revealed in Jesus. The divergence between the Book (Qur'anic guidance) and the Person (Jesus, the Redeemer) is the issue which drives a theological and practical wedge between Islam and Christianity. This divergence propels Islam toward a nomistic organization of society, whereas the Christian is more pneumatically oriented. In Islam there is tremendous concern about submitting to codified guidance, whereas in the Christian experience one is called to live in the Spirit of Jesus Christ.

Islamic perplexity concerning Christian life and commitment, however, is not necessarily contingent on the different views of the essence of revealed harmony. Rather the *umma* asks why we so often fail to commit ourselves to the one whom we profess as Lord. Jesus, as the dramatic breakthrough of the kingdom of God, announced at the beginning of his ministry that he had come to preach good news to the poor, freedom for the prisoners, sight for the blind, release for the oppressed (Lk 4:16-21). In his life Jesus revealed that this radically new kingdom order is effectuated through redemptive suffering love, supremely revealed in his crucifixion and resurrection. Cosmic harmony is, in Jesus' life, the total commitment to love, even to one's enemies. But one cannot live that way without suffering. That is the issue.

The Islamic question is really an invitation to Christians to take the *tauhid* seriously, to reflect the kingdom of God in every area of life. There is only *one* Muslim nation. The *umma* transcends nationalism. All nationalisms which segment the unity of the nation of Islam are aberrations of the reality of Islam, Dr. Ala' Eddin Kharafa, the director of the Muslim World League of North America, said in a recent assembly.

The nation-state is a recent phenomenon for Muslims. It is a residual consequence of Western imperial intrusions into the nation of Islam and the overthrow of the caliphate during the Turkish revolution (1924). In spite of the blessings of independence, there is deep disquiet among many Muslims, because the nation-state represents a fractured *umma*. Dr. Kharafa pointed out that for Muslims, any national allegiance which supersedes loyalty and commitment to the total community of faith is wrong. The Shia theologian, Dr. Ali Shari'ati (1979:82-89) refers to nationalistic division in the *umma* as *shirk,* or idolatry. *Tauhid* is harmony; it is the participation in fraternal commitment to one another; it is participation in the *Dar al Salaam* (Region of Peace) which is not fractured by nationalism.

Biblical faith also teaches that national loyalties dare not supersede loyalty to the kingdom of God; when the two conflict, the follower of Jesus has only one option, the Jesus way. Justice, peace, righteousness, the cause of the dispossessed and poor, and the urgent invitation to participate in a redeemed and joyous relationship with God and the believing community are aspects of the kaleidoscope of kingdom living. Jesus dramatically proclaimed the transnational nature of the kingdom of God by calling his disciples to seek the kingdom rather than those things which the nations seek (Lk 12:30). On the night of his arrest Jesus said, "My kingdom is not of this world: if my kingdom were of this world, then would my servants fight" (Jn 18:36 KJV).

The Islamic plea to take *tauhid* seriously should rekindle within Christians a sincere commitment to live and give witness to the fact that God's intention is "to unite all things in him, things in heaven and things on earth" (Eph 1:10). The church in mission is called by God to be an authentic sign that God's intention for the cosmos has already broken into history.

There are numerous other questions which the *umma* urgently and persistently addresses to the church; but the kingdom question is the most prescient. And it is tremendously relevant to the church and its mission among Muslims.

CHURCH GROWTH THEORY AND METHODOLOGY

How does New Testament kingdom theology affect and inform Christian mission among Muslims? At the Pattaya Consultation on World Evangelization, the mini-consultation on reaching Muslims (1980) identified five salient insights and commitments of contemporary Church Growth concerns. They are: a belief that churches ought to grow; a commitment to working with people groups; concentrating resources primarily on receptive peoples; contextualizing the gospel; and careful planning for evangelism. These rubrics are simplifications, yet they seem to state succinctly the main concerns and commitments of contemporary Church Growth missiology. At Pattaya these concepts elicited intense discussion.

I will comment on each of these rubrics from the perspective of a kingdom missiology.

CHURCHES OUGHT TO GROW

All Christian evangels rejoice when churches grow. In relation to Islam, however, church growth has been very slow. In fact for many centuries Christian communities in Islamized societies have experienced considerable attrition and assimilation. That is reverse church growth.

A cozy response to the decline of the church in Nubia or Libya, for example, is to suggest that the Christians in those countries were decadent even before the Muslim conquests. Yet this is hardly true. Nubian Christianity was explosively vigorous; the creative impact of the gospel along the Upper Nile valley contributed to an artistic and intellectual dynamism which reached far beyond the borders of Nubia. Similarly, Libyan Christians experimented with contextualization of Christian life and theology so daringly that they sometimes gained the criticisms of their more traditionally inclined fellow Christians in Egypt and elsewhere. On the eve of the Muslim conquests, Persian missionaries were proclaiming the gospel in China, and Egyptian evangels were preaching to African people groups far south of their imperial borders. These are not marks of decadent Christianity (Kealy and Shenk 1975:168-330).

Although the church of the seventh century was struggling with tremendous issues, the church as a whole was dynamic and alive. Nevertheless, many of the formerly Christianized societies of northern Africa and the Middle East are now mostly Islamized. The churches are minority communities circumscribed by the *dhimmi* system. In some countries the ancient churches are no more; over the centuries they have been slowly smothered into extinction.

During my years as an educationalist in a Muslim country, the church tried to grow. There was a fairly explicit hunger for the gospel. There were many Nicodemuses. Several times we seemed on the verge of people group movements. But these inclinations, which gave us great joy, were disconcerting to the society as a whole. With graciousness, tact, and firmness the authorities felt constrained to shackle the church. We were, for example, prohibited from visiting among the riverine peoples, who were gathering in groups of a hundred or more under the shady mango trees on Sunday afternoons to hear the gospel stories. Later a law was passed prohibiting the propagation of any religion except Islam. Religious pluralism in a country which had heretofore been 100 percent Muslim was tremendously difficult for the community to comprehend.

Nevertheless, the life and worship of the Christian congregations was affirmed. There was seldom any attempt to keep Christians from fellowshiping and praying together. Growth, however, was seriously problematical. Muslim friends often said, "Every person born in this society has the blood of Islam flowing in his veins." Everyone in that society traced genealogy, at least mythically, to the Quarish; all were kinsfolk to the Prophet. Spiritually and genealogically all were Muslim, and that fact was the foundation stone of nationhood.

Krikor Greg Haleblian, a Syrian Christian, writes, "One of the first principles most worthy of consideration is the Muslim's love for unity or oneness" (1979:79). The mosque is a supreme sign of unity in the Muslim community. All the architectural symbolism flows together, and the whole is oriented toward Mecca. Dress styles and housing patterns reveal the same affirmation of unity. How, then, can a growing church be accommodated within the unity framework? How can the *umma* accept growth pluralism, when the *umma* itself is the repository of ultimate truth?

In one Muslim community the elders met with a Christian missionary after the first two people in that community had made a profession of Christian faith. They said with deep feeling, "We would rather all our children starved to death, than that one of them should become a Christian and go to hell." It is therefore not surprising that sometime later a Christian was martyred in that community. *Tauhid* needs to be preserved.

Although we do rejoice when churches grow, is church growth the only authentic measure of effective and faithful witness? Do effective witness and ministry always lead to church growth? Does ministry in a no-growth situation suggest that the witness is not in any sense redemptive?

We need patience. Let me illustrate from a non-Muslim situation. In 1853 the first Christian missionaries arrived in Kenya. Within weeks the first missionary graves were planted on the outskirts of Mombasa, the port town of Kenya. The Church Missionary Society continued that ministry and witness for thirty years with incredible suffering and dedication. The consequence: seven baptized communicant members. Today nearly 10,000,000—or seventy percent—of the Kenyan people are professing Christians. Yet those who planted and ministered faithfully saw almost no fruit whatsoever.

In relation to Islam we also need the gift of patience. In some traditional societies we need only a decade or two of patience. In some Muslim societies we probably need a patience which endures for a century or more.

A fixation on church growth often distorts the authenticity of our witness and service. At Muslim congresses anger is frequently expressed against forms of Christian philanthropy which are a hook for church growth (Parshall 1980). I have experienced the same kinds of apprehension directed toward me when working in Muslim communities. Obviously we rejoice when congregations of believers emerge through such ministries. Nevertheless, the emergence of congregations is not the reason why we serve. We serve because God is love (Cragg 1956:210-43).

Several years ago I was heading up philanthropic Christian ministries in a Muslim society which was undergoing radical social change. Most humanitarian agencies quit. We stayed. Many times I was asked, "Why?" My response was, "Because in the Messiah, God has revealed his love. We also, as disciples of the Messiah, want to share God's love with you." That witness was acceptable, and I believe effective. We didn't experience much church growth, but the witness in deed *and* word spoke deeply. We minister because of Jesus.

How large does a church need to become before its redemptive presence is felt throughout a society? Paul Hiebert's descriptions of bounded, fuzzy, and open sets are helpful, by opening the question of the meaning of a Christ orientation (1981). As an Anabaptist, I am committed to the bounded set, an explicitly committed, visible, covenant community. Nevertheless, I also believe that the redemptive power of the community of faith is not proportionate to its size. Jesus does become present where two or three meet in his name. And the gates of hell do not prevail against the ministry of that faith community.

We cannot fully fathom the redemptive implications of the power of Jesus' presence. Recently a Muslim government official told a mission executive, "Your community is the only group who have ever left an eternal impact on my country." What did he mean? Massive multilateral aid agencies have had a high profile in that country. Yet a minuscule cluster of believers ministering in the name of Christ are especially appreciated because of their transforming quality. Is this what Jesus meant when he referred to his disciples as salt and light? To what extent can the presence of the church in a Muslim community help that community retrieve that which was lost through the traditional Muslim misperceptions of the gospel (Cragg 1956:244-331)?

The presence, life, prayer, ministry, witness, and invitation of the re-deemed cluster who meet in Jesus' name is vitally needed even in situations where the church does not grow numerically. Muslim societies need to see and experience the church. It is the authentic sign of the presence of the kingdom. The church is the only community which perceives salvation in the one born in the cattle stall of Bethlehem, in the one who loved ultimately, in the one whose open arms on the cross speak of the redemptive vulnerability of God. That witness is desperately needed everywhere. Could it be that from God's perspective, the presence of the church in a society is more significant than the growth of the church?

I am completely confident that the Holy Spirit does want the church to grow. Yet some societies have developed formidable anti-growth propensities. In those situations it seems the Holy Spirit is especially concerned about maintaining an authentic presence and witness. It seems to me, therefore, utterly disastrous when Christians ministering and witnessing in an apparently sterile no-growth situation decide to terminate their presence. The darkness cannot overcome the light, but what happens when the small light which is present emigrates?

A COMMITMENT TO WORKING WITH PEOPLE GROUPS

The church has normally been committed to the right of people to worship and express their Christian faith in their own idiom and culture. Even from the early centuries of the Christian era missionaries have translated the Bible into the languages of the peoples they evangelized. In relation to Islam, probably one of the greatest attractions the church presents is the affirmation of the right of people to read the Bible in their own mother tongue. This is in contrast to Muslim missioners who teach people to read the Arabic, because God's final revelation to humankind is the "Arabic Qur'an."

Nevertheless, an emphasis on people groups is not a panacea for world evangelism, and in some situations it might be counter-productive. Let me illustrate. I grew up in a missionary home in Tanzania. My parents were the first evangels to a particular people group (15,000 people). They learned the language and spent many hours translating the Gospel of Matthew into that people's language. Yet many of those Scripture portions remained on the shelves unsold. They were never used, because the great movement into the church in that particular people group took place at the moment when those people caught the vision of the new universal community, which could link their tiny ethnic group into a worldwide fellowship. It was the quest for universality, not locality, which was the trigger for church growth. Consequently it was the Swahili Bible, written in the national language which united all societies together in East Africa, which sold, and the Scripture portions which seemed to reinforce ethnicity were seldom used.

In many emerging nations in Africa the church is the only authentic transethnic community. It is the principal glue which holds the nation together, because it is a transcultural community. In some countries government leaders explicitly look to the church to help maintain transethnic commitments. In that context Western missiologists need to be very cautious. Overemphasizing ethnic identity is perceived by many emerging nations as being treasonable. The church is affirmed as the community which helps bring unity, not as the exacerbator of ethnic identities.

It is also so in Muslim societies. The church must minister as a unifier, not a divider of the people. Symbols of universality will be just as important as affirmations of particularity.

Another dimension is that the values of homogenous people groups are often so tightly woven into the sociological and cultural fabric that it is exceedingly difficult for an alternate commitment to break through. Consequently some of the most responsive peoples to the gospel are those who have broken out of the trappings of ethnicity. These are the upwardly mobile people, those who travel, seek education, or participate in outward expansions. The modern emphasis on individualism is prying people loose from traditional loyalties and opening them to the possibilities of involvement and commitment to other forms of community. For those modern individualists the church often provides a welcome home, for it is a primary fellowship which is also genuinely universal, and it affirms the integrity of personhood.

A people-group orientation sometimes overlooks the broad commonalities which link all Muslims together. A fixation on local cultural apparatus may obscure the amazingly consistent worldview of Muslims (Parshall 1980:63-93). The people-group emphasis tempts us to sidestep the universal theological nature of the encounter and witness.

RESOURCES SHOULD BE CONCENTRATED ON RECEPTIVE PEOPLES

A third tendency among Church Growth missiologists is to encourage the concentration of financial and personnel resources on receptive peoples. Frequently this emphasis skews resources away from Islamized peoples. The general secretary of the Kenya National Council once told me that mission agency heads frequently came to ask him where the unevangelized areas of Kenya were. He would show them a map. One third of the country was almost untouched by the gospel. These were Islamized peoples. Weeks later he would learn that instead of going to these unevangelized peoples, the new mission agencies would always settle in the evangelized areas, often in communities which were already ninety-five percent churched. Four new mission agencies came to Kenya from America every year. During my six years in that country, not one new agency decided to concentrate resources in the Islamized areas of the country, even though Kenya's secular government would have provided the most ideal circumstances for quiet evangelization.

It is disturbing that much of the new impetus for concentrating resources on ministries among Muslims is undergirded with notions that we are on the verge of a breakthrough. Certainly we give thanks for any indications of openness to the gospel among Muslims. This is a great joy. Nevertheless, for multitudes of faithful Christian evangels who are ministering among Muslims, there probably never will be a breakthrough in Church Growth terms. Consequently the resource flow for Muslim ministries will be siphoned into Muslim communities which are only marginally Islamized.

There is, of course, the biblical command to shake the dust from our feet and go elsewhere when a people reject the gospel. Nevertheless, most Muslims have never explicitly rejected the gospel. Their apparent resistance is usually related to the fact that they have never understood its message. An apparently resistant people are not necessarily a people who have rejected. In fact I have seldom interacted with any other people who seem as open to hearing the gospel as Muslims. Nevertheless, the misperceptions run deep, the theological issues are profound, and community pressures are tremendous. It takes time. Patience is required, the kind of patience which does not fit the categories of any forms of cost effectiveness analysis. It is patience borne out of commitment to Jesus Christ who also lived among a people who often painfully misunderstood his ministry.

THE GOSPEL AND THE CHURCH NEED TO BE CONTEXTUALIZED
It is imperative for the gospel to break out of the cultural repository of the missioner so that it may become truly incarnate within the culture of those receiving the message. In this, Islam and the gospel are very different. Cultural indigeneity is a far greater concern of Christianity than it is of Muslims. On the African continent this fact is dramatically obvious. The Muslim intelligentsia are calling for the purification of Islam, which in their terms means the incipient denigration of African traditional culture in favor of the Islamic *Sharia*. Within the Christian community the opposite message is heard. Everywhere Africans speak of the need to Africanize Christianity, to contextualize the gospel in African forms. This is one of the dramatic differences between the incarnational gospel of Jesus, and the Islamic perception of revelation as *tanzil* (sent down).

Therefore in the process of contextualization, let us not assume that through these devices Muslims will be painlessly attracted to Christ. The theological issues cannot be surmounted by cultural niceties.

Christians should also be aware that Muslims have a deep aversion for all forms of hypocrisy. Contextualization must not be perceived as an attempt to camouflage the reality of the gospel or the development of a redeemed community who cluster in worship in the name of Jesus. The Isawa of northern Nigeria are a case in point. These Muslims began to profess a faith in Christ, using thoroughly Muslim cultural forms. Early in this century more orthodox Muslims committed genocide against the Isawa because they seemed to be renegade Muslims. Only a small cluster of the Isawa remain today.

In all attempts at contextualization the missioner must be sensitive to the local fellowship. Contextualization must never be a camouflage for the presence of the church, and it must be deeply sensitive to the need for identity with the universal church. An African churchman said that although meat and beer would be more appropriate symbols of the eucharist from an African perspective than the traditional wine and bread, it is nevertheless necessary to use the wine and bread because in that way the church is reminded through these non-indigenous symbols that it is a part of a worldwide fellowship. In much the same manner, a cluster of Christians from a Muslim background were rather horrified when a missionary suggested using camel's milk in the eucharist. Otherness and universality are dimensions of Christian symbolism which are just as important as are the symbols of incarnational contextualization. The kingdom of God is new!

THE CHURCH SHOULD PLAN CAREFULLY FOR EVANGELISM
Much of my life I have lived among peoples who were the targets of Western missionary enterprise. I grew up among these peoples, and have listened to their feelings. On the whole I have sensed great appreciation for missionary work

borne of the love of God, but great resentment against those strategies which see people as objects to be manipulated into the church. The concern for planning is right. The manipulative plan is wrong, however. Furthermore we must always recognize that in Christ means and ends converge. The means to the kingdom and the kingdom itself are the same. Jesus is both the way and the life. Any technique or plan which is not immersed in love and genuine concern for the totality of the other person must be condemned.

It is especially important that parachurch agencies develop sensitivity to the local church. The church is already present in most Muslim countries. These Christians understand the local culture better than the expatriate ever can. Insensitive strategies can cause enormous harm. I know, for example, of several incidents where Christian Scripture portions were posted by parachurch agencies to every address in a telephone book. In each situation tremendous embarrassment was experienced by the local church.

Recently an evangelical mission was in conversation with a Muslim governmental department concerning beginning a new ministry. The mission executive asked to clarify the commitment of the mission; but the response of the Muslim officials was, "We know you completely and we trust you. That is why we welcome you!" That is the kind of open mission planning which is precious!

The overall assumptions of Church Growth theory seem to be anchored on the premise that correct missiology will produce church growth. However, is it not true that from a kingdom perspective, faithfulness, not success, is the only valid criterion of authentic mission? The cross precedes the resurrection. Mission is most authentically expressed through the suffering redemptive love of the people of God.

CONCLUDING OBSERVATION

Several years ago an independent African church, which was not begun through foreign missionary initiative, developed a concern for ministry among Muslims. They asked an overseas mission agency to join in a partnership ministry. The agency and the African church jointly appointed a Canadian family for this mission among Muslims. An African family was also appointed by the African church. Both were commissioned by the African church.

For a year the team visited Muslim villages. They met leaders. They developed a strong trust relationship with decision makers. They visited a Muslim mystical community (*Sufi Tariq*) several times. They felt that the *tariq* represented an alternate form of Islamic community which was readily adaptable to a Christian presence. So they moved into one of the largest Muslim communities in the region and began developing a Christian community on the *tariq* model.

The houses were built in the same style, with roundels for the core cluster of households, a special house for eating (communal meals with locally available foods), and another for meetings. A multiethnic group of Christians formed the core community. The pastor ministered in a manner somewhat parallel to the skeikh in the *tariq*. Teaching and worship experiences were performed on mats, with participants sitting cross-legged on the floor. All community events were punctuated with prayer, and frequently Muslims and Christians prayed together, for even jointly sponsored events needed the affirmation received through prayer.

The faith community ministered creatively to community needs, especially the needs of widows and orphans.

For some of the Bible studies, as many as thirty people have been present. Muslims who would never enter a church will come to this center for worship. Bible study courses which draw from some portions of the Qur'an as contact points for the biblical witness have been used.

When a riot broke out in the community, over a hundred houses were burned adjacent to the Christian community. Many people were killed. As the neighbors fled into the bush, they tossed their belongings across the fence into the Christian community. Although there was considerable looting, nothing was touched or harmed in the Christian community. It seemed to be an authentic sign of peace in the midst of the turmoil. Later the leaders of the factions involved in the conflagration came and asked the Christian community to give leadership to reconciliation and the reconstruction of the village.

Although contextualized, the community is distinctly Christian; although suffering, it lives and ministers in the joy of the resurrection. This small community is graciously affecting the atmosphere in the whole region. It is a precious sign of the presence of the kingdom of God, a witness to the gracious creation by God of a redeemed peoplehood.

BIBLIOGRAPHY

CHRISTIANS MEETING MUSLIMS
  1977   *WCC Papers on Ten Years of Christian-Muslim Dialogue*, Geneva: WCC.

CRAGG, Kenneth
 *1956   *The Call of the Minaret*, New York: Oxford University Press.
  1969   *Christianity in World Perspective*, London: Lutterworth Press.
  1971   *The Event of the Qur'an*, London: George Allen & Unwin Ltd.
  1975   *The House of Islam*, Belmont: Kickenson Publishing House.

DAYTON, Edward R.
  1979   *That Everyone May Hear, Reaching the Unreached*, Monrovia: MARC.

DRETKE, James P.
  1979   *A Christian Approach to Muslims, Reflections from West Africa*, Pasadena: William Carey Library.

ESPOSITO, John L.
  1980   *Islam and Development, Religion and Socio-political Change.* Syracuse: Syracuse University Press.

GIBB, H. A. R.
  1969   *Mohammedanism*, New York: Oxford University Press.

GUILLAUME, Alfred
  1979   *Islam*, New York: Penguin.

HALEBLIAN, Krikor
 *1979   "World View and Evangelization: A Case Study on Arab People" (Th.M. thesis), Pasadena: Fuller Theological Seminary.

HIEBERT, Paul G.
 *1981   "Contextualization's Challenge to Theological Education," Council of Men-

nonite Seminaries/Missionary Study Fellowship, *Conference on Theological Education in Missional Perspective*, Elkhart, Indiana, February 26-28.

HITTI, Philip K.
1973 *History of the Arabs*, London: Macmillan.

KATERREGA, Badru D. and SHENK, David W.
1980 *Islam and Christianity: A Muslim and a Christian in Dialogue*, Nairobi: Uzima. U.S. edition, 1981, Grand Rapids: Eerdmans.

KEALY, John P. and SHENK, David W.
*1975 *The Early Church and Africa*, Nairobi: Oxford University Press.

KRAFT, Charles H.
1980 *Christianity in Culture, A Study in Dynamic Biblical Theologizing in Cross-Cultural Perspective*, Maryknoll: Orbis.

LUZBETAK, Louis J.
1976 *The Church and Cultures*, Pasadena: William Carey Library.

McCURRY, Don, ed.
*1978 *The Gospel and Islam*, Monrovia: MARC.

MINI-CONSULTATION
*1980 *Mini-Consultation on Reaching Muslims*, Pattaya, Thailand, June.

PARSHALL, Phil
*1980 *New Paths in Muslim Evangelism, Evangelical Approaches to Contextualization*, Grand Rapids: Baker Book House.

REGISTER, Ray
1973 *Dialogue and Interfaith Witness with Muslims*, Kingsport: Moody Books, Inc.

RAHMAN, Fazlur
1979 *Islam*, Chicago: University of Chicago Press.

SAID, Edward W.
*1979 *Orientalism*, New York: Vintage.

SHARI'ATI, Ali
*1979 *On the Sociology of Islam*, translated from the Persian by Hamid Algar, Berkeley: Mizan Press.

VAN LEEUWEN, Arend Theodoor
1964 *Christianity in World History*, New York: Charles Scribner's Sons.

WATT, W. Montgomery
1969 *Muhammed, Prophet and Statesman*, New York: Oxford University Press.

* Indicates reference cited in chapter.

13. MISSIONS AND THE RENEWAL OF THE CHURCH

Paul G. Hiebert

"LORD, REVIVE THY WORK IN THE MIDST OF THE YEARS" (HAB 3:2)

Any long-range vision for missions must include not only the planting of new churches, but also the renewal of old ones. The former without the latter eventually leads only to lands full of dead and dying churches. The birth of new congregations is no guarantee that they will remain spiritually alive.

Many missionaries and church leaders have tried to establish "steady state" churches—churches that remain forever strong in faith and ministry. But there is no spiritual "steady state," neither in churches nor in individuals. Spiritual life, like all forms of life, is involved in processes of health and illness, of reinvigoration and decay. A church can remain vitally alive only as it periodically experiences times of life renewal. We deal here with one of the sets of processes that affect the life of a church, and, at length, with one of the types of structures for renewal.

INSTITUTIONALIZATION

Christianity is a set of allegiances and beliefs. But it is more. It is a set of relationships. Faith may be an intensely personal matter, but Christianity is also a community of believers, the church, united under the lordship of Christ.

Because the church is a corporate body of human beings, it must take on social forms. Without these forms, there would be no relationships between believers, and no visible congregation. There would also be no transmission of the gospel from one people to another, or from one generation to another, for these, too, require social structures. To be sure, the church cannot be understood solely as a social organization. It is the body of Christ, and the Spirit of God is at work within it. But to the extent that the church is made up of people and congregations in relationship to one another, it will be influenced by the social and cultural dynamics of human institutions. Among these dynamics we here look only at the process of institutionalization and its effect, both positive and negative, on local congregations and other church organizations.

Paul G. Hiebert, Pasadena, California, is Professor of Anthropology and South Asian Studies at Fuller School of World Missions. He served as a missionary to India with the Mennonite Brethren Church from 1960 to 1966. He has been a consultant to the Mennonite Brethren Board of Missions and Services since 1970 and was Associate Professor of Anthropology at the University of Washington, Seattle, Washington, from 1972 to 1977. Among his publications is Cultural Anthropology *(Lippincott, 1976).*

GENERATIONS IN AN INSTITUTION

Institutions such as churches, mission agencies, and schools undergo changes from the time of their birth to their maturity. These changes can be analyzed by looking at the successive generations of people within a particular institution.

The first generation is made up of the "founding fathers and mothers" who have some things in common. They are drawn together by a vision of something new, for which they have paid a high price. Often they have left some old institutions to join the new movement. Friends and relatives sought to draw them back and, when this failed, cut them off. Moreover, they faced high risk, for there was no assurance that the new organization they founded would survive. Cut off from their old world, they are bound together by strong ties of fellowship and oneness of purpose.

The second generation is made up of the children of the founders, or by the generation that takes over from the founders. Here a major structural change takes place. While the founders paid a high price to leave their old institutions to form the new one, the children grow up within the framework of the new institution and its programs. The cost is not so high, but neither is the commitment. Members of the second generation do grow up amid the excitement, sacrifice, and commitment of a new movement, but they acquire secondhand the vision that motivated their parents.

By the third, fourth, and fifth generations, the new movement has become "the establishment." These generations grow up within the institutional structures. In churches the children go to Sunday school and youth meetings with their friends, then with those friends they make profession of faith and are baptized. In schools and mission agencies, people work their way through the ranks to positions of leadership. For all of them, to remain within the institution is the path of least resistance and cost.

The strength of these generations is their stability and continuity over time. The life of the church like any institution depends upon one generation succeeding another. But the weakness of these successive generations is nominalism. The spiritual vision of the founders is dimmed by the routines of institutional life. What began as a movement has become a bureaucratic organization.

PROCESSES OF INSTITUTIONALIZATION

Over the generations, an institution normally grows and matures. And with maturation come the problems of middle age—a loss of vision and a hardening of the categories. This maturation or institutionalization of human organization is characterized by a number of related processes.

First, informal associations give way to formal social roles. At the beginning of a movement there are few formal roles. There is often no official or salaried custodian, or secretary, or treasurer. Different members volunteer to type correspondence, to handle finances, and to welcome newcomers. As an institution grows, more and more roles are formalized.

Second, *ad hoc* arrangements are replaced by rationally formulated rules and constitutions in which relationships are standardized and generalized. At the outset, many things are handled by casual arrangements. At the last moment the pastor may ask someone to lead the singing or read the Scriptures. Later such arrangements must be made well in advance so that the names can be put into a bulletin. In time the question arises as to who in fact can appoint the song leader, and the decision becomes part of the growing number of rules by which the church is run. Finally, when these rules become unwieldy and confusing, a constitution is drawn up to organize them into a formal whole. What began in the first generation as a casual arrangement, by the second becomes normative, by the third law, and by the fourth sacred. To change it becomes increasingly difficult.

In part, formal rules and constitutions are functions of size. They are necessary for large institutions to function smoothly. They are also functions of culture. Western cultures with their obsession for uniformity, efficiency, and rationality tend to organize institutions along the lines of bureaucracies in which tasks and relationships are divided and allocated to different people. The result is a mechanical approach to human organization, in which people become standardized parts within a "factory" which has as its goals production and gain. In many parts of the world social organizations are based on kinship and are organic in nature. Tribes, clans, lineages, and families tend to be more particularized or tailored to the individual characteristics of the persons involved. Moreover, they must be inclusive for they cannot reject kinsfolk just because they do not fit into the structure.

Third, charismatic leaders are succeeded by bureaucratic leaders. As Max Weber points out (1968), founders of new movements tend to be dynamic, prophetic leaders who command a following by means of their personal charisma. Such leaders can rarely lead a mature, established institution, for they act too much on personal impulse and outside established procedures. Formalized roles and relationships call for a priest or administrator who is selected by due institutional processes and is identified with the people and the institution. This transition from charismatic founder to bureaucratic leader is crucial for the survival of an institution. If it does not take place, the institution dies. It is for the succeeding leaders to turn the vision of the founder into reality; to do so they must build and administer a complex institution.

The most difficult leadership position to fill is that of successor to the founder, for it is here that the transition must begin. Often it is a position with little honor. Honor goes to the founder whose picture is generally central on the wall of fame. Only as personal knowledge of the founder dies and memories of him or her fade are leaders measured by their own contributions.

Finally, unity based on implicit trust in one another's faith gives way to unity based on explicit affirmation of common creeds and written confessions of faith. In the intimacy of the early gatherings, everyone knows everyone else personally. In such cases, theological differences are bridged by mutual trust. As churches and other institutions grow and become more impersonal, the bond holding members together must be formally defined. Moreover, outsiders want to know what the organization stands for. Consequently there are pressures to make explicit the beliefs and goals of the institution.

BENEFITS OF INSTITUTIONALIZATION
In a number of ways the processes of institutionalization are beneficial for the building of churches. One has been called "redemption and life"; it is found particularly in churches that spring up in poor non-Christian communities. In

many parts of the world Christian converts come from the lower classes of society. First-generation members are generally nonliterate, economically poor, and socially powerless. But many of these early converts send their children to mission or church schools so that second-generation members are school teachers and government clerks. They in turn send their children to college to become doctors, college teachers, and government officials. This rapid rise of Christian communities means that in time even churches planted among the poor become self-supporting and develop their own advanced leadership. The danger, of course, is that in this rapid social rise, the church loses contact with the community from which it came, and can no longer witness effectively to that community.

Another benefit of institutionalization is efficiency. Unformalized social organizations consume a great deal of time and energy simply to maintain themselves. New decisions must constantly be made for each activity, no matter how small. In a sense, institutionalization is for social organizations what habit formation is for individuals. It reduces the effort necessary to operate the institution by clarifying decision-making processes and by routinizing decisions.

A third benefit of institutionalization is the ability to mobilize large numbers of people and resources in order to carry out an otherwise impossible program of missions and ministry.

A final benefit is the theological maturation of the church. New converts, particularly in mission churches, are often theologically naive. Most come from non-Christian backgrounds and have little understanding of the Bible or of a biblical worldview. Their children, raised in the church and often a Christian school, have a much deeper understanding of the Bible and its message. By the third generation, there arise Bible scholars, translators, and theologians who can indigenize the gospel in their own culture far more effectively than can any missionaries. The long-range survival of the church in a land—and its remaining true to the Christian faith through the centuries—depends to a considerable extent upon the emergence of such leaders rooted in a deep understanding of the Scriptures.

DANGERS OF INSTITUTIONALIZATION

Institutionalization also has its dangers. What begins as a means to help the congregation can, in the end, strangle it.

One negative consequence of institutionalization is that the vision is often lost in the process of carrying it out. For example, in order to evangelize a neighboring community, the church forms a committee. To keep committee minutes, a secretary is hired and an office set up. In the end, the secretary, pressured to type letters and make reports, sees little connection between those tasks and the evangelization of the neighborhood.

Another danger is that the focus on goals gives way to a concern for self-maintenance. Churches are started to evangelize and minister to peoples among which no churches exist. But as time passes, more of their resources and efforts are spent on simply maintaining the institutional structures. Young churches often make do with the simplest of facilities in order to focus their efforts on their mission to the world. Older churches spend more and more on sanctuaries and parking lots for themselves and schools for their children. Older mission agencies and educational institutions tend to spend an increasing proportion of their efforts and budgets on administration.

This shift of priorities from tasks to self-maintenance is due, in part, to the fact that there is no one in the administrative structures or on the committees where decisions are made who represents the world outside and its needs. Decisions are made by the insiders—by those whose cars get muddy in the unpaved lot. The turning-inward process also occurs as the identity of members gets tied up with the organization and their roles within it.

Yet another danger is that flexibility gives way to inflexibility. In the early stages of an institution's life, decisions are made on an *ad hoc* basis. Eventually rules and procedures are created to establish order and to reduce the number of decisions that must be made, but these also reduce flexibility in decision making. Too many exceptions to administrative rules make them useless, so pressures build to insure conformity.

The fourth danger is the shift in focus from people to programs. Young institutions are generally more people oriented. There is a strong emphasis on fellowship, trust, and meeting human needs. As an institution grows, more and more emphasis is placed on building programs and maintaining institutional structures. In a showdown, institutional needs take priority over human needs.

PROCESSES OF RENEWAL

In view of these processes, which seem almost inevitable, is there no hope for institutions? True, there are some benefits, but the evils seem to outweigh them in the long run.

Some say the only hope is to get rid of institutions. Our only hope is to oppose the formation of formal social organizations and to return to a relatively unstructured way of life. Get rid of the establishment with its bureaucratic organization, its rules and procedures, and its dehumanizing power. But, as Peter Berger points out (1973), anti-structural movements have never been successful. For one, they are unable to build stable enduring societies or organize people into communities of common purpose and mutual support. At best such movements survive because they have a symbiotic relationship to a more institutionalized society. For another, they themselves are subject to the subtle forces of institutionalization. The symbols of their rebellion soon become the emblems of their identity, which they impose with institutional harshness upon their members.

The answer to the hardening of institutional categories is not anti-institutionalism, but institutional renewal. Institutions can be regenerated periodically so that their evils are tempered and their ministries enhanced.

Since we are speaking here of the renewal of the church as a human organization, we must make it clear that spiritual renewal is first and foremost the work of God, and this cannot be programmed. There is no "formula" for revival. To seek one is itself idolatry, for formulas make human gods capable of forcing God to do their bidding. But God does work through the spiritual, cultural, social, and psychological processes he created in human beings. As Edwin Orr points out (1975), God responds to sincere prayers. God also uses individuals, human experiences, sermons, songs, books, sacred places, sacred times, and other cultural symbols to move in the lives of people. When we seek renewal, we need to understand the human processes that can make us open to the possibility of renewal—that can help us to listen so that when God speaks we will hear.

CONVERSION

One pattern of institutional renewal is that of personal conversion. The emphasis in the believers' church upon personal commitment to Christ and to the church after one has reached the age of accountability in a sense recreates in each individual the costliness of leaving an old way of life and the high commitment to a new one that characterized the founders of the church. Ideally, each new generation enters with a fresh vision and new life.

In reality, however, two factors temper this ideal. First, the children are now, in fact, raised as if they were inside the church. Theologically, during their most formative years, they are rarely considered really lost. Institutionally, moreover, they are very much insiders. They attend services and are treated as participants. In the face of widespread acceptance, the meaning of their exclusion from the few technical rights of church membership often escapes them.

The second factor weakening the conversion experience is the institutionalization of conversion itself. Young people are soon expected to experience conversion at certain times in their lives, at certain occasions, and in certain ways. Furthermore, young people often act in imitation of one another. Consequently, conversion itself can become the path of least resistance rather than a costly new beginning. When all are being converted, those who hold back may have to pay a greater price.

NEW BEGINNINGS

Another pattern of renewal is the beginning of a new institution or movement. As bureaucratic inertia and nominalism make a church or denomination appear almost lifeless, there is a strong temptation among those with vital spiritual life to begin anew. The possibility of reviving the old seems almost hopeless.

Their theology does not permit the Catholics to split. Consequently their new beginnings take the form of new movements or orders within the church. For example, the Franciscans, Jesuits, Dominicans, and other Catholic organizations began as renewal movements that led eventually to fully institutionalized orders. The result, again, is a proliferation of bureaucratic structures, each of which must face the question of renewal.

INTERSECTING RENEWAL MOVEMENTS

The best modern example of crosscutting renewal movements is the East African Revival that has been continuing for more than forty years. In it, people interested in spiritual life and the renewal of the church gather in informal meetings for Bible study, prayer, confession and forgiveness of sins, and mutual exhortation. They come from many different churches and denominations. There is little or no formal structuring of the movement. The institutionalized churches raise funds, organize schools, hospitals, and church programs, build church buildings, and hire pastors. The revival groups meet informally, carry out no large organized activity, and maintain no offices or paid personnel. The result is an ongoing renewal of the established churches from within.

The pattern closest to this in Western churches is the emergence of parachurch organizations such as the Christian Business Men's Club, Navigators, InterVarsity Christian Fellowship, Youth for Christ, and Campus Crusade. However, unlike the East African Revival, these movements have led to formal organizations that, in time, have experienced the problems of institutionalization. Moreover, parachurch organizations have drawn personnel and resources from the churches and often created rivalries between the two. Because parachurch movements can limit their membership to those with talent and high spiritual commitment, they attract some of the best Christian leaders. But the church, which cannot turn away the weak, the poor, the uneducated, and the broken outcasts of society, is left weakened by the loss of talents and resources. There is often less excitement and honor in the care of those on the margins of society.

RITUALS OF RENEWAL

A fourth structure for renewal is rituals. Rituals play an important part in all religions. In them people draw apart from the secular routines of everyday life in order to focus their attention on religious matters. Ever since the Reformation, the Protestant churches in the West have tended to look at rituals with a disapproving eye. The rise of secularism (probably due in part to this anti-ritualistic stance) has only reinforced this rejection of ritual. The result has often been to stress corporate fellowship rather than worship of God as the central purpose of Sunday services, and to introduce informal, but not less rigid, ritual forms such as bulletins, special clothes, and implicit spiritual hierarchies.

It may well be that Protestants need to rediscover the importance of multivocal rituals if they wish to counteract the growing secularism of the modern age, for rituals like symbols are languages for speaking of spiritual things. As in the case of institutions, the answer to dead rituals is not no rituals, but living rituals. Such rituals are important in bringing renewal not only to individuals but to institutions as well.

RITUALS OF RENEWAL

Rituals play an important part in all religious life. This is particularly true of nonliterate peoples from whom rituals and myths are the encyclopedias in which religious knowledge is stored. Literate people store such information in books, but nonliterate peoples must do so in forms that can be readily recalled. For this reason, rituals that can be reenacted and stories that can easily be remembered are the primary means by which most people around the world retain and transmit their religious beliefs.

Religious rituals are also important in the expression of religious feelings. As Otto points out (1923), the religious experience is closely tied to a sense of mystery, awe, and fear in the face of the supernatural. Such feelings are important in giving expression and reinforcement to the beliefs we hold most deeply.

Finally, rituals call for personal response, often in some tangible form. To participate in a ritual is to reaffirm one's commitment to the beliefs it enacts.

STRUCTURE OF RITUALS

All rituals share a basic structure: they stand as sacred events in opposition to ordinary, secular life. Everyday life is semichaotic. Unexpected occurrences and accidents interrupt a sequence of events that in itself often lacks order. In the face of this disorder, secular life, left to itself, becomes increasingly meaningless.

RITUALS OF RESTORATION

Rituals can be divided into two types. The first of these, and by far the most common, are rituals of restoration. In these people gather together to restore their faith in the beliefs that order their lives, and rebuild the religious community in which these beliefs find expression.

Rituals of restoration have several basic characteristics. First, they are generally characterized by a high degree of ritual order. For example, the order of Sunday morning services is often fixed and repeated from week to week. The Lord's Prayer is recited again and again (in ordinary life such repetition appears foolish—one does not tell the same joke again and again to the same audience). The songs are generally printed and their melodies and words highly predictable. Even the congregational responses may be spelled out in detail. Only in the sermon do we allow some originality, and even there the content must remain within the normally expected theological framework. This high order restores in the participants a sense of order and meaning in the universe, in their community, and in their own lives.

Second, restorative rituals take place within the state of community. That is, people occupy formal roles and relate in institutionalized ways to one another. For example, in ordinary church services the members act as pastor, deacon, choir leader, and layperson. Many of these distinctions are reinforced by titles, differences in clothing, and special locations in the sanctuary. Role differentiation and hierarchy are evident in the organization of the service. The leader is a priest or head appointed by the institution. As such, he or she represents the people before God. Consequently, restorative rituals reinforce the authority and structures of the establishment.

Third, there is a sharp focus on religious activity and a strong sense of expectation that something will occur. People leave behind the cares of everyday life. Ordinary tasks are forgotten as full attention is given to the service at hand.

Finally, these regenerative rites are generally held in places central to the lives of the people. The church, particularly in villages and towns, is in the middle of the community and carries with it the religious feeling of home—a place where people find security, meaning, and a sense of rest.

RITUALS OF TRANSFORMATION

If restorative rituals are characterized by a high degree of structure, transformative ones are characterized by a high degree of creativity and antistructure. That is, they often reject the normal structure of an institution and seek to create a new one. In so doing, they cut through established ways of doing things and restore a measure of flexibility and personal intimacy to the organization.

Transformational rituals are found in all religions of the world, including Christianity. They include such practices as pilgrimages, camps and retreats, special revival services, festivals, mass rallies, and, in many countries, religious fairs. On the level of the individual and family they also include rites of passage associated with birth, marriage, death, and other transitions of life. In the early and medieval church transitional rituals played an important part in the lives of the people. Only in recent years, and in Western Protestant churches in secular, urban settings, have they lost much of their significance.

In some crucial ways transformative rites are the opposite of restorative rites. First, they are characterized by what Victor Turner (1969) calls "limi-nality." This is the state of being in limbo—of being torn out of the familiar settings and relationships in which we live our lives. For instance, the pilgrim leaves familiar territory to travel to a strange place where everything is new. There is a structure, but it is a totally new one characterized by flexibility, creativity, and change rather than the reinforcement of an existing order. The result is an openness to change, for the ties to everyday life that often draw us back into existing structures are broken.

Second, transformational rituals are characterized not by *community* but by *communitas*. This term introduced by Turner (1969) connotes a lack of formal roles and relationships. In other words, in *communitas* there is no rigid social structure and no hierarchy. Participants are all equals. In the presence of God, all human distinctions become meaningless. This sense of *communitas* bonds participants together into a single group and opens them up to change.

There is an exception to this state of *communitas*. For the leaders of the pilgrimage, camp, or festival, the ritual is not a place set apart from their normal lives. It is their place of work. Consequently for them these rituals are their *community*. But leaders of such rites are generally prophets. They are often charismatic leaders who in the role of addressing "the voice of God" to religious institutions and their members often pose a threat to the "priests" who run the establishment.

Communitas is a short-lived state of affairs. One cannot live in it for long without beginning to transform it into community, for *communitas* does not provide for all the requirements of ongoing social life. In time people need doctors, merchants, teachers, and a great variety of other workers to maintain the society. When Peter suggested on the Mount of Transfiguration that they build houses, he had already begun the transformation from an ethereal experience to ordinary life.

Third, rituals of transformation, like those of restoration, are associated with a high sense of focus and of expectation. Outside matters are left behind. In tranformational rituals this often includes a geographic separation that makes disengagement from the world complete.

Finally, transformative rites allow for a great deal of creativity. This creativity destroys the old order, but it also builds a new one.

The goal of transformative rites is to bring about change. The combination of liminality, *communitas,* high expectations, and antistructural creativity makes deep and lasting changes possible in short periods of time. Changes in funda-mental beliefs are often reinforced by strong emotions and a commitment to act upon the new convictions. These transformations are often spoken of as con-versions, rededications, and new commitments.

TRANSFORMATIVE RITUALS AND THE RENEWAL OF THE CHURCH

Transformative rituals were very much a part of Judeo-Christian life until recent times. In the Old Testament the levitical priests scattered throughout the land conducted the normal restorative rituals. However, three times a year all adult males, particularly heads of families who served as family priests, were expected to go to Jerusalem. There they gathered as pilgrims in the great festivals of regeneration. All ordinary social distinctions were broken down as the people assembled before the Lord. Special music, art, and even dance gave expression to the creativity of these events. It is not surprising, therefore, that the most important events in the life of Christ—his initiation into Jewish adulthood, his death, and his resurrection—took place on such occasions.

Festivals, pilgrimages, and even the Crusades played important roles in the medieval church. The toil of daily life and the routine of local services were broken by special occasions that made the people aware of a greater Christendom, of the world outside, and of the great historical heritage of their faith. The great cathedrals, the pilgrimage sites, and Palestine itself restored to many a sense of the sacred and of God's presence in human history.

Even in frontier America, transformative services played a key part in the religious life of the people. The evangelistic crusades, revival meetings, and mission conferences were annual events on the calendars of many churches.

Today, in Western urban society, our regenerative rites are largely secular—the major sports events, the political rallies, and professional conferences. In churches the revivals and crusades have been replaced by summer camps and weekend retreats. They play an important part in personal renewal, but they have less effect upon the structures of the institutionalized church. Denominational conferences, anniversary celebrations, and festivals such as Easter and Christmas do involve whole churches, but they are often controlled by the priests of the institution. Citywide crusades do break down barriers between denominations and provide Christians with a greater vision of the scope of Christianity as a whole, but they are sporadic and far between.

Restorative rites can renew commitment and vision, but only by reaffirming the institutional structures. It takes transformations and revolutions to break the stranglehold these structures can have in the church. It may well be that churches in the West may need to rediscover the importance of such regenerative rituals if they want to counter the evils of institutionalization and bring new life back into the church.

TRANSFORMATIVE RITUALS AND MISSIONS

What implications does all this have for missions? It is clear that we must strive not only to plant new churches, but to renew constantly the life of the old ones. Dead forms of Christianity are little better than non-Christian religions. Consequently, missions like churches must plan for the hundred-year span and longer.

But there is another reason why missions must take renewal rituals into account. Many of the societies in which missions are found are nonliterate societies that encode their beliefs in religious rituals. Missionaries who come from literate societies that store their beliefs in books often do not realize this and seek to get rid of rituals, dramas, stories, and other folk means for preserving knowledge. The result is that new Christians often have few ways to remember their beliefs. They cannot read the Bible. The preacher may come only on rare occasions. As P. Y. Luke and John B. Carman found (1968:127), the theology of most Indian village Christians is recorded in their songs. This "lyric theology" is memorized and sung in the homes at night, sustaining the people's faith.

The contrast between Protestant services and the people's traditional ceremonies is probably greatest in the areas of transformative rituals. Festivals, religious fairs, pilgrimages, and rites of passage such as birth, initiation, marriage, and death break the drudgery of everyday life, provide excitement, and make life more meaningful. Here modern Christian missionaries have provided the fewest functional substitutes to replace the old ways. Consequently Christianity often appears drab and uninteresting.

Several innovative attempts have been made to change this picture. J. T. Seamands began a Christian religious fair in South India that attracts Christians from a wide area for a week of meetings and excitement. The Korean churches have united to organize nationwide rallies that strengthen the believers and serve as a witness to the people of the growing church in the land.

Church planting and church renewal are the two central tasks of missions. The first without the second leads to widespread nominal Christianity; the second without the first leads to life without a mission. In fact, the two go together. An effective mission to the world often revives the home church, and renewal at home often leads to a new missionary vision.

BIBLIOGRAPHY

BERGER, Peter
  *1974   The Homeless Mind: Modernization and Consciousness, New York: Vintage
         Books.
ELIADE, Mircea
  1963   Myth and Reality, New York: Harper.
LUKE, P. Y. and CARMAN, J. B.
  *1968   Village Christians and Hindu Culture, London: Lutterworth Press, for Com-
         mission on World Mission and Evangelism, W.C.C.
ORR, Edwin
  *1975   The Eager Feet: Evangelical Awakenings 1790-1830, Chicago: Moody Press.
  1975-78 Evangelical Awakenings, 5 vols., Minneapolis: Bethany Fellowship.
OTTO, Rudolph
  *1923   The Idea of the Holy, Oxford: Oxford University Press. Originally published
         as Das Heilige in 1917.
RATZLAFF, Don
  1981   "The parachurch power shift," The Christian Leader (May 5).
TURNER, Victor
  *1969   The Ritual Process, Chicago: Aldine Publishing Company.
  1973   "The center out there: Pilgrim's goal," History of Religions, 12:191-230.
  1978   Image and Pilgrimage in Christian Cultures: Anthropological Perspectives,
         New York: Columbia University Press.
WEBER, Max
  1964   The Theory of Social Organization, New York: Free Press.
  *1968   Economy and Society, Vol. I, New York: Bacdminster Press.
*Indicates reference cited in chapter.

III. THEOLOGICAL ISSUES

14. THE OLD TESTAMENT ROOTS OF MISSION

Richard R. De Ridder

"AT FIRST SIGHT THE OLD TESTAMENT APPEARS TO OFFER LITTLE BASIS FOR the idea of mission. . . . Yet if we investigate the Old Testament more thoroughly, it becomes clear that the future of the nations is a point of the greatest concern. . . . This indeed cannot be otherwise, for from the first page to the last the Bible has the whole world in view, and its divine plan of salvation is unfolded as pertaining to the whole world" (Bavinck 1960:11).

J. H. Bavinck's thesis stands in marked contrast to the statement of Adolf Harnack who wrote, "To reject the Old Testament in the second century was an error the church rightly resisted; to maintain it in the sixteenth century was a destiny the Reformation could not escape; but still to preserve it in the nineteenth century as one of the canonical documents of Protestantism is the result of religious and ecclesiastical paralysis" (Harnack 1924:217).

By these two opinions the lines are strictly drawn and the tensions between varied viewpoints of the Old Testament clearly expressed. Did the Christian church too hastily take over the Old Testament as part of its canon without sufficient reflection? Did the church in fact violate the New Testament when it held on the one hand that the cultic and civil legislation of the Old Testament was done away in Jesus Christ (at least literally) while it continued to insist that the Old Testament was a valid and necessary part of its sacred canon? At the same time the careful reader of the New Testament can only conclude that the use which the writers of the New Testament made of the Old Testament precluded the church from rejecting the Old Testament.[1]

Choosing the side of those who affirm the unity of Scripture (Old and New Testaments), we are forced to ask in terms of the purpose of this book, Does the Old Testament have any significance for the church's mission? Are the roots of the New Testament church's mission to be found only in the New Testament? Because great prominence is given by the church today to its calling

---

1. Van Ruler (1971:10) gives a synopsis of Harnack's thesis and the response of H. Bornkamm.

Richard R. De Ridder, Grand Rapids, Michigan, is Professor of Church Polity and Missions at Calvin Theological Seminary. He has served in numerous pastorates in Christian Reformed churches and as a missionary to Sri Lanka from 1956 to 1960. Among his recent publications are Discipling the Nations *(Baker Book House, 1975),* My Heart's Desire for Israel *(Presbyterian and Reformed Publishing Company, 1974), and* God Has Not Rejected His People *(Baker Book House, 1977).*

to be a witness of its ascended Lord (Jesus), what does the Old Testament contribute to our understanding of God's redemptive purpose? Does the Old Testament constitute a significant part of the message we proclaim and the witness we bring? These questions are of great importance for the Christian mission. The way we answer them will define the content of our message.

The current practice of the church, in its corporate worship and contemporary theology as well as in its mission outreach, does not give much promise of finding a positive answer to the questions posed. In some Christian circles the Old Testament is treated as though it does not exist or was abrogated by the revelation of the New Testament. The New Testament is published separate from the Old Testament, not merely out of cost consciousness or convenience but also out of a principial assumption that the New Testament can stand alone, by itself. Old Testament books are among the last to be translated in the languages of the peoples to whom the church reaches out.

Our churches are almost completely barren of the rich Old Testament symbols, these having been long replaced by the cross alone (and often inappropriately by *three* crosses, which leads one to ask how all three of the crosses of Golgotha have such significance). The hymnology of many churches ignores almost completely the rich heritage of the Psalms and their universal themes, while experiential, sentimental substitutes replace them in our worship.

There is little awareness among many Christians that Jesus was a Jew of his day, that he spoke in terms of prevailing religious concepts and beliefs held by his contemporaries, and that it was his custom to worship in the synagogue and his feet often walked the Temple's sacred courts. While we proclaim and claim him as the Savior of the Gentiles, we seem to be saying that it looks as if God had to begin over again his dealings with humankind when in love he gave his Son, the only begotten, that the world might be saved by believing in him, as though God to have a people had to call Gentiles to faith and obedience.

No matter how difficult it is to answer the questions posed about the relationship of the Old Testament to the New Testament mission, the matter we here treat is of great importance.[2] Only because Jesus Christ is the messiah of Israel can he be the Savior of the world. The history of the church is a continuum of and an integral part of God's dealings with Israel. Israel and the Old Testament reflect what God has in mind for humankind, for the whole world. God has planted only one olive tree, subject throughout the ages to his pruning and grafting (Rom 9-11).

We must begin, therefore, at the beginning.[3] By doing so we will discover immediately that the revelation given by God is intimately bound up with history, that the faith we confess is grounded in events that took place and in which God was intimately involved. It may be well to observe at this point that Western culture has had considerable influence upon the Western church's conceptions as to what took place when God revealed himself to humankind. Our conceptions of inspiration, for example, concentrate almost completely (and very simplistically) on *words*. However, it may not be forgotten that although words do con-

2. Van Ruler (1971:11-14) sketches ten current views of the Old Testament held by the church and develops his critique of these views in succeeding chapters.
3. Blauw (1962:18) states that "the key to understanding of the whole of Scripture is found in Gen 1-11."

stitute a part of that revelation, the *words* of God's revelation are inseparably united with God's *deeds* in history. God's self-disclosures are themselves the stimuli to action.[4] Humankind's relationship to God takes precedence over all other relationships.

GENESIS 1–3

The understanding of the first three chapters of Genesis is foundational to an understanding of all that follows in Scripture. Several points will be noted, each of which to one degree or another touches the heart of the church's message.

Although stated largely in theological terms, it must not be forgotten that what we are considering is based upon acts of God in the history of the universe and of humankind. However one judges or assesses the relationship of the report to the actual event (this refers to the question of the nature of the reporting and its recording), the truth remains that God acted, events occurred, and real events were recorded.

God active everywhere. We first of all meet God in action: "In the beginning God *created*" (Gen 1:1). The significance of this statement can hardly be exhausted by a simple proposition. What is said here about God's actions characterizes all that we know of him throughout Scripture. God worked and continues to work: "My Father is always at his work to this very day" (Jn 5:17 NIV). One cannot interpret any history—whether of the world or of the church—unless one sees that God is not an absent deity who hides from humankind, but we can know him from what he has made (Rom 1:20). God's deeds, moreover, are not limited to the church but encompass the whole world. God is not only present everywhere, but active everywhere as well.

The Creator in control. The Genesis account gives no credence whatever to any form of philosophical or theological dualism, either between God and the creation or between God and the creature. God in his nature is distinct from the world and from the created order. God brought the world into existence. It is not described for us as an extension of God, but as a finite, created reality upheld only because the Creator continues to uphold it. As the New Testament teaches, when God's purposes with the present created order are fulfilled, this world and the universe will come to an end and a new heaven and a new earth will be created (Rev 21:1).

Worthy citizens in God's world. We are also clearly taught that God's creative acts produced a "good" universe and world (Gen 1:31). No possible justification can be found here for world-denial or world-flight. God affirms the goodness of creation not merely in the sense of being technically or mechanically perfect but as fit also as the habitation and workshop of humanity, God's image-bearers, moral creatures created without imperfection. The Christian message stands diametrically opposed to all worldviews which look at the world as intrinsically evil and justify humankind's flight from it. To live in God's world as God's image-bearer and joyful servant is *life*.

4. Kraft more fully explores this thesis (1979). It also agrees with the thesis of Harry R. Boer (1955) that the New Testament church did not base its witnessing activity in a specific command or commission but was being responsive to the Holy Spirit and the great redemptive acts of God in Jesus Christ.

Ruling function for man and woman. Man and woman were created in the image of God (Gen 1:26-27). Together they constituted what was necessary to function as that image. Rule over the world was given them to exercise together, a ruling function that extended over all that God made and included a moral element (Gen 2:15). Humankind is distinct from all the creatures the Lord God made by virtue of its receiving the breath of life from God (Gen 2:7). Adam's own judgment concerning his special nature—the representative for humanity—was confirmed when God brought to him all the beasts of the field and the birds of the air (Gen 2:9), among whom Adam could find no suitable helper (Gen 2:20). These acts of God distinguish the Creator from created being and humankind from all the rest which God made. Man and woman have a God-given dignity, worth, and mission that separate them from everything else.

A common and unbroken family tree. Humankind constitutes a unity through the creative act of God in bringing man and woman into being. The unity of the human race is set in the context of birth from human parents (Gen 2:23; 3:16, 20). Only Adam was the direct creation of God. Even Eve was formed out of his bone and flesh. The "Seed of the Woman" would someday be born from a human parent and partake fully of our human nature. The significance of this unity in God's redemptive plan cannot be overestimated. When God later reveals his manner of working through covenants he establishes and promises to which he binds himself, it is in a family (nation, tribe, and so on) context in which he carries this out. Race, culture, nationality are nothing. We can be one in Christ Jesus because God has made of one all nations of the earth. God did this "that they should seek God . . . and find him" (Acts 17:27).

Humans distinct from spirits. Human beings are distinct from the world of spirits (good and evil). Although fuller understanding of the identity as to who tempted Eve and led to the fall of humankind is given later in the Scriptures, the Bible is clear about the fact that the spirits are created, finite beings, subject to God. There is no eternal dualism between God and Satan, between good and evil. The created being is not the hapless victim of gods and spirits of this world. The redeemed share the triumph over their vaunted powers and self-acclaimed deity. The spirits too are subject to Jesus.

God not sidetracked by sin. The introduction of sin nowhere compromises God's complete control of creation, creature, or the spirit world. God asserted sovereignty as soon as the representative sinned and revealed clearly that, though humankind and the world will continue—although under greatly altered conditions (Gen 3)—, God remained in full control of history. History will move to the fulfillment of God's plan. Covenants are not abrogated and promises never fail because God is the Lord of history and the controller of destiny.

From every tribe and tongue. It is clearly implied that God is concerned not with a part of the human race but with all humankind. God's works are to be seen from a universal perspective. In fact, one needs to read to the twelfth chapter of Genesis before one finds any mention of the fathers of the Jewish people.

Eden exit: divine calling. It should also be clearly noted that Genesis 3 ends on a note of grace and mercy. Many have misunderstood the meaning of

God's acts of banishing and driving out Adam and Eve from Paradise as though this only indicated judgment and punishment. The words used in Genesis 3:23-24 leave a positive note, however. While on the one hand God made a separation of humans from the Garden and its Tree of Life, the act of driving out included a sense of mission, of purpose, of divine calling. It is good news that even in a creation which will continue to be subject to frustration until the glorious freedom of the children of God is complete, humankind will find this world an arena in which work and service to God are possible (Rom 8:19-22). Nothing of world-rejection or world-flight is taught in the Bible.

These propositions form a sort of bridge to the rest of the Old Testament and the understanding of its meaning for mission. If indeed the Old Testament is from the beginning a record of God's dealings with the human race, then the Christian mission is likewise an expression of this universal purpose of God. However, as soon as we say this, a host of inescapable questions intrude themselves into the discussion. Not the least important of these is the question that concerns the purposes of God's dealings with Abraham and his seed in relation to other nations and peoples. It is obvious that Genesis 12 begins a new chapter in salvation history, but how are God's acts to be understood? What did God have in mind? Was salvation henceforth to be limited to one people or nation only? If not, then what was the significance of Israel for the nations? Does the Old Testament imply that God "left off" dealing with the nations and concentrated on Abraham's seed until Messiah Jesus came? Did Israel have no message for the people of the world? Did Israel have no mission except to wait out God's time?

THE GOSPEL TO ABRAHAM

Paul in Galatians 2:8 says, "The Scripture foresaw that God would justify the Gentiles by faith, and announced the gospel in advance to Abraham: 'All nations will be blessed through you' " (NIV). This promise, found in Genesis 12:1-3, constitutes the turning point in history at which humankind's primordial history ends and the age of the promise begins. The significance of that promise can hardly be overestimated, either for the Jews or for the Gentiles. Isaiah in later years let it be clearly known to people in his day that there could be no Golden Age for Israel unless the world shared in the blessings God was prepared to dispense.

That Yahweh intended this is clearly stated in Genesis 22:18 where what is said about Abraham in Genesis 12:1-3 is transferred to his descendants: "Through your offspring all nations on earth will be blessed, because you have obeyed me" (NIV). When God entered into covenant with Abraham, he did not abandon the nations but did so for the sake of the nations. "Abraham is chosen, not just for his own glory, the good fortune of his descendants, or the misery of his enemies. . . . Abraham is the instrument for the redemption of the world" (Martin-Achard 1962:35). Abraham was God's means to an end. Genesis 12:1-3 is the keystone in the overarching purpose of God for humankind.

But why Abraham? Jew and Gentile have repeatedly asked that question. The answer cuts to the heart of the mercy and love of God. Abraham did not excel in any virtues over his fellows, no more than Israel over the other nations

(Deut 7:7-8). In fact Joshua (Josh 24:2-3) specifically mentioned that Abraham came from a family of worshipers of other gods. No wonder the rabbis called him the first proselyte! (Bab. Talmud *'Aboda Zara* 44-45; *Sukka* 232; *Hagigah* 8).

The whole history of Abraham and the story of his call and pilgrimage is a remarkable demonstration of how one who was himself dispersed by the command of God—"Leave your country, your people, and your father's household and go to the land I will show you" (Gen 12:1 NIV)—became the gracious instrument by which those who had been dispersed by the judgment of God— "So the Lord scattered them from there over all the earth" (Gen 11:8 NIV)— will again be brought back to the only source of life and into unity with each other (Gal 3:28-29). The narrative will seem to become more and more exclusive (Abraham-Isaac-Jacob-Judah-David-Jesus), but this does not mean that the purposes of God were altered in the process, nor that God surrendered claim on the nations.

In this early promise of Genesis 12:1-3 the essential features basic to the missionary task are to be found. Although, as many have correctly observed, there is here no command to evangelize the nations in the way the New Testament expressed this, Yahweh asserts lordship over the nations and will guide their destiny and accomplish his purpose. This purpose will be worked out through Abraham, whose election by Yahweh was for service, not personal advantage (De Ridder 1975:22ff).

Election may not be defined merely in terms of privilege or honor, as chosenness for an eternity of bliss. Election is always for a purpose and is based on covenant. Peter describes a chosen people as "a people belonging to God," that they "may declare the praises of him who called [them] out of darkness into his marvelous light" (I Pet 2:9 NIV). That is why we may not regard Israel's function as ended when Messiah came and the church began. If we do this, Israel becomes an isolated entity separated from the world rather than a people through whom God acts on behalf of the world. Israel (or any person) does not possess the right to withdraw itself from this purpose of God. The promise and covenant were sovereignly established; they will continue to be sovereignly administered. One can rebel, be disobedient, refuse to fulfill God's purpose. Even that kind of action does not mean that God is handicapped and consequently incapable of fulfilling his purposes.

To digress for a moment, this touches the heart of the misunderstanding of contemporary Judaism concerning its election. Election is always in the service of covenant, not vice versa. Today's Jews limit the Jewish mission to survival as a separate people and find it unnecessary to put forth any effort to bring others to the only light that can dispel the gross darkness of the peoples.

To return to what was said earlier concerning God's sovereign act of creation, Genesis 1:1 obviously constitutes the necessary basis for mission since no people or race may consider itself to be more worthy than any other people. All peoples are God's concern, and he remains their righteous judge whose very righteousness becomes the ground of our hope that his sufficient grace will bring us into full and blessed fellowship. Whenever persons contemplate what God has done for them, they must be moved to share that best of news with others.

The work of missions must be understood, therefore, as being possible only in the context of covenant. Israel has no peculiar claim on God other than what God has sovereignly committed himself to being and doing. God's people lived out their history (and God's) in the sight of the nations, not in some hidden corner of the world. Yahweh set the bounds of the nations according to the number of the people of Israel (Deut 32:8), and he set them at the crossroads of the nations. When they were dispersed or dispersed themselves, God went with them. Wherever they went, it was there they prayed that God would be gracious and bless them, so that God's way might be known on earth and his salvation among all nations (Ps 67:1-2).

Israel was a people that had no need for a missionary command because its very heart cried out, "May the peoples praise you, O God; may all the peoples praise you. May the nations be glad and sing for joy, for you rule the peoples justly and guide the nations of the earth" (Ps 67:3-4 NIV). Joy for the blessing of the Lord is not limited to fruitful fields that yield abundant harvests, but will be experienced when "all the ends of the earth will fear him" (Ps 67:7). To look for a command to carry on a witness to the peoples is to seek something which is not there because it was not needed.

The disobedience of Israel and its leaders is frequently placed too prominently in our assessment of the Old Testament people of God. One cannot dispute, of course, that then (just as now among Christians) disobedience characterized Israel's response to Yahweh and that God frequently disciplined his people, afflicting and punishing them in varied ways. At the same time we must not forget that like ourselves contemporary prophets of those days were sometimes blind to the acts of God (one even prayed for death under the juniper tree whereas God could speak of 7,000 who had not bowed to Baal!) and that even in days of widespread apostasy many remained true to God.

Whatever was happening to Israel, its history was not the kind of affair that had no meaning for others. Everything was part of God's plan, and through his acts in Israel God was stretching out his hands to the world.

We should not forget that there is a somewhat subtle difference, often overlooked, between the Old Testament and the New Testament. Whereas Israel was called on to *display* the wonderful deeds of God, the New Testament church is called on to *declare* that message to the people (Sandmel 1968:33). Abraham was before his call a representative of the *fallen* race. He and his descendants embodied God's grace and were a sign of how that grace overcomes human estrangement from God. The New Testament difference is that Genesis 3 (the story of the fall) is reenacted not in the privacy of a Garden but before the eyes of the whole world and through a people destined to be the light to the nations (Martin-Achard 1962).

THE LAW AND THE PROPHETS

Moving beyond the time of the patriarchs, it is necessary to make a brief stop at Mount Sinai. Here Israel was born as a nation, and the covenant promises made to the fathers were extended to a newly emerging nation, a people (Num 14:9). The Exodus, which was a manifestation of Yahweh's unconditioned sovereignty, was an act not of humans but of the world-God. Israel had no special status among the nations by itself except what God gave to it. The focus was not what God had *done* but *why* he acted in this way for his people. At

Sinai Israel and the world were given God's answer. In later reflection on this (Ps 136:4-9), the inevitable conclusion is drawn: The God who saves is none other than the God who created the world! At Sinai God covenanted with Israel and took Israel into partnership with himself. No area of his people's life will ever again be free from his purpose and will.[5] Israel might never be "like the nations" (Deut 4:33-35; 17).

From Sinai onward Israel became a people among the nations. Having lived as a *ger* (a stranger, resident alien) in Egypt (Ex 22:21; 23:9; Lev 19:34), Israel continued a *ger* in her assigned territory (Lev 25:23). Her treatment of the strangers in her midst, God said, must always be a conscious attempt to practice God's concern for the stranger. Too little attention has been paid, I believe, to the presence within Israel of those whose bloodlines could not be traced to Abraham (De Ridder 1975:41-48). The non-Israelite could at any time claim the right to a share in the salvation of Yahweh.

The age of the prophets made it unmistakably clear for both Israel and the world that God's purpose was universal. Although one searches in vain for specific commands to witness, the history of Old Testament Israel clearly demonstrates that wherever Israel was dispersed or wherever this people lived in voluntary dispersion, they shared their faith with the community and welcomed the Gentile into fellowship.[6]

CREATION, REVELATION, REDEMPTION

These three themes—creation, revelation, redemption—summarize the major emphasis of ancient as well as contemporary Jewish belief. They constitute the basis on which the Jews have systematized their faith. We would be misunderstanding that faith, however, if we thought that such themes were wholly otherworldly. The faith of God's people is so utterly this-worldly. For example, release from the slavery of Egypt was a call to life, to *shalom* (peace), to fullness of life and the realization of the potentials latent within full surrender of life to obedience to Israel's covenanting God. The righteousness and justice which God sought (Isa 5:7) would be the blessedness of God's continued favor if obediently rendered to him. The *shalom* of Eden would be restored to the world through Israel (Isa 9:6-7; 11:6-8) when God's mighty, liberating acts elicited from his people the righteousness and justice which alone are consistent with union in his mission and purpose.

It would be interesting to pursue this meaning of *shalom* in detail. What is important to note is that the world is always taken up in Israel's destiny. The hope of Israel is the hope of the world (Zimmerli 1976). The fulfillment of the promises will mean peace to the world (Zech 9:9-10; Isa 2:2-4; Mic 4:1-3). Passages could be multiplied. This significant relationship of God's people to the world is not the passive kind of relationship so often described as the dominant theme of the Old Testament.[7] It is rather the active participation of God's people

5. Brueggemann (1968) demonstrates how the legal material revealed at Sinai is theological in a decisive way.
6. See my work (1975—a reprint of *The Dispersion of the People of God*) for a detailed study of the extent and motivation for proselytizing in the Old Testament period.
7. This is frequently expressed by the terms "centrifugal" and "centripetal," a distinction I find increasingly difficult to maintain except in a very limited application.

in the affairs of the world. They must maintain the right relationship to God by pursuing righteousness and showing justice to others. Both together complete the covenant obedience of the law revealed at Sinai.

John Stek defines justice as humankind's vocation, as right dealing with their neighbors, as the justice of the kingdom of God, the "befriending" (*'ahab*) of fellow humans. The end, he says, is liberation:

> Liberation in the Old Testament is redemption of man from every power (social, political, economic, cultural, religious, ideological, spiritual—the "principalities and powers," Eph 3:10; 6:12; Col 2:15) that injects itself between Yahweh and man to thwart Yahweh's purpose, to demean man's true dignity, to exploit man's labor, to sterilize man's reproductive powers, to diminish man's provisions, to rob man of his appointed blessing, to cut man off from his divinely intended destiny. Liberation is unto covenant, to the re-establishment of the lord-servant relationship between God and man so that man stands once more in his full dignity directly under the claims of God and under his care and benediction. God's mission is to effect that liberation. It is also his servants' co-(m)mission (Stek 1978:133-65).

Nothing less than this is the call of the church to be the people of God in the new covenant age. Ingrafted into the olive tree, Gentile and Jew are now one in Jesus Christ. The church would do well to begin to read its sacred books in the light of all that God has revealed. The good news can neither be understood nor preached unless it be understood in the perspective of the Old Testament witness concerning God and the creation, created beings and their relationship to God, as well as their place in creation and the course of history.

Too often basic biblical concepts, foundational to the Christian message, have been ignored or abstracted from their context and the Bible made a tool for whatever program of hope we present to the world. A more submissive reading of the Bible is required of us, for only in that way can we truly hear the Lord of the Word and not just the Word of the Lord (Frei 1974). Such a way of reading salvation history will at the same time release us from "our ethnic, geographical, chronological and confessional parochialism" (Stek 1978:133).

REFERENCES CITED

BAVINCK, Johan H.
  1960   *An Introduction to the Science of Missions*, Philadelphia: Presbyterian & Reformed Publishing Company.
BLAUW, Johannes
  1962   *The Missionary Nature of the Church*, New York: McGraw-Hill.
BOER, Harry R.
  1955   *Pentecost and Missions*, Franeker: T. Wever Company.
BRUEGGEMANN, Walter
  1968   *Tradition for Crisis*, Richmond: John Knox Press.
DE RIDDER, Richard R.
  1975   *Discipling the Nations*, Grand Rapids: Baker Book House. A reprint of *The Dispersion of the People of God*, Kampen: J. H. Kok, 1971.

FREI, Hans
    1974   *The Eclipse of Biblical Narrative,* New Haven and London: Yale University Press.
HARNACK, Adolf
    1924   *Marcion: Das Evangelium vom Fremden Gott,* Leipzig: J. C. Hinrichs.
KRAFT, Charles
    1979   *Christianity in Culture,* Maryknoll: Orbis Books.
MARTIN-ACHARD, R.
    1962   *A Light to the Nations,* Edinburgh: Oliver & Boyd.
SANDMEL, Samuel
    1968   *New Testament Issues,* New York: Harper & Row.
STEK, John H.
    1978   "Salvation, Justice and Liberation in the Old Testament," *Calvin Theological Journal,* Vol. 13, No. 2, November 1978.
VAN RULER, Arnold A.
    1971   *The Christian Church and the Old Testament,* Geoffrey W. Bromiley (trans.), Grand Rapids: Eerdmans.
ZIMMERLI, Walther
    1976   *The Old Testament and the World,* John J. Scullion (trans.), Atlanta: John Knox Press.

15. THE PEOPLE OF GOD AND THE PEOPLES

John S. Pobee

GOD, IN JESUS CHRIST, MADE A NEW PEOPLE OF FAITH. THIS NEW HUMANITY spread out amid the old. It's a story with many facets, one which I propose to approach from a biblical perspective with special reference to the New Testament and in an African context.

The Bible, Old and New Testaments alike, represents a wealth of individual traditions. This fact itself expresses the vitality of the people of God, from the heart of which these documents emerged. They came out of specific situations which differ from our own modern contexts; some are lost for us. It is, therefore, impossible to reach back to what happened in the primitive church. To that extent the New Testament cannot be normative, because then all the elements and forms must be recovered and imitated. Nevertheless, the New Testament offers a model for renovation and restructuring in the face of persisting later developments, traditionalism, and legalism. New Testament principles must be given appropriate expression.

THE NEW FORCE OF THE LAW AND THE PROPHETS

In the Sermon on the Mount, Jesus declared among other things, "Think not that I have come to abolish the law and the prophets; I have come not to abolish them but to fulfil them" (Mt 5:17). The Law and the Prophets referred to the revelation which the people of God, the Jews, had received and by which they believed themselves to be guided. It was that revelation of God which constituted them the people of God, ratified by the covenant at Mount Sinai.[1] The dominical logion asserts that there is a theological thread running through from Moses, if not before, to Jesus with the result that "in Jesus there has come true what the

---

1. The cult resulting from the special revelation expresses the special relationship between the deity and the clan chief or cult founder. Hence in the Old Testament there is talk of the God of Abraham (Gen 15:1), "the Fear of Isaac" (Gen 31:1), "the Mighty One of Jacob" (Gen 49:34). Our conviction is that the pre-Moses beliefs came to be fused in the worship of the Mosaic Yahweh.

John S. Pobee, Legon, Ghana, is head of the Department for the Study of Religions and Dean of the Faculty of Arts at the University of Ghana. He has lectured in Great Britain, The Netherlands, and the USA. He has chaired the Africa Committee of Theological Education. His latest publication is The Theme of Persecution and Martyrdom in the Writings of St. Paul *(Sheffield: Society of New Testament Studies, 1982).*

laws and the prophets only announced. In him has come the fullness that was intended in them but not attained" (Schweizer 1976:107).

The Law and the Prophets, representing the revelation of God to the old people of God, Israel, remain in force as an expression of the will of God. The fulfillment of the Law and the Prophets by Jesus consists of the fact that he not only teaches it but also does its demands. If there is a difference between the old people of God on the one hand, and the new people of God, it resides in the latter trying to follow in the steps of Jesus and through Christ to live out the demands of the Law and the Prophets which Jesus also taught. The difference between the old and the new people of God is the confession by the latter of Jesus of Nazareth as Lord and Christ. Jesus claimed that he had come to make complete the revelation to the old people of God.

JESUS' FIRST MISSIONARY EMBRACE: THE LOST SHEEP OF ISRAEL

Against that background it should occasion no surprise that Jesus' ministry was in the first instance to the covenanted people of God. In the Gospels Jesus rarely went outside the confines of the covenanted people of God. One of the rare occasions of Jesus dealing with outsiders to the people of God is the story of his encounter with the Syrophoenician woman (Mk 7:14-30; Mt 15:21-28). She came asking for compassion to be shown her daughter, to which Jesus replied, "Let the children first be fed, for it is not right to take the children's bread and throw it to the dogs" (Mk 7:27).

Commentators have been quick to observe that the odds were against the woman because Tyre and Sidon were accursed cities which were consigned to total exclusion. From Tyre Jezebel, the daughter of Ethbaal, king of Tyre, had come to marry Ahab (I Kings 16:31), a marriage which led to the painful introduction of idolatrous worship and foreign ideas of monarchy into Israel, making the people of God depart from the revelation of God which constituted them the people of God.

By normal standards Jesus would not and should not have associated with them, for they were not only outside the people of God but also had in fact brought much trouble on the people of God.[2] However, at the end of the day even the woman represented "the dogs of the household" rather than "the great wild dogs infesting the eastern towns" (I Kings 14:11; II Kings 9:10). She did not dispute that designation but asserted with determination that even if the small dogs did not get the children's portion, they may yet have received the soft white part of the bread on which the hands were customarily wiped after having been dipped into the common dish. For her sense of determination and her faith, Jesus

2. Matthew from a Jewish provenance introduces three details which emphasize the claim that there could be no communication between the Jews and the non-Jews: At first Jesus would not respond to the pitiful appeal of the Gentile woman (Mt 15:23); he actually refused to oblige, declaring that he was sent only "to the lost sheep of the house of Israel" (Mt 15:24); and Jesus reproached her, saying, "It is not right to take the children's bread and cast it to the dogs" (Mt 15:26). Furthermore, whereas Mark describes her as a Greek and a Syrophoenician (Mk 7:26), Matthew describes her as a Canaanite woman, which in the light of Old Testament usage designates Gentiles as distinct from the people of God (Mt 15:21). It is not without interest that in Matthew 15:22, the impression is given that Jesus did not actually enter the Gentile region but went in that direction.

overlooked her natural category as one outside the covenanted people of God and responded favorably to her wish.

The story of Jesus' encounter with the Syrophoenician woman is one that affirms Jesus' acceptance of a covenanted people of God to whom, for the moment at any rate, he was primarily sent and to whom he primarily owed obligation. Outside them were other people, also in God's created world, still members of God's household. But if these others showed faith, determination, and sense of direction, they too could be embraced by God. This story then is a prefiguration of the future progress of the good news from the covenanted people of God, namely the Jews, to a new people of God, the Gentiles who showed faith and determination. Furthermore, if Jesus was sent to "the lost sheep of the house of Israel," then it is asserted that the covenanted people of God had not been faithful to the covenant which constituted them the people of God. But insofar as God is faithful to his part of the covenant, he seeks through Christ to bring them back to their true calling.

Again, if it is true that Jesus saw his primary responsibility to the Jews, it is also true that it does not mean the total and eternal exclusion of those who did not originally belong to the covenanted people of God. If by chance one outside the covenanted people of God stumbled onto what is involved in being a member of the people of God, that one was acceptable to God. That is precisely why in another story the Gentile centurion was highly commended (Mt 8:5-13; Lk 7:1-10). The implication is that belonging to the people of God is not primarily a matter of race, birth, and so on, but a matter of response to the invitation of God through faith and faith-deeds. Faith is not simply assent to specific doctrines; it expresses itself in vital terms.

The seeming reluctance of Jesus to go outside the covenanted people of God is even more drastically stated in Matthew 10:5-6. In the well-known mission charge, Jesus bade the twelve disciples to go only to the "lost sheep of the house of Israel" and not to go anywhere near the Gentiles and even the Samaritans who at the worst had some Jewish blood in them. Though they shared lostness with other nations, yet they belonged to Israel, the people of God, for whom God cares. This, as is often pointed out, is material peculiar to Matthew (in contrast to Mk 6:7-13) and is consistent with the theology of particularism so characteristic of Matthew. In any case, it is difficult to reconcile this particularism with the openness to Samaritans and Gentiles found elsewhere in the teaching of Jesus, as in Matthew 8:11: "I tell you, many will come from east and west and sit at table with Abraham, Isaac, and Jacob in the kingdom of heaven, while the sons of the kingdom will be thrown into the outer darkness" (Lk 10:33; Jn 4:4ff; 8:48).

I am persuaded by Schweizer's comment that

> more likely the saying goes back to a group within the primitive christian community that maintained that only those who became Jews through circumcision would be accepted into the community. . . . Later, the saying came to be understood as representing a temporal sequence: first Israel, then the gentile would receive God's word. . . . It probably derives from the period in which a strict Jewish christian community expected an influx of gentiles seeking to be incorporated into Israel, but did not expect to go on mission to the gentiles (1976:235-36).

The form-critical distinction between *Sitz im Leben Jesu* and the *Sitz im Leben Ecclesiae* has come into its own. Jesus did not totally exclude the possibility of going beyond the people of God to other peoples. At issue are the conditions under which going beyond the covenanted people of God may be undertaken. After that comes the question of what really distinguishes the original people of God from other peoples. To these questions we shall return a little later.

THE POST-RESURRECTION MISSION CHARGE

For the present we wish to turn to the post-resurrection charge to the disciples to be witnesses of Jesus, who was vested with authority before all peoples (Mt 28:18-19). This commission is peculiar to Matthew of the Synoptic Gospels. But the Acts of the Apostles has an independent tradition in which the risen Lord promised the Holy Spirit who would make them "witnesses in Jerusalem and in all Judea and Samaria and to the end of the earth" (Acts 1:8-9). Of course, the earliest community did not draw lines between the resurrection and the exaltation. Be that as it may, the passages at hand indicate that the earliest Christian community saw it as their business to go beyond the people of God to the peoples. For the people of the Old Covenant, this would be the fulfillment of the prophecy of Isaiah that the nations would at last come streaming into Zion (Isa 42:1-5; Tobit 13:11; 14:6-7; Enoch 90:30-36). But the new people were to create a community of Gentiles and Jews, not a community of naturalized Jews. Later we shall discuss this further.

The operative word in the charge is "make disciples," to which the participles "going," "baptizing," and "teaching" are subordinate. Even if before his exaltation Jesus felt called to work primarily among the covenanted people of God, now after the resurrection the earliest community which had emerged seemingly as a sect within Judaism felt called to make disciples of all nations. This development need not be a surprise for two reasons.

First, going beyond the covenanted people of God would have been the only way to make good a real situation. The Jewish leaders had rejected Jesus in no uncertain terms, having blessed the execution of Jesus as a messianic pretender by the Roman overlords of Palestine. So preaching in Palestine was probably excluded by the practical and real situation. In that situation, if they still believed in the cause of Jesus, their only platform could be with the people.

Second, making disciples of every people was the practical working out of the rule of Christ over all the world (Mt 28:18). It would be a contradiction in terms to speak of the universal lordship of Christ when some were not brought under the sovereign rule of Christ through the proclamation (I Tim 3:16). Making disciples is a peculiarly Matthean expression (Mt 28:18; 13:53; 27:57). But it is obvious from Matthew 23:8-10 that all Christians, whether Jewish or Gentile, remain in this category, whatever their qualifications. In other words, whereas before Christ race had been a key factor in the concept of the people of God, now race and progeny are not that significant. Be that as it may, the post-resurrection mission charge emphasizes that the task of the church is to create peoples, and that from Judea to the ends of the world.

Even before the Great Commission of Matthew 28:18 it is asserted that before the eschaton "the gospel must first be preached to all nations" (*panta ta ethnē*, Mk 13:10). In the Matthean parallel (Mt 24:14), instead of *panta ta ethnē*, i.e., all peoples, we have *tēi oikoumenēi*—the nations of the Roman Empire. There is no substantial difference between Mark and Matthew with respect to the theme of the universal mission. Scholars, however, contest the authenticity of the Marcan text as a dominical logion. For one thing, the vocabulary is wholly and distinctively Marcan. For yet another, this verse is in prose which interrupts the poetic arrangement of Mark 13:9, 11-13.

Furthermore, Mark 13:9 and 11 are closely related in thought, which makes verse 10 look more like an intrusion. In any case, if it were authentic, it makes it all the more difficult to account for the fact that Peter and others for long would not go out to the Gentiles (Gal 2:7ff; Acts 10–11:15). However, Taylor seems to me to be right that

> Mark truly represents the mind of Jesus (cf. vii. 27a) but does not give His *ipsissima verba*; and the deeper reason for His reserve must be found in His preoccupation with action, the fulfilment, namely of the Messianic ministry of suffering, death and resurrection (1957:508).

Whether this is a saying from Jesus or not, it is obvious that within thirty to forty years of the coming into existence of the church, the church in some quarters envisaged and prosecuted a universal mission, a mission that went beyond the confines of the original people of God to peoples called by God through Christ. And certainly already in the fourth decade of the first century Paul had no problem reaching out beyond the people of God. I wish to argue that that dimension was only the blossoming out of what was in germ, at least, in the teaching of Jesus.

THE LAST SUPPER AS MOTIVE FOR MISSION

I wish to suggest that in the movement from the people of God to the peoples, the Last Supper is of crucial importance. The words over the cup in Mark and Paul are of relevance to our study. According to I Corinthians 11:25, Jesus said over the cup of wine, "This cup is the new covenant in my blood" (compare Lk 22:20). On the other hand, according to Mark, he said, "This is my blood of the covenant, which is poured out for many" (Mk 14:24; Mt 26:28). Whatever the original form, there is no essential difference between the two versions with respect to the meaning (Taylor 1957:546).

The cup of wine is compared with blood which is shed to establish a new covenant (Jeremias 1966:170). There is an obvious parallelism with Exodus 24:8 where Moses sacrificed young bulls, sprinkled part of the blood on the altar, and made the people promise to obey the commandments of the book of the covenant, and then sprinkled the rest of the blood on them saying, "Behold the blood of the covenant." Similarly, now by the blood of Christ rather than by the blood of a bull, a new covenant is made. That there is conscious relationship between the older covenant and Christ's covenant is shown by the use of *my* with "blood." As Taylor puts it, "As of old dedicated blood was applied in blessing to the people of Israel, so now His life, surrendered to God and accepted by Him is offered to, and made available for men" (1948:138; 1957:545).

By the violent death of Christ which turns out to be a self-sacrifice, a new covenant is established which at once abrogates and represents the Old

Covenant. The newness consists in the fact that the New Covenant was sealed by the self-sacrifice of Christ which *inter alia* creates a new people of God (Behm 1965:133-34).

CONDITIONS THAT GIVE RISE TO A COMMUNITY OF FAITH

Given the fact that there was a people of God and now in Christ a new people of God, at issue now are the conditions under which one may go beyond the people of God to the peoples. First stands the failure of the people of God to live by the terms of the covenant which constituted them the people of God. This is the unanimous note of the New Testament: Jesus' reference to the "lost sheep of the house of Israel" testifies to this. Even if they are wayward, they still belong to the people of God; for their God cares (Gutbrod 1965:384-88). This waywardness could not be allowed to thwart the purpose of God; therefore, the people of God is reconstituted. Similarly, Paul in his letter to the Church of Rome harks back to this point again and again (Rom 10:21; 11:17-20).

Second is the issue of the sovereignty of God. If God is the sovereign Lord of all life and the whole world, then the Gentiles were to be considered at some stage or other. If love is the plumbline for the judgment of humankind at the eschaton, then some exposure of the people to that message is a foregone conclusion.

Third, the condition of the acceptance of people is faith. When the Syrophoenician woman showed faith, her wish was granted (Mk 7:29; Mt 15:28). The centurion's wish was granted also on the grounds of his faith: "Truly, I say to you, not even in Israel have I found such faith" (Mt 8:10). People then may be accepted on the basis of the faith they exhibit. However, the word *faith* is a loaded word.

Two types of faith. I would distinguish between simple and what I propose to call *ichthus* faith. By the former I refer to the belief that Jesus like others in the world is a man of God who could perform great deeds in the power of God. The faith of the Syrophoenician woman like that of the centurion seems to me to belong to this category. It is not without interest that in the Marcan account of the Syrophoenician woman's story Jesus is addressed only as "Sir." On the other hand, at some point, especially after the resurrection, the content of the faith would have deepened into the affirmation that Jesus Christ is the Son of God. This is *ichthus* faith.[3]

Thus, despite the continuity between the people of God and the peoples, the biblical record strikes the new note that others who originally belonged to the peoples and were outside the people of God may now belong to the people of God as long as they affirm that Jesus Christ is the Son of God. On the other hand, Paul, for example, would call the old people of God Jews because they decide against and reject both God and God's community and are excessively attached to the law. As Gutbrod writes, "In Paul . . . *Ioudaios* is almost always used in a sense which emphasized the essential, typical and suprapersonal respect of the term, whether negatively in the historical orientation towards Christ, or

3. *Ichthus* is, of course, Greek for fish. But, as is well known, it came to be used in the early church as a symbol of the church which taught that Jesus Christ is the Son of God.

positively in the commitment to the Law which determines the being of a Jew as such" (1965:381-82). In other words, belonging to the people of God is more a matter of fidelity to a covenant which is now fulfilled in Christ than a matter of descent.

Natural revelation. I referred earlier to simple faith as a condition of entry into the people of God. I wish to include, at this stage, the theology of natural revelation which is articulated in the Bible. Paul like Jesus affirmed that nature itself is a medium of God's revelation as providence, creatorship, and judgeship of the world.

I have elsewhere (Pobee 1979:72-80) demonstrated that these elements are verifiable in African traditional religions. I wish to suggest that these belong to the category I call simple faith. Through visions, dreams, and many other forms of revelation, God reveals himself even to those outside the covenanted people of God. The implication is that if only they would be faithful to that measure of revelation, they too would belong to the household of God. It is precisely because they failed to be faithful to their measure of revelation that Paul was able to charge them with sin.

The conclusion is inevitable that what constitutes the people of God is fidelity to the measure of revelation received. Yet in that general description there is differentiation on the basis of whether the revelation is too rudimentary or advanced. The peculiar note of the Jesus people is the *theologia crucis* which also happens to be the *theologia gloriae*. This, I believe, is the sum of *ichthus* faith.

WORD STUDY

This study would be incomplete without reference to some of the vocabulary involved in the distinction between the people of God and the peoples. This is undertaken with due regard to the warning given by Barr (1965) concerning the use of philological material in theological argument. A number of words come to mind: *laos, ochlos, dēmos, ethnos, Hebraios, Ioudaios, Israēlitēs.*

Hebraios in its Old Testament beginnings is in the first instance a legal term and not an ethnic term; it refers to the Israelites as aliens of inferior legal status (Ex 21:2ff; Jer 34:8). Others used it of them (Gen 39:14; Ex 1:16, 19; I Sam 4:6), though the Hebrews used it of themselves when addressing themselves to foreigners (Gen 40:15; Ex 2:7; 3:18; 9:1). At other times there is the implication that they were in opposition to other nations (Gen 43:32; Deut 15:12; I Sam 13:3). As von Rad puts it, "It carries with it a sense, not of national pride, but of humility and even contempt" (1965:309; Trench 1961:29).

In its rare occurrence in the New Testament, the term "Hebrews" denotes those who have retained the sacred Hebrew tongue as their native language. Its antithesis is *Hellenistēs,* i.e., the Jews of the Diaspora who used the language of the empire (Acts 6:1; II Cor 11:22; Phil 3:5). In other words, "Hebrew" indicates a distinction within the nation of the people of God and has no reference to those outside it.

Ioudaios is a later word coming probably from the division of the kingdom. After the division of the kingdom, the two more important tribes were designated Judea and the ten northern tribes, Israel (II Kings 16:6; Jer 32:12;

34:9). After the fall of the northern kingdom in 722 B.C., "Hebrew" was used of the whole nation of the people of God. In later usage "Jew" implies a national distinction between a member of the covenanted people and others (Rom 2:9-10; Mt 2:2; 27:29, 37). In Paul Jew stands for "a type, a spiritual or religious attitude" (Gutbrod 1965:380) by which they reject both God and his community (1 Thess 2:15).

The third word is *Israelite*. That word underlines the theocratic privileges of those so designated. Trench has argued that the word expresses "the whole dignity and glory of a member of the theocratic nation, of the people in a peculiar covenant with God" (1961:133). In other words, it is a special badge of honor, a title of honor for the Jew and that because they are descendants of Abraham (Gen 25:15; compare Gen 25:25). Acts 2:22 retains this sense of the special covenant relationship.

Originally Israelite was a sacral term which described the totality of the elect of Yahweh and of those united in the Yahweh cult (von Rad 1965:357). But when the monarchy was established, a change in the use of the name occurred because it was originally tied with the sacral league of tribes (Josh 24). After the monarchy Israel was just the northern kingdom. After 722 B.C. "Israel" was adopted by the southern kingdom. Therefore after 722 B.C. it signified the whole of God's people as a spiritual designation which transcended political titles. This became the normative use in the New Testament, i.e., Israel as the people of God to whom he has revealed himself (Mt 10:6; 15:24; Jn 1:49, 31, 47).

It is evident that the words "Jew" and "Hebrew" are used of the people of God. They carry different emphases. Israelite, however, gets widened to describe a spiritual condition.

On the other hand, there are four words for people in the New Testament. *Dēmos* (=Latin *populus*) occurs only once in Luke and then again in Acts 12:22; 7:5; 19:30, 33, and it describes a popular assembly as it asserts its rights as citizens. There is nothing theological about it, and it is not really relevant for our study. *Ochlos* is also an unorganized assembly, a multitude (Lk 9:38; Mt 21:8; Acts 14:14) (Trench 1961:344). There is nothing particularly theological about it.

When *laos* is used theological notions begin to come into play. Strathmann has shown that the usage of the word in the LXX is normative for New Testament usage (1968:30). Behind it stand at least three Hebrew words: *'am*, *leʾōm* (eleven times; sometimes translated *ethnos*), and *gôy* (twelve times in Josh 3:17; 4:1; Isa 26:2; Jer 9:8; 40:9). There is a tendency to use *laos* for Israel and *ethnos* when *'am* is not Israel (Ex 1:9; 15:14; 19:5). But even Egyptians are called *laos* (Gen 41:40), as are Ethiopians (Isa 18:2; Ps 86:6). In the LXX a *laos* is not just a crowd or population but a union (Gen 34:32). At other times it describes peoples over against their rulers. Thus the Egyptians are the people (*laos*) of Pharaoh (Gen 41:40). Then there is the specific use of *laos* of Israel, the people of God, a national union, "the national society of Israel according to its religious basis and distinction" (Strathmann 1968:35). The distinction is from other people and on the basis of religion (Ex 19:4-7; Deut 7:6-12; 22:8ff).

In the New Testament *laos* occurs 140 times. Of these, eight are in the plural (Lk 2:31; Acts 4:25, 27; Rom 15:11; Rev 7:8; 10:11; 11:9; 17:15; and possibly Rev 21:3). The usage is predominantly Lucan: thirty-six times in the

Gospel and forty-eight times in the Acts. However, in its New Testament usage *laos* designates a crowd, a population, people with no idea of national union albeit in distinction from other peoples. It covers Jew and Gentile alike.

In its New Testament usage the singular form of *ethnos* is used of the Jews by others or by themselves, and there is no element of slight (Acts 10:22; Lk 7:5; Jn 11:18). But the plural *ta ethnē* is used of all humankind outside the covenant (Deut 30:43; Acts 15:14; Lk 12:30). But even they have some knowledge of God, however imperfect and inarticulate.

SUM OF WORD STUDY

What does this study of the biblical words contribute to the present study? It is evident that even if there is a tendency to particularize the people of God as the covenanted people, the Jews, there is, nevertheless, a certain flexibility in the use of words which may exclude any rigidity in the definition of the people of God based on race. The covenant relationship is central to the idea of people of God—Sinai was the renewal of the Abrahamic covenant by which a people of God was chosen. But there are other peoples in God's household. Now in Jesus a renewal of the idea of the people of God is made on the basis of his cross, and that has no ethnic element. The crucial element is a faithful response to the invitation of God in that new covenant.

MEANING FOR MISSION IN AFRICA

But what has all this to say about the proclamation of the gospel in Africa, especially today? First, missions to Africa are in fulfillment of the commission to preach the good news to all peoples. None is excluded from the invitation to join God's household. Second, such mission as is carried out in Africa is based on the sovereignty of God and of Christ. The letters of credence come from Christ, and the content of the message is the sovereignty of God and of Christ. It has nothing to do with the power of the world rulers.

However, precisely at this point there is some confusion. The mission into Africa was carried on by North Atlantic agents who confused the accidents of the gospel with the essence of the gospel. This is what I have elsewhere called the North Atlantic captivity of the church. It is in essence the same as the Jewish expectation that Gentiles would be naturalized to become Jews when they embraced Judaism. It is no different from Jewish Christians expecting Gentiles who embraced the good news of Christ to become Jews by accepting circumcision and making a contribution to the Jerusalem Temple. The idea was that of *extra Judaeas nulla salus est*. The modern version of it is "outside the North Atlantic civilization there is no salvation," and therefore, African Christians had to be as North Atlantic Christians in their expression of the faith.

The teaching of Jesus and the picture that emerges from the Acts of the Apostles give the lie to such an approach. The African comes to Christ with African integrity and etches another color to the mosaic that is God's world. In this regard, the natural revelation that the African had before conversion has to be taken seriously, used as a starting point for evolving African Christianity in diverse forms, given the diversity and pluralism of Africa. That natural revelation is what is to be tested and weighed in the balance of the ultimacy of Christ and used to make Christianity genuine and real in Africa.

The African, like any other racial group, becomes a member of the people of God on three counts: fidelity to the natural revelation each possessed, the covenant established in Christ, and fidelity to the covenant of Christ. All these are the inheritance of the new humanity by the grace of God.

REFERENCES CITED

BARR, J.
    1965   *Semantics of Biblical Language*, Manchester: Manchester University Press.
BEHM, J.
    1965   *diathēkē, Theological Dictionary of the New Testament*, Vol. II, Gerhard Friedrich (ed.), Grand Rapids: Eerdmans.
GUTBROD, W.
    1965   *Israēl, Theological Dictionary of the New Testament*, Vol. III, Gerhard Friedrich (ed.), Grand Rapids: Eerdmans.
JEREMIAS, J.
    1966   *Eucharistic Words of Jesus*, London: SCM.
POBEE, John S.
    1979   *Toward an African Theology*, Nashville: Abingdon.
SCHWEIZER, E.
    1976   *The Good News According to St. Matthew*, London: SPCK.
STRATHMANN, H.
    1968   *laos, Theological Dictionary of the New Testament*, Vol. III, Gerhard Friedrich (ed.), Grand Rapids: Eerdmans.
TAYLOR, V.
    1948   *Jesus and His Sacrifice*, London: Epworth.
    1957   *The Gospel According to St. Mark*, London: Macmillan.
TRENCH, R. C.
    1961   *Synonyms of the New Testament*, London: James Clarke.
VON RAD, G.
    1965   *Theological Dictionary of the New Testament*, Vol. III, Gerhard Friedrich (ed.), Grand Rapids: Eerdmans.

16. A THEOLOGY OF HUMANKIND

Sidney H. Rooy

THE TASK TO WHICH WE DIRECT OUR EFFORTS IS PROFESSEDLY NOT A SCIENTIFIC and objective one. Rather, it is colored by a particular Christian commitment and by the clearly expressed goal of defining the crucial characteristics of a Christian theology of humankind. Let us also remember that the terms "Christian theology" and "humankind" are to be understood as concrete existential concepts. That is to say, I do not, indeed I must not, claim universality for the specific conclusions at which this study arrives. To do so would be pretentious. Theology in general, and Christian theology in particular, can only be reflection from one's individual and community experience, be it ecclesiastical or secular. Only in this way can one make a valid contribution to theological reflection as it is carried out in other contexts.

This introduces one more presupposition limiting the scope of this anthropological essay. Let us call it the *biblical* theology of humankind. The Bible is the source and norm for Christian theology; yet it is so in a particular way. Christian anthropology in the Scriptures reflects concrete situations, definite historical moments with differing cosmologies, from varied economic and sociopolitical realities. Each biblical author was inspired to see in the first place the truth of God's will for himself and for the people of his time. Certain normative aspects of his writing speak specifically to his historical moment, defining obedience and disobedience, faith and non-faith, true worship and idolatry. Some of these aspects, though normative for the time in which they were written, are no longer so today, such as the ceremonial Old Testament prescriptions and certain New Testament ecclesiastical practices.

Other norms of the Holy Scriptures do carry authentic and continuing validity from biblical times to the present, and until the fulfillment of human history. Though these norms are naturally clothed with the images and experiences of their times, they reveal aspects of created reality which are valid for all time. To distinguish these norms precisely and definitively is not always easy, as multiple ecclesiastical divisions testify. They confirm that church father Vincent of Lérins was overly optimistic when he thought to solve all such problems by appealing to universal acceptance as the criterion for determining the truth: "Moreover in the Catholic Church itself all possible care should be taken that

---

Sidney H. Rooy has served as dean and is professor of church history in the Instituto Superior Evangélico De Estudios Teológicos, Buenos Aires, Argentina. He is author of The Theology of Missions in the Puritan Tradition: A Study of Representative Puritans: Richard Sibbes, Richard Baxter, John Eliot, Cotton Mather, and Jonathan Edwards *(Eerdmans, 1965).*

we hold the faith which has been believed everywhere, always, and by all."[1] Vincent wrote these words in opposition to Augustine's teaching on grace and predestination. They are, ironically enough, the prelude to long anthropological discussions in medieval and modern times.

Let us say, then, that our task is a humble, though essential one. I shall attempt to define certain dimensions in a theology of humankind which characterize and are essential to a Christian anthropological approach to the mission of the church. I shall argue that a biblical and Christian approach to humanity is essential to the adoption of a correct methodology in missions and that, at the same time, the authentic biblical approach can be known only in the active carrying on of the mission. Only by the dialogical method of confronting reality with the Scriptures and at the same time confronting the Scriptures with present historical demands can a valid comprehension be found for our times.

THE UNITY OF THE HUMAN BEING

What constitutes the uniqueness of humans? First, they must be seen as *creatures* subject to God as Creator. The history and theology of the Old Testament affirm the foundational character of this relationship for human life. Clearly, human beings are no lone and solitary figures on a barren landscape; rather, they are an integral part of creation as a whole. On the one hand, the world is their habitat, given to them for the exercise of their creativity and care. But humankind is also itself dependent for its life and continued existence on this ecosystem. As living beings created in freedom, people find their support and direction in the person of their Creator. In distinction from the rest of creation, in which relations can be described as subject-object, people are subject, conscious of the relations established among themselves and with God. Thus they are qualitatively different from the person defined by much of modern anthropology as animated behavior. God is at once the goal and the origin of people's creaturely creativeness. This dynamic relationship of people to each other and to God constitutes their claim to uniqueness.

The human being as *image of God* denotes the singularity of the person. This graphic figure, image of God, Calvin uses frequently to portray the way humans, together with all creation, mirror the "workmanship" and the glory of the Creator. It mirrors, as well, the Creator's intention and goal for the whole of creation. In the original creation account the character mirrored in the divine actions portrayed is that of the Creator who with freedom and power brings all things into existence. Humans become the recipients of that character. When God symbolically entered into rest, humanity already shouldered the creaturely responsibility of continuing the work so well begun. The "image" figure is confirmed by the "likeness" figure (*homoiosis*), reminiscent of that famous christological definition of the relation of Christ to the Father which was rejected by the early church. Thus "likeness" does not imply identity of person, though it may signify unity of purpose and close similarity of action. The (creative!) communication of life in that "likeness" became the gift of God to humanity:

1. *Quod ubique, quod semper, quod ab omnibus creditum est* (*Commonitorium*, 434).

"When God created man he made him in the *likeness* of God. . . . When Adam had lived 130 years, he had a son in his own *likeness,* in his own image" (Gen 5:1-2; italics mine). The same word, *d^{e}mut,* is used here for likeness and together with *tselem* appears in the account of the creation of humankind in Genesis 1:26.

Humans do not usurp the place of God, but as God's image-bearers they work together with God to attain the projected goals for creation. As self-transcending, conscious subjects, people stand before God as responsible stewards of all creation. Their call is to care for the ground and its creatures and to pastor each other. This responsibility defines their obligation to God and constitutes their true humanity. Conversely, not to fulfill this responsibility constitutes inhumanity.

The concepts of the human being as creature and as image of God give no reason to suspect that the concept of human as *unity* would be doubted for so many centuries of Christian history, as has been the case. That a human being is a unity was fully accepted by the writers of the Old Testament. Many theological treatises and biblical word studies of "flesh," "body," "soul," "spirit," "mind," "heart," and the like, have confirmed the Platonic injection of idealistic thought into Christian categories throughout church history. This dualism represented the imprisonment of an essentially good soul (spirit) in an essentially sinful body (flesh). The efforts of Bible students to reinvest the above concepts with their original biblical meaning have been long and arduous. The most radical divorce was between the flesh and body concepts on the one hand, and the concepts of spirit and soul on the other. However, the words *flesh* (*sarx*) and *body* (*sōma*) are both related to the same Hebrew root (*bāśār*) and normally refer to the whole person who lives in solidarity with creation, thus accentuating the material aspects of human existence. In the same way, the word *soul* (*psychē-nepeš*) refers to the whole person, accenting the vital principle of biological life for human beings; the word *nepeš* is also used to indicate animal life. Likewise, the word *spirit* (*pneuma-ruach*) when used with reference to humankind denotes the active, willing center of the person in relation to God, to others, or to oneself. These four words (flesh, body, soul, spirit) express clearly the unity of the person, conceptualizing mutually supportive aspects of one indivisible reality.

The concepts of the human being as creature, as image-bearer, and as unity underscore the unique relationship to God and to fellow image-bearers. The human being is defined over against God and, reflectively, over against others. God created human beings in love and for love, in freedom and for freedom, in dependence and for responsibility. The new fact is the brokenness of humanity's love, self-enslavement, and disobedience. In Christian anthropology humans must be seen as *sinners,* a condition made possible by the uniqueness of their creation as self-transcendent, reflective beings, a condition made real by the perversion of their calling as co-laborers or co-creators with God for the further development of the original creation and for the fulfillment of its purpose.

Let us be clear on this point: Human beings do not merely commit particular sins; they are sinners. That is to say, original sin, recorded as humanity's fall into disobedience in Genesis 3, describes the actual and real condition of the human race in general and of every person in particular. Humans distort the Creator-creature relation and the creature-creature relation. Sin does not destroy the image of God, for the image constitutes humanity's uniqueness; rather, sin perverts the whole person. Sin does not change the nature of humans, nor their humanity, nor their creaturely character; rather, it affects their functioning as responsible and personally related image-bearers. The very name *sinner* means that humanity is always to be considered as human-being-before-God, and therefore, as such, subject to God's will and judgment. Sin thus does not remove this human-being-before-God-ness; rather, sin denies, distorts, and rejects the reality of humanity's creaturely position through leading each one to disobedient insubordination and autonomous self-affirmation.

Finally, the full Christian view of humanity requires the vision of humans as *renewed* by the grace of God. Christ is uniquely the new human by whose person and work all people are ultimately judged. The possibility of overcoming the contradiction between human being as creature and human being as sinner rests fully and finally on the incarnation, sacrifice, and resurrection of Jesus Christ. The humanly impossible synthesis between creatureliness and sinfulness becomes divinely realized through the forgiveness of human guilt and the grace for new life. The restoration of humanity as truly human by God's justifying act does not annul human responsibility but rather arouses in men and women their believing response and reaffirms their capacity to mirror God's love to and for creation. It is not that grace transcends nature, as in Scholastic theology; nor that nature is transcended through the affirmation of the spirit, as in Idealistic thought; nor that nature continually evolves and is extended and enriched through the potential goodness of humanity, as in modern Naturalism; nor yet that nature makes humans the victims of cosmic forces flung into an alien universe, as in Existentialism. Rather, the reconciliation between God and human beings accomplished at Calvary reveals the whole content of Christian anthropology. We do not work out two anthropologies, one for Christians and one for pagans. There is only one Mediator, one Way, one Life. According to Christian anthropology, the renewed humanity is perfectly imaged in Jesus Christ, through whom the divine image is restored in us. However, as Luther saw so clearly, we are *justified sinners*. This ambiguity reveals our present calling and its overcoming, our faith for the future.

THE UNITY OF HUMANKIND

Humankind is adequately understood only as relational being. Martin Buber can be credited with the significant contemporary definition of this Hebraic biblical reality. What is peculiar to human as human can be discovered through concrete experience better than through abstract concepts. Thus the I-Thou experiential relationships more adequately define humans than the I-It subject-object relationships. The Thou of the I-Thou relationship refers not only to God, but also to other persons and to the created world. The definition of the *wholeness* of humanity with which a Christian anthropology concerns itself needs to take these three I-Thou relationships with total seriousness.

> In virtue of his nature and his situation man has a threefold living relation. He can bring his nature and situation to full reality in his life if all his living relations become essential. And he can let elements of his nature and situation remain in unreality by letting only single living relations

become essential, while considering and treating the others as unessential (Buber 1947:177).

We will consider the wholeness and the unity of humankind in the light of these three relations.

HUMANKIND IN COMMUNITY

We have affirmed that a human being as a self-transcending person uniquely reveals a personal relation to God, to fellow humans, and to the world through the creaturely exercise of love. This signifies a reaching out to the other person, which at once requires acceptance of the other and in which a person offers self for the fulfillment of the other person's capacities and possibilities.

Christian individualism struggled for expression during early and medieval church history. However, the sociological tribal unities, the universalistic natural-theology categories, and the religious and moral authoritarianism of that time were too restrictive to permit individual liberty. The move for individual freedom in the Renaissance outstripped Christian claims (both Catholic and Protestant) for freedom by combining the mystical belief in the infinite potential of the human spirit and the close identification of humanity with nature and its processes. Thus, while every person was said to have in him- or herself the full pattern of humanity, each at the same time was said to be able to become the autonomous master of natural forces which destroy the preexistent natural harmony assumed to be at the core of life.

The Protestant search for individuality followed a different line. The belief in the fateful impotence of sinful humanity, an urgent sense of radical responsibility to God, and deep dependence upon Christ for pardon of guilt motivate an obedient discipleship born of gratitude and faith. The priesthood of all believers refused all other than direct mediation of divine grace. Each individual as a bearer of grace again was said to mirror God's image in being priest to fellow humans and to creation. But the ambiguity of the situation of humans as *justified sinners* clouded the wholeness of the Christian's relations by a too-easy identification with the optimism of renaissance, natural humanity, or by a hurried retreat from the complexities of technological and sociological structures.

These divergent views of humankind have spawned two wrong approaches with respect to people in community: an individualistic anthropology or a collectivistic sociology, neither of which reflects biblical anthropology. Each person receives God's care; each is called by name. At the same time, no one lives unto self (Rom 14:7). The individual has existence only in relation to others. Individualism proclaims self-reliance, self-dependence, and self-development. Collectivism teaches state control, state-centered decisions, and state-directed goals. Each annuls the rightful place of the other. As we cannot permit the absorption of individual freedom by the state, so we cannot assume that independent human choice guarantees what is best for society. Individuals' essential characters become reality to the extent that God's love calls them into community with each other. Only through the biblical word, "Fear God and keep his commandments," a word of love to God and to neighbor, can we be truly human. Humanity's unity is found precisely here—all people as persons before God are mutually bound to a responsible covenant with each other. God's love becomes the paradigm for human stewardship of all creation. Human freedom to love all things in Christ is at the same time the ethical norm that makes possible true self-realization-in-community, a fully social life.

However, people not only love God and each other; they must be loved in return by them. In the concreteness of human creaturely existence lies a basic in-created dependence upon a person's ecosystem and upon the ministry and support of the other referents in a relation-defined life. The basic male-female dimension of creation constitutes an interdependence within the structure of humankind's being and permeates all of its existence. To be fully human is to be ministered to and completed by the love of female (if male), or male (if female), and of all the other extensions of this basic relationship in family, tribe, ethnic community, and the race.

Individual life can be realized only in community life, and that community life has meaning to the extent that living, interrelational units create social cohesion. We cannot enter into the many implications of these concepts for the church as the community of believers that arise at this point. But for mission methodology we ought to raise a question. What is the biblical relation between the universal and the particular, between the church as the community of the people of God (the body of Christ) and the individual believer together with those natural extensions of self in tribe, social class, race, sex, and nation? Or, to ask the question another way, to what extent can the Christian bless the continuance of those extensions of individuality within an adequate definition of the unity of humankind, or more specifically, within the present reality of the church which functions as a paradigm of redeemed humanity? We shall return to this question later. Here we only affirm that the freedom, the diversity, and the responsibility of every person (and every person's extensions) are *subordinate* to the unity of all people in Christ. In Christ there is neither Jew nor Greek, bond nor free, male nor female, rich nor poor; rather, these distinctive conditions of life and existence are placed at the service of God, of the church, and of humankind. As we have seen earlier, humankind exists as creature, as image of God, as sinner, and as called to faith. In the church the differentiation in classes, natural and spiritual gifts, and nations is placed at the service of the whole.

HUMANKIND IN THE WORLD

Having briefly discussed the individual in relation to others, we now ask how the human relation to creation ought to be defined. Perhaps it is necessary to observe that no priority of relative importance can be assigned to these relations. They are equally crucial dimensions of our humanity. It is important to note this because some contemporary missiologies make a point of stressing that preaching the gospel to people is primary, while care for the world is secondary. Such an artificial separation occurs nowhere in the Scriptures, and, indeed, does injustice to the full portrait of biblical people and their world.

World as creation. First, we must see the world (*cosmos*) as created reality. As such it is good in every part; however, it is no more than that. It, like humankind, is creature—no spark of divine fire, no eternal Spirit, no coextensiveness with eternity. Sacred rivers and holy mountains do not exist for the Christian. The surprising variety and multitudinous diversity of the world coalesce into the fundamental unity of purpose and design of its Maker. Here function the regularity of natural law and the unexpectedness of miracle in service of the fulfillment of God's purpose. The world was not made merely as an instrument for humanity's good, as modern functionalism suggests; nor does God exist to guarantee nature's availability to some of us (and not to others!), as pragmatic religion claims. Rather, creation's purpose synthesizes with the fulfillment of God's purpose for humanity in history—what we may call the realization of the kingdom of God.

Created reality must not be understood as material reality so frequently is, as a static and terminated work. Biblical revelation clearly affirms the goodness and beauty of God's great creation. It likewise affirms the living and expanding character of natural life and humanity's responsibility to direct and care for that life. Human stewardship of creation does not have its primary reference to evil and to sin but to the inherent character of humankind's place in the universe before God as the life-promoter, the shepherd, the lord of creation.

Humankind's lordship is not a disinterested one. Direction, promotion, and continuance of the world as creation is a life-and-death matter for humankind. Not until this century has human dependence upon the ecosystem become so urgently clear. If people as stewards fail, they risk the continued life of humankind. People bless each other only by recognizing that they have their existence within and as a part of the creaturely ecosystem. Protecting the biosphere from dangerous radiation and providing food to children suffering from malnutrition confirm humanity's complete dependence upon created structures for the support of life.

World as sinfulness. However, biblical revelation with respect to the world as created reality comes to us exclusively from the fallen and sinful side of human history. What Moses wrote was directed toward the salvation of Israel as God's people, their liberation from bondage, and their prospective journey to the promised land. The theme of creation stimulates paeans of praise on the lips of psalmists and prophets, who sing simultaneously of deliverance from Egypt. In the New Testament, creation and salvation are closely intertwined in Christ's work (Jn 1; I Cor 8:6; Col 1; Heb 1). That is to say, humanity's role vis-à-vis created reality has a twofold character: Humankind's relation to creation is a constitutive part of its being as humanity, and this relation is totally affected by sin. With respect to the first I add only this: As a constitutive part of people's life as humanity, created reality is the essential "stuff" which goes into the coming of the kingdom of God. For this reason this relation of humankind to creation forms a primary, never a secondary, dimension of its calling.

With respect to the second aspect of humankind's role, we can distinguish various levels of evil in the world. We can speak of *circumstantial* evil, as in the case of the falling of Siloam's wall or the destruction of a tornado. Sometimes this kind of suffering accumulates in the life of a certain person or family through successive illnesses, unexpected financial losses, accidents, deaths, and the like. There are *personal* evils where it is clear that moral choices for what is wrong and undesirable have been made. These, too, may become cumulative in the sense that one becomes enslaved by certain evils (such as drunkenness or drug addiction, obsessive pride or hate)—evils which tend to warp character and destroy the person. One might question whether such a thing as "purely" personal sin exists. Since, for example, I can live only in relation to others, even my personal wrongs may affect directly or indirectly those who love me and others. *Interpersonal* evils are most common and inescapable. Our societal existence involves interactions between persons or groups who are driven by self-interest, party spirit, pride, insecurity, desire for power, patriotism, ideological convictions. Actions and reactions motivated by these factors also have a cumulative effect. We cannot escape being tempted, convinced, and molded by the pressures exerted upon us by our families, by economic situations, by political events, and by the mass media. A fourth level is *suprapersonal* evils. These are structural in character and, due to industrialization, urbanization, technological advance, and international dependence, they are growing in size, number, and power with unbelievable rapidity in our day. The international dominance and dependence patterns among the nations that took shape during the last centuries, the armaments race, and the recent growth of international corporations serve as only three examples of what affects all human beings everywhere today and what constitutes one of the greater threats to the unity of humankind. Few are those who dare to confront suprapersonal evil and unmask its idolatrous and demonic pretensions; perhaps even fewer really know how to do so.

People in the world, convinced of the beauty and goodness of God's handiwork, must clearly see evil and sin for what they are. Our conscious vocation must be the overcoming of all wrong and the proper development and use of creation for the glory of its Maker.

HUMANKIND IN CHRIST

Everyone's relation to God in Christian anthropology is defined by each individual's relation to Jesus Christ. Though Christian interpretations of the nature and extent of that relationship have varied widely throughout the history of the church, the future of humankind is defined by relation to God through Jesus Christ. This relation has two foci which we might picture as concentric circles. The inner circle signifies Christ and the new humanity, while the outer circle represents Christ and universal history.

Christ and the new humanity. The historical significance of the incarnation reaches backward and forward. Christ's life, death, and resurrection mark the crucial point of human history—we might call them the mountain pass of creation's course. The same road stretches meaningfully back from the summit's peak to creation's beginning and continues its meandering progress to the destiny of humankind. Much of Christian tradition pays at least lip service to the meaningful continuity of Jewish and Christian history, though the implications of this continuity have frequently been forgotten or passed over.

The basic affirmations of humankind's identity as the one created in the image of God and responsible for the tending and development of natural reality remain valid. These affirmations are reconstituted in the reconciling work of Jesus Christ, the authentic image of God, the new person. Here we must remember that, though we tend to think of people as individuals, the Bible thinks of them as being in community with each other. The new humanity is humankind in Jesus Christ. "His purpose was to create in himself one new man out of two, thus making peace, and in this one body to reconcile both of them to God through the cross, by which he put to death their hostility" (Eph 2:15-16). The "one new man" here is clearly a new humanity, the church composed of what was formerly two, that is, Jews and Gentiles. Since all non-Jewish nations are considered Gentiles, Paul says in effect that people from all nations and classes are reconciled into the new humanity in Christ. Christ is the second Adam: He restores humankind to its true and original humanity; he rehumanizes people; he makes possible the attainment of our vocation. In this way the will of the Redeemer God is one with the will of the Creator God.

Only by looking at Christ can we see the world as it is called to be and as it really is—*his* world, "and through him to reconcile all things, whether things on earth or things in heaven, by making peace through his blood, shed on the cross" (Col 1:19b). We have already spoken of humanity's brokenness and sin. People everywhere need healing and guidance, but they seek relief frequently on the wrong basis. Amid the plethora of proposed solutions, the church as the body of Christ is called to be the unique fellowship of reconciliation, where people are bound together in mutual dependence upon their Creator-Redeemer God, who purposes the uniting of all things in Christ. For the church, unity is more than a hope; it is a reality. Church life is constituted by the tremendous love of God in Jesus Christ. The church understands and experiences that this love posits a fellowship which humankind does not create but into which men and women are brought. This reality of the new humanity in Christ constitutes the sole basis for the future and the unity of humankind.

Christ and world history. This leads us to the conclusion that the sole purpose of world history from the perspective of Christian anthropology is the fulfillment of the Creator's purpose. We need to remind ourselves of two facts. *First*, Christian anthropology proposes one anthropology for the whole of humankind. That a person is creature, image of God, one, sinful, and called to restoration in Jesus Christ constitutes a universally valid description of all humankind. Christian historians and anthropologists deal with the same stuff of human and world history as do all other anthropologists. The Christian vision of reality is totalitarian, perhaps more so than that of most other anthropologies.

1. Biological and scientific naturalism alike view a human being as a more or less highly developed animal, and therefore tend to limit anthropological considerations to those of physical reality, often with animistic projections.

2. Classical and modern idealism tend to depreciate the physical aspects of life and to find the essence of humanness in reason or spirit.

3. Mysticism and humanistic romanticism find the core of humanness neither in the physical nor in the rational aspects of existence but rather in the mysterious, the intuitional, or the feeling aspect of the person in relationship to the totality or whole of reality.

4. Others tend to accept elements from all these anthropologies to form what Brunner calls a "*synthetic* anthropology"[2]—which does not really define what constitutes the nature of humanity.

Each of the views of humanity just mentioned is open to criticism:

1. Naturalistic anthropologies can be faulted for their denial of human responsibility, since they reject the creature–image-of-God aspects of humankind.

2. For a succinct presentation of these four views, see *The Christian Understanding of Man* (Brunner 1938:144-51). I am indebted to Brunner for several thoughts in this division of my essay.

2. Idealistic anthropologies can be faulted for their refusal to take seriously the moral ambiguity of human history by failing to see the depths of human sin.

3. Mystical anthropologies can be faulted for their rejection of knowable authority and of normative criteria for moral action—a rejection which relativizes both divine revelation and the possibility of evaluating ethical action.

4. Synthetic anthropologies can be faulted for their failure to take seriously the profound contradictions between people's created goodness and their moral depravity, between the aimlessness of their existence and the goal of human history, between the purpose of life and the seriousness of death.

Second, the totalistic character of the anthropological task directly qualifies all of history. What do we mean, then, when we speak of redemptive or salvation history in distinction from universal history? Clearly, all dualistic views are to be excluded. Universal history and salvation history do not exist side by side. If this were so, universal history would mean non-redemptive history and would therefore be either neutral or evil in character. The totalistic character of the Christian view of humanity admits neither alternative. Granted the validity of the Creator-creature disjunction, all history responds to its authority-dependence implication and must be judged accordingly, thereby precluding neutrality. Granted the radical sinfulness of humankind and the ambivalent character of people redeemed as justified sinners, human history retains its unitary character as people's response to God's redemptive action in Jesus Christ or to God's general revelation, and therefore as involving their responsibility within the created structure. "Jews and Gentiles alike are under sin . . . so that every mouth may be silenced and the whole world [be] held accountable to God" (Rom 3:9, 19).

Hendrikus Berkhof suggests three models (adapted here) which ought to be excluded in the definition of "revelation as history" (Berkhof 1979:61-65). Similar exclusions can be made concerning the relation between salvation and universal history.

1. Salvation history "does not coincide" with universal history, which evidences all too clearly humanity's rebellion and alienation from God.

2. Salvation history "is not an organic-evolutionary historical process" clearly distinguishable from universal history. The former is thoroughly embedded in, intertwined with, and synthesized into ordinary history. Rather than being a steadily developing process, God's work in maintaining people's creaturehood and in restoring their ability to image God properly is characterized by successive progress and decline, unexpected turns, and repeated struggles, blessings, and judgments.

3. Salvation history "does not consist in a series of purely momentary and vertical incursions" into general history. Consonant with God's purposes and people's actions, the accomplishment of creation's goal is progressively realized. This progressive realization occurs not so much like biological growth, but rather like the crescendo effect in classical drama or in the movements of great symphonies—movements which develop to crisis intensity, then pause, recapitulate, and carry on from this new beginning. But through it all is an "irreversible coherence" in which the exodus cannot be understood apart from the fall, nor the prophets apart from Christ, nor Paul apart from the law.

Salvation history emerges within universal history as a new historical force, redemptive in effect and purpose, which by God's grace holds within itself the destiny of all history. From creation through the Old Testament, in Jesus Christ and the New Testament church, including the post-apostolic church up to the present, divine initiatives have created a new humanity for the redemption of universal history. The Creator-Redeemer God commissions this new humanity as a missionary fellowship which lives out its calling in the midst of a humankind that stands under the sign of judgment. This is so because history as a human phenomenon apart from Jesus Christ stands condemned, but in him it becomes vibrant with expectant hope. This history of the new humanity in Christ ultimately (eschatologically) engulfs the history of the old humanity, overcomes it, and transforms it to bring all created reality "into the glory of the sons of God."

Because Jesus is the Lord of the earth, salvation history particularly includes the events transcribed into the biblical record, and yet it extends through the Spirit's working into all the supportive occurrences which reveal and further God's purpose in human history. God in Christ is the beginning, center, and goal of world history.

THE UNITY OF GOD'S MISSION

Only brief illustrative statements will be made under this heading. We begin by summarizing the salient anthropological conclusions at which I arrived in the first two divisions of this chapter. The five statements which follow illustrate areas of methodological application.

ANTHROPOLOGICAL CONCLUSIONS

1. Humankind finds its true nature in its creatureliness, both as responsible to God as Creator and as an integral part of the cosmic ecosystem.

2. Humankind mirrors God's creative and authoritative work as steward of the earth through diligent promotion of all life and responsible direction of human history.

3. In humankind the full psychosomatic unity of the human being is maintained by the rejection of all dualistic conceptions that consider the body as essentially evil in contrast to a supposed moral superiority of the soul or spirit.

4. Humankind manifests the radical depth of its brokenness as a sinner in willful disobedience to God, in willful separation from neighbors, and in selfish and indifferent abuse of the world.

5. Humankind becomes renewed from the status of a sinful creature to that of a justified sinner only through grace in Jesus Christ.

6. Humankind discovers fulfillment through the incorporation of responsible persons in responsive communities of love. The need of every person is to love and to be loved. The freedom of every person is the responsibility to subordinate personal goals to the unity of humankind in Christ.

7. Humankind stands in a double relationship to the created world: in the stewardship of creation's long journey to the fullness of the kingdom of God, and in its dependence upon creation as the indispensable ecosystem for the sustenance of human life.

8. Humankind participates fully in the distorted character of the world; indeed, humanity is responsible before the Creator, before creation, and before the courts of history for the unspeakable tragedy that affects everyone in personal and social life. The full effect of sin on the circumstantial, personal, interpersonal, and suprapersonal levels of human existence must be taken into account.

9. Humankind realizes itself finally and fully only in the new humanity constituted by Jesus Christ, the authentic image of God and the truly new Person, who restores people to true and original humanity through the church, the unique paradigm and fellowship of reconciliation.

10. Humankind reaches its destiny through universal history and does so through the redemptive mission which renewed humanity undertakes by grace in renewed fellowship with the Creator-Redeemer God.

SOME MISSIOLOGICAL IMPLICATIONS

1. God's mission restores humankind and the creation and transforms them into the fullness of his kingdom. This implies more than a mere restitution of the original creation; it involves the taking up of all creation's past and future history into the fullness of God's purpose. Therefore we can affirm that the unity of the Creator-Redeemer God confirms the unity of his purposes in nature and grace. The so-called cultural and evangelistic mandates are not to be separated, as though the first treats of original creation's fulfillment and the other of fallen humanity's restoration through the sacrifice of Jesus Christ. No such divorce exists in principle between these and other biblical mandates such as love for God and neighbor, holiness, and cross bearing. God's mission in Jesus Christ takes up into itself in an indivisible unity the creation structure of which human existence is an inseparable part.

2. God's mission appoints humankind as the personal, self-conscious, and responsible steward over and within all creation. This appointment is not revoked but continues throughout history. The character of humankind's relation to creation is dialectical. People are at once lords of creation and dependent upon it. On the one hand, their humanity calls for responsible leadership, control, and direction of historical processes for the attainment of that which is good and just for nature and for neighbors. On the other hand, people remain radically dependent on the ecosystem which supports all humankind and without which all life as we know it would become an utter impossibility.

Here we can point out the so-called inalienable (better called creaturely) rights of people from the two perspectives just mentioned. First, all humankind has the God-given right to personal, responsible decisions with respect to the stewardship of life to which people are called and for which they are answerable both to God and to each other. Second, everyone as a dependent being has the God-given right to such participation in creation's resources and human love as will make possible creative growth in and contribution to the furtherance of God's kingdom.

3. God's mission calls people in their unity and diversity as sharers in the love and freedom made real by the gospel's power. That love and freedom in Christ brings forgiveness and healing to a world in which sin has brought alienation from God, indifference to the neighbor, and gross abuse of the eco-

system which sustains life. The healing of that brokenness cannot be solely a spiritual matter. The psychosomatic unity of the human being and the inseparable dependence-upon-ecosystem character of all creaturely life demand the redemption of all existence, both spiritual and physical.

Likewise, humankind remains incomplete without full recognition of its bisexual character, in which man is incomplete without woman and woman incomplete without man. This is equally true in the projections of this mutual interdependence in family, tribe, ethnic community, and race. The essential unity of humankind excludes paternalistic mission policies that further domination and dependence. This unity excludes chauvinistic male dominance in mission structures and in the work to which Scripture appoints all believers. It promotes the sharing of gospel answers to people's ultimate problems. It incarnates Christ's love in deeds which proclaim his message and in words which are made concrete in self-giving for others.

4. God's mission constitutes the church as a special vehicle of the renewed humanity for the carrying out of the work of the kingdom. This kingdom is concentrated in the church, the body of Christ, and extends by his Word and Spirit into the whole earth. In a world divided by fierce nationalisms (Britain and Argentina, Israel and the Arabs, Iran and Iraq), widely disparate economic classes (first- and third-world differences, land or machine owners and employee-serfs, rich elite and masses of poor), and continuing racial segregation (apartheid, *de facto* segregation of churches and schools, job discrimination), the church functions as the beginning center and sign fulfillment of God's recapitulation of all things in Christ. The church must first of all be the church: a believing, repentant, restored fellowship called to a meaningful confession of Jesus as Lord through obedient discipleship in a ministering and healing service to one another and to everyone for Christ's sake. As such it becomes a paradigm, a teaching model, portraying the unity to which all people are summoned. Establishment of churches should mean new centers for a living commitment to kingdom justice.

Such rectification of humankind's inhumanities sometimes means gathering homogeneous units together where tribal, family, or group relationships have been broken by the disruptive power of sin. A contemporary example would be the Toba Indians in northern Argentina—a tribe which, like hundreds of others, fights for survival. Protestant missionaries have effectively divided this single tribe into some fifteen denominational groups, many of which proselytize to increase membership. It might be argued that mutual competitiveness has enlarged church membership. The cost, however, could be that the resultant divisions contribute to the uncertainty of the tribe's survival.

At other times, however, heterogeneous groups become a sign of the kingdom in a dehumanized world. This is particularly true in much of post-Christian Occidental society. We hardly dare to teach the world to become like the church, because the church has already become too much like the world. The church reflects all too clearly the divisions, strifes, prejudices, and animosities that are found in the world; it follows, rather than challenges, the patterns of the world. Precisely here men and women must be challenged to demonstrate that in Christ the barriers of race, social class, and nationalism have been removed (Eph 2:14-16; Gal 3:28). Costly discipleship, not cheap grace, is the gospel that Americans of both continents and Europeans need to incarnate. As an East German pastor wrote some years after the Soviet occupation: "We in the churches are fewer now, but we know who we are."

5. God's mission extends the kingdom as the standard by which all history is judged and as the eschatological norm for human conduct. Humankind's calling as *eschatological* beings signifies their participation in God's salvation history as recipients and responsible subjects. This qualitatively new historical force, initiated, sustained, and carried to fulfillment by divine grace, ultimately engulfs the already-under-judgment universal history and effectively transforms creation into newness of life, bringing it into the glory of the children of God. The revelation of the fulfillment of history in the realized kingdom of God functions as the ethical norm-goal for the redemption of humanity in the present. In this way the eschatological promises function not merely as maps for post-historical life, but especially as clear blueprints for present faithfulness and concrete action. Let us look at a few model passages by way of illustration:

"There will be no more death nor mourning or crying or pain, for the old order of things has passed away" (Rev 21:4). These words require the promotion of life and the need to remove, as far as is possible, the causes of death and human suffering. If there is to be no more mourning in the fulfillment of the kingdom, I must do all in my power to take away mourning now; likewise with crying, pain, and death.

"And all mankind will see God's salvation" (Lk 3:6). These words place squarely upon all seekers the mandate to make real and visible the presence of God in history through "fruits worthy of repentance" (3:8).

The prophets' sense of call, fulfilled in Christ but still awaiting its full eschatological realization, becomes a norm to us in the ethics of the kingdom: good news to the poor, freedom for the prisoners, sight for the blind, release for the oppressed ones, and the coming of the jubilee year for all (Isa 61:1-2).

The parameters of humankind's final judgment and full salvation finally depend upon the grace-filled response of men and women to basic human needs. "The King will reply, 'I tell you the truth, whatever you did for one of the least of these brothers of mine, you did for me' " (Mt 25:40).

The final word rests with the Creator and Giver of life. Limited now is our perception of all the implications of God's future and of what through humanity's creative response can begin to be realized. But fullness will come, and that anticipation challenges us to meaningful commitment to God's mission today.

> "They will neither harm nor destroy
>   on all my holy mountain,
> for the earth will be full of the knowledge of the Lord
>   as the waters cover the sea" (Isa 11:9).

BIBLIOGRAPHY

BABBAGE, Stuart Barton
1957   *Man in Nature and in Grace,* Grand Rapids: Eerdmans.
BERKHOF, Hendrikus
1962   *De Mens Onderweg,* 's-Gravenhage: Boekencentrum, N.V.

*1979   *Christian Faith: An Introduction to the Study of Faith,* Sierd Woudstra (trans.), Grand Rapids: Eerdmans.

BLAUW, Johannes
1961   "The Biblical View of Man in His Religion," *The Theology of the Christian Mission,* Gerald H. Anderson (ed.), New York: McGraw-Hill.
1962   *The Missionary Nature of the Church: A Survey of the Biblical Theology of Mission,* London: Lutterworth Press.

BRUNNER, Emil
1938   "The Christian Understanding of Man," *The Christian Understanding of Man,* Chicago: Willett, Clark and Company.

BUBER, Martin
*1955   "What is Man?" *Between Man and Man,* Ronald G. Smith (trans.), Boston: Beacon Press.
1965   *The Knowledge of Man,* M. Friedman and Ronald G. Smith (trans.), New York: Harper and Row.

CALVIN, John
1964   *Institutes of the Christian Religion,* Book II, Grand Rapids, Eerdmans.

COSTAS, Orlando E.
1973   *Hacia una teológia de la evangelización,* Buenos Aires: La Aurora.

CROATTO, Severino
1974   *El hombre en el mundo I,* Buenos Aires: La Aurora.

DE GRAFF, Arnold and OLTHUIS, James (eds.)
1978   *Toward a Biblical View of Man: Some Readings,* Toronto: Institute for Christian Studies.

EICHRODT, Walther
1947   *Das Menschenverständis des Alten Testaments,* Zurich: Zwingli-Verlag. English translation: *Man in the Old Testament*, K. and R. Gregor Smith (trans.), London: SCM Press, 1954.

FOWLER, Stuart
1981   *On Being Human: Toward a Biblical Understanding,* Potchefstroom: Instituut vir de Bevording van Calvinisme.

MÍGUEZ-BONINO, José
1976   *Christians and Marxists—The Mutual Challenge to Revolution,* London: Hodder and Stoughton.

MOLTMANN, Jürgen
1974   *Man: Christian Anthropology in the Conflicts of the Present*, John Sturdy (trans.), Philadelphia: Fortress Press.

MÜLLER-FAHRENHOLZ, Geiko (ed.)
1978   *Unity in Today's World,* The Faith and Order Studies on "Unity of the Church— Unity of Humankind," Faith and Order Paper No. 88, Geneva: World Council of Churches.

NIEBUHR, Reinhold
1949   *The Nature and Destiny of Man,* New York: Charles Scribner's Sons.

PANNENBERG, Wolfhart
1968   *Revelation as History,* David Granskou (trans.), New York: Macmillan.
1970   *What is Man? Contemporary Anthropology in Theological Perspective,* Duane A. Priebe (trans.), Philadelphia: Fortress Press.

RAMSEYER, Robert L.
   1973   "Anthropological Perspectives on Church Growth Theory," *The Challenge of Church Growth: A Symposium,* Wilbert R. Shenk (ed.), Elkhart, Indiana: Institute of Mennonite Studies/Scottdale: Herald Press.

ROBERTSON, Edwin H.
   1958   *Man's Estimate of Man,* London: SCM Press.

SMITH, Ronald G.
   1969   *The Free Man: Studies in Christian Anthropology,* London: Collins Clear-Type Press.

VICUÑA, Maximo
   1982   *La resurrección de los muertos,* doctoral thesis, Instituto Superior Evangélico De Estudios Teológicos, Buenos Aires, Argentina.

*Indicates reference cited in this chapter.

17. KINGDOM, MISSION, AND GROWTH

Wilbert R. Shenk

EVER SINCE THE ANTIOCH CHURCH COMMISSIONED AND SENT THE FIRST APOSTLES (Acts 13), the church has been asking how the people with whom the witness has been shared have responded to the gospel. A sending church can only rejoice when they hear how the Spirit has "opened a door of faith" to any people through apostolic witness.

What are the grounds for this rejoicing? Did the early church celebrate church growth? Do we focus on the correct issue when we speak about church growth as though it is the ultimate goal?

This chapter probes the question: What is the theological root of church growth?

MISSION ROOTED IN KINGSHIP

Jesus took as his point of departure for both his message and ministry the *basileia* (kingship) of God. The phrase "kingdom of God" does not occur in the Old Testament, but the idea of God as King occurs frequently. Some Old Testament passages describe God as King while others speak of the day when God will become King and reign over his people. The Old Testament acclaims God, therefore, as the only true God and King, but at the same time recognizes that not everyone acknowledges his kingship.

God chose to manifest his kingship through Israel, yet even Israel frequently fell away and rebelled in spite of their special covenant relationship with God. The prophets of Israel continued to call Israel back to God. They told of the coming of Messiah who would radically alter the structures of life and enable people to live together in love and justice because God himself would dwell in their midst.

THE KING ACTED UNEXPECTEDLY

A qualitative shift occurs between Old and New Testaments. What had long been anticipated has now arrived in the person and ministry of Jesus. The *basileia* (= kingship, reign, rule, kingdom) becomes personified in Jesus Christ who came to "do the will of the Father." His words and deeds breathe submission to the will of God. The message he proclaims is the call to his audiences to repent and join the new order. According to G. E. Ladd,

---

Wilbert R. Shenk, Elkhart, Indiana, is Vice President for Overseas Ministries for Mennonite Board of Missions. He served in Indonesia with the Mennonite Central Committee from 1955 to 1959. He is editor of Mission Focus *and author of* Henry Venn—Missionary Statesman *(Orbis, 1983).*

God's Kingdom, his reign, has already come into history in the person and mission of Jesus. The presence of God's Kingdom means the dynamic presence of his reign. It means that God is no longer waiting for men to submit to his reign but has taken the initiative and has invaded history in a new and unexpected way. The Kingdom of God is not merely an abstract concept that God is the eternal King and rules over all; it is also a dynamic concept of the acting God (1964:140).[1]

The kingdom of God is to be understood eschatologically. It was inaugurated by Jesus but has not yet reached its fulfillment. The earthly ministry of Jesus marked the "beginning of the end." All that Jesus did while on earth and all that he commissioned his people to do point toward that consummation which his coming again will bring. In this light, the Christian interprets present experience and all history in view of the parousia, Christ's return. The pull of the future—what we call hope—continually bears on what we are doing. This means that we must live in a tension between the "now" and the "not yet." Whenever the church becomes preoccupied with the "now" and loses touch with the "not yet," it loses power and a sense of direction. It identifies church with kingdom, and the church becomes the center of its concern and action. If the church concentrates on the "not yet," it attempts to flee the world.

The kingdom is now present, but it is visible only to the "eyes of faith." Much of the world is unaware of the kingdom of God. The church becomes confused and without sure direction the moment it no longer has a vision of the kingdom coming in fullness and power.

The kingdom of God is supernatural. Humanly speaking, we cannot manipulate it or control it. We can only submit to God's reign. Ladd (1964:189) has collected biblical references to the kingdom which describe its chief characteristics:

The Kingdom can draw near and be present to people (Mt 3:2, 4:17; Mk 1:15, etc.); it can
    come (Mt 6:10; Lk 17:20; etc.),
    arrive (Mt 12:28),
    appear (Lk 19:11),
    be active (Mt 13:13-52).
God can give the kingdom to men and women (Mt 21:43; Lk 12:32), but people do not give the Kingdom to one another.
Furthermore, God can take the Kingdom away from men and women (Mt 21:43), but they do not take it away from one another, although they can prevent others from entering it.
Women and men can enter the Kingdom (Mt 5:20, 7:21; Mk 9:47, 10:23, etc.), but they are never said to erect it or to build it.
They can
    receive the Kingdom (Mk 10:15; Lk 18:17),
    inherit it (Mt 25:34), and
    possess it (Mt 5:3),
but never establish it.

1. For surveys of the differing interpretations of the kingdom, see "Introduction," in H. Ridderbos, *The Coming of the Kingdom* (1962:xi-xxxii) and the article "Kingdom of God," in Alan Richardson (ed.), *Theological Wordbook of the Bible* (1950:119ff).

Men and women can
   reject the Kingdom, i.e.,
   refuse to receive it (Lk 10:11),
   enter it (Mt 23:13), or
   attack it violently (Mt 11:12),
but they cannot destroy it.
They can
   look for it (Lk 23:51),
   pray for its coming (Mt 6:10), and
   seek it (Mt 6:33; Lk 12:31),
but they cannot bring it.
People may be in the Kingdom (Mt 5:19, 8:11; Lk 13:29; etc.), but we are not told that the kingdom grows. Men and women can work for the sake of the Kingdom (Mt 19:12; Lk 18:29), but they are not said to act upon the Kingdom itself.
People can preach the Kingdom (Mt 10:7; Lk 10:9), but only God can give it to men and women (Lk 12:32).

JESUS DECLARES MESSIAHSHIP

Both the masses and the religious leaders of Jesus' day failed to catch the meaning of Jesus and his message. Yet he did not falter in his mission. He crystallized the central theme of his ministry in the prayer he taught his disciples, "Your kingdom come, your will be done." When at the end of his earthly ministry Jesus commissioned his disciples, he linked God's kingdom mandate with his own (Mt 28:18-20; Jn 20:21-22).

The Synoptic Gospels show Jesus inaugurating his ministry through a series of interrelated events which reveal his purpose and the content of his mission. By publicly receiving baptism at the hands of John the Baptist, Jesus identified himself with the prophetic tradition. But John also pointed to the discontinuity between Jesus and himself. He declared that Jesus would baptize with "the Holy Spirit and with fire." What sealed Jesus' messiahship was the presence of the Holy Spirit in his life. Christ/Messiah means "anointed one." What would set Messiah apart from all previous prophets, priests, and kings was that the fullness of the Spirit of God would be upon Messiah. At his baptism the Voice announced that this Jesus was "Son of God" (Ps 27; Isa 42:1). God became visibly present to the people in the form of a suffering servant. Indeed, this identification of Son of God with Suffering Servant confounded the Jews. Yet this was the way God chose to express saviorhood.

The public presentation of Jesus as Messiah was followed immediately by confrontation with Satan. "And Jesus, full of the Holy Spirit, returned from the Jordan, and was led by the Spirit for forty days in the wilderness, tempted by the devil" (Lk 4:1-2). Two kinds of power, diametrically opposed, came into conflict. Following the encounter between Jesus and Satan, Jesus began his public ministry in Galilee.

In his first utterances Jesus identified the *kingdom of God* as both the object and the content of his messiahship. In Luke's version of the inauguration of Jesus' ministry, Jesus linked himself with the messianic vision of Isaiah and other Old Testament prophets. This is simply a way of describing what Matthew and Mark assume when they say, "The kingdom of heaven is at hand" and "The

Matthew 4:17, 23	Mark 1:14-15	Luke 4:16-19
From that time Jesus began to preach, saying, "Repent, for the kingdom of heaven is at hand." And he went about all Galilee, teaching in their synagogues and preaching the gospel of the kingdom and healing every disease and every infirmity among the people.	*Jesus came into Galilee, preaching the gospel of God, and saying, "The time is fulfilled, and the kingdom of God is at hand; repent, and believe in the gospel."*	*And he came to Nazareth...and he went to the synagogue. And he stood up to read, and there was given to him the book of the prophet Isaiah. He opened the book and found the place where it was written, "The Spirit of the Lord is upon me, because he has anointed me to preach good news to the poor. He has sent me to proclaim release to the captives and recovering of sight to the blind, to set at liberty those who are oppressed, to proclaim the acceptable year of the Lord."*

time is fulfilled." The age of Messiah would be the time when the new order of God's salvation would be fully experienced, including elimination of social, physical, and personal disabilities.

The way to the realization of the kingdom, however, is through the cross. Messiah willingly gave up life itself. Therein he revealed how he deals with humankind and will reign in the life of his people. The ultimate proof that he is Messiah, that he is truly the "anointed one" who is full of the Holy Spirit, is that the Holy Spirit resurrected him, thus offering hope and life to all who acknowledge him as Lord and accept his rule in their lives. The kingdom of God is the great unifying theme of Jesus' life and mission.

Following the inauguration, Jesus selected a group of disciples, and began preaching to the crowds, healing, and delivering people from Satan's power. The Gospel of Mark emphasizes Jesus' ministry of exorcism. Through Messiah the power of God confronted and confounded the power of Satan.

The several forms of commission in the Synoptics adhere in essentials to this same pattern. Jesus came to inaugurate the kingdom of God, and his disciples are called to share in announcing the kingdom and demonstrating the meaning of this new reality (Mt 10:5-15; Mk 6:7-13; Lk 9:1-6; 10:1-12).

If *kingdom* is the prior term, then we must seek to understand church growth in relation to the kingship of God. We will take seriously the coming of God's reign and pay special attention to the signs of God's presence and how these are being manifested in the life of the church. This perspective will both challenge and enrich the meaning of church growth.

KINGDOM AND CHURCH

The relationship of church to kingdom has been the subject of controversy and confusion. Some people hold them to be two terms for the same thing. But Scripture does not equate church and kingdom. They are intimately related but two distinct realities.

When Jesus dispatched his disciples on their first missionary journeys, he did not instruct them to preach the gospel of the church but the gospel of the kingdom. The Synoptic Gospels scarcely mention the church, although "sending" is reported several times. The Synoptic writers consider kingdom to be a main theme. The post-Pentecost church never confused church and kingdom. Acts 8:12 reports that Philip "preached good news about the kingdom of God and the name of Jesus Christ" to the Samaritans who responded and were baptized into the faith (Acts 19:8; 20:25; 28:23, 31).

Kingdom and church often exist in a tension one with the other. The apostate church bears false witness to the kingdom and falls under judgment by the kingdom. In the present age the church never fully expresses the reality of God's reign. We can identify four aspects of this relationship between kingdom and church (see Ladd 1968:258-73 for full exposition).

The kingdom creates the church. The kingdom is God's dynamic rule in history to which he invites men and women to respond. It comes in answer to human hopes for a new order of existence. Those who respond to the divine invitation are incorporated into God's people on earth, the church. The church is, therefore, the people of the kingdom; but some individuals may find their way into the church who are not committed to the kingdom; they may be baptized into the church in infancy or join the church out of impure or immature motives. Committing oneself to the kingdom indeed involves participating in the life of the church, but participation in the church is no guarantee that an individual is living under God's rule.

The church witnesses to the kingdom. The church is called to witness to the world concerning God's rule. People who speak about "building the kingdom" betray not simply an imprecise use of terms; they do not grasp clearly the distinctive character of the kingdom as contrasted with the church. The Christian witness cannot establish or build the kingdom of God. Only God can do that. The church is called to proclaim joyfully God's rule. It is good news because it alone offers salvation from a world which is death-bound. The church illustrates what the reign of God means by reciting the acts of God in the past and pointing to his promises in the future. The church tells of what it has touched, seen, and heard (I Jn 1:2-3). To the extent that the church exhibits in its own life the reality of the rule of God, it visibly demonstrates what the kingdom is.

The church is the instrument of the kingdom. The church does not simply function as a news reporter for the kingdom, telling of kingdom events. The church is caught up in kingdom action. Jesus commissioned his body to continue doing the works he had begun. Following Pentecost the disciples are reported as having preached and healed and cast out demons in the same way Jesus did. The church does not escape the tension and struggle between the two kingdoms. The fact that history testifies that "the blood of the martyrs is the seed of the church" points to the fact that faithful Christians have engaged in this struggle as participants in the kingdom itself. Participation in the kingdom will involve suffering. The Holy Spirit guides the church in this witness to and identification with the kingdom.

The church acts under the authority of the kingdom. In the Old Testament the nation of Israel was steward of the rule of God, which was committed to Israel through the law. Jesus selected disciples to whom he gave the "keys of the kingdom of heaven, and whatever you bind on earth shall be bound in heaven, and whatever you loose on earth shall be loosed in heaven" (Mt 16:19). Jesus entrusted to his disciples his authority, based on spiritual knowledge. Christ's followers themselves have accepted his kingship and are, therefore, able to enter into the struggles of others as they encounter the gospel of the kingdom. The gospel is not to be treated lightly. It is not the possession of the church. The church was created by responding to the gospel and can remain true to its calling only by sharing the gospel of the kingdom with others. The church experiences its most vital solidarity with the King in obeying the King's commands.

THE MISSION OF THE CHURCH

The church, we have noted, is the instrument of the kingdom and, therefore, the church has no mission except to serve the kingdom of God. Three observations about the nature of the church are pertinent at this point.

Beginning with Abraham, God has been calling out a people. God chose an insignificant individual from an obscure tribe. Not only did God call a man with no particular assets to commend him, but the man was without a future since his wife was barren and he had no legitimate descendants. Yet God called Abraham and promised to make him the father of a mighty nation: "And by you all the families of the earth shall bless themselves" (Gen 12:3b). God's election of Abraham was an act of sheer grace, and it was election to serve rather than merely to receive God's favors. Israel was to be a "sign to the people" and a means of spreading the knowledge of God to other peoples (Isa 11:9-10; 49:1-6). The people of God are always elected in order to serve the Lord.

The New Testament describes church and mission as a unity. As Johannes Blauw wrote, "There is no other Church than the Church *sent* into the world, and there is no other mission than that of the Church of Christ" (1962:121). In the past, the church has found it difficult to keep this unity alive. A static, non-missionary understanding of the church has dominated Protestantism from the time of the Reformation. Consequently, in Protestantism missionary service has been carried out by agencies which were largely independent of the church. But a close study of the New Testament shows that the church's mission is not one activity among many legitimate responsibilities; mission is its *raison d'être*. When Jesus entrusted responsibility to the church, his body, for continuing his ministry in the world (Jn 20:19-22), he assigned to it the task of maintaining with singular clarity this unity of mission and church.

The church has a fourfold nature. The faithful church expresses kingdom reality. First, the church is by nature a witness. The New Testament employs some thirty different terms to describe the ministry of the word; three are most representative: to herald, to announce good tidings, and to witness. In each case the one who witnesses does so under the mandate of a superior and is the instrument for transmitting the news concerning events. It is news of importance and calls for action. Second, the church is by nature a fellowship. *Koinonia* is that context in which our relationships with God intersect our relationships with one another. The New Testament uses four words, each of which defines one part of the meaning of *koinonia*: fellowship, communion, participation, and contribution. Within the Christian fellowship members are to live out the divine life which they hold in common. *Koinonia* is a way of life, a powerful object lesson to the world concerning the new community God is creating. Third, the church is by nature a servant. This feature immediately sets the church off from the world. Jesus' kind of messiahship was rejected by the majority of people because he came as a servant and insistently served. The church is called to follow its Lord in service, through genuine identification with those being served. Fourth, the church is by nature called to struggle for justice, for the righteousness of God is to be expressed in the life of his people through just relationships. The world knows little of justice. The cries of the poor and the oppressed rise up continually before God. The church is called to demonstrate before the world the meaning of salvation, including the new order of relationship it brings.

The nature of the church is demonstrably missionary. Rather than describing a specific strategy or plan for world evangelization, the New Testament provides a dynamic description of the church in action through witness, service, fellowship, and righteous/just living. The Holy Spirit was the motive power sending the church out so the message of the kingdom of God spread further and further. The church has no other reason to exist than to announce the kingdom, live out the kingdom, struggle on the side of the kingdom.

KINGDOM AND MISSION

If the kingdom of God was basic to Jesus' life and ministry, we need to examine the missiological implications of the kingdom for the church.

A sovereign God. God has a purpose and plan for the world which he is effecting by introducing his rule on earth. The complement to God's rule is the response of his people whom the Apostle Paul declares were elected "before the foundation of the world, that we should be holy and blameless before him" (Eph 1:4b). The King can point to a people who acknowledge his sovereignty over them.

The displacing of Satan. The context for mission is the cosmic struggle between the kingdom of God and the kingdom of this world. Christ is displacing Satan's rule by his own. This struggle is being carried on within history. The principalities and powers oppose the kingship of Christ. To announce the gospel of the kingdom is to side against the kingdom of this world. Even though the triumph of the kingdom of God is assured, the church will face continual opposition and persecution so long as the kingdom of the world is still active. To call men and women to citizenship in the kingdom of God is to challenge them to choose. The two kingdoms are antithetical, and the individual cannot maintain loyalty to both simultaneously (see Berkhof 1962).

Submission to the reign of God. Jesus began his ministry by challenging Satan's kingship. In his encounter with Satan in the wilderness, Jesus resisted all of Satan's overtures to worship him. From the beginning of his ministry, Jesus engaged in exorcism of demons, directly confronting Satan and his minions. Immediately after calling his disciples, Jesus faced the challenge of power (Mk

3:20-27; Mt 12:22-28). Most fundamental of all, Jesus called men and women to renounce their allegiance to the prince of this world and submit to the reign of God. The New Testament amply documents the relationship between witness and opposition. Each wave of expansion of the church was preceded by persecution (Acts 8:1-3; 12; Mk 13:9-10; Rev 5:8-13).

Jesus preached and healed. Through preaching he explained to his audiences the meaning of the kingdom of God. This came as good news because it offered liberation from the bondages of this world. Jesus healed the people. Healing demonstrated the power of the kingdom over death and evil and pointed to the time when *shalom* would be experienced. The missionary witness to the kingdom of God must always include both the word preached and the word demonstrated.

The kingdom not yet present in its fullness. Mission derives its validity from this fact. Mission is carried on during this interim. The age of the Holy Spirit—the period since Pentecost—is the missionary age. The missionary witnesses to the kingdom as revealed in Jesus Christ in his first coming and in his promised return. The kingdom of this world has been routed but not yet banished. This is the day of decision when men and women must declare their loyalties. When Jesus Christ comes again he will consummate his work of redemption and judgment, and those who have elected to serve Jesus Christ as Lord will find the kingdom in its fullness.

Faithfulness. Scripture offers no grand strategy or plan of action for introducing the reign of God on earth. Even growth is not a primary focus. Jesus commissioned his disciples to live out the reign of God in their lives and interpret that reality to people throughout the world until his return. Scripture emphasizes that the faithfulness of the church is closely linked to mission. The church is not called to succeed but to be faithful. To be faithful is to be missionary. To be missionary is to risk martyrdom.

KINGDOM GROWTH

The New Testament describes a world in rebellion against God and in bondage to Satan. It enjoins the church to be a witness to freedom and new life in Christ. God loves the world. This he proved in sending his Son to redeem it. Jesus, in turn, gave to his disciples the mandate to show the same redemptive love to the world, calling men and women to accept God's rule in their lives. The Bible pictures an expanding movement of people from all nations, languages, and classes who acclaim Jesus Christ as their Lord and are living under his reign (Rev 5:7).

PARABLES OF GROWTH

Among the parables Jesus told are parables of growth (Mt 13 and Mk 4). Each one makes a point about the nature of the kingdom, not the church. Although scholars have failed to reach consensus as to how to interpret them, we can draw a number of general conclusions based on the following parables of growth: (1) the mustard seed, (2) the leaven, (3) the seed growing secretly, (4) the dragnet, (5) the tares, and (6) the sower. Jesus used these parables to teach his disciples and the crowds the meaning of the kingdom of God.

1. The parables draw a sharp contrast between popular expectations of the messianic reign and God's design. For example, the people of Israel expected Messiah to vanquish all of Israel's enemies and guarantee Israel's political preeminence and prosperity; the nations would seek shelter with the Israelites and renounce their gods. Jesus offered no such national salvation. In fact, he spoke of Messiah as a servant, one who was coming in weakness and humility. His kingdom would appear to them to be as weak and insignificant as the mustard seed. To the vast majority this kind of kingdom lacked credibility since it diverged so sharply from traditional expectations.

2. God has provided for order and growth in organic life. Similarly, he has a plan for the world, a plan for salvation, in which he is leading history toward a consummation and a new aeon (Berkhof 1966:ch. 5). The parables do not focus on growth as such, however. Growth is assumed as a normal condition. The whole of history is moving toward a climax. Jesus inaugurated "the beginning of the end," and that end is still to come. Meanwhile kingdom activity continues. Jesus discouraged all attempts to speculate about the timetable or fix the date for its consummation. He directed his disciples to call people to repentance and conversion.

3. The growth pictured in the parables is not gradualism or evolution, a process of uninterrupted movement toward a goal. The kingdom is moving toward a climax with fixed purpose. But a power struggle is on, and there are times of tribulation and catastrophe. Growth in the kingdom comes not from the normal forces of history but from God's own creative action. He holds history in his hand. He will determine the end point. Meanwhile he is continuing to act in the affairs of humankind.

4. The meaning of the kingdom can be grasped only through the eyes of faith. The kingdom remains a mystery to natural man and woman. Jesus resorted to parables to teach the meaning of the kingdom. Even the disciples had to be told repeatedly what the kingdom was. Yet God grants faith and hope to those who respond to his invitation to live under his reign as his people. When Jesus told the parable of the soils (Mk 4:3-9), he stressed the importance of hearing the word of God aright. According to C. E. B. Cranfield,

> What we have here is a parable on hearing the Word of God, the Gospel of the Kingdom, which Jesus both preaches and is. It is directed to the multitudes, not just to the disciples (though it was relevant to them too). The hearer is challenged to ask himself, "What sort of ground am I?" and let himself be the good ground. That is not to deny that it is only by God's gift that any man is good soil—does hear aright, does have faith (Mk 10:27) (1951:404).

It makes a decisive difference whether people accept or reject the kingdom. Not all who hear the gospel will respond positively to it.

5. The parables of growth emphasize the secondary role the individual plays in sowing the seed, in leavening the dough. The growth process itself remains a secret and is in someone else's control. The ultimate results will be revealed only at the end of history.

Consistent with this view of growth of the kingdom, Scripture describes another kind of growth. It speaks of "growing up into him in all things" (Eph 4:15); the disciple is called to "grow in grace and knowledge" (II Pet 3:18). The believer is destined to progress from immaturity to maturity, from being a child to becoming adult in discipleship. At best the kingdom of God is a mystery, but the meaning of the kingdom and its claims on the lives of men and women become clearer as it is mediated through discipleship before a watching world.[2]

DISCERNING GROWTH

We need to note more closely the phenomenon of growth. A living organism changes and grows. When a body loses its vitality and can no longer produce new cells, it goes into decline and dies. However, we do not consider all kinds of growth good. The most malignant cancers grow the most rapidly. Among the fastest growing religious movements in the world are cults and sects whose allegiance is not to the kingdom of God. As we noted earlier, it is possible for an individual or group to be counted as member(s) of the church without being under the reign of God. We must, therefore, look more carefully at growth and establish criteria for evaluating it.

When people are living under the reign of God, we can expect to see signs of the presence of the kingdom. As God gathers a people, they will give evidence that his Spirit is in them by producing the fruits of the Spirit. The following are among these signs of the kingdom.

1. Jesus Christ is being proclaimed as lord and savior. Men and women are being urged to accept his rule in their lives.

2. A new community is taking form which rejects race, class, tribe, or nation as the basis for its identity, for it is founded on the work of the Holy Spirit in effecting the new creation. The "dividing wall of hostility" (Eph 2:14b) has been destroyed. This is not a call to deny one's cultural background. Rather it means that human differences are revalued in light of the work of Christ and the varied cultural heritages of the people of God are brought under the lordship of Christ.

3. Biblical *shalom* is being actualized. Members of the community are experiencing a continuing and deepening work of conversion as they are being saved from their profoundest spiritual, physical, and emotional needs. Onlookers observe a new quality of life which causes them to ask questions.

4. The power of evil is being overcome. The kingdom of God liberates people by putting the evil powers to flight.

5. Those who bear witness to the power of the kingdom and give their allegiance to it experience opposition. Witness to the kingdom inevitably leads to confrontation and even persecution. Conversely, absence of such struggle and persecution is a sign that God's people are not engaging in faithful witness.

6. The eschatological prayer, "Your kingdom come," centers all worship. The kingdom is now present in only incomplete form. The disciple community yearns for the coming of Christ and his kingdom in its fullness. Having tasted the firstfruits of that new reality, it longs for that completeness of messianic promise.

2. In *The Integrity of Mission* Orlando Costas calls for "integral growth" (1979:ch. 4).

CONCLUSION

The kingdom is a mystery, the meaning of which we will never fully grasp. The kingdom is a power over which we have no control. The kingdom represents God's activity in the world. The church is but an instrument of that activity, and not all that God is doing in the world is channeled through the church. While growth in the church is important, it is neither the only nor the complete expression of growth of the kingdom.

Indeed, to focus too exclusively on church growth entails a twofold danger. In the first place, it tends to emphasize the penultimate rather than the ultimate. Second, it produces myopia in vision and discernment. We dare not look only at what happens in the church to understand what God is doing today. History is a battlefield. The conflict between Christ and anti-Christ goes on at various levels. Evil is experienced both personally and collectively. Cultures wax and wane. Doors of opportunity to witness to the gospel open and close. But Christian faith is based on the conviction that in the resurrection Jesus Christ, the Messiah, was vindicated. His kingship will ultimately be fully established throughout the world. Mission serves his kingship by bearing witness within history that he alone is worthy of human allegiance (Berkhof 1966:81-100).

REFERENCES CITED

BERKHOF, Hendrikus
    1962   *Christ and the Powers,* Scottdale: Herald Press.
    1966   *Christ the Meaning of History,* Richmond: John Knox.

BLAUW, Johannes
    1962   *The Missionary Nature of the Church,* London: Lutterworth.

COSTAS, Orlando E.
    1979   *The Integrity of Mission,* New York: Harper and Row.

CRANFIELD, C. E. B.
    1951   "St. Mark 4:1-34," *Scottish Journal of Theology,* Vol. 4, No. 4.

LADD, George Eldon
    1964   *Jesus and the Kingdom,* Waco: Word Books.

RICHARDSON, Alan, ed.
    1950   "Kingdom of God," *A Theological Wordbook of the Bible,* London: SCM.

RIDDERBOS, Herman
    1962   *The Coming of the Kingdom,* Philadelphia: Presbyterian and Reformed Publishing Company.

18. THE STRUCTURE OF MISSION: AN EXPOSITION OF MATTHEW 28:16-20

David J. Bosch

THE GREAT COMMISSION IN MATTHEW

THE GREAT COMMISSION IN CHRISTIAN MISSION

THE SO-CALLED GREAT COMMISSION, PARTICULARLY IN ITS MATTHEAN FORM (Mt 28:19-20), has always been a powerful inspiration to Protestant missions. Truth to tell, there has been a tendency in more recent years, at least in some circles, to substitute Luke 4:16-20 for Matthew 28:16-20. Most evangelicals, however, continue to regard Matthew 28:18-20 as the major—if not sole—motivation for mission. Those who do so can at least look back upon a longer history than those who turn to Jesus' words in Nazareth (Lk 4:16-20) as the key missionary passage in Scripture. Matthew 28:16-20 has for many centuries played a crucial role in this regard. This creates an urgent need for a scholarly study of the history of the exegesis of this passage in relation to the church's worldwide mission.

In the early centuries of the Christian church the conviction developed that the apostles had subdivided the world among themselves and had completed the missionary task (the Acts of Thomas, and Eusebius) (Rosenkranz 1977:40). Although Luther dismissed this as a fable, neither he nor Calvin really managed to break new ground, since they argued that the commission was binding on the apostles only and that the special office of apostle had been discontinued (Boer 1961:18-20). Philip Nicolai (who died in 1607) managed to "prove" that the Great Commission had indeed already been accomplished (Rosenkranz 1977:151-53). When Justinian von Welz in 1664 published a plea in which he advocated, on the basis of Matthew 28:18-20, a worldwide missionary enterprise, his views were dismissed by Johann H. Ursinus as advocating interference with God's plan for the nations (Rosenkranz 1977:161-63).

William Carey was the first to make inroads into the prevalent apathy about mission in his famous *An Enquiry into the Obligations of Christians to Use Means for the Conversion of the Heathens* (1792). Carey's logic was simple: If the commission to make disciples of all nations were restricted to the apostles, then the command to baptize (Mt 28:19) and the promise of Christ's abiding presence (Mt 28:20) should also be subjected to this limitation! Carey won the argument, and a large-scale Protestant missionary enterprise was launched from Europe and North America. Ever since it has been customary to base missions on the Great Commission. The Constitution of the Evangelical Foreign Missions

---

David J. Bosch, Pretoria, South Africa, is Professor of Missiology at the University of South Africa. He was a missionary in the Dutch Reformed Church in Transkei, South Africa, from 1957 to 1971. His publications include A Spirituality of the Road *(Herald Press, 1979) and* Witness to the World: The Christian Mission in Theological Perspective *(John Knox Press, 1980).*

Association in the USA explicitly affirms obedience to the Great Commission as the primary motive for mission (Bassham 1979:182). Students who applied to attend the Student Consultation on Frontier Missions in Edinburgh in October 1980 had to sign a declaration which read, in part, "I will make the Great Commission the commanding purpose of my life for the rest of my life." These are but two of many examples of the primacy still enjoyed by the Great Commission in contemporary missionary thinking. It is indeed, in some circles, regarded as the *Magna Charta* of mission.

A COMMAND TO BE OBEYED?

Coupled with this, one frequently finds a rather one-sided emphasis on *obedience* as a motive for mission. This, too, goes back to Carey, as can be deduced from his use of the word "obligation" in the title of his 1792 publication. In addition, expressions such as "we have to obey," "it becomes us," "it behoves us," "it is incumbent upon us" occur frequently in his *Enquiry*.

Whereas such an emphasis was excusable or at least understandable in Carey's time, given the then prevailing attitude to mission, it is hardly justifiable in our day. Yet it frequently persists, and is, of course, largely due to the fact that Matthew 28:18-20 is often interpreted as a *command*. In 1890 the great Dutch theologian Abraham Kuyper declared that "mission flows from God's sovereignty, not from his love or compassion"; "all mission is obedience to God's command, and the content of the message not an invitation but a charge, an order" (van 't Hof 1980:45. My translation). Even John Stott said in the opening words of his treatment of the Great Commission at the Berlin 1966 World Congress on Evangelism, "In the last resort, we engage in evangelism today not because we want to or because we choose to or because we like to, but because we have been told to. The Church is under orders. The risen Lord has commanded us to 'go,' to 'preach,' to 'make disciples,' and that is enough for us" (Stott 1967:37). Similarly, in Roman Catholic missiology the "mandatory character" of mission as an enterprise of the ecclesiastical hierarchy was traditionally identified as the main characteristic of the biblical theology of mission (one example is Ohm 1962:407-70). It tended to operate as a juridico-moral ordinance (Kollbrunner 1974:22).

The question whether Matthew 28:18-20 is primarily a missionary *command* will be dealt with in more detail below, when we attempt an exegesis of the passage. A few general and introductory remarks must suffice at this stage.

The first point that strikes the careful reader is that none of the passages which are usually referred to as parallels to the Matthean Great Commission (Lk 25:45-49; Jn 20:21; Acts 1:8) contains a *command* to do mission work. As a matter of fact, the Great Commission does not function anywhere in the New Testament. It is never referred to or appealed to by the early church. It is therefore quite clear that the early church did not embark on a mission to Jews and Gentiles simply because it had been told to do so. This would have placed mission in the context of legalism. Mission would then have been depersonalized. The "command" develops a "weight" of its own; it leads a life of its own. It becomes a marching order of a Christian militia, engaged in a holy war (van 't Hof 1980:45-47).

Where the early Christians did indeed—albeit reluctantly at first, as far as Gentiles were concerned—embark on mission, this was simply an expression of the inner law of their lives. As Roland Allen (1962 and 1968) and Harry Boer (1961) have argued cogently, the early Christian mission was an essential result of Pentecost. It was this event that became the driving force for mission (Allen 1962:4-5; Boer 1961:119, 128). The "debt" or "obligation" Paul had to Greeks and non-Greeks (Rom 1:14) was the debt of *gratitude,* not of *duty* (Minear 1961:42-48). Newbigin aptly said, "We have regarded witness as a demand laid upon us instead of seeing it as a gift promised to us" (1979:308). Or, with reference to Acts 1:8, "The word, 'You shall be my witnesses,' is not a command to be obeyed, but a promise to be trusted" (Newbigin 1978:9; Allen 1962:5).

A striking aspect of this promise or gift was, however, that it was only perceived as such in the process of mission. One still recognizes the element of astonished joy in Peter's words when he visited the Gentile Cornelius: "I now see how true it is that God has no favourites" (Acts 10:34 NEB). And it was only in the act of preaching the gospel to all people that Paul discovered the mystery "that through the Gospel the Gentiles are joint heirs with the Jews, part of the same body, sharers together in the promise made in Christ Jesus" (Eph 3:6) (Bosch 1980:81-83).

JESUS' *IPSISSIMA VERBA*?

From the foregoing it follows that the church's worldwide mission does not depend exclusively on the Great Commission. Neither is it necessary to accept that Matthew 28:19 contains the *ipsissima verba* (the very words) of Jesus. Roland Allen is correct in saying,

> Had the Lord not given any such command, had the Scriptures never contained such a form of words, . . . the obligation to preach the Gospel to all nations would not have been diminished by a single iota. For the obligation depends not upon the letter, but upon the Spirit of Christ; not upon what He orders, but upon what He is, and the Spirit of Christ is the Spirit of Divine love and compassion and desire for souls astray from God (1968:31).

Such words may sound disconcerting to evangelicals who have always accepted Matthew 28:18-20 as being the actual words spoken by Jesus. A few remarks on this issue seem, therefore, to be required.

In the period when the form-critical approach held sway in the study of the Synoptic Gospels—particularly among German New Testament scholars— it was customary to dissect and analyze every saying of Jesus as recorded by the evangelists in an attempt to lay bare the authentic words of Jesus. The suggestion seemed to be that, if it could be "proved" that Jesus could not have said what he was reported to have said, it would not be necessary to take such sayings too seriously. And since the Matthean Great Commission could indeed be proved to have been heavily redacted by the evangelist—as we will show in some detail below—the universal mission of the church appeared to be in jeopardy. Consequently evangelicals tended to rally to the defense of the Great Commission as being authentic in the sense of its containing Jesus' *ipsissima verba.* Samuel Zwemer's *Into All the World* (1943) is a classic attempt to prove that the Great Commission is both genuine and authentic, since "the command of our Risen Lord" is the "primary basis of missions" (Zwemer 1943:89-90).

Since the 1950s the emphasis in Synoptic studies has shifted from form to redaction criticism. The primary question is no longer whether it is possible to lay bare or reconstruct Jesus' actual words, but rather, to establish what the evangelists did with the tradition handed down to them. This is indeed a far more rewarding approach: Each evangelist, as Grant Osborne—himself an evangelical—observes, "sought to interpret the true meaning of Jesus' message for his own day" (Osborne 1976:80; Harrison 1973:210-14). Therefore, instead of trying to isolate authentic sayings of Jesus from possible additions and transformations by the early church, we should pose the question differently: Is the evangelists' handling of the gospel material a legitimate interpretation of the mind of Jesus or not (Bosch 1969:7)?

It was inevitable that in the process of transmission the tradition regarding Jesus would acquire the stamp of the narrator of the moment (Bosch 1980:67). The Gospel of Matthew was most probably written after the fall of Jerusalem in A.D. 70 (although J. A. T. Robinson has recently argued for a much earlier date). This was a period of dramatic change in Judaism which could not but have exerted a profound influence on the Christian community—Jewish *and* Gentile—in Palestine and surrounding areas. Jamnia Pharisaism was in the ascendancy, a development which culminated in the composition of the *Eighteen Benedictions* in about the year 85. One of these benedictions anathematized Christians (Nazarenes) and heretics (*mînîm*). Jewish Christianity, which up to that point could with some justice have been described as a Jewish sect, was now forced to determine its relationship to Judaism and to the Gentile church. It was inevitable that Matthew, writing in the crucible of the moment, would tell the Jesus story in such a way that it would help his community to understand what it meant to be Christians in the changing milieu of postwar Judaism.

This does *not* imply that Matthew was unfaithful to the tradition; only by retelling the story in such a way that it became contextual for his own community was he really faithful to the tradition. This is as true of the Great Commission as it is of every other pericope in Matthew's Gospel. Therefore, instead of asking whether Matthew recorded the *ipsissima verba* of Jesus and the *ipsissima facta* about him, we should rather ask whether he was faithful to the *ipsissima intentio*—the true intention—of Jesus (Hahn 1980:43). Ernst Lohmeyer, in his inimitable poetic way, put it as follows: We ought to regard the Great Commission as "a saying in the Lord" (*ein Logion im Herrn*) rather than as "a saying of the Lord" (*ein Logion des Herrn*) (Lohmeyer 1956:423).

This does not imply that the first evangelist invented the episode to which Matthew 28:16-20 refers. Whereas a few scholars do indeed believe that the entire pericope is a creation of the evangelist (Lange 1973; Kingsbury 1974:573), most, after a critical analysis, come to the conclusion that Matthew definitely used an earlier tradition (Hahn 1980:32; Meier 1977a; Hubbard 1976:113-23; Strecker 1962:208-11), even if it is no longer possible to reconstruct it (although Hubbard, 1976:122-23, boldly attempts to do so). In our discussion below we will suggest reasons for believing that a common tradition underlies the Great Commission and its so-called parallels in the other Gospels and Acts. It is generally recognized that Matthew's version of the Great Commission consists of three main elements: a statement concerning Jesus' exaltation and authority, a missionary charge, and a promise of Jesus' abiding presence (Hubbard 1976:128;

Trilling 1964:47; Meier 1977a:411-16). The way in which the first evangelist has shaped his tripartite schema reveals, successively, his messianic lordship Christology, his discipleship ecclesiology, and his inaugurated eschatology (Osborne 1976:83). Typically Matthean language is used practically throughout the pericope.

THE LITERARY FORM OF MATTHEW 28:16-20

A lot of time and energy has been spent on attempts to establish the literary form or *Gattung* of Matthew 28:16-20. A bewildering variety of solutions has been suggested, some of which overlap with others. Otto Michel and Joachim Jeremias thought that the literary form is that of an enthronement hymn; Bultmann called it a cult legend (*Kultlegende*), whereas M. Dibelius referred to it as "a revelation . . . of a mythological person" and J. Munck as a farewell speech (*Abschiedsrede*). E. Lohmeyer believed that it resembles the Old Testament *Shema*, W. Trilling that it follows the Old Testament pattern of divine speech (*Gottesrede*). H. Frankemölle detected a parallel in the covenant formula (*Bundesformular*), and B. Malina in the official decree of Cyrus in II Chronicles 36:23, which concludes the Hebrew Old Testament in the same way that Matthew intended to conclude his "New Testament."[1]

The most comprehensive attempt in recent years was that of B. J. Hubbard, who concluded that in this passage we have the Matthean redaction of a primitive apostolic commissioning modeled on the literary form of the Old Testament "commissioning narrative" (Hubbard 1976). Meier has, however, shown that, the considerable merit of Hubbard's case notwithstanding, his suggested *Gattung* was too broad, general, and unfixed to qualify as a specific *Gattung* at all (Meier 1977a:421-24). Meier concludes, I believe correctly, that none of the many suggestions to establish a *Gattung* for Matthew 28:16-20 is satisfactory; we have here a pericope which is *sui generis* and eludes the labels of form criticism (Meier 1977a:424; Schieber 1977:301). We shall nevertheless continue to refer to it as the Great Commission, for the simple reason that this is how it is most widely known.

It is important to read the closing pericope of Matthew against the background of the entire Gospel (something which evangelicals in particular frequently fail to do). Some scholars have, of course, argued that these verses are a foreign body in the Gospel since they contradict the rest of the work, particularly statements such as Matthew 10:5-6 and 15:24. Matthew 28:16-20 has therefore occasionally been classified as a later addition. Harnack for one toyed with the idea that here we have an interpolation, but he later (reluctantly?) rejected the suggestion (Harnack 1961:40-41, n. 2). Nobody today would seriously consider this view. Otto Michel states categorically, "The entire Gospel is written only from the theological presupposition of Matthew 28:16-20. . . . [These verses are] the key to the understanding of the whole book" (Michel 1950/51:21. My translation). And John Meier says, "There are certain great pericopes in the Bible which constantly engender discussion and research, while apparently never admitting of definite solutions. Matthew 28:16-20 seems to be

---

1. For a survey and discussion of these suggestions, see Hubbard (1976:2, 23); Schieber (1977:291-300); Meier (1977a:417-18); O'Brien (1976:67-71).

such a pericope. The one thing scholars are agreed upon is the pivotal nature of these verses" (Meier 1977a:407).

THE LATE START OF THE GENTILE MISSION

In view of the above there can be little doubt that Matthew himself understood the last verses of chapter 28 to be the key to his entire Gospel. Nor can it be doubted that these verses, in their present form, show clear signs of Matthean redaction. The tradition on which these verses rest appears, however, to be suspect. Two arguments are advanced in this regard. We shall very briefly examine each.

First, it has often been pointed out that the early church was slow in launching the Gentile mission. There is an early account, cited by Clement in his *Stromateis* as coming from Peter, that Jesus had said to his disciples, "After twelve years, go out into the world, lest any should say, we have not heard"; this is, however, clearly to be understood as an apologetic attempt to explain the late start in "foreign" missions (Harnack 1961:45).

It appears that the Cornelius episode reported in Acts 10 was the major catalyst of the Gentile mission from the Jerusalem church. As Schuyler Brown points out, Peter is led to admit Gentiles to the church not because of an encounter with the risen Lord but through a vision on a rooftop in Joppa. On this basis, Brown dismisses Matthew 28:18-20 as well as the tradition behind it, since it clearly contradicts the events referred to in Acts 10 (Brown 1980:199, 204). However, Brown ignores the fact that Luke himself, not once, but twice, refers to a pronouncement about a worldwide mission. Thus, in reporting the Cornelius episode in Acts, Luke was well aware of what he himself wrote earlier and he clearly did not experience this as an insurmountable difficulty. Luke 24:47-49 and Acts 1:8 reflect a tradition similar to that behind Matthew 28:18-20; it is therefore not permissible to reject only the *Matthean* pericope with a reference to Acts 10.

Even so, problems remain. According to all records the Gentile mission started late. Not so the mission to *Jews*. With Jerusalem as its base the early church launched an unprecedented missionary work among fellow-Jews. "The missionary zeal of this still young church was immense" (Hengel 1970/71:31). Christian churches among Jews in the Dispersion also started early. Only a few years after the crucifixion of Jesus. Paul journeyed to Damascus in an effort to destroy a Jewish Christian community there. And the Roman writer Suetonius reports that, in A.D. 49, Emperor Claudius "expelled the Jews from Rome because they were indulging in constant riots at the instigation of Chrestus (=Christus)" (see also Acts 18:2). This means that less than twenty years after the crucifixion there was already in the imperial capital a sizable community of Jewish Christians whose presence and activities were such that they attracted the attention of Caesar's court.

It is equally clear that the Christian message found a much more ready acceptance among Greek- than among Aramaic-speaking Jews, as the events behind Acts 6 testify. "Hellenistic" Jews were, moreover, far less traditional in their views than their compatriots. Stephen's critical attitude (Acts 6:13) to the temple and the law—the two pillars upon which Judaism rested (Hengel 1970/71:26)—in essence probably goes back to his pre-Christian period.

The missionary outreach to Gentiles did not, however, begin only after Peter baptized the Cornelius household. After all, one of the seven, Nicolas of Antioch, was himself a former convert to Judaism (Acts 6:5), which proves at the very least that Gentiles felt accepted and at home in the Christian community. There can, however, be little doubt that these early converts were circumcised when they became Christians, if they had not already been circumcised as proselytes (Kasting 1969:117). It can nevertheless be surmised that here and there Gentiles were accepted into the (Hellenistic) Jewish church without circumcision, but that these conversions were not recognized by the Aramaic-speaking leaders. The entire issue came to a head, according to Luke, when nobody less than Peter baptized Cornelius and his household without first circumcising them.

This, then, was the real issue in the early church—not whether Gentiles should be evangelized, but whether they should be required to be circumcised and to keep the Torah. Even after Cornelius' baptism the issue was not settled once for all. It surfaced again in Antioch, not because it was *new* but because it now became clear that there was a danger that Gentiles might enter the church in such numbers that the Jewish character of the movement would be in jeopardy. The overwhelming majority of early Jewish Christians, both Aramaic- and Greek-speaking, originally regarded the new movement as a renewal movement *within* Judaism, with a smaller or larger Gentile contingent. There was nothing in Jesus' conduct and words, as they understood them, that could have led them to believe otherwise, even if we accept the Great Commission as containing Jesus' *ipsissima verba*. It was only because of the rapid growth of a distinctly Gentile Christianity in Antioch and the increasing Jewish resistance to the Christian message that their eyes were opened to a development that had not been foreseen. And it was Paul who elaborated the theological consequences of this new development, suggesting among other things that precisely the worldwide Gentile mission would provoke the conversion of the Jews (Rom 9–11).

The fact of the late start of the Gentile mission is thus not itself a convincing argument against the reliability of the tradition behind the Great Commission (Hubbard 1976:127). Peter (in Acts 10) cannot, as Kasting suggests, be designated as the "proto-missionary" (1969:86-89); that would give Peter a primacy for which there is no support in the sources. Hengel is correct when, after carefully weighing the evidence, he concludes that Jesus' own preaching surely had no less a missionary character than that of his disciples after Easter and that the real inspiration of the early Christian mission was Jesus' own conduct. "If at all, one should call him the 'proto-missionary' " (Hengel 1970/71:36; 33-37).

CONTRADICTIONS IN MATTHEW'S GOSPEL

The second main argument against the reliability of the tradition behind the Great Commission is found in the apparent contradiction *within* the Gospel of Matthew itself. The universalism of the Great Commission, so it is contended, can in no circumstances be reconciled with the exclusivism of sayings such as Matthew 10:5-6 and 15:24.

A bewildering variety of solutions to this problem has been suggested.[2] To a considerable extent the issue revolves around the question as to whether the

2. For a brief survey of the debate until 1968, see Bosch (1969:3-19).

author of the first Gospel was a Jew or a Gentile. For many years he passed indubitably as a Jew, even "a converted Jewish rabbi," as E. von Dobschütz once called him. In more recent years, however, a case for the Gentile authorship of the Gospel has from time to time been advanced. As early as 1947, K. W. Clark stated, "The gentile bias is the primary thesis in Matthew, and such a message would be natural only from the bias of a gentile author" (Clark 1980:4). This thesis was taken up and developed further by Georg Strecker (1962:15-35) and Rolf Walker (1967:*passim*) among others. Scholars such as these tend to explain the "particularistic" sayings in the first Gospel as deriving from the debates on mission in the early church and thus as *not* truly reflecting Matthew's own position, nor that of his community, which was almost, if not exclusively, *Gentile* (Strecker 1962).

The majority of modern scholars, however, are still convinced that the first evangelist was a Jew. I believe that these scholars are correct. This does not at all imply that Matthew consistently "rejudaized" the tradition in order to win the confidence of his Jewish Christian community which was still lukewarm toward the idea of a mission among Gentiles, nor that he simply could not omit Matthew 10:5-6 from his Gospel because of the "importance assigned to it within the Matthean community" (Brown 1977:26-28). It is far more likely that we have in Matthew's Gospel a case of "periodizing": The ministry of the earthly Jesus was confined to the Jews; the ministry of the exalted Christ would be universal (Strecker 1962; Walker 1967). This explains why the "particularistic" sayings are found in the early part of the Gospel, and the "universalistic" in the latter part, with Matthew 21:43 marking the turning point.

Matthew thus did not regard the sayings of Jesus in 10:5-6 and 15:24 as being absolutely irreconcilable with those in 24:14 and 28:19. The two sets of sayings belong to two dispensations. And yet, even during the first dispensation, before Israel rejected him, Jesus in principle transcended the narrow confines of contemporary Judaism. Matthew gives expression to this in several ways. Among these are the inclusion of four women—who were probably all pagan—in Jesus' genealogy, the contrasts between pagan astrologers and Herod as representative of the Jewish people (Mt 2), and between the faith of a Gentile army officer and that of the Jews (8:11-12). Above all he, like the other evangelists, portrays Jesus as having a boundless compassion for all who are poor, ostracized, unclean—the victims of society or prejudice (Bosch 1980:53-57). Because of such factors the early church "saw in Jesus *the archetype of the missionary*" (E. Grässer, quoted in Hengel 1970/71:36).

Matthew indeed stood between two worlds, the Jewish and the Gentile. "That he once was a Jew cannot be doubted. That he had had Jewish training in Palestine prior to the war is probable. That he belongs to a Hellenistic community is obvious. That this community includes gentiles is sure" (Stendahl 1968:xiii). In this peculiar position Matthew is involved in a double polemic: against the particularism of (Jamnia?) Pharisaic Judaism (and possibly some anti-Gentile elements in Jewish Christianity) and against Gentile Christian tendencies toward antinomianism and enthusiasm (Stendahl 1968:xi; Trilling 1964:124ff; Zumstein 1972:29-31).

The way in which Matthew conducts this polemic is to portray Jesus and his coming as the fulfillment of the Old Testament covenant, as the numerous formula quotations (*Reflexionszitate*) indicate. Matthew directly cites the Old Testament forty-four times, twenty of which are not derived from his Markan source nor found in Luke (see particularly Stendahl 1968:*passim*). Jesus is, in a way, the "new Moses," as the allusions to the Moses story show (Hubbard 1976:92-94). The epitome of the fulfillment motif is to be found in the idea of the Lord's presence with his people. This finds expression in the Immanuel name (Mt 1:23; Isa 7:14), which is closely related to the rabbinic notion of the *shekinah*. Matthew begins his Gospel with this notion of "God with us"; he closes it in similar fashion, with the Resurrected One saying, "I will be with you always" (Trilling 1964:40-43; Strecker 1962:213; O'Brien 1976:77), thus recapitulating his entire Gospel in this final punch-line.

The last verses of Matthew 28 in fact in several respects constitute a summary of the Gospel. Several motifs that play an important role throughout the Gospel are here reiterated for the last time: the disciple group, Galilee, the mountain, the disciples' doubt, and their worshiping Jesus (Hahn 1980:29). More specifically, the final pericope may be regarded as a parallel to the story of Jesus' temptation (Mt 4:1-11), which immediately preceded his public ministry. These two antithetic passages in fact frame Jesus' entire ministry and refer, respectively, to a wrong and the right interpretation of the mission of the Son of God (Matthey 1980:165-66).

This perhaps explains why Jesus still appears so very human in the final pericope. He is still called Jesus; the disciples (or some of them) still have doubts about him; and no ascension nor any outpouring of the Holy Spirit is reported. There is remarkable restraint in the way Matthew describes the entire scene; the concentration is almost exclusively on Jesus' *words* (Bosch 1959:188; Matthey 1980:166). In fact, whereas Matthew is usually given to quoting the Old Testament in order to authenticate what Jesus is and does, no such formula quotation appears here; the readers have to accept the words of the Resurrected One on the basis of their own authority (Hahn 1980:32). It is as if Matthew is saying to those who go out into all the world to make disciples of all nations that this is a most precarious enterprise, without any objective guarantees.

EXPOSITION OF MATTHEW 28:16-20

THE MEETING IN GALILEE

Against this wider canvas we may now attempt a brief exegesis of Matthew 28:16-20. In doing so we must, as far as possible, transpose ourselves to Matthew's first-century community and read these verses as he intended them to be understood by his first readers. Naturally any Christian can read and understand the Bible, but in this process "short-circuiting" inevitably occurs. It then becomes the theologian's responsibility to call the reader back to the context and intention of the biblical author and to draw attention to the distance that separates the present situation from that of the biblical story. A creative tension must be maintained between these two contexts, and we do ourselves a disservice if we immediately read our own situation back into the Bible. If we accept that the Bible is the historical document about God's dealings with his people, then its historical dimension must be taken seriously. What Matthew wrote in his Gospel was primarily intended for his first readers. It has meaning for us only in a derived sense. What is more, the better we know that original setting and identify with Matthew's first readers, the better we will be able to make the transition to our own time and to model *our* mission in such a way that it is true to the intention of the evangelist, who here interprets his Lord's word to the church.

Matthew does not record any appearance of the resurrected Jesus to his disciples in Jerusalem. During a brief encounter of Jesus with the women outside the tomb (28:9-10) they are instructed to tell his disciples to go to *Galilee*. This is where Jesus' earthly ministry began, where the whole story of discipleship began, and where the renewed call to discipleship will be issued. Matthew also knows it as "Galilee of the Gentiles"; this is frontier country, far away from the Jewish metropolis, on the very borders of Syria from where people once came to Jesus (4:24).

The eleven disciples go to the *mountain* where Jesus had told them to meet him. The mountain remains unidentified and is, in fact, unimportant as a geographical location, for in Matthew the mountain is usually understood to be the place of revelation. Wherever Jesus reveals himself in a special way, that locality in Matthew's eyes takes on the shape of a mountain! Where, according to Luke, the devil merely "led [Jesus] up" during the temptation account (Lk 4:5), Matthew says that the devil took him to a "very high mountain" (4:8). Whereas Luke records a "Sermon on the Plain" (Lk 6:17), Matthew has a "Sermon on the Mount" (5:1). The mountain is also connected with times of special communication between the Father and the Son (14:23). Thus, by styling the venue in Galilee a mountain, Matthew alerts his readers to the fact that what now follows is of very special significance.

BETWEEN DOUBT AND WORSHIP

Matthew 28:17: "When they saw him, they fell prostrate before him, though some doubted."

We have already referred to the *restraint* of the narrative; "they saw him" (v. 17), "he approached them" (v. 18). The Resurrected One is identified only as *ho Iēsous,* the same name given to him in the gospel narrative (Matthey 1980:166). There is no attempt at describing the event as such. "The account . . . is so brief, that the emphasis does not fall on the appearance itself, but on the subsequent words of Jesus" (Barth 1961:123. My translation. Zumstein 1972:20, 23).

Two verbs in verse 17 clearly reveal Matthean redaction: "fall prostrate" (or "worship") and "doubt." Worship (*proskynein*) appears thirteen times in Matthew, as compared with twice each in Mark and Luke. In several instances Matthew introduces *proskynein* where he is following Mark, e.g., in 8:2; 9:18; 15:25; and 20:20 (Hubbard 1976:75). The verb refers to a gesture that should be reserved for expressing submission to and adoration of God alone, as Jesus' answer to Satan (4:10) explicitly states. When the disciples fall at Jesus' feet in the boat, exclaiming, "You are the Son of God" (Mt 14:33, no parallel), they give expression to their belief in his oneness with God. The verb already assumes liturgical overtones here (Matthey 1980:164).

In Matthew 28:17 *proskynein* is however strangely juxtaposed to another verb, *distazein,* "doubt," which is not found anywhere in the New Testament outside Matthew. What is more, the two verbs are also closely connected in Matthew 14:31 and 33 (the parallel account in Mark has neither). The two *themes,* nevertheless, are also found in the other Gospels. Worship and joy are parallel ideas, as are doubt and disbelief. The juxtaposition of these two sets of emotions belongs to the common tradition behind the commissioning accounts in all the Gospels (Hubbard 1976:77, 114; Zumstein 1972:20).

Verse 17 can be translated as asserting either that *some* disciples doubted or that *all* doubted. The latter translation is preferable (Zumstein 1972:23-24). It is also not said that their doubt is removed. "It is precisely those disciples who submit themselves to him but still have fundamental doubts that Jesus sends out in mission. The Great Commission is not only addressed to those who have overcome their doubt. Christians are called to mission as people who confess Jesus as Son of God and King, but who also experience crises in their faith" (Matthey 1980:165; Zumstein 1972:20, 24).

ALL AUTHORITY

Matthew 28:18: "Then Jesus approached and said to them, All authority in heaven and on earth has been given to me."

The sentence construction introducing the actual commission is another typically Matthean device. The verb *proserchomai* (approach) occurs fifty-two times in the first Gospel, compared to only five times in Mark and ten times in Luke (Meier 1977a:409; Hubbard 1976:6). The same verb is frequently used with reference to the earthly Jesus. Thus, though exalted, Jesus is still with his disciples and does not speak from heaven (Matthey 1980:164).

Jesus' first words are a statement about what has already happened. It is idle to attempt to establish at which precise point in history full authority (*exousia*) was given (*edothē*; aorist passive) to Jesus; only the fact of the giving is of importance (Zumstein 1972:25). Authority is in any case not given to him only now for the first time. During his earthly ministry he already had authority to teach, to heal, to cast out demons, to forgive sins, but that authority was never unlimited, cosmic. Now Jesus has full or all authority. What is new, therefore, is not the fact of Jesus' authority, but its universal extension (Meier 1977a:413; Zumstein 1972:24; Strecker 1962:211-12; Matthey 1980:166-67). There is some parallel between this verse and Matthew 11:27, a fact which led Lange to regard the Great Commission as a new edition of Matthew 11:27 (Lange 1973:*passim*). The vague *panta* there has now, however, become explicit: "In heaven and on earth" here refers to the entire universe; Jesus is Lord of the whole creation (Zumstein 1972:25). "What has already taken effect in heaven still has to be realized on earth" (Hahn 1980:38. My translation). What the disciples were taught to pray for (Mt 6:10) is now coming true. We may have here an allusion to the accession of Daniel's "son of man" to the throne (Dan 7:13-14), as Otto Michel in particular has argued (Michel 1950/51).

Verse 18 is linked to the actual Great Commission in verse 19 with an emphatic "therefore" (*oun*). The universal mission flows from Jesus' universal authority. The proclamation of the gospel is the proclamation of his lordship; mission is the manifestation of his universal dominion (Blauw 1974:84; quoting Otto Michel).

"Go Ye Therefore"(?)

Matthew 28:19-20a: "Go therefore and make disciples of all nations, baptizing them in the name of the Father and of the Son and of the Holy Spirit, teaching them to observe all that I have commanded you."

We now come to what has traditionally been regarded as the Great Commission proper, and all too frequently quoted and appealed to in isolation from its proper context.

Within the threefold division of Jesus' words to his disciples, Matthew 28:19-20a constitutes the center. It is framed by the statement of authority (v. 18) and the assurance of Jesus' abiding presence (v. 20b). The three sections are tied together by the fourfold *all*: "all authority" (v. 18), "all nations" (v. 19), "teaching . . . all" (v. 20), and "with you always" (v. 20).

The verb *poreuthentes*, the aorist participle of *poreuomai* (to go), has been of special importance in Western missionary thinking, particularly since Carey. Says Blauw, "The fact that this *participium* is put first . . . places the emphasis on going, on travelling. One will have to pass Israel's boundaries consciously and intentionally to be able to fulfil the order" (Blauw 1974:86). Elsewhere *poreuthentes* is described as a Matthean technical term for mission (Matthey 1980:167; Zumstein 1972:26). Hubbard points out that it is characteristic of commissioning narratives in general (1976:67, 83-84).

Hubbard's argument in favor of translating *poreuthentes* as an imperative verb separate from the imperative of the main verb depends, however, on the existence of a distinct commissioning *Gattung* and, as shown above, the existence of such a *Gattung* is highly doubtful. For other reasons also the translation of *poreuthentes* as an imperative, "Go!", is to be questioned on two grounds.

First, we have here a construction which Matthew frequently uses and about which Schlatter says, "When two actions are connected with a single event, Matthew puts the aorist participle of the preparatory action before the aorist of the main verb. This sentence construction is so common that it may be designated a characteristic of Matthew's style" (Schlatter 1948:23. My translation). This means that in Matthew 28:19 both *poreuthentes* and *mathēteusate* (make disciples) refer to *one* event.

Second, Matthew frequently uses the verb *poreuomai* (in various forms) as an auxiliary verb together with the imperative of another verb (2:8; 9:13; 11:4; 17:27; 28:7) in a *pleonastic* sense (Strecker 1962:209; Baumbach 1967:890; Kingsbury 1974:576). The "going" is not separate from the event expressed in the verb in the imperative mood. It does not necessarily suggest a traveling from one geographical point to another. However, this does not mean that *poreuthentes* is redundant; rather, it serves to *reinforce* the action of the main verb (O'Brien 1976:72) and adds a note of *urgency* to it (Rogers 1973:261). This is clearly the case in Matthew 28:19. *Poreuthentes* serves to underline the urgency and primacy of *mathēteusate*.

Due to the standard Western translations of *poreuthentes* as "Go ye (therefore)!" and the like, a peculiar conception of mission developed. The emphasis tended to be on the "going" rather than on the "making disciples" (Hesselgrave 1979:199). The locality, not the task, determined whether someone was a missionary or not; one qualified if one was commissioned by an agency in one locality to go and work in another. The greater the distance between these two places, the clearer it was that the individual was a missionary (Bosch 1980:46). In addition, the imperative voice appealed to an activist people. It was easy to rally popular support around the vision of conquering unknown territory and pioneering on distant frontiers (Shenk 1980:42). Chaney indicates the implications of this understanding for nineteenth-century North America: "Home missions" became a technique for maintaining Christian America. "Mission" now signified exclusively *foreign* mission, and Matthew 28:19, with its "Go ye therefore" was singled out as a proof-text. On the home front the chief concern was to check the spread of weeds. "Home missions became the great divine hoe, for keeping the garden clean" (Chaney, quoted in Bosch 1980:151-52).

If, however, we translate *poreuthentes* not as a separate command, but as adding emphasis and urgency to *mathēteusate*, a different picture of mission emerges. It then refers to bringing people to Jesus as Lord, wherever they may be (O'Brien 1976:73). Mission then loses its preoccupation with the geographical component and becomes mission in six continents.

MAKE DISCIPLES

So we move on to *mathēteusate* (make disciples), which is without doubt the principal verb in the Great Commission, as a structural analysis of the pericope shows (*contra* Schieber 1977 who concludes that the phrase, "baptizing them in the name of the Father and of the Son and of the Holy Spirit," constitutes the center). The two modal participles "baptizing" and "teaching" (to which we shall return below) are clearly subordinated to "make disciples," describing the form the disciple-making is to take (Hahn 1980:35; Osborne 1976:79; Trilling 1964:39-40; Matthey 1980:168).

In several of his writings Donald McGavran emphatically agrees that *mathēteusate* is the key verb in the Great Commission. However, he regards this as the first stage, to be followed later by the second, which Matthew calls "baptizing" and "teaching." For the first stage McGavran coins the new verb "to disciple"; the second he calls "to perfect."

"Discipling" is used by McGavran as a synonym for "evangelizing" and consists, in his view, of going to unreached people with the gospel and persuading them to "turn from idols to serve the living and true God" (I Thess 1:9-10). It therefore concerns only the initial conversion experience of a homogeneous group of people. Any further activity toward the building up of these converts is covered by Jesus' "teaching them all things" and is designated "perfecting," a term found in Ephesians 4:12 (KJV). McGavran defines it as the "bringing about of an ethical change in the discipled group, an increasing achievement of a thoroughly Christian way of life for the community as a whole, and the conversion of the individuals making up each generation as they come to the age of decision" (McGavran 1957:15).

The last part of the sentence above reveals another peculiarity of McGavran's terminology: Discipling can take place only once in the history of a given community; what follows in subsequent generations may not be thus described. He says,

> The discipling of a people takes place only on new ground. It does not take place in a nominally Christian land. For example, the conversion of

ten thousand individuals in an evangelistic campaign in London is not the discipling of a people. The peoples of Britain were discipled centuries ago. The conversion of each new generation is a continuing task of the churches, but it is not the discipling of the British peoples (McGavran 1957:15).

This definition of McGavran is closely linked to his interpretation of the *panta ta ethnē* (all the nations) that follows *mathēteusate* in the Great Commission. We shall deal with this issue below. For the time being, let us return to McGavran's distinction between discipling and perfecting.

McGavran's missiology is clearly biased toward discipling (as he defines it). His emphasis is, however, aimed at redressing a serious imbalance he detects in much contemporary missionary thinking, where there "is a constitutional bias toward perfecting. The Churches gravitate toward caring for what they have. Their built-in nature prefers perfecting" (McGavran 1966:93).

However legitimate McGavran's censure of the contemporary missionary movement may be, his building of his case on Matthew 28:19 is untenable for two reasons. First, it is impossible to read the text as describing discipling and perfecting as two successive activities (the participle "teaching" qualifies the main verb "to make disciples" and is not a separate enterprise); second, his definition of the verb *mathēteuein* is not consistent with Matthew's use of this verb.

The fact that some objections have been raised to McGavran's use of the two terms, coupled with the fact that Church Growth exponents (including McGavran himself) began to use "discipling" in a way not strictly consistent with his 1955 definition, led McGavran in 1979 to distinguish three meanings of the verb. He designated them D1 (the turning of a non-Christian society for the first time to Christ), D2 (the turning of any individual from non-faith to faith in Christ and his incorporation in a church—D2 would therefore apply as well in an already "Christianized" society), and D3 (teaching a Christian to become an informed, illuminated, thoroughly dedicated follower of Jesus Christ—which would make D3 for all practical purposes a synonym of "perfecting") (McGavran 1979:265-70; 1980:170). Elsewhere he says, "The Church lives faithful to her Master when she disciples and perfects in a *single continuous motion*" (1980:172; Wagner 1973:*passim*).

These later refinements in McGavran's terminology have helped us considerably toward clarifying the entire issue. However, they still do not do justice to the nuances in Matthew 28:19 (Hesselgrave 1979:199-200). Let us therefore turn to the first Gospel.

The verb *mathēteuein* (to make disciples) does not appear in the Septuagint and occurs only four times in the entire New Testament, three of which are in Matthew (13:52; 27:57; and 28:20) and one in Acts (14:21). In Matthew 27:57 it is used with reference to Joseph of Arimathea, "who had himself become a disciple of Jesus" (literally, "who had been discipled unto Jesus"). The Markan parallel (15:43) reads, "who was looking forward to the kingdom of God." Matthew wants to say materially the same as Mark, which means that he sees a close connection between the kingdom of God and Jesus (Trilling 1964:29). In Matthew 13:52 reference is made to a scribe who "had been discipled unto the kingdom of heaven." A comparison with Matthew 27:57 once again underlines this close connection.

Whereas the verb *mathēteuein* is rare, the noun *mathētēs* (disciple) is common—at least in the Gospels and Acts—although it is not found once outside of these five books. Paul never uses it. *Mathētēs* is more central in Matthew's Gospel than in the others. It occurs seventy-three times in Matthew, forty-six times in Mark, and forty-seven times in Luke. Where Mark usually refers to the small circle around Jesus as "the twelve," Matthew prefers to call them "the disciples" (Trilling 1964:30). Even where the word itself does not occur, Matthew calls attention to the *idea*, for he uses *akolouthein* (to follow) far more frequently than do the other evangelists. In Matthew 8:23, for example, Matthew explicitly mentions "and his disciples followed"; this is omitted in the parallels in Mark and Luke (Kasting 1969:35-36). The English word "discipleship" is thus a correct rendering of the German *Nachfolge*.

Although there are clear parallels between being a disciple of Jesus and being a disciple of a Jewish rabbi, there are also distinct differences. The disciples did not attach themselves to Jesus but were called by him. He himself, not the Torah, stands at the center of the relationship. Discipleship is therefore not a transitional stage, ending in the disciple himself becoming a rabbi (Mt 23:8); it describes a permanent relationship with Jesus. Nowhere does Jesus debate with his disciples, only with his opponents. Ultimately the disciples would not become the transmitters of his teaching, but his witnesses (Bornkamm 1961:37; Rogers 1973:265, quoting Rengstorf). To follow Jesus also suggests sharing his fate (Hengel 1970/71:35).

In Matthew's time the word *disciple* and related terms had acquired a clearly circumscribed meaning for his community. It had become a major ecclesiological term, as in Acts 14:27 and 28, where *disciples* and *church* are clearly interchangeable (Trilling 1964:31; Osborne 1976:79; Grundmann 1968:578; Matthey 1980:162; Gerber 1980:36-41). Paul Minear is correct when he states "that in the early Church the stories of the disciples were normally understood as archetypes of the dilemmas and opportunities that later Christians experienced. Each Gospel pericope became a paradigm with a message for the Church, because each Christian had inherited a relationship to Jesus similar to that of James and John and the others" (Minear 1977:146).

It is against this background that we have to understand Matthew's use of the verb *mathēteusate* in 28:19—the only instance where the verb occurs in the imperative mood. In the pre-Easter period the key word was *kēryssein* (to proclaim or to preach), often linked with "the gospel (of the kingdom)," as in Matthew 4:23; 9:35; 24:14; and 26:13. It was the classical term for the ministry of Jesus, and in Matthew 10:7 also that of the disciples. Now *mathēteusate* replaces *kēryssete*, which in a way causes a stylistic unevenness, as the latter would correspond better to the object "all the nations." The substitution dramatically signals the new situation which obtains for Matthew and his community: When the Master still walked this earth, proclaiming the kingdom or the gospel were appropriate terms; now he is himself the Kingdom and the Gospel (Lohmeyer 1956:418).

The task of the disciples is no longer merely that of proclaiming, but of enlisting people into their fellowship (Trilling 1964:47, 50). To this end they are now empowered. To become a disciple implies a commitment both to the Master and to each other (Minear 1977:146-48). It is, moreover, no small step to take, as Matthew has already warned his readers (10:37-38). Matthew is clearly not thinking of first-level decisions only, to be followed at a later stage by a second-level decision (Newbigin 1979:310). He has no two separate stages in mind, nor two different types of Christians, one of which has only been discipled, the other already perfected. This does not mean that there is no process involved. Certainly there is. After all, following Jesus suggests a journey which, in fact, never ends in this life (Schweizer 1973:351).

Baptizing and Teaching

We have already pointed out that the phrase, "baptizing them . . . and teaching them to observe all that I have commanded you," should be read as further qualifying and describing the main verb, "make disciples," and not as independent activities. We shall now trace the consequences of this in some detail.

First, it is important to observe that the author of the first Gospel is not referring here to the catechetical training of later times which usually, in the case of converts from paganism, preceded baptism. The fact that in Matthew 28:19 the teaching is mentioned after the baptizing may therefore not be used in favor of the argument that converts should be baptized immediately and only then taught. Catechesis as an institution was not, as yet, established in Matthew's community, which was probably not at that time fully settled. Teaching here merely refers to the upbuilding of the church. The evangelist wishes only to underline the indissoluble unity of Jesus' teaching and baptism in his name; a disciple is somebody who has been incorporated into the community of believers and who keeps Jesus' commandments (Trilling 1964:39-40; Grundmann 1968:579; Zumstein 1972:27; Hahn 1980:36).

Matthew is, once again, using the language of his own time to reflect faithfully the mind of Jesus. The Lucan parallel to Matthew's Great Commision does not mention baptism, but it does mention "repentance bringing the forgiveness of sins" which, in turn, is wanting in Matthew. That does not suggest that the first evangelist did not know about the forgiveness of sins! In fact, he early (Mt 1:21) refers to this as the main purpose of Jesus' coming; he also adds it to the text of the institution of the Lord's Supper (Mt 26:28). Here in chapter 28, however, Matthew uses "ecclesiastical" language: His "baptizing them" is materially the same as Luke's "proclaiming repentance and the forgiveness of sins." The practice of baptism here already suggests the institutionalized form of the exercise of the power to forgive sins. "Baptism is here a sign of the present activity of the exalted one, who even now bestows salvation on those who accept the gospel" (Hahn 1965:67; Trilling 1974:32; Grundmann 1968:578; Zumstein 1972:27; Matthey 1980:169-70).

The next participle is "teaching," which in the first Gospel is always to be distinguished from both "preaching" (Hahn 1980:42) and "making disciples" (Trilling 1964:36). *Didaskein* (to teach) is characteristic of Matthew, in spite of the fact that this verb occurs more frequently in Mark and Luke. We should, however, *weigh* rather than simply *count* the occurrences (Trilling 1964:36).

"All That I Have Commanded You"

In making disciples people should be taught "to observe all that I have commanded you." Once again the language is typically Matthean. The verb *tērein* (to observe or to practice) is absent in Luke and occurs only once in Mark. Matthew uses it six times, half of these in the sense of "keeping the commandments" (Zumstein 1972:27). The verb *entellesthai* (to command) that Matthew uses in 28:19 is related to the noun *entolē* (commandment) which he employs as a technical term for the commandments of the Old Testament, particularly the Torah—5:19; 15:3; 19:17; 22:36 (Matthey 1980:171). Once again a comparison of the three Synoptic Gospels is illuminating: Luke summarizes the content of Jesus' proclamation as "repentance toward the forgiveness of sins" (24:47); Mark calls it the *euangelion* (13:10; 14:9); and Matthew refers to "that which [Jesus] has commanded" (Zumstein 1972:28).

Protestant Christians, in particular, may feel embarrassed by this emphasis on commandments that have to be observed, as it suggests the possibility of salvation by works. It should, however, be pointed out that Matthew uses these expressions in a fierce polemic against (Jamnia) Pharisaism. In doing so, Matthew consciously uses the Torah according to the Jewish tradition, but in such a way that the discrepancy between teaching and doing on the part of his opponents is exposed. The issue at stake is therefore the correct interpretation of and obedience to the law: The true teacher of the law, says the author in 13:52, is one "who has been discipled unto the kingdom" (Bornkamm 1961:22, 28; Hahn 1980:306).

The verb *entellesthai* (command) occurs here in the aorist, so the reference is not to a *new* revelation, but to what the earthly Jesus has already taught his disciples. It remains normative, now and forever. The message of the Resurrected One is the same as that of the earthly Jesus. The *Kyrios* is none other than the teacher from Nazareth (Zumstein 1972:28; Matthey 1980:171).

What, then, is his commandment? It is more than the moral and ceremonial law or than a purely religious, otherworldly rule of life. It is nothing less than the command to love God and people. In the story of the rich young man, Matthew has edited Mark thus: "If you would enter life, keep [*tērēson*] the commandments [*tas entolas*]" (Mt 19:17). The words in Matthew 28 are a clear allusion to those in Matthew 19 (Hubbard 1976:91; Hahn 1980:36; Bornkamm 1961:28). But Jesus radicalizes these commandments in a specific direction: To love one's neighbors means to have compassion on them (see also Luke's Good Samaritan) and to see that justice is done. Thus *dikaiosynē* (justice) becomes another key concept in Matthew's Gospel. The disciples are challenged to a life of righteousness (=justice) which infinitely surpasses that practiced by the Pharisees (Mt 5:20) and to seek God's kingdom and his justice (Mt 6:33). Justice is, as in the Old Testament, practically a synonym for compassion or almsgiving, as the famous parable in Matthew 25:31-46 demonstrates (Barth 1961:*passim*; Bornkamm 1961:22; Brown 1977:25; Hahn 1980:36; Matthey 1980:170-73; Scott 1980:164-71).

All this has consequences for our understanding of the Great Commission and of the command to make disciples. Waldron Scott rightly sees the Great Commission within a wider context than many of his fellow-evangelicals. He says, "I am proposing that we view the larger mission, the ultimate mission, as the establishment of justice" (1980:xvi). And Jacques Matthey says, "According to Matthew's Great Commission, it is not possible to make disciples without telling them to practise God's request of justice for the poor. The love commandment, which is *the* basis for the churches' involvement in politics, is an integral part of the mission commandment" (1980:171). If this is correct—and I believe that our exegesis has proved that it is—it is evident that neither McGavran's juxtaposition of discipling and perfecting as two consecutive stages, nor his definition of making disciples as calling a people to an initial turning to Christ, is tenable. To become a disciple is to be incorporated into God's new community through baptism and to side with the poor and the oppressed. To put it differently, it is to love God and our neighbor. This is what Jesus has commanded his disciples (Mt 28:19). And of course, for Matthew this obedience is determined not by a conformity to any impersonal commandment but by the relation to Jesus himself (Blauw 1974:86).

ALL THE NATIONS

Those who are to be made disciples are described as *panta ta ethnē* (all the nations). It would be correct to say that this expression occupies a key position in the entire Church Growth missiology. McGavran, who frequently cites *panta ta ethnē* untranslated, interprets it as referring to "the classes, tribes, lineages, and peoples of earth" (1980:22). Thus *ethnē* is interpreted in an ethnological or sociological sense; it refers to homogeneous units of people sharing common characteristics, particularly a common racial, linguistic, and class heritage.

Researchers in Pasadena have established that there are still some 16,000 identifiable affinity groups who have not yet been evangelized effectively. It was homogeneous units of people such as these that Jesus had in mind when he used the expression *panta ta ethnē*, and not modern nation-states. "He had in mind families of mankind—tongues, tribes, castes, and lineages of men. That is exactly what *ta ethnē* means . . . in Matthew 28:19" (McGavran 1980:56). McGavran therefore applauds the Hindi translation of Matthew 28:19 which reads "disciple the *castes*" (1980:348).

McGavran's co-workers concur with his interpretation: "The Great Commission was expressed in ethnic terms" (Tippett 1970:30; cf. 32). The apostles were to disciple "all the ethnic units" (Yamamori 1980:49). Of special importance in this regard is C. Peter Wagner's recent *Our Kind of People* (Wagner 1979). He finds the homogeneous unit principle not only in Matthew 28:19, but in all of the New Testament. In fact, it becomes a hermeneutical key to understanding the New Testament documents. Why did Jesus refuse to accept the former demoniac into his community (Mk 5:18-19)? Because he was a Gadarene and belonged to a different homogeneous unit (Wagner 1979:118). Why did Jesus react so brusquely to the Syrophoenician woman (Mt 15:24)? Because "the general lines of his strategy of ministry had been determined in accordance with the homogeneous unit principle" (Wagner 1979:119).

When, according to Acts 6, it was decided to form two separate homogeneous congregations in Jerusalem, the Christian movement spread with increasing rapidity (Wagner 1979:123). As a matter of fact, had the New Testament churches not been homogeneous unit churches, they could not have multiplied as rapidly as they did (Wagner 1979:117). As regards the rapid growth of the church in Antioch, it is "reasonable to postulate" that a cluster of house churches with Gentile membership was established quite separately from the Jewish groups, perhaps not even in the same section of the city (Wagner

1979:124-25). In Rome, too, there were "in all probability [nothing other than] basically homogeneous unit churches" (Wagner 1979:130-31). And the two epistles to the Thessalonians were perhaps written to "two separate and homogeneous congregations" in that city, "one Jewish and one Gentile" (Wagner 1979:131).

On the slender basis of the interpretation of Matthew 28:19 as meaning that Jesus commissioned the discipling of separate homogeneous units, the Church Growth movement has erected an imposing superstructure. There is, of course, validity in the argument that the gospel should be communicated in an intelligible way and be contextualized in the culture of the people who are being evangelized. Nobody can fault this. The question is, however, whether this is what Matthew 28:19 says. Has not a modern problem been read back into the text (Liefield 1978:177)? The evidence shows that this is indeed what has happened.

Ethnē, in the plural, is in the Septuagint the normal rendering of *gôyim* (nations). As such, the term *can* have a sociological or ethnological meaning, particularly in the singular, *ethnos*. Bertram has, however, shown that in more recent parts of the Old Testament the plural *gôyim* is to be understood almost exclusively in a religioethical sense, as the collective designation not for nations but for Gentiles or pagans (Bertram 1935:364-66). In this sense it was introduced into the Septuagint and Hellenistic Judaism as *ethnē*. It became for all practical purposes a technical term for Gentiles in contrast to Jews (Schmidt 1935:367; De Ridder 1975:188).

"Jew," too, is in this period to be understood primarily as a religious, not ethnic, designation (Bertram 1935:362). In view of this it is unlikely that *ethnē* in Matthew 28:19 should be understood in the sense of separate ethnic units. It *could* bear that sense, but there were far more suitable Greek words to give expression to that shade of meaning: words such as *phylē* (people as a national unit of common descent), *laos* (people as a political unit with a common history; this is the Greek word most frequently used for the Jews as a people), and *glōssa* (people as a linguistic unit) (Liefield 1978:175; Hesselgrave 1979:200 and 1980:50-51).

When *panta* (all) is added to *ethnē*, as in Matthew 28:19, yet another nuance is created. As the parallels and other related passages show, *panta ta ethnē* is for all practical purposes a synonym for *holē hē oikoumenē* (the whole inhabited world) (Mt 24:14—the parallel Mk 13:10 has *panta ta ethnē*), for *holos (hapas) ho kosmos* (the whole world of man) (Mk 16:15; Mt 26:13), and for *pasa hē ktisis* (the entire human world as created by God) (Mk 16:15). The words *kosmos, oikoumenē*, and *ktisis* were taken over from the colloquial Greek, whereas *panta ta ethnē* reveals Old Testament thinking (Trilling 1964:31; Hahn 1965:71, 124; Hubbard 1976:84-85). Within the context the emphasis is clearly on the entire world of humanity; the expression is used "in view of the worldwide mission" (Hahn 1965:71; Trilling 1964:31). An unbiased reading of Matthew 28:19 can therefore not take it to imply that the Christian mission is to be carried out "people by people," but that it is to reach far beyond the confines that existed up to that time (Liefield 1978:176).

There is, nevertheless, some disagreement among New Testament scholars about the the exact meaning of *panta ta ethnē*. The question is, however, *not* whether *panta ta ethnē* means ethnic units, but whether it refers to Gentiles only, or to nations, including the Jews. Those who believe that the author of the first Gospel was not a Jew but a Gentile, tend to interpret *panta ta ethnē* as excluding the Jews. Since Israel has rejected its Messiah, it now falls outside the boundary of his salvific will. The command in Matthew 10:5-6 is not simply extended but canceled; the time for a mission to Israel is past; those who had not been invited are now approached; and those who had been invited are rejected (Walker 1967:111-12; Hare and Harrington 1975:359-69).

Most scholars, however, accept that *panta ta ethnē* is used here in a completely unrestricted sense, referring to Gentiles and Jews alike. A careful analysis of the material in Matthew supports this interpretation. Where *ethnē* excludes Israel in the first Gospel, we have either an Old Testament quotation or material of non-Matthean origin (Meier 1977b:94-102). Where the term is introduced by Matthew himself, particularly in the final part of his Gospel, and even more particularly where *ta ethnē* is used together with *panta*, it means "all the nations." There is in addition some allusion to *ethnē* as signifying everybody outside God's new people, the church—a meaning that one also finds in the Pauline epistles (Bosch 1959:190-91; Matthey 1980:168, n. 14; Trilling 1964:26-28; Hahn 1965:125; Zumstein 1972:26).

The issue behind the use of the word *ethnē* is thus completely unrelated to the question of homogeneous units. It is the issue of *salvation history*: The New Covenant is to be absolutely universal, and the only point that has to be discerned is whether the Jews are still included or not. I agree with those scholars who say they are, and that *panta ta ethnē* is to be interpreted without any restriction whatsoever.

Moreover, the tensions in the early church between Jews and Gentiles were essentially theological, not cultural. The question as to whether Gentiles should be circumcised had nothing to do with the homogeneous unit issue, as becomes clear from Paul's letters. The point he makes throughout is salvation-historical: The crucified and risen Messiah has superseded the law as the way of salvation. Some early church leaders, such as James, probably subscribed to the idea that God's eschatological community consisted of *two* peoples, namely, Israel and the new people made up of Gentiles. There were two different *dispensations,* and, in a way, two different but parallel ways of salvation. The Gentiles who had come to share in Israel's faith were not subject to the law and therefore not obliged to undergo circumcision. Jewish Christians, however, remained subject to both (Brown 1980:208). The continuing validity of the law as a way of salvation for the Jews entailed the refusal of Jewish Christians to violate the law by sharing meals and eucharists with Gentile Christians (Brown 1980:210-12).

However, once again, this had nothing to do with the existence of separate homogeneous units but with different understandings of salvation history; it was a matter of theology, not communications theory. Moreover, several early church leaders, Paul foremost among them, passionately opposed the theology of two separate dispensations and pleaded unceasingly for the *unity* of the church made up of *both* Jews and Gentiles. Paul still accepted the principle of division of labor as far as the mission to Jews and Gentiles was concerned (Gal 2:7), but the salvation-historical difference between the two had been abrogated: The law was a tutor only until Christ came (Gal 3:24). The essential difference between

Jews and Gentiles was never ethnic but always salvation-historical, and even this difference had now been annulled. The idea of the homogeneous-unit approach thus finds no support in the terminology of the Great Commission.

It is important, however, to realize that the Church Growth movement was not the first to interpret *panta ta ethnē* in Matthew 28:19 as furnishing the scriptural basis for the founding of separate ethnic churches. This exegesis first came in vogue in the nineteenth century in German missionary circles. German missions originated in Pietism which, particularly in its later developments, laid an almost exclusive emphasis on *Einzelbekehrung,* the conversion of individuals. By the middle of the nineteenth century the inadequacy of this approach was recognized and exposed, and the aim of mission was modified to that of the planting of self-governing, self-propagating, and self-supporting churches (Venn and Anderson). To this the Germans added that these autonomous younger churches had to be *bodenständige Volkskirchen* (autochthonous ethnic churches). The debate about the choice between *Einzelbekehrung* (conversion of individuals) and *Volkschristianisierung* (the conversion of people as a homogeneous ethnic unit) dominated the entire German missiological scene for decades. In this discussion the concept *Volk* (people as an ethno-cultural unit) increasingly became a normative factor. In the course of time this was to color the exegesis of *panta ta ethnē* in Matthew 28:19.

The best example of this is to be found in the writings of the doyen of German missiology, Gustav Warneck. He subscribed to the exegetical evidence that *panta ta ethnē* is primarily a religious and not an ethnographic concept and admitted that the entire issue about *Einzelbekehrung* and *Volkschristianisierung* lies beyond the horizon of the Great Commission (Warneck 1902:247-50). But he then proceeds to argue in favor of the translation of *panta ta ethnē* as *Völker* (peoples as ethnic units) "even if scientific exegesis has raised some not unfounded objections to this translation" (Warneck 1902:251. My translation). After all, in the practical execution of the missionary command the religious antithesis in which the *ethnē* stood to Israel becomes an ethnographic one (Warneck 1902:250). History thus proves the correctness of the suggested translation; moreover, it should be remembered "that the facts of history are also an exegesis of the Bible, and in the final analysis they speak the decisive word when the theological interpretation remains in dispute" (Warneck 1902:258. My translation).

From Warneck the path in due time led to people such as Bruno Gutmann, Christian Keysser, and many others. German missiology would show a remarkable parallel development with German political thinking in general. The concept *Volk,* deeply influenced by Romanticism, was given a theological weight that could not but secularize the theological and biblical concept. It derived its content not from Scripture but from the contemporary scene (Hoekendijk 1948:186, 232). For Gutmann the fellow-Christians are hardly distinguishable from the compatriots; through their sharing in the *urtümliche Bindungen* (primordial ties) they are sociologically circumscribed. There is therefore an abiding connection between church and *Volk* (Hoekendijk 1948:150-52). Thus "the foundations of the Church are sought as much in anthropological as in soteriological considerations, and in the end the anthropological elements crowd the soteriological into a corner" (Boer 1961:172).

This is not to suggest that what the Church Growth movement has in mind with its interpretation of *panta ta ethnē* is in all respects the same as that which German missionary thinkers in the latter part of the nineteenth and early part of the twentieth century read into this expression. At an early stage of the development of the Church Growth movement Harry Boer already cautioned that by "peoples" McGavran did not have in mind an anglicized version of the German conception of *Volk,* with its idea of the socially unifying and integrating power that arises from the bonds of common blood and common soil (Boer 1961:179, 169).

Boer is correct in his warning. Nevertheless, some uneasiness remains. Is it merely accidental that Wagner's explanation for Jesus' refusal to minister among non-Jewish peoples tallies exactly with that of Gutmann (Wagner 1979:118, 119; for Gutmann, see Hoekendijk 1948:157)? And what are we to deduce from the fact that Keysser's major treatise *Eine Papua Gemeinde* (first published 1929) has recently been "discovered," translated, and published by the Church Growth movement (Keysser 1980)? In that book Keysser went so far as to assert categorically, "Der Stamm ist zugleich die Christengemeinde" ("The tribe is at the same time the Christian Church," German edition:235).

Undoubtedly there is validity in the Church Growth movement's honoring of the homogeneous unit principle as a communications guideline. We may, however, not take a communications principle and make it an ecclesiological norm by reasoning that (1) homogeneous churches grow more rapidly than others; (2) all churches should grow more rapidly; and (3) therefore all churches should be culturally and socially homogeneous. This reasoning cannot but lead to a wrong view of the church (Showalter 1979:11).

Class prejudices and people's alienation from each other only become more deeply ingrained into the human heart where ethnicity is regarded as an intrinsic feature of the church, as W. A. Saayman's contribution to this volume illustrates. A contemporary South African theologian has written that the church is structured by the *Volk,* from which follows "that the members of an autonomous church are chosen from the ranks of an autonomous people." And he adds, "Our own history confirms this" (Potgieter 1978:29. My translation). Once again history, in a simplistic way, has been taken as a source of divine revelation.

Nor is the problem solved by elevating the unity of the church to the "supra-congregational relationship of believers in the total Christian body" (Wagner 1979:132), by which it becomes something almost exclusively spiritual, "which impinges only at certain periodic points in the life of the congregation" (Recker 1980:304). Rather, the new fellowship transcends every limit imposed by family, class, or culture. We are not winning people like ourselves to ourselves but sharing the good news that in Christ God has shattered the barriers that divide the human race and has created a new community. The new people of God has no analogy; it is a "sociological impossibility" (Hoekendijk 1948:237) that has nevertheless become possible.

The early church gave expression to this by calling the Christians the *triton genos,* the third race next to the existing two races of Jews and Gentiles. "Beside or over against these two 'peoples' [Paul] places the church of God as a new creation . . . which is to embrace both Jews and Greeks, rising above the differences of both peoples" (Harnack 1961:243; Hoekendijk 1948:237). This is the mystery revealed to Paul, "that through the gospel the Gentiles are heirs together with Israel, members together of one body, and sharers together in the promise in Christ Jesus" (Eph 3:6 NIV).

Exclusive groupings of believers, whether around individual leaders for theological or other reasons (I Cor 1:10-13) or around homogeneous cultural units, are unacceptable in the Christian church. Neither is the problem solved by regarding this as only an initial stage which will later develop into a greater openness to other Christians; the Machiavellian principle of doing evil that good may come does not work in the church. Recker, in a review of Wagner's *Our Kind of People,* thus rightly warns against "a growing virus in the body of Christ" that fosters the formation of different denominations "upon the basis of very questionable distinctives." He adds, "When individual believers refuse any longer to entertain the biblical injunction to be reconciled to their brothers but rather simply run off to find some congregation which mirrors their own foibles, fears, suspicions, prejudices, or what not in the name of feeling 'at home' or comfortable, then something is radically wrong in the body of Christ" (Recker 1980:303-04).

THE PROMISE

We now come to the final verse of the first Gospel. The promise which it contains is linked directly to the preceding commission with *kai idou* (and see) in the sense of "surely," or "therefore, be assured." The expression is once again characteristic of Matthew, as is the wording of the promise itself.

The "I am with you" theme was first broached in Matthew 1:23 ("they will call him Immanuel, which means 'God with us' ") and repeated in Matthew 18:20. As we have noted earlier, the theme as such hails from the Old Testament and is related to the rabbinic concept of the *shekinah.* In the Old Testament it is used particularly when a dangerous mission is to be undertaken, as in Joshua 1:5 and Isaiah 43:2, 5. So Matthew's Gospel is to be understood as the fulfillment of the Old Testament covenant, the epitome of which was the Lord's presence with his people. Here in 28:20 Jesus promises his disciples the same assistance of which the Jews were assured by Yahweh, and he does it by virtue of the authority *(exousia)* entrusted to him and in view of the mission they have to undertake (Strecker 1962:213; Trilling 1964:40-43; Zumstein 1972:28; O'Brien 1976:77).

Jesus' presence with his disciples is to last *pasas tas hēmeras heōs tēs synteleias tou aiōnos* (always, until the end of time). The expression *[hē] synteleia [tou] aiōnos* is found *only* in Matthew (13:39-40, 49; 24:3; 28:20). The closest parallel is *synteleia tōn aiōnōn* in Hebrews 9:26. Matthew's redactional work is therefore once again demonstrated beyond doubt.

The first Gospel mentions neither the ascension nor the outpouring of the Holy Spirit. "The interest in [the ascension and coming of the Spirit] appears to be absorbed into the experience of the always near, comforting, and empowering presence of the Kyrios" (Trilling 1964:43. My translation). Even the delay of the parousia is not really a problem any more: "The consciousness of the present experience of the Kyrios is so overpowering that it can embrace all future times. That which is a reality now, holds good for all time. Here the faith of the Church, not apocalyptic speculation, is speaking" (Trilling 1964:43-44. My translation). Thus all attention is focused on the present; there is no hint whatsoever as to the precise moment of the end. Within this context Jesus neither announces his departure nor does he actually depart; he promises, on the contrary, to remain with his disciples always. This is the overriding impression with which Matthew leaves his readers (Trilling 1964:45; Hubbard 1976:15). And the disciples' mission will last as long as his presence lasts: until the end of time. The mission itself thus becomes an integral part of the parousia expectation; it becomes, in effect, a "proleptic parousia" (Osborne 1976:82).

THE STRUCTURE OF MISSION

We have come to the end. We have argued that the pericope of Matthew 28:16-20 has its foundation in tradition, though it is expressed predominantly in Matthean language. We have added that it cannot be read and understood on its own, but only against the background of the entire first Gospel and of the exigencies of the community to which the author belonged.

In the process we have exposed some weaknesses which we believe are to be detected in Church Growth missiology, particularly in its use of the Great Commission. *Hermeneutically* there is in the Church Growth movement—and surely not only there—the tendency to handle the biblical material too self-confidently and to build on one text the whole mystery of mission. *Exegetically* there is the unjustified, one-sided emphasis on *going* (which Church Growth exponents share with other evangelicals), the disjunction between discipling and perfecting, and the interpretation of *panta ta ethnē* in ethnological categories.

More *generally* there is the issue of ecclesiology and of a too narrow definition of mission. Regarding the latter it has to be pointed out that the Church Growth movement has not yet dynamically related its missiology to the pressing problems of social ethics facing the church, notwithstanding Wagner's attempt in *Church Growth and the Whole Gospel* (1981).

Although it would be illegitimate to erect the entire edifice of the New Testament witness concerning the church's mission on Matthew 28:16-20 (Matthey 1980:161), we can infer some significant guidelines on the basis of our exegesis of this pericope, employing it, with all the necessary qualifications, as a paradigm for our mission today.

Mission is always contextual. Mission is related to a specific time and place and situation. Thus Matthew is not simply repeating a word uttered long ago, but is reinterpreting it for his own context. The history of the Master with his disciples is foundational and paradigmatic, and as such nourishes and challenges the present. Faith is thus realized in what Kierkegaard has called *contemporaneity,* where there is, in the final analysis, no absolute discontinuity between the history of Jesus and the time of the church. By speaking of the condition and activities of those who accompanied Jesus on his way to the cross, the evangelist is speaking to the church of his own time. And it is precisely the dialectic between the history of Jesus and the existence of the believer that justifies, for Matthew, the writing of the Gospel in the way he does (Zumstein 1972:30, 33; Matthey 1980:162).

A precarious existence. Matthew's community lived at a frontier. They experienced difficulty in defining their own identity in a context where they occupied the borderline between increasingly hostile Jews and as yet alien Gentiles. They experienced, to put it mildly, a crisis of identity. For us this means that mission never takes place in self-confidence and megalomania but in the knowledge of our own weakness. The missionary is no hero but stands, like the disciples in Galilee, in the dialectical tension between faith and doubt, between worship and fear (Mt 28:17). In the midst of that tension, however, the missionary knows—by faith—that all authority in heaven and on earth has been given to Jesus. Therefore, although the missionary's own situation may be precarious, it is never hopeless.

Mission means servanthood. Although now invested with all power in the universe, the resurrected Christ is still Jesus of Nazareth who walks as a migrant through Galilee and calls his disciples to follow him to the cross. His church has to follow *that* path to glory, and *not* the alternative route suggested to him by the Devil in Matthew 4:8-9. This means that a church which wields earthly power and on that basis imposes its views on others is a church that has fallen to the Devil's temptation and is therefore disqualified from being called to the mission of Jesus. "[God] will only reach the nations if the bearers of the Gospel of the kingdom, the evangelizing disciples, come as poor, exposed, defenseless men and women, living with and not above those to whom they bring healing" (Matthey 1980:173).

Mission is incarnational. John's version of the Great Commission has Jesus saying to his disciples, "As the Father sent me, so I send you" (20:21). Thus the sending of the disciples is grounded in the sending of Jesus by the Father. Mission is *missio Dei.* Therefore baptism, the decisive act of incorporation into the church and of signifying the forgiveness of sins, takes place "in the Name of the Father and of the Son and of the Holy Spirit" (Mt 28:14).

Incarnational mission is comprehensive in nature. Those who emulate Jesus are to be characterized by boundless compassion (Bosch 1980:53-57), fellowship, and worship. They are involved in service, preaching, witness—in short, in disciple-making. The true disciple is, however, the one who is being "discipled unto the Kingdom" (Mt 13:52), which is the same as "being discipled unto Jesus" (Mt 27:57; notice the parallel in Mk 15:43: "who expected the kingdom of God"). It is well known that "the kingdom of heaven" occupies a key place in the first Gospel. The same is true of that other typically Matthean concept, *dikaiosynē.* This is not in every respect the same as Paul's "justification." It is, rather, justification, righteousness, and justice in one: "God's righteousness and human righteousness [=justice] do not exclude each other, but are identical" (Strecker 1962:155. My translation).

Moreover, in the first gospel *dikaiosynē* and *basileia* (kingdom) are intimately related. Although they are not synonyms, they are mutually dependent: "The way to the *basileia* leads only via the *dikaiosynē*" (Strecker 1962:155. My translation). When the disciples are charged to teach "all that I have commanded you" as part of the disciple-making process (Mt 28:19), the pursuit of *dikaiosynē* lies at the center. The way of Jesus is "the way of justice" (this would be the English title of Strecker's book on Matthew). Waldron Scott is therefore correct when he relates the Great Commission to the larger mission and adds, "I am proposing that we view the larger mission, the ultimate mission, as the establishment of justice" (Scott 1980:xvi).

It follows from this that Christian social involvement may never be downgraded from its status as an inherent and essential part of the good news to the position of a mere adjunct of the gospel as an editorial in *Christianity Today* (1980) would have it, for "one must understand discipleship in order to make disciples, and discipleship is not fully biblical apart from a commitment to social justice" (Scott 1980:xvi).

Mission (or disciple-making) avoids becoming a heavy burden, a new law, a command to obey. The disciples' involvement in mission is a *logical consequence* of their being "discipled unto Jesus" and of the "full authority" given to him (notice the "therefore" in Mt 28:19). "You are my witnesses *because* you have been with me" (Jn 15:26). To be involved in mission is to receive a gift, not to obey a law; to accept a promise, not to bow to a command. Christ's promised presence (Mt 28:10) "is not a reward offered to those who obey: it is the assurance that those who are commanded will be able to obey" (Allen 1968:25). So the Great Commission is not a commission in the ordinary sense of the word, but rather a creative statement, in the manner of Genesis 1:3 and elsewhere, "Let there be . . ." (Bosch 1980:81).

Mission involves the church. In Matthew's understanding the church is God's chosen messenger in the world. Of course, he does not use the word church in the Great Commission (though he is the only evangelist who uses it at all, in Mt 16:18 and 18:17). He talks about disciples and disciple-making, but in his thinking this is the same as "being a member of the Church" and "incorporating people into the Christian community" (Trilling 1964:31; Hahn 1980:38; also Strecker 1962:191-226).

Discipleship ecclesiology. Matthew's "discipleship ecclesiology" (Osborne 1976:83) highlights the fact that the believer follows a Master. The *Master-disciple relationship* is prominent in the final pericope of the first Gospel. The risen Christ is still Jesus; he is thus, paradoxically, identical to the earthly Master. The same parallelism applies to the believer: the disciple in Matthew's own community is, equally paradoxically, identical to the Twelve. The intimate relationship and unconditional allegiance which applied during Jesus' earthly ministry still applies in Matthew's community (Zumstein 1972:29, 31-33).

The structure of mission. Mission is indeed *structured,* not amorphous, antinomian, and purely enthusiast. On the other hand, mission should never become *established,* institutionalized, ecclesiasticized. Within his community Matthew is involved in a double polemic against these two opposite heresies, embodied respectively in the early forms of Ebionitism on the one hand and enthusiastic Gentile Christianity on the other (Zumstein 1972:29-31; Trilling 1964:124ff).

The horizon of mission is unlimitedly universal. He who has been given all authority in heaven and on earth sends his disciples into all the world to make disciples of all nations. Nothing is said about the communication methods involved. That lies outside the scope of the Great Commission. The emphasis is entirely on the fact that the horizon has become unlimited, that the old restrictions have fallen away entirely. So the disciples see before them not so many separate tribes and tongues, but the whole of humankind that has to be discipled.

The permanence of Jesus' presence. Jesus' authority is universal ("heaven and earth"), his commission is worldwide ("all the nations"), and his *presence is permanent* ("always, until the end of time"). Ultimately, then, it is Jesus' abiding presence with his disciples "which transforms an imperative into an inspiration" (Warren 1955:114). Even if Matthew does not mention the Holy Spirit in 28:20, Jesus' presence with his disciples is to be understood pneumatologically.

REFERENCES CITED

ALLEN, Roland
1962   *The Ministry of the Spirit,* Grand Rapids: Eerdmans.
1968   *Missionary Principles,* London: Lutterworth.

BARTH, Gerhard
1961   "Das Gesetzverständnis des Evangelisten Matthäus," *Ueberlieferung und Auslegung im Matthäusevangelium,* G. Bornkamm, G. Barth, and H. J. Held, Neukirchen: Neukirchener Verlag.

BASSHAM, Roger C.
1979   *Mission Theology 1948-1975, Years of Worldwide Creative Tension: Ecumenical, Evangelical, and Roman Catholic,* Pasadena: William Carey Library.

BAUMBACH, Günther
1967   "Die Mission im Matthäus-Evangelium," *Theologische Literaturzeitung* 92:12.

BERTRAM, G.
1935   Art. *ethnos, ethnikos,* in *Theologisches Wörterbuch zum Neuen Testament,* Vol. 2, Stuttgart: Kohlhammer.

BLAUW, Johannes
1974   *The Missionary Nature of the Church,* Grand Rapids: Eerdmans.

BOER, Harry R.
1961   *Pentecost and Missions,* London: Lutterworth.

BORNKAMM, G.
1961   "Enderwartung und Kirche im Matthäusevangelium," *Ueberlieferung und Auslegung im Matthäusevangelium,* G. Bornkamm, G. Barth, and H. J. Held, Neukirchen: Neukirchener Verlag.

BOSCH, David J.
1959   *Die Heidenmission in der Zukunftsschau Jesu,* Zürich: Zwingli Verlag.
1969   " 'Jesus and the Gentiles'—a Review after Thirty Years," *The Church Crossing Frontiers, Essays on the Nature of Mission in Honour of Bengt Sundkler,* Lund: Gleerup.
1980   *Witness to the World: The Christian Mission in Theological Perspective,* Atlanta: John Knox.

BROWN, Schuyler
1977   "The Two-fold Representation of the Mission in Matthew's Gospel," *Studia Theologica* 31:1.
1980   "The Matthean Community and the Gentile Mission," *Novum Testamentum* 22:3 (July).

CHRISTIANITY TODAY
1980   Editorial, *Christianity Today,* August 8, 1980.

CLARK, K. W.
1980   *The Gentile Bias and Other Essays,* Leiden: Brill (the first essay in this volume was originally published in 1947).

GERBER, Vergil
1980   *Discipling through Theological Education by Extension,* Chicago: Moody.

GRUNDMANN, Walter
1968   *Das Evangelium nach Matthäus,* Berlin: Evangelische Verlagsanstalt.

HAHN, Ferdinand
1965   *Mission in the New Testament,* London: SCM Press.
1980   "Der Sendungsauftrag des Auferstandenen: Matthäus 28, 16-20," *Fides pro mundi vita,* Theo Sundermeier (ed.), Missionstheologie heute, Hans-Werner Gensichen zum 65. Geburtstag, Gütersloh: Gerd Mohn.

HARE, Douglas R. A. and HARRINGTON, Daniel J., S. J.
1975   " 'Make Disciples of all the Gentiles' (Mt 28:19)," *The Catholic Biblical Quarterly* 37:3.

HARNACK, Adolf
1961   *The Mission and Expansion of Christianity in the First Three Centuries,* New York: Harper & Brothers (first published in German in 1902).

HARRISON, Everett F.
1973   "Did Christ Command World Evangelism?" *Christianity Today* 18:4 (Nov. 23).

HENGEL, Martin
1970/71   "Die Ursprünge der christlichen Mission," *New Testament Studies* 18:1.

HESSELGRAVE, David J.
1979   "Confusion Concerning the Great Commission," *Evangelical Missions Quarterly* 15:4 (Oct.).
1980   Letter on "Meaning of the Great Commission," *Evangelical Missions Quarterly* 16:1 (Jan.).

HOEKENDIJK, J. C.
1948   *Kerk en volk in de duitse zendingswetenschap.* Amsterdam: Drukkerij Kampert & Helm.

HUBBARD, B. J.
1976   *The Matthean Redaction of a Primitive Apostolic Commission: An Exegesis of Matthew 28:16-20,* Missoula: Society of Biblical Literature and Scholar's Press Dissertation Series, No. 19.

KASTING, H.
1969   *Die Anfänge der urchristlichen Mission, Eine historische Untersuchung,* Munich: Christian Kaiser.

KEYSSER, Christian
1980   *A People Reborn,* Pasadena: William Carey Library (translation of *Eine Papua Gemeinde,* first published 1929).

KINGSBURY, Jack Dean
1974   "The Composition and Christology of Matthew 28:16-20," *Journal of Biblical Literature* 93:4.

KOLLBRUNNER, Fritz
1974   *The Splendour and Confusion of Mission Today,* Gwelo (Zimbabwe): Mambo Press.

LANGE, J.
1978   *Das Erscheinen des Auferstandenen im Evangelium nach Matthäus,* Würzburg: Echter Verlag.

LIEFIELD, Walter L.
1978   "Theology of Church Growth," *Theology and Mission,* D. J. Hesselgrave (ed.), Grand Rapids: Baker.

LOHMEYER, Ernst
1956   *Das Evangelium des Matthäus*, Göttingen: Vandenhoeck & Ruprecht.

McGAVRAN, Donald A.
1957   *The Bridges of God*, London: World Dominion Press (first published 1955).
1966   *How Churches Grow: The New Frontiers of Mission*, New York: Friendship Press (first published 1959).
1979   "How about that New Verb 'to disciple'?" *Church Growth Bulletin* 15:5 (May).
1980   *Understanding Church Growth* (fully revised), Grand Rapids: Eerdmans.

MATTHEY, Jacques
1980   "The Great Commission according to Matthew," *International Review of Mission* No. 274 (April).

MEIER, John P.
1977a   "Two Disputed Questions in Matthew 28:16-20," *Journal of Biblical Literature* 96:3.
1977b   "Nations or Gentiles in Matthew 28:19?" *The Catholic Biblical Quarterly* 39:1.

MICHEL, Otto
1950/51   "Der Abschluss des Matthäusevangeliums," *Evangelische Theologie* 10:1.

MINEAR, Paul S.
1961   "Gratitude and Mission in the Epistle to the Romans," *Basileia. Walter Freytag zum 60. Geburtstag*, Stuttgart: Evang. Missionswerk.
1977   *Images of the Church in the New Testament* (third printing), Philadelphia: Fortress Press.

NEWBIGIN, Lesslie
1978   "The Church as Witness," *Reformed Review* 35:1 (March).
1979   "Context and Conversion," *International Review of Mission* No. 271 (July).

O'BRIEN, P.
1976   "The Great Commission of Matthew 28:18-20: A Missionary Mandate or Not?" *The Reformed Theological Review* 35:3 (Sept.-Dec.).

OHM, Thomas, O.S.B.
1962   *Machet zu Jüngern alle Völker, Theorie der Mission*, Freiburg: Erich Wewel Verlag.

OSBORNE, Grant R.
1976   "Redaction Criticism and the Great Commission: A Case Study Toward a Biblical Understanding of Inerrancy," *Journal of the Evangelical Theological Society* 19:2.

POTGIETER, F. G. M.
1978   "Eenheid en veelvormigheid prinsipieel verantwoord," *Veelvormigheid en eenheid*, J. D. Vorster (ed.), Cape Town: N. G. Kerk-Uitgewers.

RECKER, Robert
1980   Review of C. Peter Wagner, *Our Kind of People*, in *Calvin Theological Journal* 15:2 (Nov.).

DE RIDDER, Richard R.
1975   *Discipling the Nations*, Grand Rapids: Baker.

ROGERS, Cleon
1973   "The Great Commission," *Bibliotheca Sacra* No. 519 (July-Sept.).

ROSENKRANZ, Gerhard
1977   *Die christliche Mission, Geschichte und Theologie*, Munich: Christian Kaiser Verlag.

SCHIEBER, Hans
1977   "Konzentrik im Matthäusschluss, Ein form- und gattungskritischer Versuch zu Mt 28, 16-20," *Kairos* 19:4.

SCHLATTER, Adolf
1948   *Der Evangelist Matthäus,* Stuttgart: Calwer.

SCHMIDT, Karl Ludwig
1935   Art. *ethnos* in *Theologisches Wörterbuch zum Neuen Testament,* Stuttgart: Kohlhammer.

SCHWEIZER, Eduard
1973   *Das Evangelium nach Matthäus,* Göttingen: Vandenhoeck & Ruprecht.

SCOTT, Waldron
1980   *Bring Forth Justice: A Contemporary Perspective on Mission,* Grand Rapids: Eerdmans.

SHENK, Wilbert R.
1980   "The Great Commission," *Mission Focus: Current Issues,* Wilbert R. Shenk (ed.), Scottdale: Herald Press.

SHOWALTER, Richard
1979   "Church Growth Principles and Christian Discipleship," *Mission and the Peace Witness,* Robert L. Ramseyer (ed.), Scottdale: Herald Press.

STENDAHL, Krister
1968   *The School of St. Matthew, and its use of the Old Testament* (with a new introduction by the Author), Philadelphia: Fortress (first published in 1954).

STOTT, John R. W.
1967   "The Great Commission," *One Race, One Gospel, One Task,* Vol. 1. C. F. H. Henry and W. S. Mooneyham (eds.), Minneapolis: World Wide Publications.

STRECKER, Georg
1962   *Der Weg der Gerechtigkeit, Untersuchung zur Theologie des Matthäus,* Göttingen: Vandenhoeck & Ruprecht.

TIPPETT, Alan R.
1970   *Church Growth and the Word of God, The Biblical Basis of the Church Growth Viewpoint,* Grand Rapids: Eerdmans.

TRILLING, Wolfgang
1964   *Das wahre Israel, Studien zur Theologie des Matthäusevangeliums,* Munich: Kösel.

VAN'T HOF, I. P. C.
1980   "Gehoorzaamheid aan het zendingsbevel," *Kerk en Theologie* 37:1 (Jan.).

WAGNER, C. Peter
1973   "What is 'Making Disciples'?" *Evangelical Missions Quarterly* 9:5 (Fall).
1979   *Our Kind of People, The Ethical Dimensions of Church Growth in America,* Atlanta: John Knox.
1981   *Church Growth and the Whole Gospel,* New York: Harper and Row.

WALKER, Rolf
1967   *Die Heilsgeschichte im ersten Evangelium,* Göttingen: Vandenhoeck & Ruprecht.

WARNECK, Gustav
1902   *Evangelische Missionslehre III/1* (second edition), Gotha: Perthes.

WARREN, Max
1955   *The Christian Imperative,* London: SCM Press.

YAMAMORI, Tetsunao
  1980   Letter on "Meaning of the Great Commission," *Evangelical Missions Quarterly* 16:1 (Jan.).
ZUMSTEIN, Jean
  1972   "Matthieu 28:16-20," *Révue de Théologie et de Philosophie* 22:1.
ZWEMER, Samuel M.
  1943   *"Into all the World," The Great Commission: A Vindication and an Interpretation,* Grand Rapids: Zondervan.

19. THE HOLY SPIRIT AND CHURCH GROWTH

Harry R. Boer

THE SPIRIT'S WORK IN CREATION

THE FIRST SCRIPTURE REFERENCE TO THE HOLY SPIRIT DOES NOT RELATE TO redemptive activity but rather to the Spirit's role in the creation of the world: "And the Spirit of God was moving over the face of the waters." It suggests the Spirit's energizing power ready to effectuate the tenfold "and God said" which made cosmos out of chaos. This is the Creator Spirit by whom the heavens and their hosts were made, and in that creation the Holy Spirit remains omnipresent. In the world there is no place private to the Spirit's eye (Ps 139:7-12). The Spirit bestows gifts on humans—artistic skill, rulership, courage, physical strength, guidance—as we read again and again in the sacred record.

When Paul spoke of whatever is true, honorable, just, pure, lovely, gracious, excellent, and worthy of praise (Phil 4:8), he had in mind good gifts of the Spirit granted us with our creation which we are to make fruitful by the power of the Redeemer Spirit. And this is true no less of the qualities which Paul designated as "fruits of the Spirit" listed in Galatians 5:22: love, joy, peace, patience, kindness, goodness, faithfulness, gentleness, self-control. The intercession of the Spirit with sighs too deep for words when we do not know how to pray (Rom 8:26) is not to be separated from God's solicitude for the groaning of the tortured creation as it awaits the revelation of the glorious liberty of the children of God (Rom 8:21).

THE SPIRIT'S WORK IN REDEMPTION

We must remember with strictest consistency and relevance that the Spirit's work in salvation, though based solely on the work of Christ, is restorative of the Spirit's work in creation. The Redeemer Spirit's renewing redemption has as its

---

Harry R. Boer, Grand Rapids, Michigan, is a retired missionary. His service includes U.S. Navy chaplain, 1942-46; study and mission work in Nigeria, 1946-50; Professor of Missions at Calvin Seminary, 1950-52; doctoral study at the Free University of Amsterdam, 1953-55; and principal of the Theological College of Northern Nigeria, 1955-71. From 1972 to 1978 he authored textbooks for African theological students. He wrote the seminal work Pentecost and Missions *(1961), and more recently he published* A Short History of the Early Church *(1976),* The Book of Revelation *(1980),* The Bible and Higher Criticism *(1981), and* The Four Gospels and Acts: A Short Introduction *(1982), all by Eerdmans.*

object the Creator Spirit's fallen creation. The Redeemer God *is* the Creator God. As the Father of our Lord and Savior Jesus Christ is one and the same as the Father of him through whom the world was made, as the world that he redeems is one and the same as the world that he created, so the Spirit that brought the created world back from death to life is one and the same as the Spirit that brought the world to birth. The end of all the Holy Spirit's work is a *new* heaven and a *new* earth in which shall dwell a *new* humanity. But this is not *another* humanity than the humanity that God created; it is that *same* humanity, resurrected and reborn to live in the reconstituted universe.

The life of the new creation is constituted in the same manner as the life of the old creation. The Holy Spirit is the originator and principle of the new life in Christ, and out of and through that life gifts and graces bestowed by the Creator Spirit are sanctified to perform service in the kingdom of God. In re-creation as in creation, the life-giving principle is the Holy Spirit of God, and out of the life so given flow all the beauty and diversity that exist in the work of God in grace, as do the beauty and diversity of the work of God in nature from the Creator Spirit.

ONE SPIRIT A UNITY INDIVISIBLE

The correlation between the Spirit as Creator and the Spirit as Redeemer is much overlooked in theology, and not least in missiology. It is a breathtaking thought that the Holy Spirit given at Pentecost is one and the same Spirit as he who moved over the face of the primordial waters. The relationship between the two did not escape Roland Allen, missionary of the Society for the Propagation of the Gospel of Great Britain the first half of this century. He was preeminently a missionary thinker.

In Allen's thought the work of the Holy Spirit was the point of departure, and it was his point of constant reference. The major works in which he developed his missionary theology are *Missionary Methods, St. Paul's or Ours?* (1912), *Missionary Principles* (1913), and *The Spontaneous Expansion of the Church and the Causes Which Hinder It* (1927). Allen is often associated with the "three selfs" of missionary practice in the founding of churches: self-propagation, self-support, and self-government. He certainly gave prominence to these, but in his view they had little merit apart from the context in which he developed their meaning and value.

This context constitutes the central contribution of Roland Allen to missiology. For him the whole of missionary outreach should basically be determined by the nature of the Holy Spirit. He is the life-giving Spirit who empowers the witness of the gospel messenger; he is the indwelling Spirit who creates the new person in Christ in the converts. The new life which he inspires in them makes them spontaneous witnesses to the truth of the gospel. That same new life enables them to have all necessary sufficiency to live their lives in terms of their own spiritual resources and spiritual judgment. The support which they effect among themselves relates not only to finance, but to mutual help, to ministry, to the provision of places of worship. The Spirit also gives them ability to govern themselves.

Allen regarded the failure of the missionary community to recognize these Spirit-given abilities and qualities in the converts as the chief cause of missionary paternalism and all the retardation which that occasioned in developing virile younger churches. He encapsulated his philosophy in the famous dictum: We have done much *for* our converts, we have done little *with* them. Self-propagation, self-support, and self-government are therefore not, in Allen's view, independently valuable characteristics of the newborn church, but they are rather visible expressions of a profoundly spiritual reality, namely, the reality of the Spirit living within the converts individually and corporately.

Believers, therefore, once they are constituted through confession and baptism as a church of Christ, are competent, independent, and should be masters in their own house. Because this has so often not been acknowledged by the missionaries, people who were the object of paternalistic attitudes and policies could not distinguish them from the exercise of colonial power. It seemed to them that wherever they met the Westerner, whether in commerce, in education, in hospitals, in politics, or in missionary attitudes and administration they met a person who sought to dominate, however kindly. The Spirit, said Allen, is no respecter of persons. One who has the Spirit is a fully redeemed human being and must be accorded the respect, the trust, the confidence that befit God's redeemed humanity.

We must be careful, however, to understand what Allen meant by the Holy Spirit. The general tendency is to understand simply the person and work of the Holy Spirit as these come to expression in redemption, the Holy Spirit who regenerates the heart, illumines the mind, steels the will, sanctifies the life, and comforts the believer in the pilgrimage from new birth to consummation. Such an understanding, however, does not do justice to Allen's magisterial vision. He operated not one whit less with the Holy Spirit as Creator than with the Holy Spirit as Redeemer. For him the freedom, the spontaneity, the sense of self-respect and independence which the gift of the Spirit confers arise out of the restoration of natural gifts bestowed in creation to their true position in life. Again and again, one cannot escape the impression, especially in Allen's *The Spontaneous Expansion of the Church* (1927), that for him the distinction between the work of the Spirit in redemption and his work in creation has practically fallen away. It is not that the one is swallowed up by the other; it is rather that the two are seen as a unity indivisible. The Holy Spirit who-redeems-what-he-created seems to stand front and center.

In *Spontaneous Expansion* Allen speaks about the meaning of *spontaneous*. He writes:

> If we seek for the cause which produces rapid expansion when a new faith seizes hold of men who feel able and free to propagate it spontaneously of their own initiative, we find its roots in a certain natural instinct. . . . But in Christians there is more than this natural instinct. The Spirit of Christ is a Spirit who longs for, and strives after, the salvation of the souls of men, and that Spirit dwells in them. That Spirit converts the natural instinct into a longing for the conversion of others . . . (12, 13).

> Where this instinct for expression, this divine desire for the salvation of others has free course, there it exercises a most extraordinary power (13).

Spontaneous expansion begins with the individual effort of the individual Christian to assist his fellow, when common experience, common difficulties, common toil have first brought the two together. It is this equality and community of experience which makes the one deliver his message in terms which the other can understand, and makes the hearer approach the subject with sympathy and confidence . . . (13).

But perhaps it may be said that what we fear is not the free expression of this natural instinct, still less of this divine grace; what we fear is the expression of human self-will and self-assertion. . . . We cannot possibly open the door to an unrestricted freedom for the expression of the natural instinct and the spiritual grace without opening it also to the expression of self-will; and that we dare not do.

That is quite true; but unhappily it is also true that we cannot check the license of self-will without checking at the same time the zeal which springs from the natural instinct and the grace of the gospel. We cannot distinguish the activity of the one from the activity of the other (20).

Neither the natural instinct, nor the grace of the gospel, nor the self-will of man can be permanently eradicated by any external authority. . . . We are in far greater danger of serious disorder when, in fear of the expression of self-will, we restrain a God-given instinct, than when we accept the risks involved in giving it free play (22).

It is more than clear in these quotations that in Allen's view the Holy Spirit of redemption works mightily with and in the human spirit as constituted by the Holy Spirit in creation. The intermingling of, or correlation between, "that natural instinct and that God-given grace," and in similar couplets, illustrates that Allen was not only a theologian of special but also of general revelation. He had learned the lesson that Calvin had so effectively taught, the lesson that the world of nature from microcosm to macrocosm with humans at the center is indeed a revelation of God which, when it is viewed through "the spectacles of Scripture," is seen for what it truly is (*Institutes of the Christian Religion,* I:14:1). Moreover, this understanding would seem to imply that the revelation in nature, so perceived, becomes in its turn a pair of spectacles through which the revelation in Scripture is to be viewed. The two revelations thus undergo interaction and become mutually enriching.

PLACE OF THE SPIRIT IN EVANGELICAL CHRISTIANITY

This enlightening emphasis of Allen's is little in evidence in what is generally referred to as evangelical Christianity. To read it, to hear it, one would think that heaven is profoundly concerned to save a lost humanity that came out of nowhere. It is therefore hardly surprising that there is little concern to find in that first creation, marred though it is, patterns, directions, and building blocks for the construction of the new edifice that is redemptively in the making. In missionary reflection and practice, too, we must remember that all things are ours, that we are Christ's who has made them ours, and Christ is God's, from whom, through whom, and to whom are all things.

CLAIM TO THE PRACTICAL OVER THE THEOLOGICAL

In discussing the relationship between Church Growth and the Holy Spirit, it is of the greatest importance to distinguish between theological doctrine concerning the Holy Spirit, on the one hand, and the existential efficacy of the Holy Spirit's work in the hearts of people on the other. The difference is akin to the fact that one can be deeply religious while yet being quite innocent of theological doctrine. To know God, fortunately, does not depend on intellectual comprehension of him and his works. Such knowledge is personal, intimate, and affective, and the person blessed with it can be an instrument of great good in God's hand. Still, the Bible and God's revelation in nature are both profound and intertwining magnitudes to the understanding of which the image-bearers of God must address themselves. It is neither necessary nor possible that all believers should do this. It is, however, incumbent on those working in the theological area to search out the ontological realities lying unsensed behind our religious experience that they may somehow be diffused in the church for the profit of all and the greater glory of God whose wisdom, power, and majesty lie no less in the manner in which he saves than in the fact that he saves.

With respect to theological reflection on the person and work of the Holy Spirit in the church's discharge of the missionary task, I see Church Growth in the position of devout Christians who are deeply gripped by God's saving power and respond to it in terms of an impressively ordered theoretical and practical missionary activism. There is in Church Growth writing a considerable awareness of the Holy Spirit's power and presence. One need not delve deeply into the literature before sensing its greatly felt dependence on the Holy Spirit's enabling blessing. This awareness is not, however, orchestrated into a theologically structured whole. A striking example of this aspect of Church Growth literature is found in Dayton and Fraser's *Planning Strategies for World Evangelization* (1980), which in the index lists sixty-four scriptural references to the Holy Spirit. Every one of them is what may be called an "awareness reference" designating the work of the Holy Spirit in terms of a word or phrase and developing none of them anywhere. The Spirit is related to convicting of sin, church as new creation, power, indwelling, gifts, indispensability of, voice of, unity, regeneration, fruits of, leading of, use of means, and others. Two things stand out here: a massive awareness of the Spirit's power and presence in the work of missions, and the failure of this awareness to pass over into theological integration and articulation.

STRENGTH AND WEAKNESS IN CHURCH GROWTH MOVEMENT

Donald McGavran's *The Bridges of God* (1955), which may be called the beginning of Church Growth literature, contains no theology of the Holy Spirit, but again and again the sense of dependence on the work of the Spirit obtrudes. This kind of relationship to the Spirit, theologically weak on the one hand and religiously strong on the other, has remained constant both in McGavran's writings and in other Church Growth literature. The Holy Spirit is the assumed basis of all missionary proclamation, witness, and service, and stands in no need of elaboration or explication.

Church Growth may therefore be seen as a facilitator of the communication of the Spirit with a view to a more rapid and consistent increase in the numbers of new believers organized into churches or brought into existing churches by the application of systematic research, planning, and execution. As such, Church Growth is part and parcel of the ongoing effort to establish the Christian faith where churches have not yet been planted or in areas where churches are found but stand in need of a revival of their evangelism. It is nondenominational in character, and this is in important respects an advantage. It is thereby free from obligation to include or emphasize certain historic theological positions and is thus able to develop methodological patterns which can fit into any theological, liturgical, or ecclesiastical tradition. The service it renders is indeed a service to the church universal. This, however, is not the cause of its theological simplicity. It is possible to discuss missions theologically along broad spectrums without entering into controversial territory. This is especially true in connection with the missionary doctrine of the Spirit, which has not been developed consistently in any tradition. Roland Allen's books have definite theological underpinnings, yet they have been received widely and appreciatively in many parts of the worldwide church.

Few will, I believe, agree with these observations more readily than Dr. McGavran himself. He has taken full note of the criticism that his missionary vision is short on theology, and it bothers him not at all. He replies to this effect: If you feel that Church Growth needs more rootage theologically, there is nothing at all to prevent you from investing Church Growth principles with theological foundations and elaboration. Speaking about this matter, he observes, "Put it in your own *patois*."[1] This needed saying. Too often in reading literature critical of Church Growth, one gets the impression that it is to be taken as Pasadena has delivered it or not at all. We meet a kind of insistence in such writing that Church Growth people think theologically as well as methodologically.

The writers of the New Testament are responsible for the books they have written; we do not chide them for having withheld theological articulation. That has been provided as need arose. In some such way we may say that Church Growth has provided us with methods for more effective church planting. If in the history and experience of their application in missionary practice theological questions are raised, the Lutheran, the Catholic, the Reformed, the Methodist, the Pentecostal may deal with these questions each in their own way. That, I take it, is what McGavran meant by the need to theologize in one's own *patois*.

This does not mean to suggest that the Church Growth movement would not be greatly served by larger theological concern than it manifests. The contrary is true, and that particularly in the area of theological interest in the work of the Holy Spirit, specifically in the relationship of the Creator Spirit to the Redeemer Spirit. Of this I cite three examples.

LESSONS FROM MISSIONARY HISTORY

Pioneer missionaries were wonderfully resourceful and versatile people. In them were combined the preacher, the teacher, the medic, the linguist, the builder, the keeper of accounts, the gardener, the general fix-it person. Expanding work inevitably brought specialization. Builders, doctors, nurses, teachers, and bookkeepers came to take over work that the evangelist missionary had been forced to do. But many of these newcomers had a problem. They had come to be

---

1. This reference is cited out of one of those irritating experiences, surely familiar to every writer, of knowing *that* you have read, that you have recorded *what* you read, but are unable to recall *where* you read it.

missionaries, but can a person really be a missionary when the whole day is taken up with building, bookkeeping, and teaching general school subjects? I have seen competent and devout missionaries feeling unfulfilled in their official work if they could not also do some "spiritual" work. This perplexity was variously dealt with. Some were brought to see that their work made possible the "true" missionary task of preaching, Bible teaching, and church organization. Others were given some "spiritual work" to do. Still others were given to understand that education, medical work, and agriculture were come-on devices to bring people under the hearing of the gospel. And, in all this, the idea of establishing a "Christian presence" of Western civilization was not altogether wanting.

Such thinking forgets that redemption *has no independent value*. True redemption is always the redemption of something. This something in the redemptive work of Christ is a lost humanity, a humanity that is lost on all fronts, not only religiously. It forgets that the work of the Pentecostal Spirit embodies teamwork with the Creator Spirit. In any missionary undertaking that goes beyond the pioneer stage, there is much work to do, the character of which is derived from creation. This work is not only essential for the execution of the directly religious aim of the mission; it also has a value of its own, a subduing of the earth, the demonstration of a sense of responsibility and stewardship, the opening up to the seeing eye of God's wonders and power in nature. These are the works of the Creator Spirit. Indeed, it is to the performance of such works that the purposes of redemption are also directed.

A similar possibility of missionary perplexity stands ready, I believe, to enter the Church Growth movement if it has not already done so. Its preparatory and all-important work of survey and analysis stands on a par with the missionary services mentioned above. Taking into account anthropological and sociological dimensions, the work of analysis and interpretation, the use of graphs and charts, the calculation of percentages of gain or loss, of causes of growth and decline, of weighing numerical against spiritual loss, and of distinguishing between homogeneous and heterogeneous units and between E-0, E-1, E-2, E-3 as four kinds of evangelism are all aspects of Church Growth planning, the execution of which falls, on the whole, more under the skills conferred by the Creator Spirit than under the power conferred by the Redeemer Spirit. It is not surprising, therefore, that Ebbie C. Smith states that doing surveys and interpreting the facts of growth, while neither light nor unimportant tasks, "are, however, only preliminary" (1967:6-7).

There would seem to be something definitely out of order in the rather imposing missionary movement known as Church Growth when its central conception of planning—survey, analysis, and interpretation—is viewed as preliminary to the main action of evangelism. As Church Growth leaders present it, the church cannot grow as it should unless these methods become part and parcel of its evangelism. American naval terminology regards as one the navy ashore and the navy afloat. The former is useless without the latter, and the latter is powerless without the former. Together they constitute a mighty instrument of national security. The answer to the problem of seeing true missionary worth in those aspects of missionary service that do not involve direct verbal communication of the gospel undoubtedly lies in bringing down to laypeople's earth the theological correlation between redemption and creation with the one Spirit of God functioning with equal worth and power in each.

BASIS FOR CONFRONTATION WITH CHRISTIAN HUMANISM

Were evangelical missionary theologians to take the creation-redemption correlation as the starting point for a more thorough theology of the Holy Spirit, the way would be open for a more decisive confrontation with Christian humanism in the area of missions. The extent of humanistic penetration into this area is clearly set forth in *Eye of the Storm* (1972), admirably conceived and edited by Donald McGavran. In it he takes to task the World Council of Churches' Uppsala pronouncement "Renewal in Mission" (*The Uppsala Report* 1968). The issue presented by this declaration was well summarized by John R. W. Stott in one of the discussion articles:

> Is the new humanity experienced as the result of a personal new creation ("If any one is in Christ, he is a new creation"—2 Cor. 5:17, RSV) or as a result of the establishment of justice and peace in society? Is the gift of "new manhood" or "reconciliation" bestowed indiscriminately on all mankind through Christ, or is it received by faith? Do people become Christians by conscious commitment to a Christ made known to them, or are many non-Christians in reality incognito Christians, serving a Christ they neither know nor profess? Is Christian witness a testimony to Christ in word and deed (that is, in words corroborated by deeds) or is it merely a silent professional competence? (Stott 1972:267).

What Stott is basically asking here is whether Christian witness is from the Spirit of Pentecost joined with the Creator Spirit (words corroborated by deeds), or from the Creator Spirit only (professional competence).

Christian humanism is so taken with innate human potential for good that it seriously underrates the power of sin and consequently the importance of the specific measures God has taken for the redemption of people from the hold that it has on them. This humanistic underestimation of the forces that redemption seeks to conquer and of the instruments of that redemption to effect the conquest is so great that, were it not for determined evangelical criticism and opposition, this kind of humanism might well lose its Christian moorings altogether.

In meeting such theology in the household of faith, the evangelical may be tempted to take issue with it as a manifestation of "autonomous man," "secularism," "humanism" pure and simple, "bootstrap theology," and the like. In doing so in all sincerity a person is, nevertheless, in danger of overlooking the fact that humanist concerns cannot be disposed of all that easily. The malconditions that they seek to alleviate or overcome are wholly opposed to God's good creation and therefore to the Creator Spirit who breathed into mortals the breath of life and constituted us as image-bearers of God.

The defender of evangelical missionary witness and service must be careful not to set the Holy Spirit of Pentecost against the Holy Spirit of creation. The Spirit is long-suffering with the unbalanced insights of his children, but he never surrenders his integrity. He does not permit his laws and intentions governing humans' natural life to be denigrated in the interests of an unscriptural spirituality. The Spirit of creation and the Spirit of Pentecost are one and the same Spirit. All attempts to make him a house divided against itself always prove in the end to have been shattering boomerangs.

What the Christian humanist does not sufficiently appreciate is that the Creator Spirit is no longer *simply* the Creator Spirit, no longer avails himself *only* of those powers with which he brought the world and humankind into being, no longer regards either that world or that humankind as amenable to or controllable by the governance under which he placed them in the structure of creation. Therefore the Creator, still cherishing his creation, though fallen, has become Restorer, Healer, Reconciler. His instrument is Christ, and his effectuator is the Redeemer Spirit. The Creator Spirit, while fully retaining his integrity as Creator, has also become the Redeemer Spirit. Only in this team relationship can he restore the integrity of the gifts bestowed at creation. For this reason the ignoring or underestimation of the Spirit given at Pentecost is so disastrous, so spiritually fruitless in all Christian work, not least in that of missions, which is preeminently a work of the Holy Spirit of Pentecost.

The humanist involved in mission should never be permitted to forget the fact that the Bible is a book of *redemption*. In the nature of the case it begins with and never loses it from its purview. To restore the fallen creation is *what redemption is all about*. It has no other function, end, or meaning. Christ makes *all things* new. Even now, until the work of redemption is completed, "all things hold together" in Christ (Col 1:17).

By the same token, the evangelical can forget only to his or her hurt that the Bible and with it all redemption has creation as its point of departure, as its constant focus, and the new creation as its all-controlling purpose. To confine religious and theological vision to the redemption of people with only tangential reference to the also-to-be-redeemed creation is a grievous impoverishment of the gospel. What is a person without the environing world which consumed by far the larger part of God's creative will and plan and effort? "What," asked the psalmist viewing with wonder the starry heavens, "is man that thou art mindful of him?" Does not humankind's greatness arise wholly out of its relationship to that world as God's vicar to govern it? A human being is indeed the capstone of creation, and a capstone is a capstone only because it holds together the central arch of the edifice.

Even so, it is not to be supposed that the humanist and the evangelical are equally deficient—the one in understressing redemption, the other in understressing creation. The fact of the matter is that one cannot be guided and formed by the Spirit of Pentecost without at the same time being in some degree gripped by the Spirit of creation. To have the Spirit of Pentecost is to be not-without the Spirit of creation. That is why strongly oriented Fundamentalist missions sooner or later—usually sooner—get into education, medical work, agriculture, handcrafts, vocational training, schools for the blind, and similar areas. They may get into them for reasons not altogether flattering to the Creator Spirit, but they get into them, and that rather substantially. A corresponding interest in the specific works of the Spirit of Pentecost is hardly characteristic of missions pursued on the Christian humanist basis.

THEOLOGICAL VALIDATION OF CHURCH GROWTH

Finally, permit me to return to the significance of such disciplines as anthropology, sociology, psychology, and statistical analysis for a deeper grounding of missions in a theology of the Holy Spirit. Church Growth, as it stands, must experience some embarrassment by taking to itself, and that so extensively, so necessarily, such thoroughly "secular" supporting disciplines. It is perfectly true that in historic mission work the fruits of these disciplines were in various ways used. But such use was ancillary; it stood far more in a supporting role than it does in the Church Growth movement. After all, in it we are dealing with church *growth.*

How does this growth come about? By more dedicated preaching, more systematic instruction, more simple or more persistent preaching? Not at all. The quality of earlier evangelical missions in these areas is nowhere challenged by Church Growth. Its distinctiveness lies in preaching, teaching, witness *in a carefully calculated pattern.* It is this pattern which, if rightly conceived and rightly executed and blessed by the enabling Spirit, constitutes the framework within which *the growth,* in Church Growth understanding, will take place; and without which, in Church Growth understanding, it will probably *not* take place.

The use of the disciplines and methods mentioned is therefore a *sine qua non* of Church Growth success. That being the case, and Church Growth being a specific activity and expression of the church of Christ, the use of these methods should be theologically validated. I suggest that the Creator-Redeemer Spirit correlation not only offers a possibility of such validation but indeed requires it. Were this to be done, it might conceivably prevent recurrences similar to those which have often enough happened in history when the theologians or the politicians or the colonialists or the philosophers or educators or capitalists ran off with the church.

If the church is to remain the church and God's kingdom is to remain God's kingdom, let the church so construe its calling that the statistician and the sociologist and the preacher shall always, like the angels, be ministering spirits sent forth to serve those who shall be heirs of salvation.

BIBLIOGRAPHY

ALLEN, Roland
 *1912   *Missionary Methods, St. Paul's or Ours?* reprinted, 1962, Grand Rapids: Eerdmans.
  1913   *Missionary Principles,* reprinted, 1964, Grand Rapids: Eerdmans.
 *1927   *The Spontaneous Expansion of the Church,* reprinted, 1962, Grand Rapids: Eerdmans.
BAVINCK, Herman
  1908   *Gereformeerde Dogmatiek, Vol. II, Second Edition,* Kampen: J. H. Bos.
BOER, Harry R.
  1961   *Pentecost and Missions,* Grand Rapids: Eerdmans.
CONN, Harvey M., ed.
  1976   *Theological Perspectives on Church Growth,* Nutley, New Jersey: Presbyterian and Reformed.
DAYTON, Edward R. and FRASER, David A.
 *1980   *Planning Strategies for World Evangelization,* Grand Rapids: Eerdmans.
HESSELGRAVE, D. J.
  1978   *Theology and Mission,* Grand Rapids: Baker Book House.

KUYPER, Abraham
 1888   *Het Werk Van Den Heiligen Geest, Vol. I,* Amsterdam: J. A. Wormser.

McGAVRAN, Donald A.
 *1955   *The Bridges of God,* World Dominion Press; distributed in the United States
        by Friendship Press, New York. New edition, 1981.
 1970   *Understanding Church Growth, Second Edition,* Grand Rapids: Eerdmans.
        New edition, 1980.

McGAVRAN, Donald A., ed.
 *1972   *Eye of the Storm,* Waco: Word Books.

McGAVRAN, Donald A. and BRANNER, John K.
 1972   "McGavran Speaks on Roland Allen," an interview. *Evangelical Missions
        Quarterly,* Spring.

SHENK, Wilbert R., ed.
 1973   *The Challenge of Church Growth—A Symposium,* Elkhart, Indiana: Institute
        of Mennonite Studies/Scottdale: Herald Press.

SMITH, Ebbie C.
 *1976   *A Manual for Church Growth Surveys* (Preliminary Edition), South Pasadena:
        William Carey Library.

STOTT, John R. W.
 *1972   "Does Section Two Provide Sufficient Emphasis on World Evangelism?" *Eye
        of the Storm,* Donald A. McGavran (ed.), Waco: Word Books.

TAYLOR, John V.
 1972   *The Go-Between God: The Holy Spirit and the Christian Mission,* Philadelphia:
        Fortress Press.

TIPPETT, A. R., ed.
 1973   *God, Man, and Church Growth,* Grand Rapids: Eerdmans.

UPPSALA REPORT, THE
 *1968   Official report of the Fourth Assembly of the World Council of Churches,
        Uppsala, July 4-20, Norman Goodall (ed.), Geneva: World Council of Churches.

*Indicates references cited in chapter.

20. STRATEGY FOR MISSION IN THE NEW TESTAMENT

Frederick W. Norris

EARLIEST CHRISTIAN MISSION APPEALED TO AND INVOLVED NOT ONLY THE POOR and downtrodden, but also the rich and powerful, as well as many in between. If the following treatment of the New Testament evidence demonstrates that assessment, then the two major understandings of Christian mission in the contemporary period should review their claims. Those within the Church Growth movement who employ the homogeneous unit principle should look again at the biblical data if they wish to continue their insistence that they represent a broadly based New Testament position. And those called Liberation Theologians who concentrate on the poor at times to the exclusion of the rich need to reassess the biblical foundation upon which they insist.

The defense of this thesis might be handled in various ways. An investigation of its theological warrants is needed. Yet the manner selected here is a historical description from New Testament evidence of the sociological setting and class structure of early Christian groups.

This approach is particularly appropriate for two reasons. First, significant advances in research have been made in this area during the last two decades, even though it is quite difficult to obtain and interpret the data necessary for the description. Few opponents in the first century had much interest in Christian assemblies since those associations were so small. Certainly the level of information which begins to appear during the fourth century is totally lacking for the first. Within the New Testament only Acts seems to be intentionally concerned with questions one might pose about social status. As we shall see, that intention has caused some scholars to question the accuracy of Acts in reporting the situation. Indeed the evidence which one would like to have— "housing arrangements, rates of wages," and other such concrete details—is lacking (Von Dobschütz 1904:xxiv). Therefore many answers which would be relevant will not be forthcoming. Yet Harnack's claim that more information is available concerning Christianity than for any other religion in the Roman Em-

Frederick W. Norris, Johnson City, Tennessee, is Professor of Christian Doctrine, Emmanuel School of Religion, and held an Andrew W. Mellon Fellowship in Early Christian Studies, The Catholic University of America, Washington, D.C., in 1981-82. He is editor of Patristics *and earlier was Lecturer in New Testament in the Protestant Faculty, University of Tübingen, Germany. In addition to various scholarly articles, he is at work on a commentary:* The Theological Orations of Gregory Nazianzen.

pire before Constantine continues to be unchallenged (1924:xiv). The major problem is the paucity of materials for any religion during that period.

Second, since nearly all Christians take at least part of their cues for contemporary mission theology and strategy from the New Testament, a picture of the earliest churches is helpful. The more important the place given to the New Testament in the formation of Christian mission, the more significant becomes the wrestling with the materials assembled in this chapter. If one claims under any definition that the New Testament serves a normative function in the description of Christian mission, then the data compiled here must be dealt with even if the interpretation or the conclusions are rejected.

THE SOCIAL WORLD OF EARLY CHRISTIANITY

At the turn of this century there was a consensus concerning the social identity of early Christians, one perhaps best illustrated in the work of Deissmann. Particularly influenced by his research on Egyptian papyri and their similarity to the vocabulary and style of the Greek New Testament, Deissmann stated that Paul and those with whom he worked and those to whom he preached were located socially among the urban poor (1912:465-67).

This placement was secure in the minds of most historians. Even the suggestions of Engels and Kautsky that such evidence demonstrated the proletarian character of early Christianity did not move scholars who opposed socialist or communist principles to take another look at the data (Marx/Engels 1904:316; Kautsky 1953:272-396). As late as 1974 Gager could insist that Christians did not come from the upper classes of society until the fourth century. Basing his judgments on the work of such noted historians as Nock, Dodds, and Jones, Gager claimed not only that Christian mission operated among the urban poor at least during the first two hundred years, but that its social identity was to be found among the poorer classes within the cities even during the fourth century (1975:94-113).

To provide a backdrop against which the Christian materials can be set, Gager divided the society of the Roman Empire into six classes and listed them from top to bottom.

The senatorial aristocracy. This class was quite wealthy and small. Augustus limited the number of senators to six hundred whose individual capital worth had to be a minimum of 1,000,000 sesterces. These people occupied positions of great influence, including the governorship of "the most important provinces, the chief civil magistracies (roads, treasuries, judiciary), and the top ranks within the Roman legions." The involvement of old Roman aristocratic families in these levels was steadily weakening. "In the thirty years between Nero and Nerva, the number of Roman senatorial families declined by one half."

The equestrian order. This class was just below that of the senatorial. These persons were citizens of free birth who needed a capital worth of 400,000 sesterces. They were "the capitalists in business, commerce, and industry, with regular responsibility for overseeing the financial management of the substantial imperial farms." Governors in Judea came from this group almost continuously from Christian Era 6 to 66.

Municipal bureaucracies. The last level of the "unofficial aristocracy" was the "municipal bureaucracies." Conquered peoples, including the Jews both in Palestine and in the Diaspora, dominated this rank because of the Roman decision to allow the upper strata of local populations to rule themselves. Often in cities such arrangements were created under municipal charters granted by the Roman senate. Within this stratum were the decurions and magistrates of a city who often came from the older, conservative, wealthy families of the region.

The plebs. Underneath this three-tiered aristocracy were the plebs, "the amorphous category of lower class freeborn citizens both urban and rural." Although the urban plebs were protected by law and listed for bread doles, they were not well off financially. They did not possess enough wealth to compete with the larger capitalists from the upper levels of society and were restricted in their movement into menial work areas by the existence of so many slaves. In fact, the position of slaves was often so much better—since slaves were teachers, business managers, and so on—that by about 100 C.E. it would have been more secure to live as the slave of a rich family than as a poor, freeborn citizen.

Freedmen. This class was made up of released slaves. Their numbers were large, "perhaps as much as five-sixths of the citizens in the early Empire." They often kept their former jobs and on occasion were able to amass considerable wealth. "As a class freedmen became a powerful force in Roman finance, commerce, and foreign trade." They might well be designated as the largest segment of a "middle class in the early Empire."

Slaves. The slaves were proportionately the largest part of society within the Empire during the first centuries B.C.E. and C.E. (Gager 1975:96-106).

Even though Gager's depiction is painted with sweeping strokes, it is relatively accurate. Furthermore it provides a structure against which to test his thesis that Christians came from the lower three classes. Yet even at the outset this framework must be adjusted in certain ways. First, Gager warned that wealth and education did not play a large role in this period (1971:100). That is probably true for the masses of people within such a hierarchical society. But MacMullen insists that both wealth and education were quite significant in specific instances. In as little as one or two generations, a family could move from the position of slave to that of local aristocracy. A slave who was well educated for particular business tasks could earn freedom and accumulate wealth through use of skills. If a son were born to him after he had been freed, that son was considered freeborn. And the wealth could procure position within the local aristocracy. An inscription from Pompeii in 63 C.E. speaks of a freedman who, by rebuilding the Isis temple of the city, gained admittance for his son to the city senate, even though the son was only six years old. Such an incident was not without parallels (CIL X, no. 846; MacMullen 1974:88-120; Duff 1958).

Second, freeborn citizens are described as being in far worse conditions than freedmen. That observation is too general. A number of people named within the New Testament appear to have come from a middle-class situation, one in which they had some status, some wealth, and the ability to travel. It cannot be assumed that anyone of that description must previously have been a slave and was now a freedman. Obviously some of the urban freeborn citizens were able to lead relatively satisfying lives. Some mentioned in the New Testament did not belong to the local aristocracy but are not described as slaves. They could have been part of the urban plebs, who lived fairly well.

Third, E. A. Judge has been reluctant to employ such a framework for several reasons. One of those is the heavy concentration of senatorial and equestrian classes in Rome. Even when the senate became dominated by families who were not native Romans, new senators often moved to the city. Therefore, in the Greek-speaking East, penetration into the highest available levels of society was determined more by the inclusion of people from the municipal bureaucracies or local aristocracy than by membership from senatorial or equestrian classes (Judge 1960:52, 60). Jones has even noted that Roman citizenship was relatively rare in the East until the second century C.E., another indication of how the social structure of the East was different from that in the West (1963:4).

One final interpretive point is in order. There is no reason to assume that society in the Roman Empire during the first few centuries of the Christian era was not statistically distributed in a shape which represents something similar to a triangle. The bulk of the population was to be found at the bottom of the various levels, with only a small number of families located at the top. Therefore the mention of only a few names which can be traced to the upper strata of society would not necessarily represent unusual exceptions, but would indicate considerable success at that level, particularly since there were so few occupying those places.

THE CORINTHIAN CHURCH PARADIGM

The consensus stated by Deissmann and reiterated by Gager—that Christians were located socially among the urban poor—has come under considerable pressure in recent years. In fact, Malherbe speaks of a new consensus which places the social status of early Christians on a level higher than that previously described (1977:31, 86, 87; Judge 1980:201-09). The only way to adjudicate the issue is to look directly at the New Testament materials themselves. Because historical, critical study of the New Testament has questioned the accuracy of Acts and the authenticity of the Pastoral and the Catholic Epistles, it is best to begin a survey with the so-called genuine letters of Paul. Among these epistles the most extensive information about the social identity of one church comes from the Corinthian and Roman correspondence concerning the congregation at Corinth.

The situation at Corinth is crucial because so many scriptural interpreters have insisted that I Corinthians 1:26, "Not many of you were wise according to worldly standards, not many were powerful, not many were of noble birth," is evidence for the lower-class status of early Christianity. Yet recent studies by Judge and particularly Wuellner have indicated that "to use I Corinthians 1:26-28 as the most important text in the whole New Testament for allegations of Christianity's proletarian origins is indefensible and no longer tenable simply and chiefly on grammatical grounds" (Judge 1960:60; Wuellner 1973:666-72).

It is, however, the work of Theissen on the social status of Christians in Corinth which is persuasive. He also notes that I Corinthians 1:26 must imply that some Christians in Corinth were from the upper levels of society (1982:69-119). Romans 16:23 refers to Erastus as the city treasurer. Theissen studies the evidence quite thoroughly and concludes, particularly on the basis of an inscription from Corinth, that Erastus was most probably the city treasurer of Corinth, a Roman citizen—status rare for the East—a freedman and a person of some wealth who rose even higher in the local administrative structure of Corinth before his death. In terms of the societal structure described above, this suggests that Erastus had risen from slave level to the municipal bureaucracy level, and thus belonged to the local aristocracy at the time of his involvement with the Christian congregation.

Gaius, who is described in Romans 16:23 as the host of the whole church, probably also came from the level of the local aristocracy. His home had to be large to house the whole church, if we assume that the building was big enough to accommodate the various household groups which are specifically mentioned: that is, Chloe's people (I Cor 1:11), Stephanas' household (I Cor 1:16), any persons connected with Crispus (I Cor 1:14), and those from the family units of Erastus and Gaius himself, as well as unnamed persons who might have been present.

The information offered by Acts about the church at Corinth provides a similar picture, but with few added details. Titius Justus is said to have permitted Paul to use his house for teaching after Paul stopped arguing with the Jews in the synagogue next door (Acts 18:1, 4-7). Titius Justus is described as a "worshipper of God," a point which may well be helpful in ascertaining his social status. Both Gülzow and Stuhlmacher have noted that as a rule the "God-fearers" or "devout worshippers of God" came from a higher social status than proselytes (Gülzow 1969:13ff; Stuhlmacher 1968:99, 201). Here is another man of wealth and some status who is a member of the Corinthian church.

Crispus, mentioned in I Corinthians, is described in Acts as having been the leader of the synagogue who became a Christian along with his household during Paul's stay in the city (Acts 8:18). As a synagogue ruler, he would probably have been a person of means and respect within the Jewish community. Jewish inscriptions demonstrate that often such people were called upon either to build or to maintain the synagogue.[1] Plausibility rests therefore with the suggestion that Crispus also belonged to local aristocracy, this time the upper class of the Jewish community.

The ability of those named as Christians in Corinth to travel suggests that a number of them were at least members of artisan or commercial groups. Of the seventeen names, nine are found on various journeys. Eight of the seventeen are Latin, a fact which suggests that the strong Roman element in the city of Corinth was represented within the church. The presence of people with Roman names is not of any assistance in determining their social status, but it does suggest the possibility of more areas of heterogeneity within the Corinthian congregation. Although one cannot be certain of the exact wealth and power represented in the church, the mention of the various households, the participation of people from the municipal bureaucracy and local aristocracy, and the ability to travel all indicate that levels above those of the urban poor had been penetrated. Theissen suggests that the general pattern of social status within Hellenistic churches is best illustrated by the Corinthian situation.

To say that the Corinthian congregation contained people from the level

---

1. Although the title could be honorary, here it marks Crispus as a prominent man in the synagogue. See Kirsopp Lake and Henry J. Cadbury (1933:148, 149, 225, 226) for references to the Jewish inscriptions.

of the local aristocracy, however, is not to say that those of the lower strata of society were absent. The conflict at Corinth about the Lord's Supper points out the problems which the heterogeneity created. The well-to-do could begin their worship early and be both drunk and stuffed by the time that the poor were able to arrive (I Cor 11). Slaves are mentioned (I Cor 7). And when they were discriminated against—when the rich were foolish enough not to share their wealth—Paul attacked the wealthy vigorously on theological grounds concerning the body of Christ.

But how are we to assess Theissen's claim that this heterogeneous pattern is to be seen within most of the Hellenistic churches? Unfortunately, the other so-called genuine epistles of Paul do not provide detailed information about congregations in other cities. Philippians 1:13 and 4:22 note that Paul in Rome had some access to the important Praetorian Guard and even to the household of Caesar. There were converts in Caesar's household, but we are not told what social level those persons occupied. Paul's faith was known among the Praetorian Guard, but his letter to Philippi does not speak of any converts among those guards. I and II Thessalonians offer little information about the social status of the church members there with the exception of the appeals about work, and Galatians also has no special interest in our questions even though it does tell us some things about Paul himself.

HETEROGENEITY OF HELLENISTIC CHURCHES TESTED IN ACTS

If we are to test Theissen's claim, then, we must turn to the Book of Acts. That creates significant difficulties, since—as noted above—in the history of modern New Testament research, the reliability of Acts has been so heavily questioned. Haenchen's commentary is doubtless the epitome of such careful and indeed important criticism (1971). In his remarks concerning the various incidents he points out intricate difficulties with the actual texts. For him, many of the events are legendary. There is no opportunity in an article of this size to analyze each of his arguments for any information employed from Acts. Only some general rejoinders can be made.

First, although he sees many of the events related to Paul as unhistorical, Haenchen does suggest that they could have been formed from the experience of Christian communities in Luke's time. Such a concession means that even in Haenchen's view Christianity might have reached the upper levels in Roman society before the end of the first century.

Second, Haenchen insists, however, that Luke has a *Tendenz* which moves him to emphasize the rich and powerful. For Haenchen that *Tendenz* even distorts the *Sitz im Leben* of churches in Luke's time. But Haenchen fails to notice that it is Luke who in his first volume emphasized Jesus' commitment to the oppressed in the speech at Nazareth, and who in his rendering of the Beatitudes stressed social reality (Lk 4:18-19; 6:20, 31). Perhaps the two viewpoints taken together—that the gospel had effect among both rich and poor, powerful and powerless—is indeed the true extent of the story. At least the two *Tendenze* balance each other.

Third, recent studies by those who were educated both in classics and ancient history, and who also have interests in the New Testament, emphasize the plausibility of Luke's accounts when they are compared with materials from that age (Hengel 1980). The above presentation of the information about Corinth shows how similar the Acts account is to that of the epistles. Obviously each case of correlation is not so easily handled. Every theory about the relationship of Galatians and Acts fails to explain some of the details. Yet more and more the burden of proof appears to rest on those who insist that a Lukan *Tendenz* has radically distorted the materials which he employed to write his history.

If we can use the narratives of Acts to test Theissen's claim that Hellenistic churches were heterogeneous, we find more support for his statement. Many Jews and God-fearers in Antioch of Pisidia spoke favorably to Paul and Barnabas after the first encounter, so that a much larger group gathered the next time. When on that occasion they spoke out boldly concerning the Gentiles' access to salvation, "the Jews incited the devout women of high standing and the leading men of the city" with the result that Paul and Barnabas were driven from the city (Acts 13:13-50). At Iconium both Jews and Gentiles believed, but the city was divided. When it was learned that the opposing Jews and Gentiles had "with their rulers" planned to destroy them, Paul and Barnabas fled (Acts 14:1-7). The incidents suggest that access to the local aristocracy was already available to the Jews and becoming present for Christians but that there was no certainty of success.

At Ephesus Paul was able to have some success with Jews, but after three months he went to the Hall of Tyrannus. We do not know the exact status of Tyrannus, or for that matter if the hall was owned by him or named after him. But it is clear that Paul used the hall because of either Tyrannus' influence or wealth. Tyrannus was not part of the urban poor. Paul's chief opponent in Ephesus was the silversmith Demetrius, a man of some importance, perhaps in a guild whose business was threatened by the doctrine which Paul preached. Furthermore, not only the disciples but also the Asiarchs pleaded with Paul not to go into the theater to address the crowd (Acts 19:8-40). Here again there is only some hint that the gospel was successful among the local aristocracy, but there is no doubt that Paul had an entree into the highest social ranks. The Asiarchs were important citizens within the city and were either well disposed toward Paul in order to avoid the wrath of Rome which would fall on a rioting city, or they were actually Paul's friends as Acts 19:31 states.

At Philippi, Lydia, a seller of purple from Thyatira, was converted, as was a jailer. There is little reason to assume that either of these people was of high social standing, but they would not have been part of the urban poor. Both of them would have had reasonable incomes, with Lydia's possibly being of some substance since purple was a luxury item for the rich. Luke also says that at Philippi Paul and Silas pressed their Roman citizenship with the magistrates of the city (Acts 16:12-40). The Philippian letter does not mention either Lydia or the jailer. But silence about the two of them is merely a lack of information, not proof of the inaccurate character of Luke's narrative. The epistle does suggest that Paul had access to the Praetorian Guard and the household of Caesar in Rome, information which is somewhat ambiguous but certainly not against the claim that the same Paul could have had contact with middle- and upper-class people in Philippi.

I and II Thessalonians do indicate that the problem of work was a serious one. But the lack of named people of higher social standing does not negate

Luke's report that "a great many of the devout Greeks and not a few of the leading women" of the city were converted. A man named Jason offered Paul and Silas hospitality in his house, and he may have been among those devout Greeks (Acts 17:1-9). We have no letters from Paul to Berea or Athens, but the same pattern of the gospel's attractiveness to the upper classes is found in Acts. Many Jews, "with not a few Greek women of high standing as well as men," believed in Berea (Acts 17:10-14). In Athens the status of Damaris is not stated, but Dionysius was an Aeropagite, a member of the city council, and thus socially among the local aristocracy. Damaris herself may have been one of the women from an upper-class status (Acts 17:32-34).

Luke indicates that while Paul and Barnabas were in Cyprus, they spoke to the proconsul of the island, Sergius Paulus, and he believed. A proconsul of even a small island like Cyprus most probably came from at least the equestrian class. Sergius Paulus is depicted as having had close contact with Judaism through a false prophet and magician named Bar Jesus (Acts 13:4-12). There is no corroborating evidence from inscriptions or coins for a proconsul of Cyprus named Sergius Paulus. Yet the ability of Judaism to penetrate even the family of the Roman emperor Domitian before the end of the century is attested. T. Flavius Clemens and his wife Domitilla were put to death because of their conversion. Some have thought them to be Christians, but the better interpretation is that they were Jews (Dio Cassius 67.14.2). Yet this ability of an Eastern religion to make its way into the center of Roman power does suggest that the conversion of a proconsul to Christianity is plausible, even if the evidence still available to us does not establish the fact securely.

The pattern which Acts offers is consistent with that which Theissen describes for the church at Corinth. Various hints in the Pastoral and Catholic Epistles also imply the presence of wealth and status. Judge suggests that the ring mentioned in James might well have been that of an equestrian (Jas 2:1-7) (Judge 1960:60). The ability of certain women to adorn themselves with the best hair styles, gold, pearls, and fine cloth makes the best sense of some passages, even though the rebukes could be stock quotations without reference to specific situations (I Tim 2:9; I Pet 3:3-4). The exhortations which specifically mention what should be said to the rich imply that people of means were within the churches and were expected to be there (I Tim 6:17-19; Jas 2:1-7).[2]

A CLOSER READING OF PAUL'S SOCIAL POSITION

If we continue to employ the combined information of the Epistles and Acts, we can gain a picture of Paul which suggests that Deissmann's view of him as a member of the urban poor is highly idealistic. Deissmann drew his sketch primarily on the basis of the resemblance between New Testament language and that of the papyri. But Nock has insisted that anyone who has read the papyri and the New Testament knows the differences as well as the similarities (1972:346).

One recent avenue of research has looked into the rhetorical style and argumentation of Paul's epistles. That investigation indicates that Paul was a

2. Martin Dibelius (1976:135) notices the implications and problems of such materials.

rather well-educated man in terms of his knowledge and use of rhetoric. The three major rhetorical genre—deliberative, forensic, and demonstrative—have now been identified as forming the basic structure of at least three of his letters (Betz 1975:353-79; Wuellner 1976:330-51; Church 1978:17-33). Paul does not betray the Atticism of some well-known orators of the late century, for instance Dionysius of Halicarnassus or Plutarch. But if we knew more about the Asianic style of rhetoric we might know much more clearly the level of education which Paul had received. Bornkamm suggests that Paul had been trained to fill the role of a Jewish apologist before he became a Christian (1971:12). Such a description makes sense of Paul's own insistence on his zealousness for the law (Phil 3:4-6) as well as the hint of his contact with Gamaliel in Jerusalem (Acts 22:3) and Luke's depiction of him quoting Greek philosophers at the Areopagus in Athens (Acts 17:22-32).

Hock has investigated Paul's trade as a tentmaker (Hock 1980; Judge 1980:213-14). He works out the implications from contemporary sources, noticing how much time it would have taken and how tiring it would have been. On the basis of Paul's comments in the Thessalonian correspondence Hock suggests that Paul came from a middle-class situation in which he suffered from the toils of his labor, but did teach in the shop as other philosophers had done before him. The background of tentmaking, then, is Hellenistic rather than Jewish, and the link is to philosophers, not rabbis. But if we take the account in Acts with seriousness and the occasional mention in the epistles of financial aid sent to Paul, then we may suggest that he did not always spend the long, hard hours necessary to earn his livelihood from his trade. The possibility still remains that Paul had time for discussions and teaching which the fullest involvement in his trade would have restricted.

Judge's view that Paul was at least on occasion free to visit the various salons of the ancient cities is also a picture supported by biblical texts (Judge 1972:19-36). Perhaps Paul's success in persuading people to become Christians led to his being freed at times from the long hours. His point in the Thessalonian correspondence is that people should be responsible and do a day's work. But he also insists that the ox who treads the grain should not be muzzled (I Thess 2:9; 4:11-12; II Thess 3:6-12; I Cor 9:9).

A look at the names of those mentioned by Paul raises more questions than answers, but it perhaps reveals a certain penetration into the upper classes. Both Paul and Silas are said to have been Roman citizens (Acts 16:37). Judge in an unpublished onomasticon of the Pauline circle noted that the name Paul appears somewhat frequently among inscriptions concerning senatorial families and that of Silas among inscriptions concerning families of veterans. Since Roman citizenship was rare in the East during the first century, we should probably see Paul and Silas possessing unusual privileges.

Zenas is referred to as a lawyer (Tit 3:13) and Luke as a physician (Col 4:14). Even in the first century such positions in society were rewarded with both honor and wealth. Most of the other names and the ability of those named to travel imply that these are middle-class people who rose above some of the difficulties found among freedmen or the urban plebs. There is no sign that those named within the traveling circle of Paul were primarily from the urban poor. Philemon was an owner. Most of these persons appear to have come at least from a middle-class status. On the other hand, Onesimus was a slave. It is also certain that a number of people within the earliest congregations were from the lowest social ranks of society. None of the evidence for upper-class participation would change that fact.

SOCIAL STRUCTURE IN THE JERUSALEM CHURCH

When we turn to the Jerusalem church, one which was not primarily Hellenistic in orientation even though Hellenists were present within it, we find it difficult to distinguish social status. We are not told that particular people were members of the local aristocracy. In fact, events involving Peter and John show that the rulers of Judaism were quite opposed to the preaching of Christ resurrected (Acts 4:1-2, 5-6, 13). Yet there is evidence of some wealth possessed by particular members. Barnabas was a Levite who owned a field which he sold for the sake of the community. And Ananias and Sapphira did possess property which they mishandled (Acts 4:32–5:6). The priests mentioned in Acts 6:7 probably were from lower levels of society. But some of the Hellenists may have been people of means. The "devout men" who buried Stephen fit the suggestion made by some students of the New Testament that such people were often rather well off (Acts 8:2).

One part of the agitation over the widows of the Hellenists in Jerusalem may have been because some Hellenists had indeed provided their share of support, and perhaps even more. That implication would help explain why the Jerusalem church suffered from poverty after the persecution drove the Hellenists and their supporters away from the city. It seems, then, that the Jerusalem congregation contained people of wealth who shared their means even to the point of selling what they had and giving to those in need. The social structure may not have been much different from that in the Hellenistic congregations.

SOCIAL STRUCTURE IN JESUS' MINISTRY

Even when one looks at the ministry of Jesus, some evidence of penetration into the local aristocracy is present. He was heard by scribes and Pharisees. At first they came, puzzled to discover who he was and what he taught. Although they most often concluded that he was a dangerous opponent, some were not antagonistic. Lawyers came to taunt, but the rich ruler appears to have been sincerely interested and saddened (Mt 19:16-22; Mk 10:17-22; Lk 18:30).

Other rulers responded with positive commitment. Jairus' wish to have his daughter healed was granted (Mk 5:22-43; Lk 8:41-56). We know little of Joseph of Arimathea, except that he was a member of the Jerusalem council, became a disciple of Jesus, and offered his tomb for Jesus' burial (Mt 27:57-61; Mk 15:42-47; Lk 23:50-56; Jn 19:38-42). All three of these men were members of the local aristocracy. In an incident at Capernaum a centurion, one who had already built a synagogue for some Jews in that city, went to Jesus pleading for a sick servant. His request was granted (Mt 8:5-13; Lk 7:1-10; Jn 4:46-53). The rank of centurion in the Roman army often meant power and wealth in relation to others at a local level. Jesus also had contact with women of means who gave for his needs and those of his disciples. Among the women was "Joanna, the wife of Chuza, Herod's steward" (Lk 8:1-3; Mk 15:40-41; Mt 27:55-56). Jesus' message had by that time reached the court of the local political ruler.

The circle of Jesus' closest disciples, sometimes called apostles, does not appear to have included men of the highest local status. The lists containing their names do not correspond perfectly (Mt 10:2-4; Mk 3:16-19; Lk 6:14-16; Acts 1:13). Nor do these or other passages give us status information about all those mentioned. Philip is said to have been from Bethsaida, as were Peter and Andrew, but he is not listed as a fisherman (Jn 1:44). We have no descriptions of the hometowns or occupations of Bartholomew, Thaddaeus, Judas Iscariot, Judas the son of James, or Simon the Zealot (unless "Canaan" is taken as a reference to the area from which Simon came, instead of being understood as the Aramaic for "Zealot"). At least six within the inner circle were fishermen. Peter, Andrew, and Zebedee's sons, James and John, were called away from their nets (Mt 4:18-22; Mk 1:16-20).

In another incident, not only Peter, James, and John were fishing, but also Thomas the Twin and Nathanael. Two other unnamed disciples of Jesus were involved in this event, perhaps raising the total of fishermen in the inner circle to eight (Jn 21:1-4). There is little reason to assume that fishermen were in the upper strata of society, although they were not to be counted among the poorest. Zebedee's business involved not only his two sons but also hired servants (Mk 1:20).

The only other occupation mentioned for this group is that of tax collector. Matthew held that position (Mt 9:9; 10:3). If Levi, the son of Alphaeus, is not identical with Matthew, then he represents a second tax collector (Mk 2:14; Lk 5:27). And if the variants of Mark 2:14 are correct, James the son of Alphaeus would either be identical with Levi, or a third tax collector.

Jesus himself is described as having lived in the family of a builder. Whether Joseph was a carpenter or a contractor is not clear. Jesus had four brothers and some sisters (Mt 13:55; Mk 6:3). Thus if his father were only a carpenter, the family would have been a very humble one. But if Joseph were a contractor, the family's financial status might have been considerably better (Buchanan 1964:195-207). Perhaps that is how Joseph and Mary were able to afford a flight to Egypt. Earlier they had intended to stay in an inn at Bethlehem. It was the overcrowding, not their necessary lack of means, which put them in the stable. But even if Joseph were a contractor, that occupation would not have been highly valued by Jewish society.

The rejection at Nazareth is tied not merely to the fact that people there had known Jesus, but also that they wondered how a builder's son could have such wisdom (Mt 13:54-56). The same kind of puzzlement is reflected in the Pharisees' questions concerning Jesus' eating with "tax collectors and sinners" (Mt 9:11; Mk 2:16; Lk 5:30). The rulers, elders, and scribes looked upon the fishermen Peter and John as uneducated, common men (Acts 4:13). This stigma came from those within Jewish society and involved religious aspects as well. Yet generally within the ancient world, builders, fishermen, or tax collectors would have aroused little but disdain among the uppermost classes.

In the face of this evidence, then, the only time in which Christianity had not penetrated the upper classes available to it—that is, the municipal bureaucracy or local aristocracy—was in the first few months of Jesus' ministry. The later Jerusalem church appears to have had some people of wealth and influence. We would be certain if we knew that men such as Jairus, Nicodemus, and Joseph of Arimathea and women such as Joanna were a part of the Jerusalem congregation. The Hellenistic congregations did contain people from the local aristocracy. Furthermore it is possible that even within the earliest months of Jesus' ministry those of higher status than his inner circle came to him and believed.

If this evidence about penetration into the upper levels of society from almost the very beginning is correct, then there was no major shift upward in any period until perhaps the time of the establishment from Constantine through Theodosius. Even then, part of the increase in the number of Christians among the upper classes of society must be attributed to the general increase in the number of Christians within all classes of society in the empire.

TWO CONCLUSIONS

The emerging consensus among specialists on the social world of early Christianity is that Christian groups were never composed exclusively of the urban poor or the working proletariat. The presence of those from the lower levels of society is always quite clear. The mention of collections for the needy and the involvement of slaves is without question a major part of any description of early congregations (II Cor 8:9; I Cor 7:20-24; Philem; Eph 6:5-9). But with the possible exception of the first few months of Jesus' ministry, believers in him came from all levels of society from the highest available, that is, the local aristocracy, to the poorest of the poor.

Second, combining the obvious evidence for the poor and oppressed with these assembled materials concerning the rich and well placed, these same specialists now claim that early Christianity did not occur in homogeneous units. In fact, when compared with contemporary associations and groups within the Roman Empire, Christianity can be viewed as being more heterogeneous in the social status of its members than other communities. Because of this comparison it would be quite difficult to explain away the characteristic as a fluke of some particular aspect of the social context in the first century. Indeed passages concerning elements as crucial as the Lord's Supper and communal relations demonstrate the heterogeneity both as sociological fact and theological-ethical demand (I Cor 11-14). As Judge says,

> By setting powerful new ideas to work within and upon the most familiar relationships of life, Paul created in the church a social force of a unique kind. The domestic framework was soon outstripped, as the movement of thought and belief generated institutions that were to become an alternative society to the civil order as a whole. It was not a "popular" movement as though it simply sprang up from below. There was too much talented initiative, promotion and sponsorship for that. But it deserved to be called popular in the sense that it broke through social barriers and encompassed people of every level of community life in a way that had never before been the case with any movement of ideas of an organized kind (1980:215-16).

Making the step from historical description to prescription for the present remains precarious, but it must be taken. If these two conclusions are true, then any who wish to claim biblical validity for their positions should give attention to the data and conclusions offered above. Brushing them aside as naive or not heremeneutically sophisticated still leaves the evidence to be interpreted.[3] What is one to do with the fact that early congregations were not exclusively poor or proletarian, that indeed they were quite heterogeneous?

APPLICATION TO CHURCH GROWTH PRINCIPLES

The first modern effort in missions which should restudy the materials presented here is that assembled under the general title of Church Growth. One of the most influential leaders within this body of specialists has been Donald McGavran. It can perhaps be fairly said that he pioneered the concept of homogeneous unit evangelism. McGavran has insisted upon the need for a firm biblical basis for Christian mission. Some of his writings have confessed the New Testament as an inerrant norm of Christian faith. If that inerrant guide depicts early Christianity as constituting itself in congregations of heterogeneous unity, then on his grounds the experience of anthropology, sociology, or modern mission practice cannot be used to override the inerrant guide. In at least one of his publications McGavran did notice that New Testament communities were more heterogeneous than a number of contemporary "successful" mission congregations. But he found that to be an exception, not the rule (McGavran 1970).[4]

James Smith has written a Fuller School of World Mission dissertation on McGavran's homogeneous unit concept (1976). If his selection from the entire literature of McGavran on the development of the concept is correct—and I have no reason to suggest that it is not—then McGavran paid little attention to the evidence which is discussed here. Yet only a full investigation of the social character of early Christian congregations would allow Church Growth advocates to continue to claim a biblical norm for their efforts. They are certainly correct in every sense of the term to insist that evangelism in mission was a hallmark of early Christianity. Under no circumstance should that most positive contribution be lost. Yet if the research cited here is correct, then Church Growth is too much a twentieth-century, pragmatic, sociological phenomenon which has too little connection with New Testament or early Christian history.

Apparent distinctions between discipling and perfecting, between what must be said in evangelizing and what can be left for the task of edification and growth must be examined quite closely in light of what we have in the earliest literature of Christianity. Those distinctions will be of lesser significance if the evidence demonstrates that discipling, evangelizing Christian communities of the New Testament were the most heterogeneous units in their societies. Why were the congregations more heterogeneous than other voluntary associations? One reason may well be that their heterogeneity was by theological-ethical design. If that is true, then advocates of a Church Growth understanding of world mission must tell us how their contribution relates to the New Testament mate-

---

3. When I published much of this material in *Gospel in Context* (1979:4-14, 27-28), a number of the respondents (14-27) preferred to speak of presuppositions rather than to deal with the evidence itself.

4. McGavran sees exceptions (1970:214-15), but he does not recognize (192-202), as does Judge (1980:215), the importance of the heterogeneous house church.

rials. I suspect that if it could be demonstrated that their positions do not reflect the majority of evidence within the New Testament, such a conclusion would be a serious reason for modification among their ranks. Apparently most of them sincerely do want to follow the New Testament as a significant norm.

APPLICATION TO LIBERATION THEOLOGY

Liberation Theology has also claimed to be quite biblical in its orientation, and has insisted that concern for the poor and oppressed is one biblical theme which has been largely ignored by contemporary Christians. Nothing cited here would invalidate that perspective. There is no evidence that those of lower social status were excluded from the Christian community. In fact both within the life of Jesus and under later Christian leaders, concern for injustice and oppression was intense.

Jesus had compassion for the widows, the lame, the blind, and even for lepers. He identified his ministry with the bringing of release to the downtrodden (Mk 12:41-44; Mt 15:29-31; Lk 17:11-19). Origen (*Contra Celsum* 3:55-58) insisted that all those whom Celsus snobbishly condemned as the dregs of the empire could be found and indeed warmly received in Christian fellowships. John Chrysostom's career involved sharp criticism of the rich and deep concern for the oppressed (Hom. 21:5 in I Cor). The Christian gospel cannot be described without taking serious notice of this theme and recognizing more than just intellectually that ethical practice is as biblical as orthodox doctrine. It must be lived.

But descriptions such as those found in Gutierrez' essay (1977) must come to grips with newer research concerning the social status of early Christians. "City workers, slaves, freedmen and women" were members of Christian congregations and did for the most part come from "the lower strata of society." But since there were never many people among the elite of that society, the presence of any at all from the upper classes was significant. A heterogeneous unit, representative of Roman society, would have been for the most part from the poor. But that is not the point. There were criticisms of the rich in Luke and James and instances of economic aid in Acts and the Pauline epistles. Yet it is not the case that Christianity "originally developed in the lower strata of society," entering "the privileged strata . . . only at the end of the second century" (Gutierrez 1977:5-6).

Since Gutierrez is considered by some within the movement to be its best historian, then he and other Liberation Theologians need to revise such statements. If the conclusions of the emerging consensus are correct, then Liberation Theology is warranted by biblical precedent to make its appeal to the rich and free for justice and mercy on behalf of the poor and oppressed. Certainly one way of doing that is to remember that the accumulation of wealth and status can be enormously oppressive; thus those in such positions can be freed by learning new styles of living which would allow them to assist the poor from their resources.

From the Corinthian congregation we know that a disparity of wealth and position created great internal difficulties. Thus the preaching of the gospel demands that those with such wealth continue to see its "possession" as in God's hands and not their own. Discipleship will require radical questions being asked about the accumulation of riches at the expense of the starving. There must be an identification with the poor. But that should be understood as being set over against a worldly status quo which has the rich protecting their interests from the poor who struggle to get them.

What was unique about the early Christians was their effort to develop communities in which rich and poor shared. Of course, it is true that justice, let alone love, does require different aspects of discipleship for poor or rich. Numerous biblical passages make that unmistakably clear. But salvation is for all, even though the ethical demands will vary greatly according to worldly status (Moltmann and Meeks 1978:310-17).

A TIMELY CAUTION

What needs to be avoided by both of these and any other views of mission is the stance so well described by Socrates (*Historica ecclesiastica* IV.28) in his depiction of the conflict between Cornelius and Novatus many years ago:

> Thus as these two persons wrote contrary to one another, and each confirmed his own procedure by the testimony of the Divine Word, as it usually happens, everyone identified himself with that view which favored his previous habits and inclinations.

•

REFERENCES CITED

BETZ, H. D.
  1975   "The Literary Composition and Function of Paul's Letter to the Galatians," *New Testament Studies* 21.
BORNKAMM, Gunther
  1971   *Paul,* D. M. G. Stalker (trans.), New York: Harper & Row.
BUCHANAN, George Wesley
  1964   "Jesus and the Upper Class," *Novum Testamentum* 7.
CHURCH, F. Forrester
  1978   "Rhetorical Structure and Design in Paul's Letter to Philemon," *Harvard Theological Review* 71.
DEISSMANN, Adolf
  1912   *St. Paul: A Study in Social and Religious History,* L. R. M. Strachan (trans.), London: Hodder and Stoughton.
DIBELIUS, Martin
  1976   *A Commentary on the Epistle of James,* rev. by H. Greeven, M. A. Williams (trans.), Philadelphia: Fortress Press.
DUFF, A. M.
  1958   *Freedmen in the Early Roman Empire,* Cambridge: W. Heffer.
GAGER, John
  1971   "Religion and Social Class in the Early Roman Empire," *The Catacombs and the Colosseum,* S. Benko and J. O'Rourke (eds.), Valley Forge: Judson Press.
  1975   *Kingdom and Community: The Social World of Early Christianity,* Englewood Cliffs: Prentice Hall.

GÜLZOW, Hennecke
1969   *Christentum und Sklaverei in den ersten drei Jahrhunderten,* Bonn: R. Habelt.

GUTIERREZ, Gustavo
1977   "Freedom and Truth," *Liberation and Change,* R. Shaull (ed.), Atlanta: John Knox Press.

HAENCHEN, Ernest
1971   *A Commentary,* Bernard Noble, Gerald Shinn, Hugh Anderson, and R. McL. Wilson (trans.), Philadelphia: Westminster Press.

HARNACK, Adolf
1924   *Die Mission und Ausbreitung des Christentums in den ersten drei Jahrhunderten,* Vierte Auflage, Leipzig: J. C. Hinrichs.

HENGEL, Martin
1980   *Acts and the History of Earliest Christianity,* John Bowden (tr.), Phiiadelphia: Fortress Press.

HOCK, Ron
1980   *The Social Context of Paul's Ministry: Tentmaking and Apostleship,* Philadelphia: Fortress Press.

JONES, A. H. M.
1963   "The Greeks Under the Roman Empire," *Dumbarton Oaks Papers* 17.

JUDGE, E. A.
1960   *The Social Pattern of Christian Groups in the First Century,* London: Tyndale Press.
1972   "St. Paul and Classical Society," *Jahrbuch für Antike und Christentum* 15.
1980   "The Social Identity of the First Christians: A Question of Method in Religious History," *The Journal of Religious History* 11.

KAUTSKY, Karl
1953   *Foundations of Christianity,* H. F. Mins (trans.), New York: Russell & Russell.

LAKE, Kirsopp and CADBURY, Henry J.
1933   *The Beginnings of Christianity, Part IV,* London: Macmillan and Company.

MACMULLAN, Ramsay
1974   *Roman Social Relations: 50 B.C. to A.D. 284,* New Haven: Yale University Press.

MALHERBE, Abraham
1977   *Social Aspects of Early Christianity,* Baton Rouge: Louisiana State University Press.

MARX, Karl and ENGELS, Friedrich
1964   *On Religion,* New York: Schocken Press.

McGAVRAN, Donald
1970   *Understanding Church Growth,* Grand Rapids: Eerdmans.

MOLTMANN, Jürgen with MEEKS, M. Douglas
1978   "The Liberation of Oppressors," *Christianity and Crisis* 25.

NOCK, A. D.
1972   "The Vocabulary of the New Testament," *Essays on Religion and the Ancient World,* Stewart (ed.), Cambridge: Harvard University Press.

NORRIS, Frederick W.
1979   "The Social Status of Early Christianity," *Gospel in Context,* Vol. 2, No. 1.

SHERWIN-WHITE, A. N.
1963   *Roman Society and Roman Law in the New Testament,* Oxford: Clarendon Press.

SMITH, James
   1976   "Without Crossing Barriers: The Homogeneous Unit Concept in the Writings of Donald Anderson McGavran," unpublished doctoral dissertation, Pasadena: Fuller School of World Mission.

STUHLMACHER, Peter
   1968   *Das Paulinische Evangelium,* Göttingen: Vandenhoeck & Ruprecht.

THEISSEN, Gerd
   1982   "Social Stratification in the Corinthian Community: A Contribution to the Sociology of Early Hellenistic Christianity," *The Social Setting of Pauline Christianity: Essays on Corinth,* John H. Schütz (trans.), Philadelphia: Fortress Press.

VON DOBSCHÜTZ, Ernst
   1904   *Christian Life in the Primitive Church,* Brenner (trans.), New York: G. P. Putnam's Sons.

WUELLNER, Wilhelm
   1973   "The Sociological Implications of I Corinthians 1:26-28 Reconsidered," "Studia Evangelica IV," *Texte und Untersuchungen* CXII.
   1976   "Paul's Rhetoric of Argument in Romans," *Catholic Biblical Quarterly* 38.

21. THE SOCIAL SHAPE OF THE GOSPEL

John H. Yoder

THE HOEKENDIJK/MCGAVRAN DEBATE

DONALD MCGAVRAN CHOSE TO BEGIN HIS SYMPOSIUM *Eye of the Storm* (1972:41ff) with an exchange with Johannes C. Hoekendijk, whose article "The Call to Evangelism"[1] had been concerned to distinguish between evangelism and institutional self-aggrandizement. Hoekendijk had insisted that churches which are identified with nationalism, colonialism, and class stratification are by their definition denying Christian *koinonia* and thereby incapable of communicating the good news: "The acts of your koinonia speak so loudly that we cannot hear the words of your kerygma."

THE CHALLENGE DEFINED

McGavran responds to Hoekendijk's warning by taking it apart in smaller pieces. He agrees (a) that reconciliation beyond class barriers is a good thing. However, he denies that imperfect churches are therefore either (b) released from the obligation to evangelize or (c) unable to do so. Hoekendijk would have agreed with both of these points. Thinking he has answered Hoekendijk, McGavran can then ignore the rest of what Hoekendijk was saying: (d) that as a matter of fact, in the experience of communication, a church committed to social segregation does not communicate well a message of reconciliation, and (e) that as a matter of intrinsic honesty, a church which is committed to segregation does not in fact believe that reconciliation is good news.

To explain further what McGavran accepts and what he does not, he provides two elements of further clarification. One is the notion of a time line of organic growth in the Christian movement's understanding. He uses the parallel with the early Christian communities, where in the first generations Jewish dietary regulations were respected, after which in the age of Paul they were outgrown. "Till A.D. 50 I am on the side of Peter. After A.D. 50 I am on the

1. The original sources of the essays in the symposium are not indicated by McGavran. The Hoekendijk text originally appeared in the *International Review of Missions* (1950) (thus well before the debate the rest of McGavran's book is about) and was reprinted in his *The Church Inside Out*.

John H. Yoder, Elkhart, Indiana, is Professor of Theology at Goshen Biblical Seminary and the University of Notre Dame. He formerly was an administrative assistant, consultant, and member of the Overseas Committee of Mennonite Board of Missions. Among his writings are Karl Barth and the Problem of War *(Abingdon, 1970),* The Original Revolution *(Herald Press, 1971), and* The Politics of Jesus *(Eerdmans, 1972).*

side of Paul" (McGavran 1972:61). To take that way of identifying the issue would seem seriously to undercut the ongoing validity of the McGavran thesis: for with regard to any particular phenomenon of class stratification which we see as constituting a present barrier in the fellowship of our communities, we are all situated "after A.D. 50." Putting ourselves in the place of the mind of the church before then is a helpful intellectual exercise, but we cannot as a global Christian community or as Christian leaders return to an age of innocence about the way in which segregation denies the gospel.

The other means of distinction which McGavran suggests is ethical: "Much depends on what segregation means. If it means deifying racial pride, it is sinful and must go. If it means an arrangement of convenience pleasing to some subculture . . . it may, under some circumstances, be in harmony with God's will" (61). Here again, McGavran's differentiation would seem, if taken seriously, to work against his own thesis. If there can ever be a time when we say of something that it "is sinful, and must go," then the point has been conceded to Hoekendijk for at least some cases. We need only discuss which cases that applies to. McGavran does not. The qualification "under some circumstances" indicates awareness that the acceptability of segregation is not unqualified but must be conditional. It is a demonstration of his not understanding Hoekendijk's point, when McGavran cites as arguments on his side the need to talk Swedish to Swedes and Spanish to Puerto Ricans.

Especially with regard to racial reconciliation in the American South or the Northern urban ghetto, we are far past "A.D. 50." In the American South, where segregation is the most deeply entrenched, many white segregationists are born-again Baptists whose fathers and grandfathers were also born-again Baptists. Their commitment to segregation is not a matter of not having gotten around to perfection in the first flush of becoming disciples; it is rather the alliance between a formal Christian commitment and a lifestyle which denies the gospel itself, except verbally.

McGavran continues: "Peter or Paul would never have said, 'The hollowness of your koinonia cancels the effectiveness of your kerygma. Stop and perfect yourselves before you say another word about Jesus Christ' " (63). If the question were whether God uses fallible people, earthen vessels, even disobedient churches to proclaim his word despite the vices of the carriers, I would not disagree, and I doubt that Hoekendijk would. The question is whether this same benevolent cloak of forbearance can be equally well thrown over explicit denial of the meaning of the gospel, a question which McGavran cannot handle directly because he lacks a concept of apostasy.

Hoekendijk, coming out of the struggle for the renewal of Christendom where it has been the politically and economically dominant religious culture for a millennium, is concerned for the authenticity of the message, and he entertains the possibility that an unfaithful Christianity might be communicating something other than the gospel. McGavran, although his personal origins were in the American restoration movement, does not read the Christian millennium in Europe as failure, much less as apostasy, but only as incomplete. He sees the world mission as the continuing propagation of an always imperfect Christianity, without which, it is obvious to him, there will be nothing on which ever to base a call to renewal.

ADJUDICATING THE DIALOGUE

We have come upon one of the reasons the dialogue around church growth has been so confusing and shown so little progress. People like Hoekendijk, although he was a member of a "national church," represent the vision of the church and its mission which the historians call "believers' church" or "radical reformation," according to which the situation of the established institutions of Christendom was not mere imperfection or incompleteness but denial of the faith. Although he belongs to a "free church" denomination, McGavran, using evangelical language and attracting support in America from an evangelical public, proceeds from a multitudinist and establishmentarian view of the church.

Being neither McGavran nor Hoekendijk, I must ask how one would adjudicate this difference if there were to be a fully open dialogue instead of an exchange of mortar fire from entrenched positions. One could try to resolve the difference by taking a poll, but Hoekendijk would not agree because the voices of disobedient church members should not count the same as those of authentic witnesses, and McGavran probably would not agree either, because the great majority of members of imperfect Christian churches would not agree with him on the priority of evangelism.

I might just leave them there as witnesses to the unsolved problem and the fruitlessness of that kind of debate, and strike out on my own for some third better answer. But how would that answer be supported?

I might analyze their sterile polarization and seek from the analysis to learn something: perhaps to identify some common questionable assumption they both make or some element of the truth which each of them in a different way ignores. But if that approach were to be convincing, it would need some validation for that extra "missing truth."

SCRIPTURE REEXAMINED

I propose therefore the simpler approach of going back to the Scriptures with the question with which the initial exchange of 1972 ended. Can it be that an empirical Christian community can be unfaithful in such a way as not to be communicating the gospel at all? Do we think of the sins of Christendom as blemishes of incompleteness and imperfection, or as denials of the faith and reputation of the message?

We could try to answer this question on social science grounds by measuring somehow comparatively the evangelistic effectiveness of churches in correlation with their different degrees of unfaithfulness: distinguishing according to what they are unfaithful about, which elements of the gospel they deny, how blatant the denial is, and the other relevant differentiating factors which a social scientist would help us to look out for. McGavran does this sometimes with a dramatic sweep over all of history, but without identifying significant variables and without looking for negative evidence.

Another way to proceed would be to join the method, used by theologians for ages, of distinguishing between the "essence" of the Christian faith and its "nonessentials." Then that distinction would be used in turn to measure the validity of a given church's witness not by its success but by its adequacy when measured by that "essential" criterion. McGavran could then say that of course a church which denies the essence is unfaithful, whereas the imperfections with which he is willing to be more indulgent are all nonessentials. That would not ultimately resolve our question since the task of defining essentials would itself be just another version of this present debate on another level, or rather on two other levels. There would be a discussion of just what is essential and just what is not, and a second discussion of where one is to apply the yardstick: to every baptized person, or to the most saintly evangelist, or to the doctrinal statements a group makes, or. . . ?

We seem, then, to be left with the procedure of adjudication which would have seemed to me to be normal in the first place: namely, to ask whether there is any biblical basis for the notion that the people of God can be or can have been so fundamentally unfaithful that their presence is a denial rather than a representation of the witness to the true God with which they have been charged. The statement that "Peter and Paul never would have said, 'The hollowness of your koinonia cancels the effectiveness of your kerygma. Stop and perfect yourselves before you say another word . . .' " is one concerning which we can go back to the text.

One wonders whether McGavran's putting Peter and Paul together in the above sentence was an effort to claim that his view could somehow bridge over the difference reported in Galatians 2. It is a matter on which the two men differed. Paul lets us surmise that he won Peter to his own view, since Peter had taken the other position out of weakness and not out of conviction. Of that very issue, Paul says to the Galatians that if they think otherwise, then what they believe is not the gospel at all.

Paul does not say that it is an elementary or a rudimentary or an immature gospel needing to grow up. He does not say that Galatia as a whole has been Christianized[2] and needs only to be perfected, nor even that the Jewish population in Galatia as a homogeneous unit had been Christianized and had not yet learned mature Christian ethics about brotherhood. He rather says that they are denying the true gospel, or preaching a false gospel, if the overcoming of the barrier of the Jew and Gentile is not being lived out in their daily communal and sacramental life. What they are practicing is a different gospel (1:6), a gospel contrary (1:9) to what he is free to preach. They deny the gospel because they think they can have valid messianic faith without overcoming the barrier between Jew and Greek.

WHAT IS THE GOSPEL?

The point of this question is therefore not a matter of personal ethics[3] or of

2. That a nation "as a whole" becomes Christian is said most strongly by McGavran in "God Has Often Done it Before," in *The Discipling of a Nation,* written jointly with James H. Montgomery (1980:25ff). The forced conversion of nations "as a whole" across northern Europe, before and after Charlemagne, is described as proving that such is "The manifest will of God for all nations." Those who question this are said to be naive, stupid, and cheaply sneering.

3. C. Peter Wagner (1978:12-19) considers ethnic reconciliation as "requirement," "barrier," "demand," "load," rather than as good news.

social ethics (Wagner 1979) or of social action.[4] Each of those questions is important in its own right. Each does surface in any context of cross-cultural communication. Such matters have always divided missionary Christians, including evangelical missionary Christians. But the issue here is not on the level of ethics and social action, except derivatively. It is first of all a question of what the gospel is, and whether a particular community is believing and celebrating and preaching the gospel of Jesus Christ or something else.

Paul distinguishes this from questions of imperfection and immaturity. In Romans 14 he deals sensitively with matters of diversity of maturity ("strength and weakness"). In Philippians he even expresses himself approvingly about the people who are proclaiming the gospel with the motivation of taking away from his reputation. He thus makes a distinction which, as far as I can see, the McGavran apologetic refuses to recognize. Paul separates the kinds of shortcoming which are legitimately put to the account of limited information, newness to the community, immaturity, and ordinary human frailty, from other more fundamental kinds of shortcomings which represent express disobedience in the light of better knowledge, whether on the part of individuals or subgroups, or even on the part of an entire religious culture as spoken for by its accepted leaders.

The fact that the problem has been perceived as one of ethics rather than of the nature of salvation and of the church does open the door to one other way of testing the notion that "reform" or "perfecting" should not be expected in the first generation. It should be possible to have an empirical study about whether elements of moral concern from completely different segments of the ethical agenda are dealt with in similar ways, in missionary work in general, and in the McGavran/Wagner corpus more particularly, as matters it is acceptable to leave for later. Marital fidelity, the wrongness of theft, and truthtelling are, like love of the enemy and reconciliation with the Gentile, portions of the gospel message. Are they likewise relegated by McGavran to the status of ideals which it would be stupid or naive to ask of first-generation Christians?[5] Or does McGavran give "ideal" status only to the transcending of ethnic selfishness and enmity through the cross, because it is only in this instance that a question is raised about some particular moves in mission method?

The point which Paul makes has been spelled out at some length already (Yoder 1972:215ff; more fully in Yoder 1980:115ff). In this context let it suffice

---

4. In *Church Growth and the Whole Gospel* (1981) C. Peter Wagner adopts and redefines for his own purposes the term "cultural mandate" from Reformed social thought. Since McGavran has himself not carried on the conversation on these questions, it is not clear whether these several defenses by Wagner (1978, 1979, 1981) should be taken to represent McGavran's mind completely, but they are all that the person wanting to be fair to the Pasadena school has to go by. Each of the Wagner arguments would be worthy of direct dialogue for its own sake, but that would be a different theme from the above, since our point here is that these characterizations of the issue as matters of ethics or social action are inadequate.

5. The three Wagner texts seem at least not to indicate concern to avoid that in these ethical areas new believers be put off by "requirements," "demands," "barriers to salvation." In the *Occasional Bulletin* text (1978:16) he does provide another concept, that of the "point of guilt," which is unelucidated, but which might, if examined, make segregationism an issue after all.

for us to see spelled out in Ephesians the same point which those earlier texts developed from II Corinthians. The Apostle Paul indicates that the particular message in question is his own specific contribution to the articulation of the meaning of the gospel. He calls it "my insight into the mystery." This does not mean to deny that it was already there implicitly in the words and work of Jesus, but it could only be articulated as Paul does it in the context of the Pauline world ministry, where for the first time the issues came to be formulated in that way. The word *mystery* refers to an intention which, although hidden to the Jewish believers, was clearly present and defined in the mind of God. Its manifestation is a matter of concrete historical experience under the guidance of "apostles and prophets by the Spirit."

This guidance of apostles and prophets must have followed lines something like the developments we find recorded in the Book of Acts, although there is no reason to assume that only the events which Luke reports there contributed to the process. The message is not about social action, not even about social ethics or ethics at all: it is about the meaning of the death of Christ, which was to "make peace" between two categories of humanity. Humanity under the law and humanity without law had for a long time—ever since Noah, ever since Abraham, ever since Moses—been two categorically opposed ways to be human. They are so different that they can be spoken of as having a wall between them. There literally was a wall in the Jerusalem temple, of course, excluding the Gentiles from the inner courts.

What changes the relationship of these two histories is the work of Christ. There is no reference in this connection to the specific teachings of Jesus or to specific strategies of his early missioners. It is the cross itself which destroyed the wall. It brought those who had been far away into the same room and to the same table with those who were near. The description (Eph 2:11ff) of having been far away, without God and without hope, is not a statement about the spiritual perdition of every unbeliever but a socio-historical statement about Gentile humanity. The cross of Jesus, by cracking open the synagogue and the Jewish household to receive Christians in prayer and table fellowship,[6] is a change in relationship between two ethnic groups, neither of which may henceforth exist for itself.

It is not the case that Judaism as a whole has accepted Christianity nor that Gentilism as a whole has accepted Christianity, even in one place. To think of ethnic units existing and acting "as a whole" is pre-gospel. The gospel divides them. Some Jews believe, but many do not. Some Gentiles believe though many do not. Together those who believe form the new humankind (Eph 2:15). What has happened is the creation of a new socio-history which is neither Jew nor Greek, or is both Jew and Greek (you can say it either way as Paul does). The reality is so new that the words Paul uses for it are *new creation* (not only in

6. Wagner (1978:17) interprets the Jerusalem Council as determining that "Gentiles could enter the Kingdom and still be Gentiles without feeling guilty for not being circumcised . . . just as there was never a demand for the Jews to become anything but culturally authentic Jews" (1978:17). Let us ignore the red-herring reference to "feeling guilty." In that Jerusalem decision Gentiles were given four specific restrictions, which meant changing their family mores and their ritually oriented eating patterns. The Jews were told to open their table fellowship to Gentiles. As Galatians abundantly testifies, that did not go down easily. Jewish believers thought it a burden.

II Corinthians but also in Galatians) and *new humanity*. In none of these usages (new creation, new humanity) is the new thing Paul is talking about an individual. But neither is he talking about an existing ethnic group. He is talking about a new group which is so much like an ethnic group that it can be called a *nation* or a *people,* but whose constitutive definition is that it is made up of both kinds or many kinds of people.

This unprecedented phenomenon in their social experience is at the center of what Ephesians 3:18 calls "the breadth and length and height and depth. . . ," and what verse 19 calls "the fullness of God." It is what Paul (4:1) looks back on as "the calling with which you have been called," leading to a particular style of life in community worthy of the divinely worked oneness. That gift of "oneness" then spills over into other dimensions like the multiplicity of ministries. The term *new humanity* occurs again (4:24) in reference to the practice of the communal virtues of telling the truth (v. 25), working and sharing economically (v. 28), building one another up (v. 29), and being kind (v. 32). These expressions of communal virtue no longer relate specifically to the Jew/Gentile reconciliation as did chapters 2 and 3 and 4:17-24; but they still describe the gift of the gospel in terms that transcend the merely ethical, which themselves constitute parts of the good news.

There are those who doubt that Ephesians was written with his own hand by the first-generation missionary Paul. For our purposes this is immaterial. The same point was made in other words in the unchallenged Corinthians text. If some later disciple found it appropriate to write these majestic phrases of Ephesians as if they were from the hand of Paul, this simply confirms that even after the apostle was no longer arguing his case it was still held to be convincing.

SCRIPTURAL INTEGRITY OR ANOTHER GOSPEL

The gospel itself does have a preferred social shape, I have here reaffirmed. It is communicated most integrally where the reconciliation of different kinds of people can be directly experienced by the very generation of those who first hear the message. This does not mean that an individual cannot have all by herself or himself a valid religious experience. Nor does it mean that there cannot be valid Christianity in mono-cultural or homogeneous situations. It does not mean that young churches or new Christians must be morally perfect. It does, however, mean that when we seek for trans-cultural and trans-generational ecumenically usable criteria to measure which expressions of the gospel are more or less authentic, and which strategies for its propagation are more or less adequate, we must certainly include the element which Paul in Ephesians claimed had been revealed especially through him, and of which in Galatians he claimed that to deny it is to advocate another gospel entirely.

"If one is in Christ, there is a whole new world. Ethnic standards have ceased to count. . . ."

REFERENCES CITED

HOEKENDIJK, Johannes C.
   1950   "The Call to Evangelism," *International Review of Missions,* Vol. 59, April.
   1960   *The Church Inside Out,* Philadelphia: Westminster Press.

McGAVRAN, Donald, ed.
  1972   *Eye of the Storm,* Waco, Texas: Word Books, Inc.

MONTGOMERY, James H. and McGAVRAN, Donald A.
  1980   *The Discipling of a Nation,* Santa Clara: Global Church Growth Bulletin.

WAGNER, C. Peter
  1978   "How Ethical is the Homogeneous Unit Principle?" *Occasional Bulletin of Missionary Research,* Vol. 2, No. 1 (January).
  1979   *Our Kind of People,* Atlanta: John Knox Press.
  1981   *Church Growth and the Whole Gospel,* San Francisco: Harper & Row.

YODER, John H.
  1972   *The Politics of Jesus,* Grand Rapids: Eerdmans.
  1980   "The Apostle's Apology Revisited," *The New Way of Jesus,* William Klassen (ed.), Newton, Kansas: Faith and Life Press.

22. THE UNITY OF THE CHURCH AND THE HOMOGENEOUS UNIT PRINCIPLE

C. René Padilla

THROUGHOUT THE ENTIRE NEW TESTAMENT THE ONENESS OF THE PEOPLE OF God as a oneness that transcends all outward distinctions is taken for granted. The thought is that with the coming of Jesus Christ all the barriers that divide humankind have been broken down and a new humanity is now taking shape *in* and *through* the church. God's purpose in Jesus Christ includes the oneness of the human race, and that oneness becomes visible in the church.

In the first part of this chapter we shall examine the New Testament teaching on the oneness of the church in which God's purpose to unite all things in Jesus Christ is expressed. In the second part we shall examine the historical unfolding of God's purpose of unity in apostolic times. Finally, in the last part, we shall evaluate Donald McGavran's homogeneous unit principle, according to which "men like to become Christians wihtout crossing racial, linguistic or class barriers" (McGavran 1970:198), in the light of our previous analysis of scriptural teaching and apostolic practice.

GOD'S PURPOSE OF UNITY IN JESUS CHRIST

The Bible knows nothing of the human being as an individual in isolation; it knows only of a person as a *related* being, a person in relation to other people. Much of its teaching is colored by the Hebrew concept of human solidarity, for which H. Wheeler Robinson coined a well-worn label—"corporate personality." Accordingly, the church is viewed in the New Testament as the solidarity that has been created in Jesus Christ and that stands in contrast with the old humanity represented by Adam. The Adam-solidarity is humankind under the judgment of God. Its oneness is a oneness of sin and death. But where sin abounded, grace has abounded all the more. As a result, the Adam-solidarity can no longer be viewed in isolation from Christ's world, in which God has justified sinners. Over against the darkness of death that fell upon humanity through the first Adam, the light of life has broken into the world through the last Adam (Rom 5:12-21). By means of the first Adam, the kingdom of death was established among humankind; humanity as a whole slipped into the void of meaningless

C. René Padilla, Buenos Aires, Argentina, is Associate Editor of Editorial Caribe *and pastor at La Lucila Baptist Church. He edited the post-Lausanne Congress book* The New Face of Evangelicalism *(1976), and has been active in the Latin American Theological Fraternity. This chapter is reprinted with permission from* International Bulletin of Missionary Research, *Vol. 6, No. 1 (January 1982).*

existence out of fellowship with God and under his judgment. By means of the last Adam, a new humanity comes into existence, in which the results of the fall are undone and God's original purpose for humanity is fulfilled.

The letter to the Ephesians assembles a number of insights regarding the new humanity brought into being by Jesus Christ. It opens with a doxology (1:3-14) in which the unity of Jew and Gentile in the church is viewed in the light of God's eternal purpose, which includes the creation of a new order with Christ as the head. The whole universe is depicted as intended by God to be "summed up" or "recapitulated" in Christ, moving toward an *anakephalaiōsis* — a harmony in which "all the parts shall find their centre and bond of union in Christ" (Lightfoot 1961:33). In that context, the unity of Jew and Gentile (Eph. 1:13-14) can only be understood as a proleptic fulfillment of that which God is to accomplish in the "fullness of time" (v. 10).

Both Jews and Gentiles may now receive the seal of the Spirit by faith. Circumcision, which in former days was the sign of participation in the Abrahamic covenant, in the new order becomes irrelevant—it is merely an outward sign and it has been superseded by the "circumcision made without hands" (Col 2:11). With the coming of Christ, "neither circumcision counts for anything, nor uncircumcision, but a new creation" (Gal 6:15; 5:6). God has brought into being a new humanity in which the barriers that separated the Gentiles from the Jews are broken down (Eph 2:11ff). Out of the two large homogeneous units whose enmity was proverbial in the ancient world God has made one; two enemies have been reconciled in "one body" (v. 16). In his death Jesus Christ removed the wall that stood between the two systems under which "the people" (*'am*) and "the nations" (*gôyim*) had lived in former days. Now both Jews and Gentiles stand as equal in the presence of God (v. 18), as members of a new fellowship that may be described as a city, a family, and a building (vv. 19-20). Thus the unity that God wills for the entire universe according to the first chapter of Ephesians becomes historically visible in a community where reconciliation both to God and to one another is possible on the basis of Christ's work.

Further on, in chapter 3, Paul claims that God's purpose of unity in Jesus Christ has been made known to him "by revelation" (v. 3). He is a steward of a "mystery" that was hitherto faintly perceived but that has now been revealed, namely, that in Christ "the nations" have a share in the blessings of the gospel, together with "the people," on the common ground of God's grace. Unmistakably, the unity of Jew and Gentile is here said to be *the gospel*—not simply a result that should take place as the church is "perfected," but an essential aspect of the kerygma that the apostle proclaimed on the basis of Scripture (vv. 8-9). Furthermore, it is conceived as an object lesson of God's manifold wisdom, displayed for the instruction of the inhabitants of the celestial realms, both good and evil (v. 10).

The unity resulting from Christ's work is not an abstract unity but a new community in which life in Christ becomes the decisive factor. The only peoplehood that has validity in the new order is that related to the church as "a chosen race, a royal priesthood, a holy nation, God's own people" (I Pet 2:9). Although made up of Jews and Gentiles, the church is placed together with Jews and Greeks (non-Jews) as a third group (I Cor 10:32). It is viewed as "the seed of Abraham" in which, since one is incorporated without any conditions apart from faith in Jesus Christ, "There is neither Jew nor Greek, there is neither slave nor free, there is neither male nor female; for you are all one [*heis*] in Christ Jesus" (Gal 3:28). No one would, on the basis of this passage, suggest that Gentiles have to become Jews, females have to become males, and slaves have to become free in order to share in the blessings of the gospel. But no justice is done to the text unless it is taken to mean that in Jesus Christ a new reality has come into being—a unity based on faith in him, in which membership is in no way dependent upon race, social status, or sex. No mere "spiritual" unity, but a concrete community made up of Jews and Gentiles, slaves and free, men and women, all of them as equal members of the Christ-solidarity—that is the thrust of the passage. And, as Donald Guthrie puts it, "Paul is not expressing a hope, but a fact" (Guthrie 1969:115).

A similar idea is conveyed again in Colossians 3:11, where Paul states that for those who have been incorporated into the new humanity created in Jesus Christ, the divisions that affect the old humanity have become irrelevant: "Here there cannot be Greek and Jew, circumcised and uncircumcised, barbarian, Scythian, slave, free man, but Christ is all, and in all." Race loses its importance because all believers, whether Jews or Gentiles, belong to the "Israel of God" (Gal 6:16). Religious background is neither here nor there because "the true circumcision" (Phil 3:3) is made up of Jews who are Jews inwardly, whose circumcision is "real circumcision . . . a matter of the heart, spiritual and not literal" (Rom 2:28-29). Social stratifications are beside the point because in the new humanity the slave becomes his own master's "beloved brother" (Philem 16); the slave is called to serve the Lord and not humankind (Col 3:22); and the free person is to live as one who has a Master in heaven (Col 4:11). Here—in the corporate new human, in the new homogeneous unit that has been brought into being in Jesus Christ—the only thing that matters is that "Christ is all and in all." Those who have been baptized "into one body" (I Cor 12:13) are members of a community in which the differences that separate people in the world have become obsolete. It may be true that "men like to become Christians without crossing racial, linguistic or class barriers," but that is irrelevant. Membership in the body of Christ is not a question of likes or dislikes, but a question of incorporation into a new humanity under the lordship of Christ. Whether a person likes it or not, the same act that reconciles one to God *simultaneously* introduces the person into a community where people find their identity in Jesus Christ rather than in their race, culture, social class, or sex, and are consequently reconciled to one another. "The unifier is Jesus Christ and the unifying principle is the 'Gospel' " (Mackay 1953:84).

God's purpose is to bring the universe "into a unity in Christ" (Eph 1:10 NEB). That purpose is yet to be consummated. But *already,* in anticipation of the end, a new humanity has been created in Jesus Christ, and those who are incorporated in him form a unity wherein all the divisions that separate people in the old humanity are done away with. The original unity of the human race is thus restored; God's purpose of unity in Jesus Christ is thus made historically visible.

THE UNITY OF THE CHURCH AND THE APOSTOLIC PRACTICE

A cursory examination of the New Testament shows the way in which the teaching on the new unity of the church developed in the foregoing section was implemented by the apostles. Furthermore, it brings into focus the difficulties that the early church faced as it sought to live in the light of God's purpose of unity in Jesus Christ. The breaking down of the barriers between Jew and Gentile, between slave and free, and between male and female could no more be taken for granted in the first century than the breaking of the barriers between black and white, between rich and poor, and between male and female today. But all the New Testament evidence points to an apostolic practice consistent with the aim of forming churches in which God's purpose would become a concrete reality.

JESUS' EXAMPLE

The apostles had no need to speculate as to what a community in which loyalty to Jesus Christ relativized all the differences would look like; they could look back to the community that Jesus had gathered around himself during his earthly ministry. True, he had not demanded a rigidly structured uniformity, yet he had attained the formation of a community that had been held together by common commitment to him, in the face of which all the differences that could have separated them had been overcome. Members of the revolutionary party (like "Simon who was called the Zealot," Lk 6:15) had become one with "publicans"—private businessmen in charge of collecting taxes for the government of the occupying power (like Matthew, in Mt 9:9-13; Lk 19:1-10). Humble women of dubious reputation (Lk 7:36-39) had mixed with wealthy women whose economic means made the traveling ministry of Jesus and his followers possible (Lk 8:1-3). Women had been accepted on the same basis as men, despite the common view, expressed by Josephus, that a woman "is in every respect of less worth than a man" (Jeremias 1971:223ff).

To be sure, Jesus had limited his mission to the Jews and had imposed the same limitation on his apostles before his resurrection. Yet, as Jeremias has demonstrated, he had anticipated that the Gentiles would share in the revelation given to Israel and would participate in God's people (Jeremias 1958). Accordingly, he had commanded his disciples to proclaim the gospel to "all nations"; the Gentile mission was to be the means through which the Gentiles would be accepted as guests at God's table (Mt 8:11; Isa 25:6-8).

THE JERUSALEM CHURCH

On the day of Pentecost, the gospel was proclaimed to a large multitude of pilgrims that had come to Jerusalem for the great Jewish Feast of the Weeks (Acts 2:1-13). The heterogeneous nature of the multitude is stressed in the narrative by reference to the variety of languages (vv. 6-8) and lands and cultures (vv. 9-11) represented among them. Granted that the "devout men" (*andres eulabeis*) mentioned in verse 5 should be taken as Jews rather than as Gentile God-fearers, the fact that Luke wants to press home upon us is that "every nation under heaven" was represented and that the mighty works of God were proclaimed in the indigenous languages and dialects of many lands. The worldwide proclamation of the gospel—the proclamation to be portrayed in the succeeding chapters of Acts—was thus anticipated in one single event in which even the linguistic barriers were miraculously broken down for the sake of the spread of the gospel "to the end of the earth" (1:8). The point here is that at Pentecost people became Christian with people from "every nation under heaven" (2:5), including "visitors from Rome, both Jews and proselytes" (v. 10). Accordingly, Peter understood Pentecost—the gift of the Spirit—as the means whereby the promise of the gospel (that "all the nations of the earth shall be blessed," Gen 12:3) was extended not only to those present but also to their descendants, as well as to "all that are far off" (v. 39).

The Christian community that resulted from Pentecost was, of course, made up mainly of Jewish Christians. What else could be expected before the Gentile mission? Yet it would be a great mistake to conclude that it was in their Jewishness that they found their identity. No racial homogeneity, but Pentecost, was the basis of their unity. Only in the light of the outpouring of the Spirit are we able to understand how it was possible for the early Jerusalem church to include in its constituency "unlearned and ignorant men" (*agrammatoi . . . kai idiotai,* Acts 4:13; *'ammê hā'āretz,* "people of the land," according to rabbinical terminology) and educated priests (6:7), and, at a later stage, Pharisees (15:5; 11:2); poor people in need of help and wealthy landlords (2:44-45; 4:32-37), possibly members of a well-to-do foreign community (Judge 1960:55); Jews (Aramaic-speaking, most of them natives of Palestine), "Hellenists" (Greek-speaking Jews from the Dispersion) (6:1ff), and at least one Gentile from Syrian Antioch (v. 5).

Luke's record shows that the basic ecclesiastical unit for both preaching and teaching was the house church (Acts 2:46; 5:42; 12:12, 17; 21:18). But there is nothing in Acts to support the view that "the mixed church at Jerusalem divided along homogeneous unit lines" (Wagner 1979:122-23),[1] or to lead us as much as to imagine that there were different house churches for the educated and for the uneducated, for the rich and for the poor, for the Palestinian Jews and for the Jews from the Dispersion. All the evidence points in the opposite direction. One of Luke's main emphases as he describes the church growing out of Pentecost is, in fact, that the believers were "together" (*epi to auto,* with a quasi-technical sense; Acts 2:44); that they had "all things in common" (2:44; 4:32); that they were "of one heart and soul" (4:32). The burden of proof lies with anyone who, despite Luke's description, continues to hold that the early church in Jerusalem was organized according to homogeneous units.

A problem that soon arose in the early Jerusalem church was due precisely to the heterogeneous nature of the community—the "Hellenists" complained against the "Hebrews" because their widows were not receiving a fair share from the common pool that had been formed (Acts 6:1). No clearer illustration of the way in which the apostles faced the problems of division in the church can be found than the one recorded here. A modern Church Growth

---

1. If both Jews and Gentiles were divided into "numerous important homogeneous units" (Wagner 1979:114), why does Wagner argue that the Jerusalem church was divided into only two groups, the Hellenists and the Hebrews?

expert might have suggested the creation of two distinct denominations, one for Palestinian Jews and another one for Greek Jews. That would have certainly been a *practical* solution to the tensions existing between the two conflicting homogeneous units! We are told, however, that the apostles called the community together and asked them to choose seven men who would be responsible for the daily distribution (vv. 2-6). The unity of the church across cultural barriers was thus preserved.

THE CHURCH IN SYRIAN ANTIOCH

Following Stephen's martyrdom, a great persecution arose against the Jerusalem church, apparently mainly against the Hellenist believers with whom Stephen had been identified (Acts 8:1). A result of the persecution, however, was that the first large-scale evangelization outside Palestine was launched by exiles who traveled as far as Phoenicia, Cyprus, and Syrian Antioch (11:19).

According to Luke's report, these exiles, aside from a few, shared the gospel with "none except Jews" (v. 19). Why so? one may ask. No explicit answer is given in the narrative, yet this statement is used by Donald McGavran to support the claim that in the years following Pentecost the church made "early adjustments" that favored the spread of the gospel and resulted in "one-race congregations" that "arose by the dozens; perhaps by the hundreds" (McGavran 1974:23). Luke's record, however, does not substantiate the thesis that the apostles deliberately promoted the formation of "one-race congregations" and tolerated Jewish prejudices against the Gentiles for the sake of numerical church growth. In order to claim that it does, one needs to come to Scripture with the preconceived ideas that the apostles shared the modern theory that race prejudice "can be understood and should be made an aid to Christianization" (McGavran 1955:10), and that the multiplication of the church invariably requires an adjustment to the homogeneous unit principle. Without this unwarranted assumption, one can hardly miss the point made by Acts that the extension of the gospel to the Gentiles was such a difficult step for the Jerusalem church that it took place only with the aid of visions and commands (Acts 8:26ff; 10:1-16) or under the pressure of persecution (8:1ff; 11:19-20).

No suggestion is ever given that Jewish Christians preached the gospel to "none except Jews" *because of strategic considerations*. All the evidence points to the fact that restrictions placed on the proclamation of the gospel even by Greek-speaking Jews were due to scruples that would have to be overcome (as in Peter's case when he was sent to Cornelius) if the Gentiles were to receive the Word of God and if the Jews were to see that "God shows no partiality" (as in the case of those in Judea who heard that Cornelius and his kinsmen and friends had believed). As long as Jewish Christians allowed inherited prejudices to persist, probably because of their fear that this contact with Gentiles might be interpreted by fellow Jews as an act whereby they were "traitorously joining a strange people" (to borrow McGavran's expression), they could preach "to none except the Jews." Who would have thought that their approach, based on such a limited outlook, would be used as a pattern for evangelism in the twentieth century?

The evangelists who took the new step of preaching the gospel to Gentiles in Syrian Antioch were unnamed "men of Cyprus and Cyrene" (11:20). The importance of this step can hardly be overestimated. Antioch was the third largest city in the world, "almost a microcosm of Roman antiquity in the first century, a city which encompassed most of the advantages, the problems, and the human interests, with which the new faith would have to grapple" (Green 1970:114). Soon the church there would become the base for the Gentile mission.

There is no evidence that those who received the gospel in Antioch were relatives to the exiles coming from Jerusalem. Perhaps they were, but this is merely a conjecture and lends no solid support to the idea that "in Antioch for both the Jerusalem refugees and the resident Christians we have bridges of relationship into the Greek people" (McGavran 1955:24). Furthermore, nothing Luke says leads us to the conclusion that the evangelization of Gentiles in this city took place in the synagogue. That might have been the case, but if the correct reading in verse 20 is *Hellēnas* rather than *Hellēnistas,* Gentiles of Greek culture would be meant. Floyd Filson may be right in believing that the evangelized were "Gentiles who had had no previous contact with the synagogue" (Filson 1965:191). The message that was preached to them was centered in Jesus as Lord (*Kyrios*) and was thus cast in terms not entirely unfamiliar to people living in a cosmopolitan city where salvation was being offered by many cults and mystery religions in the name of other lords. God's power was with the evangelists, and as a result many believed.

Unless we are to assume that for the sake of numerical growth the "great number" of those who believed were immediately separated into homogeneous unit house churches (Wagner 1979:124), the clear implication is that the church that came into being embraced both Jewish and Gentile believers *on an equal basis* and that there was no thought that the latter had to accept Jewish practices as a prerequisite. At a later stage, as we shall see, the question of the place of Jewish ceremonial law in the church was to become a matter of debate. But there is no evidence that at the start of the Antioch church the evangelists resorted to the homogeneous unit principle in order to accomplish their task. How was unity preserved when there were many members who did not keep the Jewish ceremonial law and there were others who did? We are not told. We can imagine that difficulties would arise. "But," as Adolf Schlatter has commented, "the early Church never shirked difficulties: it attacked bravely. So nothing more is said about these difficulties, and we do not hear how intercourse in the mixed communities was secured" (Schlatter 1961:59).

An insight into the degree to which people from a variety of backgrounds worked together in the Antioch church is found in the list of leaders provided by Luke in Acts 13:1: "Barnabas, Simeon who was called Niger, Lucius of Cyrene, Manaen a member of the court of Herod the tetrarch, and Saul." A more heterogeneous group could hardly be suggested! Barnabas was a Levite, a native of Cyprus (4:36). Simeon, as his nickname Niger ("Black") suggests, was a Jew (or proselyte?) apparently of dark complexion, perhaps to be identified with Simon of Cyrene who carried Jesus' cross. Lucius was a Gentile (or a Jew with a Roman name?), a native of the African city of Cyrene, perhaps one of the men who had first preached the gospel in Antioch. Manaen was a "foster-brother" (*syntrophos*) to Herod Antipas, the tetrarch of Galilee, with whom he had been reared. Saul was an ex-Pharisee, a "Hebrew of Hebrews" and (as a Roman citizen) a member of a small, privileged minority in the eastern Mediterranean (Judge 1960:52, 58). What could glue these men together aside from a common experience?

THE EARLY GENTILE CHURCHES AND THE "CIRCUMCISION PARTY"

As long as the church was made up mainly of Jews, apparently it was not a great problem for Jewish Christians to accept Gentile converts as full members of the church without demanding that they become Jews. Peter's report on the way Cornelius and his household had received the Word of God was enough to silence the criticism that the circumcision party in Jerusalem had raised against the apostle (Acts 11:1-18). Later on, the news concerning the numerical growth of the church in Syrian Antioch was welcomed in the mother church, which then sent one of its most outstanding leaders with the commission to instruct the new believers (11:22ff). When the leaders of the Gentile mission (Barnabas and Saul) visited Jerusalem in connection with the relief sent from Antioch for the brethren in Judea (11:27-30), they had a meeting with James (Jesus' brother), Peter, and John, as a result of which they were given "the right hand of fellowship"; the understanding was reached that "We," says Paul, "should go to the Gentiles and they to the circumcised" (Gal 2:9). The presence of a young Greek convert named Titus with the delegation from Antioch at that time could be taken as a further confirmation that the Jewish Christian would not expect Gentile converts to be circumcised (Gal 2:1-3).

The spread of the gospel throughout south Galatia brought about by the travels undertaken by Paul and Barnabas, with the resulting increase of Gentile converts, finally raised the whole issue of the basis on which the Gentiles could participate as full members in the people of God. Was faith to be regarded as sufficient, as the missionaries were preaching? Granted that the gospel was meant to be preached to all men and women, whether Jews or Gentiles, should not the Gentile converts be circumcised? Should they not be required to conform to Jewish ceremonial laws and food regulations? Should they not be expected to "take upon themselves the yoke of the commandments," like the proselytes to Judaism? The issue was pressed by a circumcision party within the Jerusalem church, made up of people who had previously been associated with the Pharisees (Acts 15:1, 5).

It is likely that the episode that Paul narrates in Galatians 2:11-14 should be viewed in connection with the visit that according to Acts 15:1 these members of the circumcision party made to Antioch. Before their coming Peter had felt free to share a common table with Gentile Christians, for he had learned in Joppa not to call anything "common" (or "unclean") if God had purified it. When they came, however, "he drew back and separated himself, fearing the circumcision party" (Gal 2:12). His attitude can best be understood when it is viewed in the light of a historical context in which those Jews who sat at a table where food would not be kosher thereby opened themselves to the accusation of "traitorously joining a strange people." According to Paul, those who induced Peter to act inconsistently with his Gentile brethren had been sent by James. Pauls' words need not mean that they had been personally commissioned by James to spy out the Jewish-Gentile relations, but from all we know the conservative party may have forced James to take action against a practice that went against their own taboos. T. W. Manson's suggestion therefore carries weight, that a message from James was brought to Peter, couched more or less in the following terms: "News has come to Jerusalem that you are eating Gentile food at Gentile tables, and this is causing great scandal to many devout brethren besides laying us open to serious criticism from the Scribes and Pharisees. Pray discontinue this practice, which will surely do great harm to our work among our fellow-countrymen" (Manson 1962:181).

Be that as it may, Peter's action, however justified it may have been in his own opinion, was strongly opposed by Paul, who saw in it a "play-acting" (hypokrisis) that compromised the truth of the gospel (Gal 2:13). To be sure, Peter had not agreed with the conservative party on the question of keeping the law as a Christian requirement. His failure had been to give up table fellowship with his Gentile brethren, not because of his own convictions but because of a fierce pragmatism in the face of the danger of being regarded as a traitor to his own race. Although he himself believed with Paul that "neither circumcision counts for anything, nor uncircumcision, but a new creation" (6:15), prompted by fear of others he had adopted a course of action that was totally inconsistent with that conviction. And because of his influence, he had carried with him the rest of the Jewish Christians, including Barnabas (2:13), thereby destroying Christian fellowship and denying the truth of the gospel, according to which for those who have been incorporated into Jesus Christ all the barriers that separate people have been abolished (3:28).

Peter's action showed how real was the danger facing the apostolic church to be divided into two "denominations"—a Jewish Christian church and a Gentile Christian church, each with its own emphases, serving its own homogeneous unit. The situation was so serious that a meeting was held in Jerusalem in order to discuss the problem with the apostles and elders of the local church and with Paul and Barnabas as delegates from Antioch (Acts 15:1ff). The circumcision party that had provoked the Jewish-Gentile incident in Antioch presented its case, but the "council" vindicated Paul and Barnabas and sent them back to Antioch with a letter summarizing the decision that had been reached (vv. 22-29).

The "Jerusalem Decree" provided the basis for Jewish and Gentile Christians to live in unity, as equal members of the body of Christ. It clearly exemplifies the apostolic practice in the face of problems arising out of racial, cultural, or social differences among Christians. In the first place, the Gentile converts would not have to be circumcised in order to be accepted as full members of the people of God. Faith in Jesus Christ was thus affirmed as the only condition for salvation. And the repudiation of the attempt made by the conservative party of the Jerusalem church to impose circumcision on the Gentile Christians was archetypical of the Christian rejection of every form of "assimilationist racism" (to use Wagner's expression). Clearly the apostles would have agreed with the claim that "any teaching to the effect that Christianity requires a person to adapt to the culture of another homogeneous unit in order to become an authentic Christian is unethical because it is dehumanizing" (Wagner 1979:99).

In the second place, it was taken for granted that Jewish and Gentile Christians would continue to have regular social intercourse as members of interracial local congregations, and provision was therefore made to prevent conflicts arising out of cultural differences. There is nothing at all in the Book of Acts or the epistles to lend support to the theory that the apostles ever contemplated the idea of adopting Peter's approach as described in Galatians 2:11-14: the separation of Jews and Gentiles in different one-race churches that would then endeavor to show their unity in Christ exclusively in "the supracongregational relationship of believers in the total Christian body over which Christ himself is the head . . ." (Wagner 1979:132). *The apostles rejected imperialistic uniformity but they also rejected segregated uniformity.* It was precisely because they assumed that Christians, whether Jews or Gentiles, would normally eat and worship *together* that they took measures to remove the most obvious obstacle to Christian fellowship in interracial churches. As F. F. Bruce has rightly observed,

> The Jerusalem decree dealt with two questions—the major one, "Must Gentile Christians be circumcised and undertake to keep the Mosaic law?" and the subsidiary one, "What are the conditions with which Gentile Christians should comply if Jewish Christians are to have easy social relations with them?" The second question would not have been raised had the first question been answered in the affirmative. If Gentile Christians had been required to follow the example of Gentile proselytes to Judaism, then, when these requirements were met, table-fellowship and the like would have followed as a matter of course. But when it was decided that Gentile Christians must not be compelled to submit to circumcision and the general obligations of the Jewish law, the question of table-fellowship, which had caused the recent trouble in Antioch, had to be considered (Bruce 1969:288).

The decision reached was that the Gentiles would abstain from practices that were particularly offensive to Jews, namely (according to the most probable reading), from the flesh of animals that had been offered in sacrifices to idols, from meat with blood (including therefore the flesh of animals that had been strangled), and from "unchastity" in the sense of the degrees of consanguinity and affinity contemplated in Leviticus 18:16-18 (Bruce 1969:287). If the Jerusalem "Council," having set out to deal with the question of circumcision, ended with regulations related to table fellowship, the obvious explanation is that, once the matter of principle was settled, the effort was made to provide a *modus vivendi* for churches in which Jews and Gentiles would continue to have table fellowship together. And it is quite likely that the regulations included in this arrangement were basically the same as those that had always provided a basis for intercourse between Jews and "God-fearing" Gentiles in the synagogues throughout the empire (Ramsey 1949:169).[2]

According to Alan R. Tippett, the Jerusalem Decree "against the forcing of the cultural patterns of the evangelizing people on the unevangelized, is written into the foundation of the Church and cries aloud today at the expressly westernizing missionary" (Tippett 1970:34). True. But a closer look at the historical

2. C. Peter Wagner recognizes that "Most synagogue communities in the Roman provinces were made up of a core of Hellenistic Jewish residents, some Gentile proselytes who had converted to Judaism and been circumcised, and a number of so-called God-fearers who were Gentiles attracted to the Jewish faith but who had not wished to be circumcised and keep the Mosaic law" (Wagner 1979:127). If that kind of pluralism was possible in a Jewish context, Wagner's thesis that "New Testament churches were homogeneous-unit churches" (Wagner 1979:117) can be discarded *a priori* as an unwarranted assumption.

situation shows that the Jerusalem Decree also cries aloud at every attempt to solve the conflicts arising out of cultural differences among Christians by resorting to the formation of separate congregations, each representing a different homogeneous unit. The regulations given by the Jerusalem conference were formulated on the assumption that table fellowship between Jewish and Gentile Christians was to continue despite the difficulties. *Unity in Christ is far more than a unity occasionally expressed at the level of "the supracongregational relationship of believers in the total Christian body"; it is the unity of the members of Christ's body, to be made visible in the common life of local congregations.*

The working arrangement represented by the Jerusalem Decree was entirely consistent with Paul's attitude expressed later in I Corinthians 8:7ff and Romans 14:13ff. There was no compromise on a matter of principle, but the Gentiles were asked to forego their freedom with regard to practices that caused offense to their Jewish brothers and sisters. At least for Paul, the way to solve the conflicts in the church was neither imperialistic uniformity nor segregated uniformity but love, for love alone "binds everything together in perfect harmony" (Col 3:14).

THE GENTILE MISSION

A well-attested fact regarding evangelism in the early church is that almost everywhere the gospel was first preached to both Jews and Gentiles *together,* in the synagogues. Luke provides no evidence to support McGavran's claim that family connections played a very important role in the extension of the faith throughout the Roman Empire (McGavran 1955:27ff), but there is no doubt that the "God-fearers" on the fringe of the Jewish congregation served in every major city as the bridgehead into the Gentile world (Ramsay 1949:276-77). That these Gentiles who had been attracted to Judaism should be open to the Christian message is not surprising. If (according to the Mishnah) even the proselytes could only refer to God as "O God of *your* fathers," how much less would the "God-fearers"—who were not willing to be circumcised and to comply with food laws—be regarded as qualified for membership in the chosen people. In F. F. Bruce's words,

> By attending the synagogue and listening to the reading and exposition of the sacred scriptures, these Gentiles, already worshippers of the "living and true God," were familiar with the messianic hope in some form. They could not inherit this hope and the blessings which accompanied it until they became full converts to Judaism, and this was more than most of them were prepared for. But when they were told that the messianic hope had come alive in Jesus, that in him the old distinction between Jew and Gentile had been abolished, that the fullest blessings of God's saving grace were as readily available to Gentiles as to Jews, such people could not but welcome this good news just as every ancestral instinct moved Jews to refuse it on these terms (Bruce 1969:276-77).

A cursory study of the Pauline mission shows that time after time on arriving in a city the apostle would first visit the synagogues and then, when the break with the Jewish authorities was produced, he would start a Christian congregation with the new Gentile believers and a handful of converted Jews (Acts 13:5; 14:1; 17:1, 10, 17; 18:4, 19; 19:8). Such an approach had a theological basis—the offer of the gospel was to be made "to the Jew first" (Rom 1:16; 2:9-10; Acts 3:26), according to a conviction going back to Jesus himself, that the Gentiles could only be incorporated into the kingdom after Israel had had the opportunity to return to the Lord (Jeremias 1958:71ff; Manson 1955). But it also made it possible for the church to start almost everywhere with a nucleus of believers who already had the background provided them by Judaism, with all the obvious advantages that this background implied. From that nucleus the gospel would then spread to Gentiles with a completely pagan outlook.

It would be ridiculous to suggest that Jews and Gentiles heard the gospel *together* in the synagogues, but then those who believed were instructed to separate into segregated house churches for the sake of the expansion of the gospel. Such a procedure would have been an open denial of apostolic teaching concerning the unity of the church. It would have also meant that the door of the church was made narrower than the door of the synagogue, where Jews and Gentiles could worship together. The suggestion is so farfetched that it can hardly be taken seriously.

All the New Testament evidence, however, points in the opposite direction, namely, in the direction of an apostolic practice whose aim was the formation of churches that would live out the unity of the new humanity in Jesus Christ. The apostles knew very well that if the acceptance of "people as they are" was to become more than lip-service acceptance it had to take place at the level of the local congregations. Accordingly, they sought to build communities in which right from the start Jews and Gentiles, slaves and free, poor and rich would worship together and learn the meaning of their unity in Christ, although they often had to deal with difficulties arising out of the differences in backgrounds or social status among the converts. That this was the case is well substantiated by a survey of the dealings of the apostles with the churches in the Gentile world, as reflected in the New Testament. For the sake of brevity two examples will suffice.

THE CHURCH IN CORINTH

It is in the context of a chapter dealing with the diversity not of homogeneous unit *churches* but of the *members* of the church that Paul states: "For just as the body is one and has many members, and all the members of the body, though many, are one body, so it is with Christ. For by one Spirit we were all baptized into one body—Jews or Greeks, slaves or free—and all were made to drink of one Spirit" (I Cor 12:12-13). The emphasis on the nature of the oneness of Christians representing various racial and social groups can be best explained when it is viewed in relation to the situation of the church in Corinth.

According to Luke's report in Acts, the initiation of the church in that city followed the pattern characteristic of the Gentile mission. Paul began his preaching ministry in the synagogue, where Jews and Gentiles heard the gospel *together* (Acts 18:4). Later on he was compelled to leave the synagogue, but by then there was a nucleus of converts, including "God-fearing" Gentiles like Gaius Titius Justus (Acts 18:7; I Cor 1:14) and Stephanas and his household (I Cor 1:16; according to 16:15, "the first converts in Achaia"), and Jews like Crispus, the ruler of the synagogue, and his household (Acts 18:8; I Cor 1:14). Gaius' house was located next door to the synagogue (Acts 18:7), and it became the living quarters for Paul and the meeting place for "the whole church" consisting of Jews such as Lucius, Jason, and Sosipater, and Gentiles such as Erastus and Quartus (Rom 16:21, 23).

There are other hints regarding the constituency of the Corinthian church given in I Corinthians. The clear inference from 1:26 is that the majority of the members came from the lower strata of society—they were not wise, or powerful, or of noble birth "according to worldly standards." At least some of the members were slaves, while others were free (7:21-22). On the other hand, the community also included a few well-to-do members, notably Gaius (presumably a Roman citizen), Crispus (the ex-ruler of the synagogue), Erastus (the city treasurer, Rom 16:23), and possibly Chloe (as suggested by the reference to her "dependents," who may have been slaves, I Cor 1:11).

It would be absurd to take Paul's exhortation to each Corinthian Christian to remain "in the state in which he was called" (I Cor 7:20) as lending support to the idea that each one was to belong to a homogeneous unit church representing his or her own race or social class (see Wagner 1979:133). The whole point of the passage (I Cor 7:17-24) is that in the face of God's call both race and social status have become irrelevant; the only thing that really matters is faithfulness to Jesus Christ. The apostle is teaching here neither that slaves should remain in slavery nor that they should take freedom, should the opportunity for manumission come, but that the Christian's experience is no longer determined by one's legal status but by the fact that he or she has been called by God. The slave's slavery is irrelevant because the slave is "a freedman of the Lord"; the free person's freedom is equally irrelevant because he is "a slave of Christ" (v. 22). This is not a piece of advice to reject or to accept manumission—to leave or to remain in one's homogeneous unit—but an exhortation to see that, whatever one's social status may be, he or she is to "remain with God" (v. 24). In Bartchy's words, "Since God had called the Corinthians into *koinonia* with his crucified Son, it was *this* fellowship and not any status in the world which determined their relationship to God" (Bartchy 1973:182). This relationship to God was in turn to be the basis for the relationship among Christians.

The racial, social, and cultural diversity among the people that made up the church in Corinth goes a long way to explain the problems of dissension that Paul addresses in I Corinthians 1:10ff. Although the Christians continued to meet together at Gaius' house (Rom 16:23), they tended to divide into at least four groups, each claiming to follow a different leader (I Cor 1:12). We cannot be certain regarding the distinctive claims made by each group, but the least we can say is that the Petrine party was made up of Jews who insisted on the food regulations formulated by the Jerusalem Council (I Cor 8:1ff; 10:25ff), while the "Christ party" was probably made up of Gentiles who regarded themselves as "spiritual men," opposed Jewish legalism, and denied the Jewish doctrine of the resurrection (Manson 1962:190ff). To complicate things even further, the communal meals, in the course of which the believers participated in the Lord's Supper, had become a sad picture of the division of the church according to economic position. C. K. Barrett is probably right in inferring from the text that "the members of the church were expected to share their resources, the rich, presumably, to bring more than they needed and to make provision for the poor" (Barrett 1971:263). Instead of sharing, however, the rich would go ahead and eat their own supper and even get drunk, while the poor would go hungry. The natural result was that the poor felt ashamed and the supper became a display of lack of brotherliness (I Cor 11:20-22).

It seems clear that, despite the divisions, the whole Christian community in Corinth continued to come together regularly in one assembly (11:17, 20; 14:23, 26; Rom 16:23). There may be some exaggeration in Johannes Munck's description of the Corinthian church as "The Church Without Factions" (Munck 1959:135ff), but it is undeniable that all the evidence points in the direction of disunity and bickering, but not of separate churches representing the various positions in conflict.

The important thing here is to notice that the whole epistle exemplifies again the apostolic practice in the face of problems of division caused by racial, cultural, or social differences among the members of the church. Not the least suggestion is ever made that the solution to such problems is to be found in homogeneous unit churches that would then seek to develop "intercongregational activities and relationships" (Wagner 1979:150). Again and again the emphasis falls on the fact that believers have been incorporated into Jesus Christ, as a result of which all the differences deriving from their respective homogeneous units are now relativized to such a degree that in the context of the Christian community they can be viewed as nonexistent. Indeed the call to unity is central to the whole epistle.

THE CHURCH IN ROME

This church, in contrast to the one in Corinth, seems to have broken up into separate groups, some of which may have been made up of people representing diverse homogeneous units in society. In Bruce's words, "Perhaps some local groups consisted of Jewish Christians and others of Gentile Christians, and there were few, if any, in which Jewish and Gentile Christians met together" (Bruce 1969:394). It may well be that it was because of this situation that Paul addressed his epistle to the Romans "to all God's beloved in Rome" (1:7) rather than "to the church of God which is at Rome." A better sign of this situation, however, is the mention made in Romans 16 of at least five house churches, associated with the names of Prisca and Aquila (v. 3), Aristobulus (v. 10), Narcissus (v. 11), Asyncritus (v. 14), and Philologus (v. 15).

If this reconstruction of the situation of the church in Rome is correct, are we then to conclude that it lends support to the theory that the apostolic practice was aimed at the formation of homogeneous unit churches? So to conclude would be to disregard completely what was undoubtedly Paul's main purpose in writing the epistle, namely, "to bring about the obedience of faith" (1:5) in congregations where, as Paul S. Minear has argued (Minear 1971), Christians representing a given position would not worship side by side with Christians representing another position. Only by a partial reading of Minear's work can the evidence adduced by him be used as lending support to the theory that the apostolic church consisted largely of homogeneous unit congregations or that the situation of the church in Rome reflected the apostolic practice (see Wagner 1979:130-31).

Quite to the contrary, Minear's claim is that the epistle to the Romans was written with the hope that "a larger number of segregated house churches would at last be able to worship together—Jews praising God among Gentiles and Gentiles praising God with his people" (Minear 1971:16-17). Accordingly he shows how the entire epistle develops the idea that through the coming of Jesus Christ all human distinctions have been broken down, and concludes that faith required that the various groups in Rome should welcome one another notwithstanding their opposing views on foods and days. Thus, for Minear the situation viewed by Paul in chapters 14 and 15 was "the target of the whole epistle" (Minear 1971:33).

Paul's approach to the problem in Rome was consistent with the apostolic practice with regard to churches threatened by division. There is no evidence that he would have approved of the modern device to solve the problem of disunity, that is, the forming of segregated congregations open to communications with other segregated congregations. All his letters make it overwhelmingly clear that he conceived oneness in Christ as an essential aspect of the gospel and therefore made every effort to see that Christians would together "with one voice glorify the God and Father of our Lord Jesus Christ" (Rom 15:5).

Other New Testament writings reflect the same apostolic concern for church unity across all the barriers separating people in society. No research is necessary to verify that the congregations that resulted from the Gentile mission normally included Jews and Gentiles, slaves and free, rich and poor, and were taught that in Christ all the differences derived from their respective homogeneous units had become irrelevant (Eph 6:5-9; Col 3:22–4:1; I Tim 6:17-19; Philem 16; Jas 1:9-11; 2:1-7; 4:13; I Pet 2:18; I Jn 3:17).

The impact that the early church made on non-Christians *because of Christian brotherhood across natural barriers* can hardly be overestimated. The abolition of the old separation between Jew and Gentile was undoubtedly one of the most amazing accomplishments of the gospel in the first century. Equally amazing, however, was the breaking down of the class distinction between master and slave. As Michael Green comments, "When the Christian missionaries not only proclaimed that in Christ the distinctions between slave and free man were done away as surely as those between Jew and Greek, but actually lived in accordance with their principles, then this had an enormous appeal" (Green 1970:117-18). In F. F. Bruce's words, "Perhaps this was the way in which the gospel made the deepest impression on the pagan world" (Bruce 1957:277).

AN EVALUATION OF THE "HOMOGENEOUS UNIT PRINCIPLE"

How are we to evaluate the use of the homogeneous unit principle, advocated by Donald McGavran and his followers, in the light of the foregoing discussion of the apostolic teaching and practice regarding the unity of the church?

Before attempting to answer that question, two observations are necessary for the sake of clarity. In the first place, it cannot be denied that from a biblical perspective the (quantitative) growth of the church is a legitimate concern in the Christian mission (Costas 1981:2ff). If God "desires all men to be saved and to come to the knowledge of the truth" (I Tim 2:4), no Christian is in harmony with God's desire unless he or she also longs to see all coming to Jesus Christ. Moreover, it is clear that this longing will have to be expressed in practical terms (which may well include the use of anthropological and sociological insights) so that the gospel is in fact proclaimed as widely as possible. The issue in this evaluation, therefore, is not the employment of principles that can help in the expansion of the church. In the second place, it is a fact that hardly needs verification that the growth of the church takes place in specific social and cultural contexts and that people generally *prefer* to become Christians without having to cross the barriers between one context and another. This, again, is not the issue in this evaluation.

The real issue is whether church planting should be carried out so as to enable people to become Christians without crossing barriers (McGavran 1970:198ff); whether this principle is "essential for the spread of the Gospel" and biblically and theologically defensible. Enough has been said in the two previous sections on the apostolic teaching and practice bearing on the subject for me to draw the following conclusions, all of which are amply supported by exegesis:

1. In the early church the gospel was proclaimed to all people, whether Jews or Gentiles, slaves or free, rich or poor, without partiality. More often than not during the Gentile mission *Jews and Gentiles heard the gospel together.* The New Testament provides no indication that the apostolic church had a missionary strategy based on the premise that church planting would be "more effective" if carried on within each separate homogeneous unit and was therefore to be conducted along racial or social lines.

2. The breaking down of the barriers that separate people in the world was regarded as *an essential aspect of the gospel,* not merely as a result of it. Evangelism would therefore involve a call to be incorporated into a new humanity that included all kinds of people. Conversion was never a merely religious experience; it was also a way of becoming a member of a community where people would find their identity in Christ rather than in their race, social status, or sex. The apostles would have agreed with Clowney's dictum that "The point at which human barriers are surmounted is the point at which a believer is joined to Christ and his people" (Clowney 1976:145).

3. The church not only grew, but *it grew across cultural barriers.* The New Testament contains no example of a local church whose membership had been taken by the apostles from a single homogeneous unit, unless that expression is used to mean no more than a group of people with a common language. By contrast, it provides plenty of examples of how the barriers had been abolished in the new humanity.

4. The New Testament clearly shows that the apostles, while rejecting "assimilationist racism," never contemplated the possibility of forming homogeneous unit churches that would then express their unity in terms of interchurch relationships. Each church was meant to portray *the oneness of its members* regardless of their racial, cultural, or social differences, and in order to reach that aim the apostles suggested practical measures. If "authentic unity is *always* unity in diversity" (Wagner 1979:96. Emphasis added), the unity fostered by the apostles could never be one that eliminated plurality in the membership of local churches. Unity was not to be confused with uniformity either among local congregations or among individual church members. In Ignatius' words, "Where

Jesus Christ is, there is the whole Church." Each local congregation was therefore to manifest both the unity and the diversity of the body of Christ.

5. There may have been times when the believers were accused of traitorously abandoning their own culture in order to join another culture, but there is no indication that the apostles approved of adjustments made in order to avoid that charge. They regarded Christian community across cultural barriers, not as an optional blessing to be enjoyed whenever circumstances were favorable to it or as an addendum that could be left out if deemed necessary to make the gospel more palatable, but as *essential to Christian commitment.* They would have readily included any attempt to compromise the unity of the church among those adjustments to which Christianity objects as "adjustments which violate essential Christian teachings" (McGavran 1974:20).

If these conclusions are correct, it is quite evident that the use of the homogeneous unit principle for church growth has no biblical foundation. Its advocates have taken as their starting point a sociological observation and developed a missionary strategy; only then, *a posteriori,* have they made the attempt to find biblical support. As a result the Bible has not been allowed to speak. A friendly critic of the Church Growth movement has observed that "lack of integration with revelation is the greatest danger in Church Growth anthropology" (McQuilkin 1973:43). The analysis above leads us to conclude that the Church Growth emphasis on homogeneous unit churches is in fact directly opposed to the apostolic teaching and practice in relation to the expansion of the church. No missionary methodology can be built without a solid biblical theology of mission as a basis. What can be expected of a missiology that exhibits dozens of books and dissertations dealing with the Church Growth approach, but not one major work on the theology of mission?

We must admit that at times "The witness of separate congregations in the same geographical area on the basis of language and culture may have to be accepted as a necessary, but provisional, measure for the sake of the fulfilment of Christ's mission" (Newbigin 1977:124). But the strategy of forming homogeneous unit churches for the sake of (quantitative) church growth has nothing to say in the face of "the fear of diversity and the chauvinistic desire to ignore, barely tolerate, subordinate or eliminate pluralism" which, according to C. Peter Wagner, "has perhaps done more to harm church life in America than has heretofore been recognized" (Wagner 1979:147). Because of its failure to take biblical theology seriously, it has become a missiology tailor-made for churches and institutions whose main function in society is to reinforce the status quo. What can this missiology say to a church in an American suburb, where the bourgeois is comfortable but remains enslaved to the materialism of a consumer society and blind to the needs of the poor? What can it say to a church where a racist "feels at home" because of the unholy alliance of Christianity with racial segregation? What can it say in situations of tribal, caste, or class conflict? Of course, it can say that "men like to become Christians without crossing racial, linguistic and class barriers." But what does that have to do with the gospel concerning Jesus Christ, who came to reconcile us "to God *in one body* through the cross"?

The missiology that the church needs today is not one that conceives the people of God as a quotation taken from the surrounding society, but one that conceives it as "an embodied question-mark" that challenges the values of the world. As John Poulton says, referring to the impact of the early church on society: "When masters could call slaves brothers, and when the enormities of depersonalizing them became conscious in enough people's minds, something had to go. It took time, but slavery went. And in the interim, the people of God were an embodied question-mark because here were some people who could live another set of relationships within the given social system" (Poulton 1973:112).

Only a missiology in line with the apostolic teaching and practice with regard to the extension of the gospel will have a lasting contribution to make toward the building of this kind of church—the firstfruits of a new humanity made up of persons "from every tribe and tongue and people and nation" who will unitedly sing a new song to the Lamb of God (Rev 5:9).

REFERENCES CITED

BARRETT, C. K.
    1971   *A Commentary on the First Epistle to the Corinthians,* London: Adam and Charles Black.

BARTCHY, S. Scott
    1973   *First Century Slavery and I Corinthians,* Missoula, Montana: University of Montana Press.

BRUCE, F. F.
    1957   *Commentary on the Epistle to the Colossians,* London: Marshall, Morgan & Scott.
    1969   *New Testament History,* Garden City, New York: Doubleday & Company.

CLOWNEY, Edmund P.
    1976   "The Missionary Flame of Reformed Theology," *Theological Perspectives on Church Growth,* Harvie M. Conn (ed.), Nutley, New Jersey: Presbyterian and Reformed Publishing Company.

COSTAS, Orlando E.
    1981   "Church Growth as a Multidimensional Phenomenon: Some Lessons from Chile," *International Bulletin of Missionary Research,* Vol. 5, No. 1, January.

FILSON, Floyd
    1965   *A New Testament History,* London: SCM Press.

GREEN, Michael
    1970   *Evangelism in the Early Church,* London: Hodder and Stoughton.

GUTHRIE, Donald
    1969   *Galatians,* London: Thomas Nelson & Sons.

JEREMIAS, Joachim
    1958   *Jesus' Promise to the Nations,* London: SCM Press.
    1971   *New Testament Theology: The Proclamation of Jesus,* London: SCM Press.

JUDGE, E. A.
    1960   *The Social Patterns of Christian Groups in the First Century,* London: Tyndale Press.

LIGHTFOOT, J. B.
    1961   Quoted by F. F. Bruce in *The Epistle to the Ephesians,* London: Pickering & Inglis.

MACKAY, John A.
1953 *God's Order: The Ephesian Letter and the Present Time*, London: Nisbet & Company.

MANSON, T. W.
1955 *Jesus and the Non-Jews*, London: Athlone.
1962 In *Studies in the Gospels and the Epistles*, M. Black (ed.), Manchester: University Press.

McGAVRAN, Donald
1955 *The Bridges of God: A Study in the Strategy of Missions*, London: World Dominion Press.
1970 *Understanding Church Growth*, Grand Rapids: Eerdmans.
1974 *The Clash between Christianity and Culture*, Washington: Canon Press.

McQUILKIN, J. Robertson
1973 *How Biblical Is the Church Growth Movement?* Chicago: Moody Press.

MINEAR, Paul S.
1971 *The Obedience of Faith: The Purpose of Paul in the Epistle to the Romans*, London: SCM Press.

MUNCK, Johannes
1959 *Paul and the Salvation of Mankind*, London: SCM Press; reprinted in 1977, Atlanta: John Knox Press.

NEWBIGIN, Lesslie
1977 "What Is 'A Local Church Truly United'?" *The Ecumenical Review*, Vol. 29, No. 2, April.

POULTON, John
1973 *People Under Pressure*, London: Lutterworth Press.

RAMSAY, W. M.
1949 *St. Paul the Traveler and the Roman Citizen*, Grand Rapids: Baker Book House.

SCHLATTER, Adolf
1961 *The Church in the New Testament Period*, Paul P. Levertoff (trans.), London: SPCK.

TIPPETT, Alan R.
1970 *Church Growth and the Word of God*, Grand Rapids: Eerdmans.

WAGNER, C. Peter
1979 *Our Kind of People: The Ethical Dimensions of Church Growth in America*, Atlanta: John Knox Press.

GENERAL INDEX

Abraham, the gospel to and mission of, 175-77, 212
Adam-solidarity, 285
Africa, mission in, 189-90
Aging leadership, 70
Agriculture image of church growth, 126
Allen, Roland, 51, 250-52, 254
All the nations, 235-40. *See also Panta ta ethnē*
Anderson, Rufus, 133, 238
Anthropology: Christian, 199; cultural, 108-16, 118-19
Antioch, the church in, 290-92
Apartheid, 132, 139, 141-42
Apostolic practice of church unity, 288-99

Baptism, 242
Baptizing, 233
Behavioral sciences, use of in mission, 108-09, 115-16
Bible: as historical document, 226; teaching in Indonesia, 43

Called to faith, humankind as, 196
Calvin, John, 218, 252
Calvinism, 124
Carey, William, 218-19
Catholicity of the church, 88-89
Charismatic movements in Indonesia, 29, 33-34
Christ: humankind in, 198-201; and the new humanity, 198-99; unity in, 196; and world history, 199-201
Christianity, associated with Western culture, 4, 8-9
Christ-solidarity, 287
Church: as different from the kingdom of God, 203, 207-08, 211-12, 217, 243; nature of the, 98-101; self-propagating, 5, 7; as transethnic community, 151-52
Church growth: agriculture image of (*see* Agriculture image); criteria for evaluating contextually, 125-28; dimensions of, 102-03; evaluation and measurement of, 103-06; fixation on as distortion of authenticity, 150; popular theories of, 6-9; qualities of, 101-02; theological root of, 207; wholistic, 95-107

Church Growth: model, theory, methodology, or principles of, 117-19, 125-27, 272-73; theological validation of, 257-58
Church Growth Bulletin, 64, 85
Church meetings, 45-46
Church planting, 167
Church renewal. *See* Renewal of the church
Church unity, 140 (*see also* Unity of the church); apostolic practice of (*see* Apostolic practice of church unity)
Circumcision, 292-95
Communism, 18
Communitas, 165
Community, 86-89, 216, 232-33; eschatological, 237; of faith (*see* Faith, community of); humankind in, 195-96, 198, 201; new, 239
Contextualization, 65, 103, 117-31; among Muslims (*see* Muslims, contextualization among)
Corinth, the church in, 296-98. *See also* Corinthian church paradigm
Corinthian church paradigm, 263-65. *See also* Corinth, the church in
Corporate personality, 285
Covenant, 86-89, 176, 181, 185-87, 190
Covenant Solidarity Principle, 86, 88-89
Creation: human stewardship of, 197, 201-02; major theme of Jewish belief, 178; new, 282-83; world as, 196-97, 249, 256
Creator God, 199, 201-02, 250. *See also* Creator Spirit
Creator Spirit, 249-51, 254-58. *See also* Creator God
Creature, human being as, 192-93, 196, 201
Cultural anthropology. *See* Anthropology, cultural
Cultural relativism, 122-24
Cultural universals, 122-24
Culture, 69, 82-84, 140; affirming or denying, 122, 124-25; as divisive force, 112; related to church growth, 8-10, 45, 53-57, 103, 126-27; theological significance of, 140
Culture change, understanding of, 110-15

304

INDEX OF
SCRIPTURE REFERENCES

266

67066